Programming in C

Fourth Edition

Developer's Library

ESSENTIAL REFERENCES FOR PROGRAMMING PROFESSIONALS

Developer's Library books are designed to provide practicing programmers with unique, high-quality references and tutorials on the programming languages and technologies they use in their daily work.

All books in the *Developer's Library* are written by expert technology practitioners who are especially skilled at organizing and presenting information in a way that's useful for other programmers.

Key titles include some of the best, most widely acclaimed books within their topic areas:

Programming in Objective-C
Stephen G. Kochan
ISBN 978-0-321-96760-2

MySQL
Paul DuBois
ISBN-13: 978-0-321-83387-7

Linux Kernel Development
Robert Love
ISBN-13: 978-0-672-32946-3

Python Essential Reference
David Beazley
ISBN-13: 978-0-672-32978-4

PostgreSQL
Korry Douglas
ISBN-13: 978-0-672-32756-8

C++ Primer Plus
Stephen Prata
ISBN-13: 978-0-321-77640-2

Developer's Library books are available in print and in electronic formats at most retail and online bookstores, as well as by subscription from Safari Books Online at **safari. informit.com**

Developer's Library
informit.com/devlibrary

Programming in C

Fourth Edition

Stephen G. Kochan

◈Addison-Wesley

Upper Saddle River, NJ • Boston • Indianapolis • San Francisco
New York • Toronto • Montreal • London • Munich • Paris • Madrid
Cape Town • Sydney • Tokyo • Singapore • Mexico City

Programming in C, Fourth Edition

Copyright © 2015 by Pearson Education, Inc.

ISBN-13: 978-0-321-77641-9

ISBN-10: 0-321-77641-0

Library of Congress Control Number: 2014944082

Printed in the United States of America

Fourth Printing: September, 2015

Trademarks

All terms mentioned in this book that are known to be trademarks or service marks have been appropriately capitalized. The publisher cannot attest to the accuracy of this information. Use of a term in this book should not be regarded as affecting the validity of any trademark or service mark.

Warning and Disclaimer

Every effort has been made to make this book as complete and as accurate as possible, but no warranty or fitness is implied. The information provided is on an "as is" basis. The author and the publisher shall have neither liability nor responsibility to any person or entity with respect to any loss or damages arising from the information contained in this book.

Special Sales

For information about buying this title in bulk quantities, or for special sales opportunities (which may include electronic versions; custom cover designs; and content particular to your business, training goals, marketing focus, or branding interests), please contact our corporate sales department at corpsales@pearsoned.com or (800) 382-3419.

For government sales inquiries, please contact governmentsales@pearsoned.com.

For questions about sales outside the U.S., please contact international@pearsoned.com.

Acquisitions Editor
Mark Taber

Managing Editor
Sandra Schroeder

Project Editor
Mandie Frank

Copy Editor
Charlotte Kughen

Indexer
Brad Herriman

Proofreader
Debbie Williams

Technical Editor
Siddhartha Singh

Editorial Assistant
Vanessa Evans

Designer
Chuti Prasertsith

Compositor
Mary Sudul

❖

For my mother and father

❖

Contents at a Glance

Table of Contents

About the Author

Stephen G. Kochan has been developing software with the C programming language for more than 30 years. He is the author of several best-selling titles on the C language, including *Programming in C, Programming in Objective-C*, and *Topics in C Programming*. He has also written extensively on Unix and is the author or coauthor of *Exploring the Unix System* and *Unix Shell Programming*.

Contributing Author, Fourth Edition

Dean Miller is a writer and editor with more than 20 years of experience in both the publishing and licensed consumer products businesses. He is coauthor of the most recent editions of *Sams Teach Yourself C in One Hour a Day*, and *Sams Teach Yourself Beginning Programming in 24 Hours*.

Acknowledgments

I wish to thank the following people for their help in the preparation of various versions of this text: Douglas McCormick, Jim Scharf, Henry Tabickman, Dick Fritz, Steve Levy, Tony Ianinno, and Ken Brown. I also want to thank Henry Mullish of New York University for teaching me so much about writing and for getting me started in the publishing business.

At Pearson, I'd like to thank Mark Taber and my project editor Mandie Frank. Thanks also to my copy editor, Charlotte Kughen, and my technical editor, Siddhartha Singh. Finally, I'd like to thank all the other people from Pearson who were involved on this project, even if I did not work with them directly.

We Want to Hear from You!

As the reader of this book, *you* are our most important critic and commentator. We value your opinion and want to know what we're doing right, what we could do better, what areas you'd like to see us publish in, and any other words of wisdom you're willing to pass our way.

We welcome your comments. You can email or write directly to let us know what you did or didn't like about this book—as well as what we can do to make our books better.

Please note that we cannot help you with technical problems related to the topic of this book, and that due to the high volume of mail we receive, we might not be able to reply to every message.

When you write, please be sure to include this book's title and author, as well as your name and phone number or email address.

Email: feedback@developers-library.info

Mail: Reader Feedback
Addison-Wesley Developer's Library
800 East 96th Street
Indianapolis, IN 46240 USA

Reader Services

Visit our website and register this book at www.informit.com/register for convenient access to any updates, downloads, or errata that might be available for this book.

Introduction

The C programming language was pioneered by Dennis Ritchie at AT&T Bell Laboratories in the early 1970s. It was not until the late 1970s, however, that this programming language began to gain widespread popularity and support. This was because until that time C compilers were not readily available for commercial use outside of Bell Laboratories. Initially, C's growth in popularity was also spurred on in part by the equal, if not faster, growth in popularity of the Unix operating system. This operating system, which was also developed at Bell Laboratories, had C as its "standard" programming language. In fact, well over 90% of the operating system itself was written in the C language!

The enormous success of the IBM PC and its look-alikes soon made MS-DOS the most popular environment for the C language. As C grew in popularity across different operating systems, more and more vendors hopped on the bandwagon and started marketing their own C compilers. For the most part, their version of the C language was based on an appendix found in the first C programming text—*The C Programming Language*—by Brian Kernighan and Dennis Ritchie. Unfortunately, this appendix did not provide a complete and unambiguous definition of C, meaning that vendors were left to interpret some aspects of the language on their own.

In the early 1980s, a need was seen to standardize the definition of the C language. The American National Standards Institute (ANSI) is the organization that handles such things, so in 1983 an ANSI C committee (called X3J11) was formed to standardize C. In 1989, the committee's work was ratified, and in 1990, the first official ANSI standard definition of C was published.

Because C is used around the world, the International Standard Organization (ISO) soon got involved. They adopted the standard, where it was called ISO/IEC 9899:1990. Since that time, additional changes have been made to the C language. The most recent standard was adopted in 2011. It is known as ANSI C11, or ISO/IEC 9899:2011. It is this version of the language upon which this book is based.

C is a "higher-level language," yet it provides capabilities that enable the user to "get in close" with the hardware and deal with the computer on a much lower level. This is because, although C is a general-purpose structured programming language, it was originally designed with systems programming applications in mind and, as such, provides the user with an enormous amount of power and flexibility.

This book proposes to teach you how to program in C. It assumes no previous exposure to the language and was designed to appeal to novice and experienced programmers alike. If you have previous programming experience, you will find that C has a unique way of doing things that probably differs from other languages you have used.

Every feature of the C language is treated in this text. As each new feature is presented, a small *complete* program example is usually provided to illustrate the feature. This reflects the overriding philosophy that has been used in writing this book: to teach by example. Just as a picture is worth a thousand words, so is a properly chosen program example. If you have access to a computer that supports the C programming language, you are strongly encouraged to download and run each program presented in this book and to compare the results obtained on your system to those shown in the text. By doing so, not only will you learn the language and its syntax, but you will also become familiar with the process of typing in, compiling, and running C programs.

You will find that program readability has been stressed throughout the book. This is because I strongly believe that programs should be written so that they can be easily read—either by the author or by somebody else. Through experience and common sense, you will find that such programs are almost always easier to write, debug, and modify. Furthermore, developing programs that are readable is a natural result of a true adherence to a structured programming discipline.

Because this book was written as a tutorial, the material covered in each chapter is based on previously presented material. Therefore, maximum benefit will be derived from this book by reading each chapter in succession, and you are highly discouraged from "skipping around." You should also work through the exercises that are presented at the end of each chapter before proceeding on to the next chapter.

Chapter 1, "Some Fundamentals," which covers some fundamental terminology about higher-level programming languages and the process of compiling programs, has been included to ensure that you understand the language used throughout the remainder of the text. From Chapter 2, "Compiling and Running Your First Program," on, you will be slowly introduced to the C language. By the time Chapter 15, "Input and Output Operations in C," rolls around, all the essential features of the language will have been covered. Chapter 15 goes into more depth about I/O operations in C. Chapter 16, "Miscellaneous and Advanced Features," includes those features of the language that are of a more advanced or esoteric nature.

Chapter 17, "Debugging Programs," shows how you can use the C preprocessor to help debug your programs. It also introduces you to interactive debugging. The popular debugger gdb was chosen to illustrate this debugging technique.

Over the last decade, the programming world has been abuzz with the notion of object-oriented programming, or OOP for short. C is not an OOP language; however, several other programming languages that are based on C are OOP languages. Chapter 18, "Object-oriented Programming," gives a brief introduction to OOP and some of its terminology. It also gives a brief overview of three OOP languages that are based on C, namely C++, C#, and Objective-C.

Appendix A, "C Language Summary," provides a complete summary of the language and is provided for reference purposes.

Appendix B, "The Standard C Library," provides a summary of many of the standard library routines that you will find on all systems that support C.

Appendix C, "Compiling Programs with gcc," summarizes many of the commonly used options when compiling programs with GNU's C compiler gcc.

In Appendix D, "Common Programming Mistakes," you'll find a list of common programming mistakes.

Finally, Appendix E, "Resources," provides a list of resources you can turn to for more information about the C language and to further your studies.

This book makes no assumptions about a particular computer system or operating system on which the C language is implemented. The text makes brief mention of how to compile and execute programs using the popular GNU C compiler gcc.

Some Fundamentals

This chapter describes some fundamental terms that you must understand before you can learn how to program in C. A general overview of the nature of programming in a higher-level language is provided, as is a discussion of the process of compiling a program developed in such a language.

Programming

Computers are really very dumb machines indeed because they do only what they are told to do. Most computer systems perform their operations on a very primitive level. For example, most computers know how to add one to a number or how to test whether a number is equal to zero. The sophistication of these basic operations usually does not go much further than that. The basic operations of a computer system form what is known as the computer's *instruction set*.

To solve a problem using a computer, you must express the solution to the problem in terms of the instructions of the particular computer. A computer *program* is just a collection of the instructions necessary to solve a specific problem. The approach or method that is used to solve the problem is known as an *algorithm*. For example, if you want to develop a program that tests if a number is odd or even, the set of statements that solves the problem becomes the program. The method that is used to test if the number is even or odd is the algorithm. Normally, to develop a program to solve a particular problem, you first express the solution to the problem in terms of an algorithm and then develop a program that implements that algorithm. So, the algorithm for solving the even/odd problem might be expressed as follows: First, divide the number by two. If the remainder of the division is zero, the number is even; otherwise, the number is odd. With the algorithm in hand, you can then proceed to write the instructions necessary to implement the algorithm on a particular computer system. These instructions would be expressed in the statements of a particular computer language, such as Java, C++, Objective-C, or C.

Higher-Level Languages

When computers were first developed, the only way they could be programmed was in terms of binary numbers that corresponded directly to specific machine instructions and locations in the computer's memory. The next technological software advance occurred in the development of *assembly languages*, which enabled the programmer to work with the machine on a slightly higher level. Instead of having to specify sequences of binary numbers to carry out particular tasks, the assembly language permits the programmer to use symbolic names to perform various operations and to refer to specific memory locations. A special program, known as an *assembler*, translates the assembly language program from its symbolic format into the specific machine instructions of the computer system.

Because a one-to-one correspondence still exists between each assembly language statement and a specific machine instruction, assembly languages are regarded as low-level languages. The programmer must still learn the instruction set of the particular computer system to write a program in assembly language, and the resulting program is not *portable*; that is, the program will not run on a different processor type without being rewritten. This is because different processor types have different instruction sets, and because assembly language programs are written in terms of these instruction sets, they are machine dependent.

Then, along came the so-called higher-level languages, of which the FORTRAN (FORmula TRANslation) language was one of the first. Programmers developing programs in FORTRAN no longer had to concern themselves with the architecture of the particular computer, and operations performed in FORTRAN were of a much more sophisticated or higher level, far removed from the instruction set of the particular machine. One FORTRAN instruction or *statement* resulted in many different machine instructions being executed, unlike the one-to-one correspondence found between assembly language statements and machine instructions.

Standardization of the syntax of a higher-level language meant that a program could be written in the language to be machine independent. That is, a program could run on any machine that supported the language with few or no changes.

To support a higher-level language, a special computer program must be developed that translates the statements of the program developed in the higher-level language into a form that the computer can understand—in other words, into the particular instructions of the computer. Such a program is known as a *compiler*.

Operating Systems

Before continuing with compilers, it is worthwhile to understand the role that is played by a computer program known as an *operating system*.

An operating system is a program that controls the entire operation of a computer system. All input and output (that is, I/O) operations that are performed on a computer system are channeled through the operating system. The operating system must also manage the computer system's resources and must handle the execution of programs.

One of the most popular operating systems today is the Unix operating system, which was developed at Bell Laboratories. Unix is a rather unique operating system in that it can be found on many different types of computer systems, and under different "flavors," such as Linux or Mac OS X. Historically, operating systems were typically associated with only one type of computer system. But because Unix was written primarily in the C language and made very few assumptions about the architecture of the computer, it has been successfully ported to many different computer systems with a relatively small amount of effort.

Microsoft Windows is another example of a popular operating system. That system is found running primarily on Intel (or Intel-compatible) processors.

Of more recent vintage are operating systems that were developed to run on portable devices such as cell phones and tablets. Apple's iOS and Google's Android operating systems are the two most popular examples.

Compiling Programs

A compiler is a software program that is, in principle, no different than the ones you will see in this book, although it is certainly much more complex. A compiler analyzes a program developed in a particular computer language and then translates it into a form that is suitable for execution on your particular computer system.

Figure 1.1 shows the steps that are involved in entering, compiling, and executing a computer program developed in the C programming language and the typical Unix commands that would be entered from the command line.

The program that is to be compiled is first typed into a *file* on the computer system. Computer installations have various conventions that are used for naming files, but in general, the choice of the name is up to you. C programs can typically be given any name provided the last two characters are ".c" (this is not so much a requirement as it is a convention). So, the name prog1.c might be a valid filename for a C program on your system.

A text editor is usually used to enter the C program into a file. For example, vim is a popular text editor used on Unix systems. The program that is entered into the file is known as the *source program* because it represents the original form of the program expressed in the C language. After the source program has been entered into a file, you can then proceed to have it compiled.

The compilation process is initiated by typing a special command on the system. When this command is entered, the name of the file that contains the source program must also be specified. For example, under Unix, the command to initiate program compilation is called cc. If you are using the popular GNU C compiler, the command you use is gcc. Typing the line

gcc prog1.c

has the effect of initiating the compilation process with the source program contained in prog1.c.

In the first step of the compilation process, the compiler examines each program statement contained in the source program and checks it to ensure that it conforms to the syntax and semantics of the language[1]. If any mistakes are discovered by the compiler during this phase,

---

1. *Technically speaking, the C compiler normally makes a prepass of the program looking for special statements. This preprocessing phase is described in detail in Chapter 12, "The Preprocessor."*

they are reported to the user and the compilation process ends right there. The errors then have to be corrected in the source program (with the use of an editor), and the compilation process must be restarted. Typical errors reported during this phase of compilation might be due to an expression that has unbalanced parentheses (syntactic error), or due to the use of a variable that is not "defined" (semantic error).

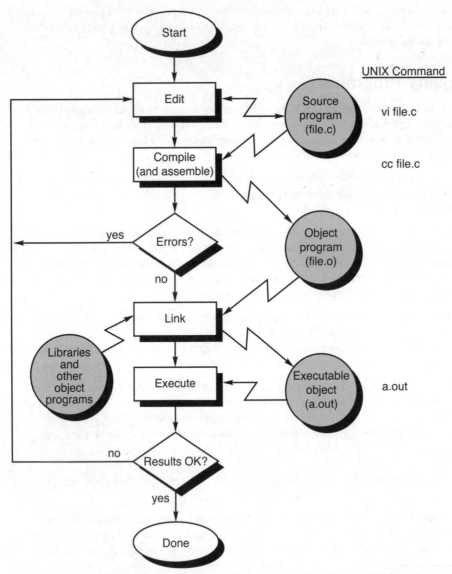

Figure 1.1 Typical steps for entering, compiling, and executing C programs from the command line.

When all the syntactic and semantic errors have been removed from the program, the compiler then proceeds to take each statement of the program and translate it into a "lower" form. On most systems, this means that each statement is translated by the compiler into the equivalent statement or statements in assembly language needed to perform the identical task.

After the program has been translated into an equivalent assembly language program, the next step in the compilation process is to translate the assembly language statements into actual machine instructions. This step might or might not involve the execution of a separate program known as an *assembler*. On most systems, the assembler is executed automatically as part of the compilation process.

The assembler takes each assembly language statement and converts it into a binary format known as *object code*, which is then written into another file on the system. This file typically has the same name as the source file under Unix, with the last letter an "o" (for *object*) instead of a "c". Under Windows, the suffix letters "obj" typically replace the "c" in the filename.

After the program has been translated into object code, it is ready to be *linked*. This process is once again performed automatically whenever the cc or gcc command is issued under Unix. The purpose of the linking phase is to get the program into a final form for execution on the computer. If the program uses other programs that were previously processed by the compiler, then during this phase the programs are linked together. Programs that are used from the system's program *library* are also searched and linked together with the object program during this phase.

The entire process of compiling and linking a program is often called *building*.

The final linked file, which is in an *executable object* code format, is stored in another file on the system, ready to be run or *executed*. Under Unix, this file is called a.out by default. Under Windows, the executable file usually has the same name as the source file, with the c extension replaced by an exe extension.

To subsequently execute the program, all you do is type in the name of the executable object file. So, the command

```
a.out
```

has the effect of *loading* the program called a.out into the computer's memory and initiating its execution.

When the program is executed, each of the statements of the program is sequentially executed in turn. If the program requests any data from the user, known as *input*, the program temporarily suspends its execution so that the input can be entered. Or, the program might simply wait for an *event*, such as a mouse being clicked, to occur. Results that are displayed by the program, known as *output*, appear in a window, sometimes called the *console*. Or, the output might be directly written to a file on the system.

If all goes well (and it probably won't the first time the program is executed), the program performs its intended functions. If the program does not produce the desired results, it is necessary to go back and reanalyze the program's logic. This is known as the *debugging phase*, during which an attempt is made to remove all the known problems or *bugs* from the program. To do this, it will most likely be necessary to make changes to the original source program. In that case, the entire process of compiling, linking, and executing the program must be repeated until the desired results are obtained.

Integrated Development Environments

The individual steps involved in developing C programs were outlined earlier, showing typical commands that would be entered for each step. This process of editing, compiling, running, and debugging programs is often managed by a single integrated application known as an Integrated Development Environment, or IDE for short. An IDE is a windows-based program that allows you to easily manage large software programs, edit files in windows, and compile, link, run, and debug your programs.

On Mac OS X, Xcode is an IDE supported by Apple that is used by many programmers. Under Windows, Microsoft Visual Studio is a good example of a popular IDE. All the IDE applications greatly simplify the entire process involved in program development so it is worth your while to learn how to use one. Most IDEs also support program development in several different programming languages in addition to C, such as Objective-C, Java, C#, and C++.

For more information about IDEs, consult Appendix E, "Resources."

Language Interpreters

Before leaving this discussion of the compilation process, note that there is another method used for analyzing and executing programs developed in a higher-level language. With this method, programs are not compiled but are *interpreted*. An interpreter analyzes and executes the statements of a program at the same time. This method usually allows programs to be more easily debugged. On the other hand, interpreted languages are typically slower than their compiled counterparts because the program statements are not converted into a low-level form in advance of their execution.

BASIC and JavaScript are two programming languages in which programs are often interpreted and not compiled. Other examples include the Unix system's *shell* and Python. Some vendors also offer interpreters for the C programming language.

2

Compiling and Running Your First Program

In this chapter, you are introduced to the C language so that you can see what programming in C is all about. What better way to gain an appreciation for this language than by taking a look at an actual program written in C?

This chapter is short, but you'll be surprised at how much ground you can cover in a brief chapter, including

- Writing your first program.
- Modifying it to change its output.
- Understanding the main() function.
- Outputting information with the printf() function
- Improving your program's readability with comments

To begin with, you'll choose a rather simple example—a program that displays the phrase "Programming is fun." in your window. Program 2.1 shows a C program to accomplish this task.

Program 2.1 **Writing Your First C Program**

```
#include <stdio.h>

int main (void)
{
    printf ("Programming is fun.\n");

    return 0;
}
```

In the C programming language, lowercase and uppercase letters are distinct. In addition, in C, it does not matter where on the line you begin typing—you can begin typing your statement at any position on the line. This fact can be used to your advantage in developing programs that are easier to read. Tab characters are often used by programmers as a convenient way to indent lines.

Compiling Your Program

Returning to your first C program, you first need to type it into a file. Any text editor can be used for this purpose. Unix users often use an editor such as vi or emacs.

C compilers recognize filenames that end in the two characters "." and "c" as C programs. So, assume you type Program 2.1 into a file called prog1.c. Next, you need to compile the program.

Using the GNU C compiler, this can be as simple as issuing the gcc command at the terminal followed by the filename, like this:

```
$ gcc prog1.c
$
```

If you're using the standard Unix C compiler, the command is cc instead of gcc. Here, the text you typed is entered in bold. The dollar sign is your command prompt if you're compiling your C program from the command line. Your actual command prompt might be some characters other than the dollar sign.

If you make any mistakes keying in your program, the compiler lists them after you enter the gcc command, typically identifying the line numbers from your program that contain the errors. If, instead, another command prompt appears, as is shown in the preceding example, no errors were found in your program.

When the compiler compiles and links your program, it creates an executable version of your program. Using the GNU or standard C compiler, this program is called a.out by default. Under Windows, it is often called a.exe instead.

Running Your Program

You can now run the executable by simply typing its name on the command line:[1]

```
$ a.out
Programming is fun.
$
```

You can also specify a different name for the executable file at the time the program is compiled. This is done with the -o (that's the letter O) option, which is followed by the name of the executable. For example, the command line

```
$ gcc prog1.c -o prog1
```

---

1. *If you get an error like this:* a.out: No such file or directory, *then it probably means the* current *directory is not in your* PATH. *You can either add it to your* PATH *or type the following at the* command prompt: ./a.out.

compiles the program `prog1.c`, placing the executable in the file `prog1`, which can subsequently be executed just by specifying its name:

```
$ prog1
Programming is fun.
$
```

Understanding Your First Program

Take a closer look at your first program. The first line of the program

```
#include <stdio.h>
```

should be included at the beginning of just about every program you write. It tells the compiler information about the `printf()` output routine that is used later in the program. Chapter 12, "The Preprocessor," discusses in detail what this line does.

The line of the program that reads

```
int main (void)
```

informs the system that the name of the program is `main()`, and that it *returns* an integer value, which is abbreviated "int." `main()` is a special name that indicates precisely *where* the program is to begin execution. The open and close parentheses immediately following `main()` specify that `main()` is the name of a *function*. The keyword `void` that is enclosed in the parentheses specifies that the function `main()` takes no arguments (that is, it is *void* of arguments). These concepts are explained in great detail in Chapter 7, "Working with Functions."

> **Note**
>
> If you're using an IDE, you may find that it generates a template `main()` for you. In such a case, you may find the first line of `main()` looks more like this:
>
> ```
> int main(int argc, char *argv[])
> ```
>
> This won't affect your program's operation, so just ignore the differences for now.

Now that you have identified `main()` to the system, you are ready to specify precisely what this routine is to perform. This is done by enclosing all program statements of the routine within a pair of curly braces. All program statements included between the braces are taken as part of the `main()` routine by the system. In Program 2.1, you have only two such statements. This statement specifies that a routine named `printf()` is to be invoked or *called*. The parameter or *argument* to be passed to the `printf()` routine is the string of characters

```
"Programming is fun.\n"
```

The `printf()` routine is a function in the C library that simply prints or displays its argument (or arguments, as you will see shortly) on your screen. The last two characters in the string, namely the backslash (\) and the letter n, are known collectively as the *newline* character. A newline character tells the system to do precisely what its name implies—that is, go to a new line. Any characters to be printed after the newline character then appear on the next line of the display. In fact, the newline character is similar in concept to the carriage return key on a typewriter. (Remember those?)

All program statements in C *must* be terminated by a semicolon (;). This is the reason for the semicolon that appears immediately following the closing parenthesis of the printf() call.

The last statement in main() that reads

```
return 0;
```

says to finish execution of main(), and return to the system a status value of 0. You can use any integer here. Zero is used by convention to indicate that the program completed success-fully—that is, without running into any errors. Different numbers can be used to indicate different types of error conditions that occurred (such as a file not being found). This exit status can be tested by other programs (such as the Unix shell) to see whether the program ran successfully.

Now that you've finished analyzing your first program, you can modify it to also display the phrase "And programming in C is even more fun." This can be done by the simple addition of another call to the printf() routine, as shown in Program 2.2. Remember that every C program statement must be terminated by a semicolon.

Program 2.2

```
#include <stdio.h>

int main (void)
{
    printf ("Programming is fun.\n");
    printf ("And programming in C is even more fun.\n");

    return 0;
}
```

If you type in Program 2.2 and then compile and execute it, you can expect the following output in your program's output window, sometimes called the "console."

Program 2.2 **Output**

```
Programming is fun.
And programming in C is even more fun.
```

As you will see from the next program example, it is not necessary to make a separate call to the printf() routine for each line of output. Study the program listed in Program 2.3 and try to predict the results before examining the output. (No cheating now!)

Program 2.3   **Displaying Multiple Lines of Output**

```
#include <stdio.h>

int main (void)
{
    printf ("Testing...\n..1\n...2\n....3\n");

    return 0;
}
```

Program 2.3   **Output**

```
Testing...
..1
...2
....3
```

Displaying the Values of Variables

The printf() routine is the most commonly used routine in this book. This is because it provides an easy and convenient means to display program results. Not only can simple phrases be displayed, but the values of *variables* and the results of computations can also be displayed. In fact, Program 2.4 uses the printf() routine to display the results of adding two numbers, namely 50 and 25.

Program 2.4   **Displaying Variables**

```
#include <stdio.h>

int main (void)
{
    int sum;

    sum = 50 + 25;
    printf ("The sum of 50 and 25 is %i\n", sum);

    return 0;
}
```

Program 2.4   **Output**

```
The sum of 50 and 25 is 75
```

In Program 2.4, the first C program statement *declares* the *variable* sum to be of type *integer*. C requires that all program variables be declared before they are used in a program. The declaration of a variable specifies to the C compiler how a particular variable will be used by the program. This information is needed by the compiler to generate the correct instructions to store and retrieve values into and out of the variable. A variable declared as type int can only be used to hold integral values; that is, values without decimal places. Examples of integral values are 3, 5, -20, and 0. Numbers with decimal places, such as 3.14, 2.455, and 27.0, for example, are known as *floating-point* numbers.

The integer variable sum is used to store the result of the addition of the two integers 50 and 25. A blank line was intentionally left following the declaration of this variable to visually separate the variable declarations of the routine from the program statements; this is strictly a matter of style. Sometimes, the addition of a single blank line in a program can help to make the program more readable.

The program statement

```
sum = 50 + 25;
```

reads as it would in most other programming languages: The number 50 is added (as indicated by the plus sign) to the number 25, and the result is stored (as indicated by the *assignment operator*, the equal sign) in the variable sum.

The printf() routine call in Program 2.4 now has two items or *arguments* enclosed within the parentheses. These arguments are separated by a comma. The first argument to the printf() routine is always the character string to be displayed. However, along with the display of the character string, you might also frequently want to have the value of certain program variables displayed. In this case, you want to have the value of the variable sum displayed at the terminal after the characters

```
The sum of 50 and 25 is
```

are displayed. The percent character inside the first argument is a special character recognized by the printf() function. The character that immediately follows the percent sign specifies what *type* of value is to be displayed at that point. In the preceding program, the letter i is recognized by the printf() routine as signifying that an integer value is to be displayed.[2]

Whenever the printf() routine finds the %i characters inside a character string, it automatically displays the value of the next argument to the printf() routine. Because sum is the next argument to printf(), its value is automatically displayed after the characters "The sum of 50 and 25 is " are displayed.

Now try to predict the output from Program 2.5.

---

2. Note that printf also allows you to specify %d format characters to display an integer. This book consistently uses %i throughout the remaining chapters.

Program 2.5   **Displaying Multiple Values**

```
#include <stdio.h>

int main (void)
{
    int  value1, value2, sum;

    value1 = 50;
    value2 = 25;
    sum = value1 + value2;
    printf ("The sum of %i and %i is %i\n", value1, value2, sum);

    return 0;
}
```

Program 2.5   **Output**

```
The sum of 50 and 25 is 75
```

The first program statement declares three variables called value1, value2, and sum all to be of type int. This statement could have equivalently been expressed using three separate declaratory statements as follows:

```
int value1;
int value2;
int sum;
```

After the three variables have been declared, the program assigns the value 50 to the variable value1 and then assigns 25 to value2. The sum of these two variables is then computed, and the result is assigned to the variable sum.

The call to the printf() routine now contains four arguments. Once again, the first argument, commonly called the *format string*, describes to the system how the remaining arguments are to be displayed. The value of value1 is to be displayed immediately following the display of the "The sum of " characters. Similarly, the values of value2 and sum are to be printed at the appropriate points, as indicated by the next two occurrences of the %i characters in the format string.

Comments

The final program in this chapter (Program 2.6) introduces the concept of the *comment*. A comment statement is used in a program to document a program and to enhance its readability. As you will see from the following example, comments serve to tell the reader of the program—the programmer or someone else whose responsibility it is to maintain the program—just what the programmer had in mind when he or she wrote a particular program or a particular sequence of statements.

Program 2.6   **Using Comments in a Program**

```
/* This program adds two integer values
   and displays the results              */

#include <stdio.h>

int main (void)
{
    // Declare variables
    int  value1, value2, sum;

    // Assign values and calculate their sum
    value1 = 50;
    value2 = 25;
    sum = value1 + value2;

    // Display the result
    printf ("The sum of %i and %i is %i\n", value1, value2, sum);

    return 0;
}
```

Program 2.6   **Output**

```
The sum of 50 and 25 is 75
```

There are two ways to insert comments into a C program. A comment can be initiated by the two characters / and *. This marks the *beginning* of the comment. These types of comments have to be *terminated*. To end the comment, the characters * and / are used without any embedded spaces. All characters included between the opening /* and the closing */ are treated as part of the comment statement and are ignored by the C compiler. This form of comment is often used when comments span several lines in the program. The second way to add a comment to your program is by using two consecutive slash characters //. Any characters that follow these slashes up to the end of the line are ignored by the compiler.

In Program 2.6, four separate comment statements were used. This program is otherwise identical to Program 2.5. Admittedly, this is a contrived example because only the first comment at the head of the program is useful. (Yes, it is possible to insert so many comments into a program that the readability of the program is actually degraded instead of improved!)

The intelligent use of comment statements inside a program cannot be overemphasized. Many times, a programmer returns to a program that he coded perhaps only six months ago, only to discover to his dismay that he could not for the life of him remember the purpose of a particular routine or of a particular group of statements. A simple comment statement judiciously inserted at that particular point in the program might have saved a significant amount of time otherwise wasted on rethinking the logic of the routine or set of statements.

It is a good idea to get into the habit of inserting comment statements into the program as the program is being written or typed in. There are good reasons for this. First, it is far easier to document the program while the particular program logic is still fresh in your mind than it is to go back and rethink the logic after the program has been completed. Second, by inserting comments into the program at such an early stage of the game, you get to reap the benefits of the comments during the debug phase, when program logic errors are being isolated and debugged. A comment can not only help you read through the program, but it can also help point the way to the source of the logic mistake. Finally, I have yet to discover a programmer who actually enjoyed documenting a program. In fact, after you have finished debugging your program, you will probably not relish the idea of going back to the program to insert comments. Inserting comments while developing the program makes this sometimes-tedious task a bit easier to swallow.

This concludes this introductory chapter on developing programs in C. By now, you should have a good feel as to what is involved in writing a program in C, and you should be able to develop a small program on your own. In the next chapter, you begin to learn some of the finer intricacies of this wonderfully powerful and flexible programming language. But first, try your hand at the following exercises to make certain you understand the concepts presented in this chapter.

Exercises

1. Type in and run the six programs presented in this chapter. Compare the output produced by each program with the output presented after each program in the text.

2. Write a program that prints the following text.

    1. In C, lowercase letters are significant.

    2. `main()` is where program execution begins.

    3. Opening and closing braces enclose program statements in a routine.

    4. All program statements must be terminated by a semicolon.

3. What output would you expect from the following program?

```
#include <stdio.h>

int main (void)
{
    printf ("Testing...");
    printf ("....1");
    printf ("...2");
    printf ("..3");
    printf ("\n");

    return 0;
}
```

4. Write a program that subtracts the value 15 from 87 and displays the result, together with an appropriate message, at the terminal.

5. Identify the syntactic errors in the following program. Then type in and run the corrected program to ensure you have correctly identified all the mistakes.

```
#include <stdio.h>

int main (Void)
(
        INT   sum;
        /* COMPUTE RESULT
        sum = 25 + 37 - 19
        /* DISPLAY RESULTS //
        printf ("The answer is %i\n" sum);
        return 0;
}
```

6. What output might you expect from the following program?

```
#include <stdio.h>

int main (void)
{
        int answer, result;

        answer = 100;
        result = answer - 10;
        printf ("The result is %i\n", result + 5);

        return 0;
}
```

## 3

Variables, Data Types, and Arithmetic Expressions

The true power of programs you create is their manipulation of data. In order to truly take advantage of this power, you need to better understand the different data types you can use, as well as how to create and name variables. C has a rich variety of math operators that you can use to manipulate your data. In this chapter you will cover:

- The `int`, `float`, `double`, `char`, and `_Bool` data types
- Modifying data types with `short`, `long`, and `long long`
- The rules for naming variables
- Basic math operators and arithmetic expressions
- Type casting

Understanding Data Types and Constants

You have already been exposed to the C basic data type `int`. As you will recall, a variable declared to be of type `int` can be used to contain integral values only—that is, values that do not contain decimal places.

The C programming language provides four other basic data types: `float`, `double`, `char`, and `_Bool`. A variable declared to be of type `float` can be used for storing floating-point numbers (values containing decimal places). The `double` type is the same as type `float`, only with roughly twice the precision. The `char` data type can be used to store a single character, such as the letter 'a', the digit character '6', or a semicolon (';') (more on this later). Finally, the `_Bool` data type can be used to store just the values 0 or 1. Variables of this type are used for indicating an on/off, yes/no, or true/false situation. These one-or-the-other choices are also known as binary choices.

In C, any number, single character, or character string is known as a *constant*. For example, the number 58 represents a constant integer value. The character string "Programming in C is fun.\n" is an example of a constant character string. Expressions consisting entirely of constant values are called *constant expressions*. So, the expression

```
128 + 7 - 17
```

is a constant expression because each of the terms of the expression is a constant value. But if i were declared to be an integer variable, the expression

```
128 + 7 - i
```

would not represent a constant expression because its value would change based on the value of i. If i is 10, the expression is equal to 125, but if i is 200, the expression is equal to –65.

The Integer Type int

In C, an integer constant consists of a sequence of one or more digits. A minus sign preceding the sequence indicates that the value is negative. The values 158, -10, and 0 are all valid examples of integer constants. No embedded spaces are permitted between the digits, and values larger than 999 cannot be expressed using commas. (So, the value 12,000 is not a valid integer constant and must be written as 12000.)

Two special formats in C enable integer constants to be expressed in a base other than decimal (base 10). If the first digit of the integer value is a 0, the integer is taken as expressed in *octal* notation—that is, in base 8. In that case, the remaining digits of the value must be valid base-8 digits and, therefore, must be 0–7. So, to express the value 50 in base 8 in C, which is equivalent to the value 40 in decimal, the notation 050 is used. Similarly, the octal constant 0177 represents the decimal value 127 (1 × 64 + 7 × 8 + 7). An integer value can be displayed at the terminal in octal notation by using the format characters %o in the format string of a printf() statement. In such a case, the value is displayed in octal without a leading zero. The format character %#o does cause a leading zero to be displayed before an octal value.

If an integer constant is preceded by a zero and the letter *x* (either lowercase or uppercase), the value is taken as being expressed in hexadecimal (base 16) notation. Immediately following the letter *x* are the digits of the hexadecimal value, which can be composed of the digits 0–9 and the letters a–f (or A–F). The letters represent the values 10–15, respectively. So, to assign the hexadecimal value FFEF0D to an integer variable called rgbColor, the statement

```
rgbColor = 0xFFEF0D;
```

can be used. The format characters %x display a value in hexadecimal format without the leading 0x, and using lowercase letters a–f for hexadecimal digits. To display the value with the leading 0x, you use the format characters %#x, as in the following:

```
printf ("Color is %#x\n", rgbColor);
```

An uppercase x, as in %X or %#X, can be used to display the leading x and the hexadecimal digits that follow using uppercase letters.

Storage Sizes and Ranges

Every value, whether it's a character, integer, or floating-point number, has a *range* of values associated with it. This range has to do with the amount of storage that is allocated to store a particular type of data. In general, that amount is not defined in the language. It typically depends on the computer you're running, and is, therefore, called *implementation-* or *machine-*dependent. For example, an integer might take up 32 bits on your computer, or perhaps it might be stored in 64. You should never write programs that make any assumptions about the size of your data types. You are, however, guaranteed that a minimum amount of storage will be set aside for each basic data type. For example, it's guaranteed that an integer value will be stored in a minimum of 32 bits of storage, which is the size of a "word" on many computers.

The Floating Number Type `float`

A variable declared to be of type `float` can be used for storing values containing decimal places. A floating-point constant is distinguished by the presence of a decimal point. You can omit digits before the decimal point or digits after the decimal point, but obviously you can't omit both. The values `3.`, `125.8`, and `-.0001` are all valid examples of floating-point constants. To display a floating-point value at the terminal, the `printf` conversion characters `%f` are used.

Floating-point constants can also be expressed in *scientific notation*. The value `1.7e4` is a floating-point value expressed in this notation and represents the value 1.7×10^4. The value before the letter `e` is known as the *mantissa*, whereas the value that follows is called the *exponent*. This exponent, which can be preceded by an optional plus or minus sign, represents the power of 10 by which the mantissa is to be multiplied. So, in the constant `2.25e-3`, the `2.25` is the value of the mantissa and `-3` is the value of the exponent. This constant represents the value 2.25×10^{-3}, or 0.00225. Incidentally, the letter `e`, which separates the mantissa from the exponent, can be written in either lowercase or uppercase.

To display a value in scientific notation, the format characters `%e` should be specified in the `printf()` format string. The `printf()` format characters `%g` can be used to let `printf()` decide whether to display the floating-point value in normal floating-point notation or in scientific notation. This decision is based on the value of the exponent: If it's less than −4 or greater than 5, `%e` (scientific notation) format is used; otherwise, `%f` format is used.

Use the `%g` format characters for displaying floating-point numbers—it produces the most aesthetically pleasing output.

A *hexadecimal* floating constant consists of a leading `0x` or `0X`, followed by one or more decimal or hexadecimal digits, followed by a `p` or `P`, followed by an optionally signed binary exponent. For example, `0x0.3p10` represents the value $3/16 \times 2^{10} = 0.5$.

The Extended Precision Type `double`

The `double` type is very similar to the `float` type, but it is used whenever the range provided by a `float` variable is not sufficient. Variables declared to be of type `double` can store roughly twice as many significant digits as can a variable of type `float`. Most computers represent `double` values using 64 bits.

Unless told otherwise, all floating-point constants are taken as `double` values by the C compiler. To explicitly express a `float` constant, append either an `f` or `F` to the end of the number, as follows:

```
12.5f
```

To display a `double` value, the format characters `%f`, `%e`, or `%g`, which are the same format characters used to display a `float` value, can be used.

The Single Character Type `char`

A `char` variable can be used to store a single character.[1] A character constant is formed by enclosing the character within a pair of single quotation marks. So `'a'`, `';'`, and `'0'` are all valid examples of character constants. The first constant represents the letter *a*, the second is a semicolon, and the third is the character zero—which is not the same as the number zero. Do not confuse a character constant, which is a single character enclosed in single quotes, with a character string, which is any number of characters enclosed in double quotes.

The character constant `'\n'`—the newline character—is a valid character constant even though it seems to contradict the rule cited previously. This is because the backslash character is a special character in the C system and does not actually count as a character. In other words, the C compiler treats the character `'\n'` as a single character, even though it is actually formed by two characters. There are other special characters that are initiated with the backslash character. Consult Appendix A, "C Language Summary," for a complete list.

The format characters `%c` can be used in a `printf()` call to display the value of a `char` variable at the terminal.

The Boolean Data Type `_Bool`

A `_Bool` variable is defined in the language to be large enough to store just the values `0` and `1`. The precise amount of memory that is used is unspecified. `_Bool` variables are used in programs that need to indicate a Boolean condition. For example, a variable of this type might be used to indicate whether all data has been read from a file.

By convention, `0` is used to indicate a false value, and `1` indicates a true value. When assigning a value to a `_Bool` variable, a value of `0` is stored as 0 inside the variable, whereas any nonzero value is stored as 1.

To make it easier to work with `_Bool` variables in your program, the standard header file `<stdbool.h>` defines the values `bool`, `true`, and `false`. An example of this is shown in Program 5.10A in Chapter 5, "Making Decisions."

---

1. *Appendix A discusses methods for storing characters from extended character sets, through special escape sequences, universal characters, and wide characters.*

In Program 3.1, the basic C data types are used.

Program 3.1 **Using the Basic Data Types**

```c
#include <stdio.h>

int main (void)
{
    int       integerVar = 100;
    float     floatingVar = 331.79;
    double    doubleVar = 8.44e+11;
    char      charVar = 'W';

    _Bool     boolVar = 0;

    printf ("integerVar = %i\n", integerVar);
    printf ("floatingVar = %f\n", floatingVar);
    printf ("doubleVar = %e\n", doubleVar);
    printf ("doubleVar = %g\n", doubleVar);
    printf ("charVar = %c\n", charVar);

    printf ("boolVar = %i\n", boolVar);

    return 0;
}
```

Program 3.1 **Output**

```
integerVar = 100
floatingVar = 331.790009
doubleVar = 8.440000e+11
doubleVar = 8.44e+11
charVar = W
boolVar = 0;
```

The first statement of Program 3.1 declares the variable `integerVar` to be an integer variable and also assigns to it an initial value of `100`, as if the following two statements had been used instead:

```c
int  integerVar;
integerVar = 100;
```

In the second line of the program's output, notice that the value of `331.79`, which is assigned to `floatingVar`, is actually displayed as `331.790009`. In fact, the actual value displayed is dependent on the particular computer system you are using. The reason for this inaccuracy is the particular way in which numbers are internally represented inside the computer. You have probably come across the same type of inaccuracy when dealing with numbers on your pocket calculator. If you divide 1 by 3 on your calculator, you get the result .33333333, with perhaps some additional 3s tacked on at the end. The string of 3s is the calculator's approximation to one third. Theoretically, there should be an infinite number of 3s. But the calculator can hold only so many digits, thus the inherent inaccuracy of the machine. The same type of inaccuracy applies here: Certain floating-point values cannot be exactly represented inside the computer's memory.

When displaying the values of `float` or `double` variables, you have the choice of three different formats. The `%f` characters are used to display values in a standard manner. Unless told otherwise, `printf()` always displays a `float` or `double` value to six decimal places rounded. You see later in this chapter how to select the number of decimal places that are displayed.

The `%e` characters are used to display the value of a `float` or `double` variable in scientific notation. Once again, six decimal places are automatically displayed by the system.

With the `%g` characters, `printf()` chooses between `%f` and `%e` and also automatically removes from the display any trailing zeroes. If no digits follow the decimal point, it doesn't display that either.

In the next-to-last `printf()` statement, the `%c` characters are used to display the single character `'W'` that you assigned to `charVar` when the variable was declared. Remember that whereas a character string (such as the first argument to `printf()`) is enclosed within a pair of double quotes, a character constant must always be enclosed within a pair of single quotes.

The last `printf()` shows that a `_Bool` variable can have its value displayed using the integer format characters `%i`.

Type Specifiers: `long`, `long  long`, `short`, `unsigned`, and `signed`

If the specifier `long` is placed directly before the `int` declaration, the declared integer variable is of extended range on some computer systems. An example of a `long  int` declaration might be

```
long int factorial;
```

This declares the variable `factorial` to be a `long` integer variable. As with `float`s and `double`s, the particular accuracy of a `long` variable depends on your particular computer system. On many systems, an `int` and a `long  int` have the same range and either can be used to store integer values up to 32-bits wide ($2^{31} - 1$, or $2,147,483,647$).

A constant value of type `long  int` is formed by optionally appending the letter L (upper- or lowercase) onto the end of an integer constant. No spaces are permitted between the number and the L. So, the declaration

```
long int numberOfPoints = 131071100L;
```

declares the variable `numberOfPoints` to be of type `long  int` with an initial value of $131,071,100$.

To display the value of a `long  int` using `printf()`, the letter l is used as a modifier before the integer format characters i, o, and x. This means that the format characters `%li` can be used to display the value of a `long int` in decimal format, the characters `%lo` can display the value in octal format, and the characters `%lx` can display the value in hexadecimal format.

There is also a `long long` integer data type, so

```
long long int maxAllowedStorage;
```

declares the indicated variable to be of the specified extended accuracy, which is guaranteed to be at least 64 bits wide. Instead of a single letter l, two ls are used in the `printf` string to display `long long` integers, as in `"%lli"`.

The `long` specifier is also allowed in front of a `double` declaration, as follows:

```
long double US_deficit_2004;
```

A `long double` constant is written as a floating constant with the letter l or L immediately following, such as

```
1.234e+7L
```

To display a `long double`, the L modifier is used. So, `%Lf` displays a `long double` value in floating-point notation, `%Le` displays the same value in scientific notation, and `%Lg` tells `printf()` to choose between `%Lf` and `%Le`.

The specifier `short`, when placed in front of the `int` declaration, tells the C compiler that the particular variable being declared is used to store fairly small integer values. The motivation for using `short` variables is primarily one of conserving memory space, which can be an issue in situations in which the program needs a lot of memory and the amount of available memory is limited.

On some machines, a `short int` takes up half the amount of storage as a regular `int` variable does. In any case, you are guaranteed that the amount of space allocated for a `short int` will not be less than 16 bits.

There is no way to explicitly write a constant of type `short int` in C. To display a `short int` variable, place the letter h in front of any of the normal integer conversion characters: `%hi`, `%ho`, or `%hx`. Alternatively, you can also use any of the integer conversion characters to display `short ints`, due to the way they can be converted into integers when they are passed as arguments to the `printf()` routine.

The final specifier that can be placed in front of an `int` variable is used when an integer variable will be used to store only positive numbers. The declaration

```
unsigned int counter;
```

declares to the compiler that the variable `counter` is used to contain only positive values. By restricting the use of an integer variable to the exclusive storage of positive integers, the accuracy of the integer variable is extended.

An `unsigned int` constant is formed by placing the letter u (or U) after the constant, as follows:

```
0x00ffU
```

You can combine the letters u (or U) and l (or L) when writing an integer constant, so

20000UL

tells the compiler to treat the constant 20000 as an unsigned long.

An integer constant that's not followed by any of the letters u, U, l, or L and that is too large to fit into a normal-sized int is treated as an unsigned int by the compiler. If it's too small to fit into an unsigned int, the compiler treats it as a long int. If it still can't fit inside a long int, the compiler makes it an unsigned long int. If it doesn't fit there, the compiler treats it as a long long int if it fits, and as an unsigned long long int otherwise.

When declaring variables to be of type long long int, long int, short int, or unsigned int, you can omit the keyword int. Therefore, the unsigned variable counter could have been equivalently declared as follows:

unsigned counter;

You can also declare char variables to be unsigned.

The signed qualifier can be used to explicitly tell the compiler that a particular variable is a signed quantity. Its use is primarily in front of the char declaration, and further discussion is deferred until Chapter 13, "More on Data Types."

Don't worry if the discussions of these specifiers seem a bit esoteric to you at this point. In later sections of this book, many of these different types are illustrated with actual program examples. Chapter 13 goes into more detail about data types and conversions.

Table 3.1 summarizes the basic data types and qualifiers.

Table 3.1   **Basic Data Types**

Type	Constant Examples	printf chars
char	'a', '\n'	%c
_Bool	0, 1	%i, %u
short int	—	%hi, %hx, %ho
unsigned short int	—	%hu, %hx, %ho
int	12, -97, 0xFFE0, 0177	%i, %x, %o
unsigned int	12u, 100U, 0XFFu	%u, %x, %o
long int	12L, -2001, 0xffffL	%li, %lx, %lo
unsigned long int	12UL, 100ul, 0xffeeUL	%lu, %lx, %lo
long long int	0xe5e5e5e5LL, 500ll	%lli, %llx, &llo
unsigned long long int	12ull, 0xffeeULL	%llu, %llx, %llo
float	12.34f, 3.1e-5f, 0x1.5p10, 0x1P-1	%f, %e, %g, %a

Type	Constant Examples	printf chars
double	12.34, 3.1e-5, 0x.1p3	%f, %e, %g, %a
long double	12.341, 3.1e-51	%Lf, $Le, %Lg

Working with Variables

Early computer programmers had the onerous task of having to write their programs in the binary language of the machine they were programming. This meant that computer instructions had to be hand-coded into binary numbers by the programmer before they could be entered into the machine. Furthermore, the programmer had to explicitly assign and reference any storage locations inside the computer's memory by a specific number or memory address.

Today's programming languages allow you to concentrate more on solving the particular problem at hand than worrying about specific machine codes or memory locations. They enable you to assign symbolic names, known as *variable names*, for storing program computations and results. A variable name can be chosen by you in a meaningful way to reflect the type of value that is to be stored in that variable.

In Chapter 2, "Compiling and Running Your First Program," you used several variables to store integer values. For example, you used the variable sum in Program 2.4 to store the result of the addition of the two integers 50 and 25.

The C language allows data types other than just integers to be stored in variables as well, provided the proper declaration for the variable is made *before* it is used in the program. Variables can be used to store floating-point numbers, characters, and even *pointers* to locations inside the computer's memory.

The rules for forming variable names are quite simple: They must begin with a letter or underscore (_) and can be followed by any combination of letters (upper- or lowercase), underscores, or the digits 0–9. The following is a list of valid variable names.

```
sum
pieceFlag
i
J5x7
Number_of_moves
_sysflag
```

On the other hand, the following variable names are not valid for the stated reasons:

sum$value	$ is not a valid character.
piece flag	Embedded spaces are not permitted.
3Spencer	Variable names cannot start with a number.
int	int is a reserved word.

int cannot be used as a variable name because its use has a special meaning to the C compiler. This use is known as a reserved name or reserved word. In general, any name that has special significance to the C compiler cannot be used as a variable name. Appendix A provides a complete list of such reserved names.

You should always remember that upper- and lowercase letters are distinct in C. Therefore, the variable names sum, Sum, and SUM each refer to a different variable.

Your variable names can be as long as you want, although only the first 63 characters might be significant, and in some special cases (as described in Appendix A), only the first 31 characters might be significant. It's typically not practical to use variable names that are too long—just because of all the extra typing you have to do. For example, although the following line is valid

```
theAmountOfMoneyWeMadeThisYear = theAmountOfMoneyLeftAttheEndOfTheYear -
        theAmountOfMoneyAtTheStartOfTheYear;
```

this line

```
moneyMadeThisYear = moneyAtEnd - moneyAtStart;
```

conveys almost as much information in much less space.

When deciding on the choice of a variable name, keep one recommendation in mind—don't be lazy. Pick names that reflect the intended use of the variable. The reasons are obvious. Just as with comments, meaningful variable names can dramatically increase the readability of a program and pay off in the debug and documentation phases. In fact, the documentation task is probably greatly reduced because the program is more self-explanatory.

Working with Arithmetic Expressions

In C, just as in virtually all programming languages, the plus sign (+) is used to add two values, the minus sign (-) is used to subtract two values, the asterisk (*) is used to multiply two values, and the slash (/) is used to divide two values. These operators are known as *binary* arithmetic operators because they operate on two values or terms.

You have seen how a simple operation such as addition can be performed in C. Program 3.2 further illustrates the operations of subtraction, multiplication, and division. The last two operations performed in the program introduce the notion that one operator can have a higher priority, or *precedence*, over another operator. In fact, each operator in C has a precedence associated with it. This precedence is used to determine how an expression that has more than one operator is evaluated: The operator with the higher precedence is evaluated first. Expressions containing operators of the same precedence are evaluated either from left to right or from right to left, depending on the operator. This is known as the *associative* property of an operator. Appendix A provides a complete list of operator precedences and their rules of association.

Program 3.2   **Using the Arithmetic Operators**

```c
// Illustrate the use of various arithmetic operators

#include <stdio.h>

int main (void)
{
    int a = 100;
    int b = 2;
    int c = 25;
    int d = 4;
    int result;

    result = a - b;        // subtraction
    printf ("a - b = %i\n", result);

    result = b * c;        // multiplication
    printf ("b * c = %i\n", result);

    result = a / c;        // division
    printf ("a / c = %i\n", result);

    result = a + b * c;    // precedence
    printf ("a + b * c = %i\n", result);

    printf ("a * b + c * d = %i\n", a * b + c * d);

    return 0;
}
```

Program 3.2   **Output**

```
a - b = 98
b * c = 50
a / c = 4
a + b * c = 150
a * b + c * d = 300
```

After declaring the integer variables a, b, c, d, and result, the program assigns the result of subtracting b from a to result and then displays its value with an appropriate printf() call.

The next statement

```c
result = b * c;
```

has the effect of multiplying the value of b by the value of c and storing the product in result. The result of the multiplication is then displayed using a printf() call that should be familiar to you by now.

The next program statement introduces the division operator—the slash. The result of 4, as obtained by dividing 100 by 25, is displayed by the printf() statement immediately following the division of a by c.

On some computer systems, attempting to divide a number by zero results in abnormal termination of the program.[2] Even if the program does not terminate abnormally, the results obtained by such a division will be meaningless.

In Chapter 5, you see how you can check for division by zero before the division operation is performed. If it is determined that the divisor is zero, an appropriate action can be taken and the division operation can be averted.

The expression

```
a + b * c
```

does not produce the result of 2550 (102 × 25); rather, the result as displayed by the corresponding printf() statement is shown as 150. This is because C, like most other programming languages, has rules for the order of evaluating multiple operations or terms in an expression. Evaluation of an expression generally proceeds from left to right. However, the operations of multiplication and division are given precedence over the operations of addition and subtraction. Therefore, the expression

```
a + b * c
```

is evaluated as

```
a + (b * c)
```

by the C programming language. (This is the same way this expression would be evaluated if you were to apply the basic rules of algebra.)

If you want to alter the order of evaluation of terms inside an expression, you can use parentheses. In fact, the expression listed previously is a perfectly valid C expression. Thus, the statement

```
result = a + (b * c);
```

could have been substituted in Program 3.2 to achieve identical results. However, if the expression

```
result = (a + b) * c;
```

were used instead, the value assigned to result would be 2550 because the value of a (100) would be added to the value of b (2) before multiplication by the value of c (25) would take place. Parentheses can also be nested, in which case evaluation of the expression proceeds outward from the innermost set of parentheses. Just be certain you have as many closed parentheses as you have open ones.

---

2. This happens using the gcc compiler under Windows. On Unix systems, the program might not terminate abnormally, and might give 0 as the result of an integer division by zero and "Infinity" as the result of a float division by zero.

You will notice from the last statement in Program 3.2 that it is perfectly valid to give an expression as an argument to printf() without having to first assign the result of the expression evaluation to a variable. The expression

```
a * b + c * d
```

is evaluated according to the rules stated previously as

```
(a * b) + (c * d)
```

or

```
(100 * 2) + (25 * 4)
```

The result of 300 is handed to the printf() routine.

Integer Arithmetic and the Unary Minus Operator

Program 3.3 reinforces what you just learned and introduces the concept of integer arithmetic.

Program 3.3   **More Examples with Arithmetic Operators**

```
// More arithmetic expressions

#include <stdio.h>

int main (void)
{
    int    a = 25;
    int    b = 2;

    float c = 25.0;
    float d = 2.0;

    printf ("6 + a / 5 * b = %i\n", 6 + a / 5 * b);
    printf ("a / b * b = %i\n", a / b * b);
    printf ("c / d * d = %f\n", c / d * d);
    printf ("-a = %i\n", -a);

    return 0;
}
```

Program 3.3   **Output**

```
6 + a / 5 * b = 16
a / b * b = 24
c / d * d = 25.000000
-a = -25
```

Extra blank spaces are inserted between int and the declaration of a, b, c, and d in the first four statements to align the declaration of each variable. This helps make the program more readable. You also might have noticed in each program presented thus far that a blank space was placed around each operator. This, too, is not required and is done solely for aesthetic reasons. In general, you can add extra blank spaces just about anywhere that a single blank space is allowed. A few extra presses of the spacebar prove worthwhile if the resulting program is easier to read.

The expression in the first printf() call of Program 3.3 reinforces the notion of operator precedence. Evaluation of this expression proceeds as follows:

1. Because division has higher precedence than addition, the value of a (25) is divided by 5 first. This gives the intermediate result of 5.

2. Because multiplication also has higher precedence than addition, the intermediate result of 5 is next multiplied by 2, the value of b, giving a new intermediate result of 10.

3. Finally, the addition of 6 and 10 is performed, giving a final result of 16.

The second printf() statement introduces a new twist. You would expect that dividing a by b and then multiplying by b would return the value of a, which has been set to 25. But this does not seem to be the case, as shown by the output display of 24. It might seem like the computer lost a bit somewhere along the way. The fact of the matter is that this expression was evaluated using integer arithmetic.

If you glance back at the declarations for the variables a and b, you will recall that they were both declared to be of type int. Whenever a term to be evaluated in an expression consists of two integers, the C system performs the operation using integer arithmetic. In such a case, all decimal portions of numbers are lost. Therefore, when the value of a is divided by the value of b, or 25 is divided by 2, you get an intermediate result of 12 and *not* 12.5 as you might expect. Multiplying this intermediate result by 2 gives the final result of 24, thus explaining the "lost" digit. Don't forget that if you divide two integers, you always get an integer result. In addition, keep in mind that no rounding occurs, the decimal value is simply dropped, so integer division that ends up with 12.01, 12.5, or 12.99 will end up with the same value—12.

As you can see from the next-to-last printf() statement in Program 3.3, if you perform the same operation using floating-point values instead of integers, you obtain the expected result.

The decision of whether to use a float variable or an int variable should be made based on the variable's intended use. If you don't need any decimal places, use an integer variable. The resulting program is more efficient—that is, it executes more quickly on many computers. On the other hand, if you need the decimal place accuracy, the choice is clear. The only question you then must answer is whether to use a float, double, or long double. The answer to this question depends on the desired accuracy of the numbers you are dealing with, as well as their magnitude.

In the last printf() statement, the value of the variable a is negated by use of the unary minus operator. A *unary* operator is one that operates on a single value, as opposed to a binary operator, which operates on two values. The minus sign actually has a dual role: As a binary operator, it is used for subtracting two values; as a unary operator, it is used to negate a value.

The unary minus operator has higher precedence than all other arithmetic operators, except for the unary plus operator (+), which has the same precedence. So the expression

```
c = -a * b;
```

results in the multiplication of -a by b. Once again, in Appendix A you will find a table summarizing the various operators and their precedences.

The Modulus Operator

A surprisingly valuable operator, one you may not have experience with, is the modulus operator, which is symbolized by the percent sign (%). Try to determine how this operator works by analyzing Program 3.4.

Program 3.4   **Illustrating the Modulus Operator**

```
// The modulus operator

#include <stdio.h>

int main (void)
{
    int a = 25, b = 5, c = 10, d = 7;

    printf("a = %i, b = %i, c = %i, and d = %i\n", a, b, c, d);
    printf ("a %% b = %i\n", a % b);
    printf ("a %% c = %i\n", a % c);
    printf ("a %% d = %i\n", a % d);
    printf ("a / d * d + a %% d = %i\n",
                a / d * d + a % d);

    return 0;
}
```

Program 3.4   **Output**

```
a = 25, b = 5, c = 10, and d = 7
a % b = 0
a % c = 5
a % d = 4
a / d * d + a % d = 25
```

The first statement inside `main()` defines and initializes the variables a, b, c, and d in a single statement.

For a reminder, before a series of statements that use the modulus operator are printed, the first `printf()` statement prints the values of the four variables used in the program. It's not crucial, but it's a nice reminder to help someone follow along with your program. For the remaining `printf()` lines, as you know, `printf()` uses the character that immediately follows the percent sign to determine how to print the next argument. However, if it is another percent sign that follows, the `printf()` routine takes this as an indication that you really intend to display a percent sign and inserts one at the appropriate place in the program's output.

You are correct if you concluded that the function of the modulus operator % is to give the remainder of the first value divided by the second value. In the first example, the remainder after 25 is divided by 5 and is displayed as 0. If you divide 25 by 10, you get a remainder of 5, as verified by the second line of output. Dividing 25 by 7 gives a remainder of 4, as shown in the third output line.

The last line of output in Program 3.4 requires a bit of explanation. First, you will notice that the program statement has been written on two lines. This is perfectly valid in C. In fact, a program statement can be continued to the next line at any point at which a blank space could be used. (An exception to this occurs when dealing with character strings—a topic discussed in Chapter 9, "Character Strings.") At times, it might not only be desirable, but perhaps even necessary, to continue a program statement onto the next line. The continuation of the `printf()` call in Program 3.4 is indented to visually show that it is a continuation of the preceding program statement.

Turn your attention to the expression evaluated in the final statement. You will recall that any operations between two integer values in C are performed with integer arithmetic. Therefore, any remainder resulting from the division of two integer values is simply discarded. Dividing 25 by 7, as indicated by the expression a / d, gives an intermediate result of 3. Multiplying this value by the value of d, which is 7, produces the intermediate result of 21. Finally, adding the remainder of dividing a by d, as indicated by the expression a % d, leads to the final result of 25. It is no coincidence that this value is the same as the value of the variable a. In general, the expression

```
a / b * b + a % b
```

will always equal the value of a, assuming of course that a and b are both integer values. In fact, the modulus operator % is defined to work only with integer values.

As far as precedence is concerned, the modulus operator has equal precedence to the multiplication and division operators. This implies, of course, that an expression such as

```
table + value % TABLE_SIZE
```

will be evaluated as

```
table + (value % TABLE_SIZE)
```

Integer and Floating-Point Conversions

To effectively develop C programs, you must understand the rules used for the implicit conversion of floating-point and integer values in C. Program 3.5 demonstrates some of the simple conversions between numeric data types. You should note that some compilers might give warning messages to alert you of the fact that conversions are being performed.

Program 3.5   **Converting Between Integers and Floats**

```
// Basic conversions in C

#include <stdio.h>

int main (void)
{
    float   f1 = 123.125, f2;
    int     i1, i2 = -150;
    char       c = 'a';

    i1 = f1;                    // floating to integer conversion
    printf ("%f assigned to an int produces %i\n", f1, i1);

    f1 = i2;                    // integer to floating conversion
    printf ("%i assigned to a float produces %f\n", i2, f1);

    f1 = i2 / 100;             // integer divided by integer
    printf ("%i divided by 100 produces %f\n", i2, f1);

    f2 = i2 / 100.0;           // integer divided by a float
    printf ("%i divided by 100.0 produces %f\n", i2, f2);

    f2 = (float) i2 / 100;     // type cast operator
    printf ("(float) %i divided by 100 produces %f\n", i2, f2);

    return 0;
}
```

Program 3.5   **Output**

```
123.125000 assigned to an int produces 123
-150 assigned to a float produces -150.000000
-150 divided by 100 produces -1.000000
-150 divided by 100.0 produces -1.500000
(float) -150 divided by 100 produces -1.500000
```

Whenever a floating-point value is assigned to an integer variable in C, the decimal portion of the number gets truncated. So, when the value of f1 is assigned to i1 in the previous program, the number 123.125 is *truncated*, which means that only its integer portion, or 123, is stored in i1. The first line of the program's output verifies that this is the case.

Assigning an integer variable to a floating variable does not cause any change in the value of the number; the value is simply converted by the system and stored in the floating variable. The second line of the program's output verifies that the value of i2 (–150) was correctly converted and stored in the float variable f1.

The next two lines of the program's output illustrate two points that must be remembered when forming arithmetic expressions. The first has to do with integer arithmetic, which was previously discussed in this chapter. Whenever two operands in an expression are integers (and this applies to short, unsigned, long, and long long integers as well), the operation is carried out under the rules of integer arithmetic. Therefore, any decimal portion resulting from a division operation is discarded, even if the result is assigned to a floating variable (as you did in the program). Therefore, when the integer variable i2 is divided by the integer constant 100, the system performs the division as an integer division. The result of dividing –150 by 100, which is –1, is, therefore, the value that is stored in the float variable f1.

The next division performed in the previous listing involves an integer variable and a floating-point constant. Any operation between two values in C is performed as a floating-point operation if either value is a floating-point variable or constant. Therefore, when the value of i2 is divided by 100.0, the system treats the division as a floating-point division and produces the result of –1.5, which is assigned to the float variable f1.

The Type Cast Operator

The last division operation from Program 3.5 that reads

```
f2 = (float) i2 / 100;      // type cast operator
```

introduces the type cast operator. The type cast operator has the effect of converting the value of the variable i2 to type float for purposes of evaluation of the expression. In no way does this operator permanently affect the value of the variable i2; it is a unary operator that behaves like other unary operators. Because the expression –a has no permanent effect on the value of a, neither does the expression (float) a.

The type cast operator has a higher precedence than all the arithmetic operators except the unary minus and unary plus. Of course, if necessary, you can always use parentheses in an expression to force the terms to be evaluated in any desired order.

As another example of the use of the type cast operator, the expression

```
(int) 29.55 + (int) 21.99
```

is evaluated in C as

```
29 + 21
```

because the effect of casting a floating value to an integer is one of truncating the floating-point value. The expression

```
(float) 6 / (float) 4
```

produces a result of 1.5, as does the following expression:

```
(float) 6 / 4
```

Combining Operations with Assignment: The Assignment Operators

The C language permits you to join the arithmetic operators with the assignment operator using the following general format: op=

In this format, *op* is any of the arithmetic operators, including +, –, ×, /, and %. In addition, *op* can be any of the bit operators for shifting and masking, which is discussed later.

Consider this statement:

```
count += 10;
```

The effect of the so-called "plus equals" operator += is to add the expression on the right side of the operator to the expression on the left side of the operator and to store the result back into the variable on the left-hand side of the operator. So, the previous statement is equivalent to this statement:

```
count = count + 10;
```

The expression

```
counter -= 5
```

uses the "minus equals" assignment operator to subtract 5 from the value of counter and is equivalent to this expression:

```
counter = counter - 5
```

A slightly more involved expression is

```
a /= b + c
```

which divides a by whatever appears to the right of the equal sign—or by the sum of b and c—and stores the result in a. The addition is performed first because the addition operator has higher precedence than the assignment operator. In fact, all operators but the comma operator have higher precedence than the assignment operators, which all have the same precedence.

In this case, this expression is identical to the following:

```
a = a / (b + c)
```

The motivation for using assignment operators is threefold. First, the program statement becomes easier to write because what appears on the left side of the operator does not have to be repeated on the right side. Second, the resulting expression is usually easier to read. Third, the use of these operators can result in programs that execute more quickly because the compiler can sometimes generate less code to evaluate an expression.

Types _Complex and _Imaginary

Before leaving this chapter it is worthy to note two other types in the language called _Complex and _Imaginary for working with complex and imaginary numbers.

Support for _Complex and _Imaginary types has been part of the ANSI C standard since C99, although C11 does make it optional. The best way to know if your compiler supports these types is to examine the summary of data types in Appendix A.

Exercises

1. Type in and run the five programs presented in this chapter. Compare the output produced by each program with the output presented after each program in the text.

2. Which of the following are invalid variable names? Why?

```
Int             char        6_05
Calloc          Xx          alpha_beta_routine
floating        _1312       z
ReInitialize    _           A$
```

3. Which of the following are invalid constants? Why?

```
123.456     0x10.5      0X0G1
0001        0xFFFF      123L
0Xab05      0L          -597.25
123.5e2     .0001       +12
98.6F       98.7U       17777s
0996        -12E-12     07777
1234uL      1.2Fe-7     15,000
1.234L      197u        100U
0XABCDEFL   0xabcu      +123
```

4. Write a program that converts 27° from degrees Fahrenheit (F) to degrees Celsius (C) using the following formula:

$$C = (F - 32) / 1.8$$

5. What output would you expect from the following program?

```c
#include <stdio.h>

int main (void)
{
    char c, d;

    c = 'd';
    d = c;
    printf ("d = %c\n", d);
```

```
    return 0;
}
```

6. Write a program to evaluate the polynomial shown here:

   $3x^3 - 5x^2 + 6$

   for $x = 2.55$.

7. Write a program that evaluates the following expression and displays the results (remember to use exponential format to display the result):

   $(3.31 \times 10^{-8} \times 2.01 \times 10^{-7}) / (7.16 \times 10^{-6} + 2.01 \times 10^{-8})$

8. To round off an integer i to the next largest even multiple of another integer j, the following formula can be used:

   ```
   Next_multiple = i + j - i % j
   ```

   For example, to round off 256 days to the next largest number of days evenly divisible by a week, values of i = 256 and j = 7 can be substituted into the preceding formula as follows:

   ```
   Next_multiple    = 256 + 7 - 256 % 7
                    = 256 + 7 - 4
                    = 259
   ```

9. Write a program to find the next largest even multiple for the following values of i and j:

i	j
365	7
12,258	23
996	4

Program Looping

One of the great powers of computers is their ability to perform repeated calculations. The C program has a few constructs specifically designed to handle these situations when you need to use the same code repeatedly. This chapter will help you understand these tools, including

- The `for` statement
- The `while` statement
- The `do` statement
- The `break` statement
- The `continue` statement

Triangular Numbers

If you arrange 15 dots in the shape of a triangle, you end up with an arrangement that might look something like this:

```
        .
      .   .
    .   .   .
  .   .   .   .
.   .   .   .   .
```

The first row of the triangle contains one dot, the second row contains two dots, and so on. In general, the number of dots it takes to form a triangle containing n rows is the sum of the integers from 1 through n. This sum is known as a *triangular number*. If you start at 1, the fourth triangular number is the sum of the consecutive integers 1 through 4 (1 + 2 + 3 + 4), or 10.

Suppose you want to write a program that calculates and displays the value of the eighth triangular number at the terminal. Obviously, you could easily calculate this number in your head, but for the sake of argument, assume that you want to write a program in C to perform this task. Such a program is shown in Program 4.1.

The technique of Program 4.1 works fine for calculating relatively small, triangular numbers. But what happens if you need to find the value of the 200th triangular number, for example? It certainly would be tedious to modify Program 4.1 to explicitly add up all of the integers from 1 to 200. Luckily, there is an easier way.

Program 4.1 **Calculating the Eighth Triangular Number**

```
// Program to calculate the eighth triangular number

#include <stdio.h>

int main ()
{
    int  triangularNumber;

    triangularNumber = 1 + 2 + 3 + 4 + 5 + 6 + 7 + 8;

    printf ("The eighth triangular number is %i\n",  triangularNumber);

    return 0;
}
```

Program 4.1 **Output**

```
The eighth triangular number is 36
```

One of the fundamental properties of a computer is its ability to repetitively execute a set of statements. These *looping* capabilities enable you to develop concise programs containing repetitive processes that could otherwise require thousands or even millions of program statements to perform. The C programming language contains three different program statements for program looping. They are known as the for statement, the while statement, and the do statement. Each of these statements is described in detail in this chapter.

The for Statement

Let's dive right in and take a look at a program that uses the for statement. The purpose of Program 4.2 is to calculate the 200th triangular number. See if you can determine how the for statement works.

Program 4.2 **Calculating the 200th Triangular Number**

```
/* Program to calculate the 200th triangular number
   Introduction of the for statement                    */

#include <stdio.h>
```

```
int main (void)
{
    int  n, triangularNumber;

    triangularNumber = 0;

    for ( n = 1;  n <= 200;  n = n + 1 )
        triangularNumber = triangularNumber + n;

    printf ("The 200th triangular number is %i\n", triangularNumber);

    return 0;
}
```

Program 4.2 **Output**

```
The 200th triangular number is 20100
```

Some explanation is needed for Program 4.2. The method employed to calculate the 200th triangular number is really the same as that used to calculate the 8th triangular number in Program 4.1—the integers from 1 to 200 are summed. The for statement provides the mechanism that enables you to avoid having to explicitly write out each integer from 1 to 200. In a sense, this statement is used to "generate" these numbers for you.

The general format of the for statement is as follows:

```
for ( init_expression; loop_condition; loop_expression )
       program statement (or statements)
```

The three expressions that are enclosed within the parentheses—*init_expression*, *loop_condition*, and *loop_expression*—set up the environment for the program loop. The program statement that immediately follows (which is, of course, terminated by a semicolon) can be any valid C program statement and constitutes the body of the loop. This statement is executed as many times as specified by the parameters set up in the for statement.

The first component of the for statement, labeled *init_expression*, is used to set the initial values *before* the loop begins. In Program 4.2, this portion of the for statement is used to set the initial value of n to 1. As you can see, an assignment is a valid form of an expression.

The second component of the for statement are the condition or conditions that are necessary *for* the loop to continue. In other words, looping continues *as long as* this condition is satisfied. Once again referring to Program 4.2, note that the *loop_condition* of the for statement is specified by the following *relational expression*:

```
n <= 200
```

This expression can be read as "n less than or equal to 200." The "less than or equal to" operator (which is the less than character < followed immediately by the equal sign =) is only one of several relational operators provided in the C programming language. These operators are used to test specific conditions. The answer to the test is "yes" or, more commonly, TRUE if the condition is satisfied and "no" or FALSE if the condition is not satisfied.

Relational Operators

Table 4.1 lists all the relational operators that are available in C.

Table 4.1   **Relational Operators**

Operator	Meaning	Example
==	Equal to	count == 10
!=	Not equal to	flag != DONE
<	Less than	a < b
<=	Less than or equal to	low <= high
>	Greater than	pointer > endOfList
>=	Greater than or equal to	j >= 0

The relational operators have lower precedence than all arithmetic operators. This means, for example, that the following expression

```
a < b + c
```

is evaluated as

```
a < (b + c)
```

as you would expect. It would be TRUE if the value of a were less than the value of b + c and FALSE otherwise.

Pay particular attention to the "is equal to" operator == and do not confuse its use with the assignment operator =. The expression

```
a == 2
```

tests if the value of a is equal to 2, whereas the expression

```
a = 2
```

assigns the value 2 to the variable a.

The choice of which relational operator to use obviously depends on the particular test being made and in some instances on your particular preferences. For example in Program 4.2, the relational expression

```
n <= 200
```

can be equivalently expressed as

```
n < 201
```

The program statement that forms the body of the `for` loop

```
triangularNumber = triangularNumber + n;
```

is repetitively executed *as long as the result of the relational test is TRUE*, or in this case, as long as the value of n is less than or equal to `200`. This program statement has the effect of adding the value of `triangularNumber` to the value of n and storing the result back in the value of `triangularNumber`.

When the `loop_condition` is no longer satisfied, execution of the program continues with the program statement immediately following the `for` loop. In your program, execution continues with the `printf` statement after the loop has terminated.

The final component of the `for` statement contains an expression that is evaluated each time *after* the body of the loop is executed. In Program 4.2, this `loop_expression` adds 1 to the value of n. Therefore, the value of n is incremented by 1 each time after its value has been added into the value of `triangularNumber` and ranges in value from `1` to `201`.

It is worth noting that the last value that n attains, namely `201`, is *not* added into the value of `triangularNumber` because the loop is terminated *as soon as* the looping condition is no longer satisfied, or as soon as n equals `201`.

In summary, execution of the `for` statement proceeds as follows:

1. The initial expression is evaluated first. This expression usually sets a variable that will be used inside the loop, generally referred to as an *index* variable, to some initial value such as `0` or `1`.

2. The looping condition is evaluated. If the condition is not satisfied (the expression is FALSE), the loop is immediately terminated. Otherwise, execution continues with the program statement that immediately follows the loop.

3. The program statement that constitutes the body of the loop is executed.

4. The looping expression is evaluated. This expression is generally used to change the value of the index variable, frequently by adding an incremental variable to it or subtracting an decremental variable from it.

5. Return to step 2.

Remember that the looping condition is evaluated immediately on entry into the loop, before the body of the loop has even executed one time. Also, remember not to put a semicolon after the close parenthesis at the end of the loop (this immediately ends the loop).

Because Program 4.2 actually generates all of the first 200 triangular numbers on its way to its final goal, it might be nice to generate a table of these numbers. To save space, however, let's assume that you just want to print a table of the first 10 triangular numbers. Program 4.3 performs precisely this task!

Program 4.3 Generating a Table of Triangular Numbers

```c
// Program to generate a table of triangular numbers

#include <stdio.h>

int main (void)
{
    int  n, triangularNumber;

    printf ("TABLE OF TRIANGULAR NUMBERS\n\n");
    printf (" n     Sum from 1 to n\n");
    printf ("---    --------------\n");

    triangularNumber = 0;

    for ( n = 1;  n <= 10;  ++n ) {
        triangularNumber +=  n;
        printf (" %i            %i\n", n, triangularNumber);
    }

    return 0;
}
```

Program 4.3 Output

```
TABLE OF TRIANGULAR NUMBERS

 n     Sum from 1 to n
---    --------------
 1             1
 2             3
 3             6
 4            10
 5            15
 6            21
 7            28
 8            36
 9            45
 10           55
```

It is always a good idea to add some extra `printf()` statements to a program to provide more meaning to the output. In Program 4.3, the purpose of the first three `printf()` statements is simply to provide a general heading and to label the columns of the output. Notice that the first `printf()` statement contains two newline characters. As you would expect, this has the effect of not only advancing to the next line, but also inserting an extra blank line into the display.

After the appropriate headings have been displayed, the program proceeds to calculate the first 10 triangular numbers. The variable n is used to count the current number whose "sum from 1 to n" you are computing, whereas the variable triangularNumber is used to store the value of triangular number n.

Execution of the for statement commences by setting the value of the variable n to 1. Remember that the program statement immediately following the for statement constitutes the body of the program loop. But what happens if you want to repetitively execute not just a single program statement, but a group of program statements? This can be accomplished by enclosing all such program statements within a pair of braces. The system then treats this group or *block* of statements as a single entity. In general, any place in a C program that a single statement is permitted, a block of statements can be used, provided that you remember to enclose the block within a pair of braces.

Therefore, in Program 4.3, both the expression that adds n into the value of triangularNumber and the printf() statement that immediately follows constitute the body of the program loop. Pay particular attention to the way the program statements are indented. It is easy to determine which statements form part of the for loop. You should also note that programmers use different coding styles. Some prefer to type the loop this way:

```
for ( n = 1;  n <= 10;  ++n )
{
    triangularNumber += n;
    printf (" %i          %i\n", n, triangularNumber);
}
```

Here, the opening brace is placed on the next line after the for. This is strictly a matter of taste and has no effect on the program.

The next triangular number is calculated by simply adding the value of n to the previous triangular number. This time, the "plus equals" operator is used, which was introduced in Chapter 3, "Variables, Data Types, and Arithmetic Expressions." Recall that the expression

```
triangularNumber += n;
```

is equivalent to the expression

```
triangularNumber = triangularNumber + n;
```

The first time through the for loop, the "previous" triangular number is 0, so the new value of triangularNumber when n is equal to 1 is simply the value of n, or 1. The values of n and triangularNumber are then displayed, with an appropriate number of blank spaces inserted in the format string to ensure that the values of the two variables line up under the appropriate column headings.

Because the body of the loop has now been executed, the looping expression is evaluated next. The expression in this for statement appears a bit strange, however. It seems like you made a typographical mistake and meant to insert the expression

```
n = n + 1
```

instead of the funny-looking expression

```
++n
```

The expression ++n is actually a perfectly valid C expression. It introduces you to a new (and rather unique) operator in the C programming language—the *increment operator*. The function of the double plus sign—or the increment operator—is to add 1 to its operand. Because addition by 1 is such a common operation in programs, a special operator was created solely for this purpose. Therefore, the expression ++n is equivalent to the expression n = n + 1. Although it might appear that n = n + 1 is more readable, you will soon become familiar with the function of this operator and will even learn to appreciate its succinctness.

Of course, no programming language that offered an increment operator to add 1 would be complete without a corresponding operator to subtract 1. The name of this operator is the *decrement operator* and is symbolized by the double minus sign. So, an expression in C that reads

```
bean_counter = bean_counter - 1
```

can be equivalently expressed using the decrement operator as

```
--bean_counter
```

Some programmers prefer to put the ++ or -- after the variable name, as in n++ or bean_counter--. This is a matter of personal preference for the example shown in the for statement. However, as you'll learn in Chapter 10, "Pointers," the pre- or post-nature of the operator does come into play when used in more complex expressions.

Aligning Output

One slightly disturbing thing that you might have noticed in Program 4.3's output is the fact that the 10th triangular number does not quite line up under the previous triangular numbers. This is because the number 10 takes up two print positions, whereas the previous values of n, 1 through 9, took up only one print position. Therefore, the value 55 is effectively "pushed over" one extra position in the display. This minor annoyance can be corrected if you substitute the following printf() statement in place of the corresponding statement from Program 4.3.

```
printf ("%2i          %i\n", n, triangularNumber);
```

To verify that this change does the trick, here is the output from the modified program (we'll call it Program 4.3A).

Program 4.3A **Output**

```
TABLE OF TRIANGULAR NUMBERS

n           Sum from 1 to n
---         ---------------
1                 1
2                 3
```

```
 3            6
 4           10
 5           15
 6           21
 7           28
 8           36
 9           45
10           55
```

The primary change made to the printf() statement was the inclusion of a *field width specification*. The characters %2i tell the printf() routine that not only do you want to display the value of an integer at that particular point, but you also want the size of the integer to be displayed to take up two columns in the display. Any integer that would normally take up less than two columns (that is, the integers 0 through 9) are displayed with a *leading* space. This is known as *right justification*.

Thus, by using a field width specification of %2i, you guarantee that at least two columns are used for displaying the value of n and, therefore, you ensure that the values of triangular-Number are lined up.

If the value that is to be displayed requires more columns than are specified by the field width, printf() simply ignores the field width specification and uses as many columns as are necessary to display the value.

Field width specifications can also be used for displaying values other than integers. You will see some examples of this in programs that are coming up shortly.

Program Input

Program 4.2 calculates the 200th triangular number—and nothing more. If you want to calculate the 50th or the 100th triangular number instead, you have to go back and change the program so that the for loop is executed the correct number of times. You also have to change the printf() statement to display the correct message.

An easier solution might be if you could somehow have the program ask which triangular number you want to calculate. Then, after you provide your answer, the program could calculate the desired triangular number for you. Such a solution can be effected in C by using a routine called scanf(). The scanf() routine is very similar in concept to the printf routine. Whereas the printf() routine is used to display values at the terminal, the scanf() routine enables you to type values *into* the program. Program 4.4 asks the user which triangular number should be calculated, proceeds to calculate that number, and then displays the results.

Program 4.4   **Asking the User for Input**

```
#include <stdio.h>

int main (void)
{
```

```
    int   n, number, triangularNumber;

    printf ("What triangular number do you want? ");
    scanf   ("%i", &number);

    triangularNumber = 0;

    for ( n = 1;  n <= number;  ++n )
        triangularNumber += n;

    printf ("Triangular number %i is %i\n", number, triangularNumber);

    return 0;
}
```

In Program 4.4 output, the number typed in by the user (100) is set in bold type to distinguish it from the output displayed by the program.

Program 4.4   **Output**

```
What triangular number do you want? 100
Triangular number 100 is 5050
```

According to the output, the number 100 was typed in by the user. The program then proceeded to calculate the 100th triangular number and displayed the result of 5050 at the terminal. The user could have instead typed in the number 10, or 30, if he desired to calculate those particular triangular numbers.

The first printf() statement in Program 4.4 is used to prompt the user to type in a number. Of course, it is always nice to remind the user what it is you want entered. After the message is printed, the scanf() routine is called. The first argument to scanf() is the format string and is very similar to the format string used by printf(). In this case, the format string doesn't tell the system what types of values are to be displayed but rather what types of values are to be read in from the terminal. Like printf(), the %i characters are used to specify an integer value.

The second argument to the scanf() routine specifies *where* the value that is typed in by the user is to be stored. The & character before the variable number is necessary in this case. Don't worry about its function here, though. Chapter 10 discusses this character, which is actually an operator, in great detail. Always remember to put the leading & in front of the variable name in the scanf() function call. If you forget, it causes unpredictable results and might cause your program to terminate abnormally.

Given the preceding discussion, you can now see that the scanf() call from Program 4.4 specifies that an integer value is to be read from the terminal and stored in the variable number. This value represents the particular triangular number that the user wants to calculate.

After this number has been typed in (and the "Return" or "Enter" key on the keyboard pressed to signal that typing of the number is completed), the program then proceeds to calculate the requested triangular number. This is done in the same way as in Program 4.2—the only difference being that instead of using 200 as the limit, number is used.

> **Note**
>
> Pressing the Enter key on a keyboard with a numeric keypad may not cause the number you enter to be sent to the program. Use the Return key on your keyboard instead.

After the desired triangular number has been calculated, the results are displayed, and execution of the program is then complete.

Nested for Loops

Program 4.4 gives the user the flexibility to have the program calculate any triangular number that is desired. However, if the user has a list of five triangular numbers to be calculated, she can simply execute the program five times, each time typing in the next triangular number from the list to be calculated.

Another way to accomplish this same goal, and a far more interesting method as far as learning about C is concerned, is to have the program handle the situation. This can best be accomplished by inserting a loop in the program to simply repeat the entire series of calculations five times. You know by now that the for statement can be used to set up such a loop. Program 4.5 and its associated output illustrate this technique.

Program 4.5 **Using Nested for Loops**

```c
#include <stdio.h>

int main (void)
{
    int  n, number, triangularNumber, counter;

    for ( counter = 1;  counter <= 5;  ++counter ) {
        printf ("What triangular number do you want? ");
        scanf  ("%i", &number);

        triangularNumber = 0;

        for ( n = 1;  n <= number;  ++n )
            triangularNumber += n;

        printf ("Triangular number %i is %i\n\n", number, triangularNumber);
    }

    return 0;
}
```

Program 4.5   **Output**

```
What triangular number do you want? 12
Triangular number 12 is 78

What triangular number do you want? 25
Triangular number 25 is 325

What triangular number do you want? 50
Triangular number 50 is 1275

What triangular number do you want? 75
Triangular number 75 is 2850

What triangular number do you want? 83
Triangular number 83 is 3486
```

The program consists of two levels of for statements. The outermost for statement

```
for ( counter = 1;   counter <= 5;   ++counter )
```

specifies that the program loop is to be executed precisely five times. This can be seen because the value of counter is initially set to 1 and is incremented by 1 *until* it is no longer less than or equal to 5 (in other words, until it reaches 6).

Unlike the previous program examples, the variable counter is not used anywhere else within the program. Its function is solely as a loop counter in the for statement. Nevertheless, because it *is* a variable, it must be declared in the program.

The program loop actually consists of all the remaining program statements, as indicated by the braces. It might be easier for you to comprehend the way this program operates if you conceptualize it as follows:

```
For 5 times
{
     Get the number from the user.

     Calculate the requested triangular number.

     Display the result.
}
```

The portion of the loop referred to in the preceding as *Calculate the requested triangular number* actually consists of setting the value of the variable triangularNumber to 0 *plus* the for loop that calculates the triangular number. Thus, you see that you have a for statement that is actually contained *within* another for statement. This is perfectly valid in C, and nesting can continue even further to any desired level.

The proper use of indentation becomes even more critical when dealing with more sophisticated program constructs, such as nested `for` statements. You can easily determine which statements are contained within each `for` statement. (To see how unreadable a program can be if correct attention isn't paid to formatting, see exercise 5 at the end of this chapter.)

`for` Loop Variants

Some syntactic variations are permitted in forming the `for` loop. When writing a `for` loop, you might discover that you have more than one variable that you want to initialize before the loop begins or more than one expression that you want to evaluate each time through the loop.

Multiple Expressions

You can include multiple expressions in any of the fields of the `for` loop, provided that you separate such expressions by commas. For example, in the `for` statement that begins

```
for ( i = 0, j = 0;   i < 10;   ++i )
    . . .
```

the value of i is set to 0 *and* the value of j is set to 0 before the loop begins. The two expressions i = 0 and j = 0 are separated from each other by a comma, and both expressions are considered part of the *init_expression* field of the loop. As another example, the `for` loop that starts

```
for   ( i = 0, j = 100;   i < 10;   ++i, j = j - 10 )
    . . .
```

sets up two index variables, i and j; the former initialized to 0 and the latter to 100 before the loop begins. Each time after the body of the loop is executed, the value of i is incremented by 1, whereas the value of j is decremented by 10.

Omitting Fields

Just as the need might arise to include more than one expression in a particular field of the `for` statement, the need might arise to *omit* one or more fields from the statement. This can be done simply by omitting the desired field and marking its place with a semicolon. The most common application for the omission of a field in the `for` statement occurs when there is no initial expression that needs to be evaluated. The *init_expression* field can simply be "left blank" in such a case, as long as the semicolon is still included:

```
for   (  ;  j != 100;   ++j )
    . . .
```

This statement might be used if j were already set to some initial value before the loop was entered.

A for loop that has its *looping_condition* field omitted effectively sets up an infinite loop; that is, a loop that is theoretically executed forever. Such a loop can be used provided there is some other means used to exit from the loop (such as executing a return, break, or goto statement as discussed elsewhere in this book).

Declaring Variables

You can also declare variables as part of your initial expression inside a for loop. This is done using the normal ways you've defined variables in the past. For example, the following can be used to set up a for loop with an integer variable counter both defined and initialized to the value 1:

```
for ( int  counter = 1; counter <= 5; ++counter )
```

The variable counter is only known throughout the execution of the for loop and cannot be accessed outside the loop. As another example, the following for loop

```
for ( int  n = 1, triangularNumber = 0; n <= 200; ++n )
    triangularNumber += n;
```

defines two integer variables and sets their values accordingly.

The while Statement

The while statement further extends the C language's repertoire of looping capabilities. The syntax of this frequently used construct is as follows:

```
while ( expression )
    program statement (or statements)
```

The *expression* specified inside the parentheses is evaluated. If the result of the *expression* evaluation is TRUE, the *program statement* that immediately follows is executed. After execution of this statement (or statements if enclosed in braces), the *expression* is once again evaluated. If the result of the evaluation is TRUE, the *program statement* is once again executed. This process continues until the *expression* finally evaluates as FALSE, at which point the loop is terminated. Execution of the program then continues with the statement that follows the *program statement*.

As an example of its use, Program 4.6 sets up a while loop, which merely counts from 1 to 5.

Program 4.6   **Introducing the** while **Statement**

```
// Program to introduce the while statement

#include <stdio.h>

int main (void)
{
```

```
    int   count = 1;

    while ( count <= 5 ) {
        printf ("%i\n", count);
        ++count;
    }

    return 0;
}
```

Program 4.6   **Output**

```
1
2
3
4
5
```

The program initially sets the value of count to 1. Execution of the while loop then begins. Because the value of count is less than or equal to 5, the statement that immediately follows is executed. The braces serve to define both the printf() statement and the statement that increments count as the body of the while loop. From the output of the program, you can readily observe that this loop is executed precisely 5 times, or until the value of count reaches 6.

You might have realized from this program that you could have readily accomplished the same task by using a for statement. In fact, a for statement can always be translated into an equivalent while statement, and vice versa. For example, the general for statement

```
for ( init_expression;  loop_condition;  loop_expression )
    program statement (or statements)
```

can be equivalently expressed in the form of a while statement as

```
init_expression;
while ( loop_condition ) {
    program statement (or statements)
    loop_expression;
}
```

After you become familiar with the use of the while statement, you will gain a better feel as to when it seems more logical to use a while statement and when to use a for statement.

In general, a loop executed a predetermined number of times is a prime candidate for implementation as a for statement. Also, if the initial expression, looping expression, and looping condition all involve the same variable, the for statement is probably the right choice.

The next program provides another example of the use of the while statement. The program computes the *greatest common divisor* of two integer values. The greatest common divisor (*gcd*) of two integers is the largest integer value that evenly divides the two integers. For example, the *gcd* of 10 and 15 is 5 because 5 is the largest integer that evenly divides both 10 and 15.

There is a procedure or *algorithm* that can be followed to arrive at the *gcd* of two arbitrary integers. This algorithm is based on a procedure originally developed by Euclid around 300 B.C., and can be stated as follows:

Problem:	Find the greatest common divisor of two nonnegative integers *u* and *v*.
Step 1:	If *v* equals 0, then you are done and the *gcd* is equal to *u*.
Step 2:	Calculate *temp = u % v, u = v, v = temp*, and go back to step 1.

Don't concern yourself with the details of how the preceding algorithm works—simply take it on faith. Focus more here on developing the program to find the greatest common divisor than on performing an analysis of how the algorithm works.

After the solution to the problem of finding the greatest common divisor has been expressed in terms of an algorithm, it becomes a much simpler task to develop the computer program. An analysis of the steps of the algorithm reveals that step 2 is repetitively executed as long as the value of *v* is not equal to 0. This realization leads to the natural implementation of this algorithm in C with the use of a while statement.

Program 4.7 finds the *gcd* of two nonnegative integer values typed in by the user.

Program 4.7   **Finding the Greatest Common Divisor**

```
/* Program to find the greatest common divisor
        of two nonnegative integer values          */

#include <stdio.h>

int main (void)
{
    int u, v, temp;

    printf ("Please type in two nonnegative integers.\n");
    scanf ("%i%i", &u, &v);


    while ( v != 0 ) {
        temp = u % v;
        u = v;
        v = temp;
    }

    printf ("Their greatest common divisor is %i\n", u);

    return 0;
}
```

Program 4.7 **Output**

```
Please type in two nonnegative integers.
150 35
Their greatest common divisor is 5
```

Program 4.7 **Output (Rerun)**

```
Please type in two nonnegative integers.
1026 405
Their greatest common divisor is 27
```

The double %i characters in the scanf () call indicate that two integer values are to be entered from the keyboard. The first value that is entered is stored in the integer variable u, whereas the second value is stored in the variable v. When the values are actually entered from the terminal, they can be separated from each other by one or more blank spaces or by a carriage return.

After the values have been entered from the keyboard and stored in the variables u and v, the program enters a while loop to calculate their greatest common divisor. After the while loop is exited, the value of u, which represents the *gcd* of v and the original value of u, is displayed at the terminal, together with an appropriate message.

Program 4.8 illustrates another use of the while statement, the task of reversing the digits of an integer that is entered from the terminal. For example, if the user types in the number 1234, you want the program to reverse the digits of this number and display the result of 4321.

To write such a program, you first must come up with an algorithm that accomplishes the stated task. Frequently, an analysis of your own method for solving the problem leads to the development of an algorithm. To reverse the digits of a number, the method of solution can be simply stated as "successively read the digits of the number from right to left." You can have a computer program "successively read" the digits of the number by developing a procedure to successively isolate or "extract" each digit of the number, beginning with the rightmost digit. The extracted digit can be subsequently displayed at the terminal as the next digit of the reversed number.

You can extract the rightmost digit from an integer number by taking the remainder of the integer after it is divided by 10. For example, 1234 % 10 gives the value 4, which is the rightmost digit of 1234, and is also the first digit of the reversed number. (Remember the modulus operator, which gives the remainder of one integer divided by another.) You can get the next digit of the number by using the same process if you first divide the number by 10, bearing in mind the way integer division works. Thus, 1234 / 10 gives a result of 123, and 123 % 10 gives us 3, which is the next digit of your reversed number.

This procedure can be continued until the last digit has been extracted. In the general case, you know that the last digit of the number has been extracted when the result of the last integer division by 10 is 0.

Program 4.8 **Reversing the Digits of a Number**

```
// Program to reverse the digits of a number

#include <stdio.h>

int main (void)
{
    int   number, right_digit;

    printf ("Enter your number.\n");
    scanf ("%i", &number);

    while ( number != 0 ) {
        right_digit = number % 10;
        printf ("%i", right_digit);
        number = number / 10;
    }

    printf ("\n");

    return 0;
}
```

Program 4.8 **Output**

```
Enter your number.
13579
97531
```

Each digit is displayed as it is extracted by the program. Notice that you did not include a newline character inside the printf() statement contained in the while loop. This forces each successive digit to be displayed on the same line. The final printf() call at the end of the program contains just a newline character, which causes the cursor to advance to the start of the next line.

The do Statement

The two looping statements discussed so far in this chapter both make a test of the conditions *before* the loop is executed. Therefore, the body of the loop might never be executed at all if the conditions are not satisfied. When developing programs, it sometimes becomes desirable to have the test made at the *end* of the loop rather than at the beginning. Naturally, the C language provides a special language construct to handle such a situation. This looping statement is known as the do statement. The syntax of this statement is as follows:

```
do
    program statement (or statements)
while ( loop_expression );
```

Execution of the do statement proceeds as follows: the *program statement* is executed first. Next, the *loop_expression* inside the parentheses is evaluated. If the result of evaluating the *loop_expression* is TRUE, the loop continues and the *program statement* is once again executed. As long as evaluation of the *loop_expression* continues to be TRUE, the *program statement* is repeatedly executed. When evaluation of the expression proves FALSE, the loop is terminated, and the next statement in the program is executed in the normal sequential manner.

The do statement is simply a transposition of the while statement, with the looping conditions placed at the end of the loop rather than at the beginning.

Remember that, unlike the for and while loops, the do statement guarantees that the body of the loop is executed at least once.

In Program 4.8, you used a while statement to reverse the digits of a number. Go back to that program and try to determine what would happen if you typed in the number 0 instead of 13579. The loop of the while statement would never be executed, and you would simply end up with a blank line in your display (as a result of the display of the newline character from the second printf() statement). If you use a do statement instead of a while statement, you are assured that the program loop executes at least once, thus guaranteeing the display of at least one digit in all cases. Program 4.9 shows this revised program.

Program 4.9   Implementing a Revised Program to Reverse the Digits of a Number

```
// Program to reverse the digits of a number

#include <stdio.h>

int main ()
{
    int  number, right_digit;

    printf ("Enter your number.\n");
    scanf ("%i", &number);

    do {
        right_digit = number % 10;
        printf ("%i", right_digit);
        number = number / 10;
    }
    while ( number != 0 );

    printf ("\n");

    return 0;
}
```

Program 4.9   **Output**
_____

```
Enter your number.
13579
97531
```
_____

Program 4.9   **Output (Rerun)**
_____

```
Enter your number.
0
0
```
_____

As you can see from the program's output, when 0 is keyed into the program, the program correctly displays the digit 0.

The **break** Statement

Sometimes when executing a loop, it becomes desirable to leave the loop as soon as a certain condition occurs (for instance, you detect an error condition, or you reach the end of your data prematurely). The break statement can be used for this purpose. Execution of the break statement causes the program to immediately exit from the loop it is executing, whether it's a for, while, or do loop. Subsequent statements in the loop are skipped, and execution of the loop is terminated. Execution continues with whatever statement follows the loop.

If a break is executed from within a set of nested loops, only the innermost loop in which the break is executed is terminated.

The format of the break statement is simply the keyword break followed by a semicolon:

```
break;
```

The **continue** Statement

The continue statement is similar to the break statement except it doesn't cause the loop to terminate. Rather, as its name implies, this statement causes the loop in which it is executed to be continued. At the point that the continue statement is executed, any statements in the loop that appear *after* the continue statement are automatically skipped. Execution of the loop otherwise continues as normal.

The continue statement is most often used to bypass a group of statements inside a loop based upon some condition, but to otherwise continue execution of the loop. The format of the continue statement is simply

```
continue;
```

Don't use the break or continue statements until you become very familiar with writing program loops and gracefully exiting from them. These statements are too easy to abuse and can result in programs that are hard to follow.

Now that you are familiar with all the basic looping constructs provided by the C language, you are ready to learn about another class of language statements that enable you to make decisions during the execution of a program. These decision-making capabilities are described in detail in Chapter 5, "Making Decisions." First, try the exercises that follow to be certain you understand how to work with loops in C.

Exercises

1. Type in and run the nine programs presented in this chapter. Compare the output produced by each program with the output presented after each program in the text.

2. Write a program to generate and display a table of n and n^2, for integer values of n ranging from 1 to 10. Be certain to print appropriate column headings.

3. A triangular number can also be generated by the formula

   ```
   triangularNumber = n (n + 1) / 2
   ```

   for any integer value of n. For example, the 10th triangular number, 55, can be generated by substituting 10 as the value for n in the preceding formula. Write a program that generates a table of triangular numbers using the preceding formula. Have the program generate every fifth triangular number between 5 and 50 (that is, 5, 10, 15, ..., 50).

4. The factorial of an integer n, written $n!$, is the product of the consecutive integers 1 through n. For example, 5 factorial is calculated as

   ```
   5!  =  5 x 4 x 3 x 2 x 1  =  120
   ```

   Write a program to generate and print a table of the first 10 factorials.

5. The following perfectly valid C program was written without much attention paid to its format. As you will observe, the program is not very readable. (And believe it or not, it is even possible to make this program significantly more unreadable!) Using the programs presented in this chapter as examples, reformat the program so that it is more readable. Then type the program into the computer and run it.

   ```c
   #include <stdio.h>
   int main(void){
   int n,two_to_the_n;
   printf("TABLE OF POWERS OF TWO\n\n");
   printf(" n     2 to the n\n");
   printf("---    --------------\n");
   two_to_the_n=1;
   for(n=0;n<=10;++n){
   printf("%2i         %i\n",n,two_to_the_n); two_to_the_n*=2;}
   return 0;}
   ```

6. A minus sign placed in front of a field width specification causes the field to be displayed *left-justified*. Substitute the following printf() statement for the corresponding statement in Program 4.2, run the program, and compare the outputs produced by both programs.

```
printf ("%-2i            %i\n", n, triangularNumber);
```

7. A decimal point before the field width specification in a printf() statement has a special purpose. Try to determine its purpose by typing in and running the following program. Experiment by typing in different values each time you are prompted.

```c
#include <stdio.h>

int main (void)
{
    int   dollars, cents, count;

    for ( count = 1;  count <= 10;  ++count ) {
        printf ("Enter dollars: ");
        scanf ("%i", &dollars);
        printf ("Enter cents: ");
        scanf ("%i", &cents);
        printf ("$%i.%.2i\n\n", dollars, cents);
    }
    return 0;
}
```

8. Program 4.5 allows the user to type in only five different numbers. Modify that program so that the user can type in the number of triangular numbers to be calculated.

9. Rewrite Programs 4.2 through 4.5, replacing all uses of the for statement with equivalent while statements. Run each program to verify that both versions are identical.

10. What would happen if you typed a negative number into Program 4.8? Try it and see.

11. Write a program that calculates the sum of the digits of an integer. For example, the sum of the digits of the number 2155 is 2 + 1 + 5 + 5 or 13. The program should accept any arbitrary integer typed in by the user.

5

Making Decisions

In Chapter 4, "Program Looping," you learned that one of the fundamental properties of a computer is its capability to repetitively execute a sequence of instructions. But another fundamental property lies in its capability to make decisions. You saw how these decision-making powers were used in the execution of the various looping statements to determine when to terminate the program loop. Without such capabilities, you would never be able to "get out" of a program loop and would end up executing the same sequence of statements over and over again, theoretically forever (which is why such a program loop is called an infinite loop).

The C programming language also provides several other decision-making constructs, which are covered in this chapter:

- The `if` statement
- The `switch` statement
- The conditional operator

The `if` Statement

The C programming language provides a general decision-making capability in the form of a language construct known as the `if` statement. The general format of this statement is as follows:

```
if  ( expression )
    program statement
```

Imagine that you could translate a statement such as "If it is not raining, then I will go swimming" into the C language. Using the preceding format for the `if` statement, this might be "written" in C as follows:

```
if ( it is not raining )
    I will go swimming
```

The `if` statement is used to stipulate execution of a program statement (or statements if enclosed in braces) based upon specified conditions. I will go swimming if it is not raining. Similarly, in the program statement

```
if ( count > COUNT_LIMIT )
    printf ("Count limit exceeded\n");
```

the `printf()` statement is executed *only* if the value of `count` is greater than the value of `COUNT_LIMIT`; otherwise, it is ignored.

An actual program example helps drive this point home. Suppose you want to write a program that accepts an integer typed in from the terminal and then displays the absolute value of that integer. A straightforward way to calculate the absolute value of an integer is to simply negate the number if it is less than zero. The use of the phrase "if it is less than zero" in the preceding sentence signals that a decision must be made by the program. This decision can be affected by the use of an `if` statement, as shown in Program 5.1.

Program 5.1   **Calculating the Absolute Value of an Integer**

```
// Program to calculate the absolute value of an integer

#include <stdio.h>

int main (void)
{
    int   number;

    printf ("Type in your number: ");
    scanf ("%i", &number);

    if ( number < 0 )
        number = -number;

    printf ("The absolute value is %i\n", number);

    return 0;
}
```

Program 5.1   **Output**

```
Type in your number: -100
The absolute value is 100
```

Program 5.1   **Output (Rerun)**

```
Type in your number: 2000
The absolute value is 2000
```

The program was run twice to verify that it is functioning properly. Of course, it might be desirable to run the program several more times to get a higher level of confidence so that you know it is indeed working correctly, but at least you know that you have checked both possible outcomes of the decision made by the program.

After a message is displayed to the user and the integer value that is entered is stored in number, the program tests the value of number to see if it is less than zero. If it is, the following program statement, which negates the value of number, is executed. If the value of number is not less than zero, this program statement is automatically skipped. (If it is already positive, you don't want to negate it.) The absolute value of number is then displayed by the program, and program execution ends.

Look at Program 5.2, which uses the if statement. Imagine that you have a list of grades for which you want to compute the average. But in addition to computing the average, suppose that you also need a count of the number of failing grades in the list. For the purposes of this problem, assume that a grade less than 65 is considered a failing grade.

The notion of keeping count of the number of failing grades indicates that you must make a decision as to whether a grade qualifies as a failing grade. Once again, the if statement comes to the rescue.

Program 5.2   **Calculating the Average of a Set of Grades and Counting the Number of Failing Test Grades**

```
/* Program to calculate the average of a set of grades and count
   the number of failing test grades     */

#include <stdio.h>

int main (void)
{
    int        numberOfGrades, i, grade;
    int        gradeTotal = 0;
    int        failureCount = 0;
    float      average;

    printf ("How many grades will you be entering? ");
    scanf ("%i", &numberOfGrades);

    for ( i = 1;  i <= numberOfGrades;  ++i ) {
        printf ("Enter grade #%i: ", i);
        scanf ("%i", &grade);

        gradeTotal = gradeTotal + grade;

        if ( grade < 65 )
            ++failureCount;
```

```
    }

    average = (float) gradeTotal / numberOfGrades;

    printf ("\nGrade average = %.2f\n", average);
    printf ("Number of failures = %i\n", failureCount);

    return 0;
}
```

Program 5.2   **Output**

```
How many grades will you be entering? 7
Enter grade #1: 93
Enter grade #2: 63
Enter grade #3: 87
Enter grade #4: 65
Enter grade #5: 62
Enter grade #6: 88
Enter grade #7: 76


Grade average = 76.29
Number of failures = 2
```

The variable gradeTotal, which is used to keep a cumulative total of the grades as they are typed in, is initially set to 0. The number of failing test grades is stored in the variable failureCount, whose value also is initially set to 0. The variable average is declared to be of type float because the average of a set of integers is not necessarily an integer itself.

The program then asks the user to enter the number of grades that will be keyed in and stores the value that is entered in the variable numberOfGrades. A loop is then set up that will be executed for each grade. The first part of the loop prompts the user to enter in the grade. The value that is entered is stored in the variable called, appropriately enough, grade.

The value of grade is then added into gradeTotal, after which a test is made to see if it is a failing test grade. If it is, the value of failureCount is incremented by 1. The entire loop is then repeated for the next grade in the list.

When all of the grades have been entered and totaled, the program then calculates the grade average. On impulse, it seems that a statement such as

```
average = gradeTotal / numberOfGrades;
```

would do the trick. However, recall that if the preceding statement were used, the decimal portion of the result of the division would be lost. This is because an integer division would be performed because *both* the numerator and the denominator of the division operation are integers.

Two different solutions are possible for this problem. One is to declare either `numberOfGrades` or `gradeTotal` to be of type `float`. This then guarantees that the division is carried out without the loss of the decimal places. The only problem with this approach is that the variables `numberOfGrades` and `gradeTotal` are used by the program to store only integer values. Declaring either of them to be of type `float` only obscures their use in the program and is generally not a very clean way of doing things.

The other solution, as used by the program, is to actually *convert* the value of one of the variables to a floating-point value for the purposes of the calculation. The type cast operator (`float`) is used to convert the value of the variable `gradeTotal` to type `float` for purposes of evaluation of the expression. Because the value of `gradeTotal` is cast into a floating-point value *before* the division takes place, the division is treated as the division of a floating value by an integer. Because one of the operands is now a floating-point value, the division operation is carried out as a floating-point operation. This means, of course, that you obtain those decimal places that you want in the average.

After the average has been calculated, it is displayed at the terminal to two decimal places of accuracy. If a decimal point followed by a number (known collectively as a *precision modifier*) is placed directly before the format character `f` (or `e`) in a `printf()` format string, the corresponding value is displayed to the specified number of decimal places, rounded. So in Program 5.2, the precision modifier `.2` is used to cause the value of `average` to be displayed to two decimal places.

After the program has displayed the number of failing grades, execution of the program is complete.

Note that if the user of the program enters 0 as the number of test grades to be recorded, the program will generate some odd results, like NaN (Not a Number) or something else; it will vary by system however, depending on how your computer deals with division by 0. You may wonder why someone would bother running a program to record test scores if there are no test scores to enter, but this is the type of possible error-checking you can add to your program.

The `if-else` Construct

If someone asks you whether a particular number is even or odd, you most likely make the determination by examining the last digit of the number. If this digit is either 0, 2, 4, 6, or 8, you readily state that the number is even. Otherwise, you claim that the number is odd.

An easier way for a computer to determine whether a particular number is even or odd is affected not by examining the last digit of the number to see if it is 0, 2, 4, 6, or 8, but by simply determining whether the number is evenly divisible by 2. If it is, the number is even; else it is odd.

You have already seen how the modulus operator `%` is used to compute the remainder of one integer divided by another. This makes it the perfect operator to use in determining whether an integer is evenly divisible by 2. If the remainder after division by 2 is zero, it is even; else it is odd.

Look at Program 5.3—a program that determines whether an integer value typed in by the user is even or odd and that displays an appropriate message at the terminal.

Program 5.3   Determining if a Number Is Even or Odd

```
//  Program to determine if a number is even or odd

#include <stdio.h>

int main (void)
{
    int  number_to_test, remainder;

    printf ("Enter your number to be tested.: ");
    scanf ("%i", &number_to_test);

    remainder = number_to_test % 2;

    if ( remainder == 0 )
        printf ("The number is even.\n");

    if ( remainder != 0 )
        printf ("The number is odd.\n");

    return 0;
}
```

Program 5.3   Output

```
Enter your number to be tested: 2455
The number is odd.
```

Program 5.3   Output (Rerun)

```
Enter your number to be tested: 1210
The number is even.
```

After the number is typed in, the remainder after division by 2 is calculated. The first if statement tests the value of this remainder to see if it is equal to zero. If it is, the message "The number is even" is displayed.

The second if statement tests the remainder to see if it's *not* equal to zero and, if that's the case, displays a message stating that the number is odd.

The fact is that whenever the first if statement succeeds, the second one must fail, and vice versa. Recall from the discussions of even/odd numbers at the beginning of this section that if the number is evenly divisible by 2, it is even; *else* it is odd.

When writing programs, this "else" concept is so frequently required that almost all modern programming languages provide a special construct to handle this situation. In C, this is known as the if-else construct and the general format is as follows:

```
if   ( expression )
     program statement 1
else
     program statement 2
```

The if-else is actually just an extension of the general format of the if statement. If the result of the evaluation of *expression* is TRUE, *program statement 1*, which immediately follows, is executed; otherwise, *program statement 2* is executed. In either case, either *program statement 1* or *program statement 2* is executed, but not both.

You can incorporate the if-else statement into Program 5.3, replacing the two if statements with a single if-else statement. The use of this new program construct actually helps to reduce the program's complexity and also improves its readability, as shown in Program 5.4.

Program 5.4   **Revising the Program to Determine if a Number Is Even or Odd**

```
// Program to determine if a number is even or odd (Ver. 2)

#include <stdio.h>

int main ()
{
    int  number_to_test, remainder;

    printf ("Enter your number to be tested: ");
    scanf ("%i", &number_to_test);

    remainder = number_to_test % 2;

    if ( remainder == 0 )
        printf ("The number is even.\n");
    else
        printf ("The number is odd.\n");

    return 0;
}
```

Program 5.4   **Output**

```
Enter your number to be tested: 1234
The number is even.
```

Program 5.4   **Output (Rerun)**

Enter your number to be tested: **6551**
The number is odd.

Remember that the double equal sign == is the equality test and the single equal sign is the assignment operator. It can lead to lots of headaches if you forget this and inadvertently use the assignment operator inside the if statement.

Compound Relational Tests

The if statements that you've used so far in this chapter set up simple relational tests between two numbers. In Program 5.1, you compared the value of number against 0, whereas in Program 5.2, you compared the value of grade against 65. Sometimes, it becomes desirable, if not necessary, to set up more sophisticated tests. Suppose, for example, that in Program 5.2 you want to count not the number of failing grades, but instead the number of grades that are between 70 and 79, inclusive. In such a case, you do not merely want to compare the value of grade against one limit, but against the two limits 70 and 79 to make certain that it falls within the specified range.

The C language provides the mechanisms necessary to perform these types of compound relational tests. A *compound relational test* is simply one or more simple relational tests joined by either the *logical AND* or the *logical OR* operator. These operators are represented by the character pairs && and || (two vertical bar characters), respectively. As an example, the C statement

```
if ( grade >= 70  &&  grade <= 79 )
    ++grades_70_to_79;
```

increments the value of grades_70_to_79 only if the value of grade is greater than or equal to 70 *and* less than or equal to 79. In a like manner, the statement

```
if ( index < 0  ||  index > 99 )
    printf ("Error - index out of range\n");
```

causes execution of the printf() statement if index is less than 0 *or* greater than 99.

The compound operators can be used to form extremely complex expressions in C. The C language grants the programmer ultimate flexibility in forming expressions. This flexibility is a capability that is often abused. Simpler expressions are almost always easier to read and debug.

When forming compound relational expressions, liberally use parentheses to aid readability of the expression and to avoid getting into trouble because of a mistaken assumption about the precedence of the operators in the expression. You can also use blank spaces to aid in the expression's readability. An extra blank space around the && and || operators visually sets these operators apart from the expressions that are being joined by these operators.

To illustrate the use of a compound relational test in an actual program example, write a program that tests to see whether a year is a leap year. A year is a leap year if it is evenly divisible by 4. What you might not realize, however, is that a year that is divisible by 100 is *not* a leap year unless it also is divisible by 400.

Try to think how you would go about setting up a test for such a condition. First, you could compute the remainders of the year after division by 4, 100, and 400, and assign these values to appropriately named variables, such as rem_4, rem_100, and rem_400, respectively. Then, you could proceed to test these remainders to determine if the desired criteria for a leap year are met.

If you rephrase the previous definition of a leap year, you can say that a year is a leap year if it is evenly divisible by 4 and not by 100 or if it is evenly divisible by 400. Stop for a moment to reflect on this last sentence and to verify to yourself that it is equivalent to our previously stated definition. Now that you have reformulated our definition in these terms, it becomes a relatively straightforward task to translate it into a program statement as follows:

```
if ( (rem_4 == 0  &&  rem_100 != 0) ||  rem_400 == 0 )
    printf ("It's a leap year.\n");
```

The parentheses around the subexpression

```
rem_4 == 0  &&  rem_100 != 0
```

are not required because that is how the expression will be evaluated anyway.

If you add a few statements in front of this test to declare your variables and to enable the user to key in the year from the terminal, you end up with a program that determines if a year is a leap year, as shown in Program 5.5.

Program 5.5 **Determining if a Year Is a Leap Year**

```
// Program to determine if a year is a leap year

#include <stdio.h>

int main (void)
{
    int  year, rem_4, rem_100, rem_400;

    printf ("Enter the year to be tested: ");
    scanf ("%i", &year);

    rem_4 = year % 4;
    rem_100 = year % 100;
    rem_400 = year % 400;


    if ( (rem_4 == 0  &&  rem_100 != 0)  ||  rem_400 == 0 )
        printf ("It's a leap year.\n");
    else
        printf ("Nope, it's not a leap year.\n");

    return 0;
}
```

Program 5.5 **Output**

```
Enter the year to be tested: 1955
Nope, it's not a leap year.
```

Program 5.5 **Output (Rerun)**

```
Enter the year to be tested: 2000
It's a leap year.
```

Program 5.5 **Output (Second Rerun)**

```
Enter the year to be tested: 1800
Nope, it's not a leap year.
```

The previous examples show a year that was not a leap year because it wasn't evenly divisible by 4 (1955), a year that was a leap year because it was evenly divisible by 400 (2000), and a year that wasn't a leap year because it was evenly divisible by 100 but not by 400 (1800). To complete the run of test cases, you should also try a year that is evenly divisible by 4 but not by 100. This is left as an exercise for you.

As mentioned previously, C gives you a tremendous amount of flexibility in forming expressions. For instance, in the preceding program, you did not have to calculate the intermediate results rem_4, rem_100, and rem_400—you could have performed the calculation directly inside the if statement as follows:

```
if ( ( year % 4 == 0  &&  year % 100 != 0 )  || year % 400 == 0 )
```

The use of blank spaces to set off the various operators still makes the preceding expression readable. If you decide to ignore adding blanks and remove the unnecessary set of parentheses, you end up with an expression that looks like this:

```
if(year%4==0&&year%100!=0)||year%400==0)
```

This expression is perfectly valid and (believe it or not) executes identically to the expression shown immediately prior. Obviously, those extra blanks go a long way toward aiding understanding of complex expressions.

Nested **if** Statements

In the general format of the if statement, remember that if the result of evaluating the expression inside the parentheses is TRUE, the statement that immediately follows is executed. It is perfectly valid that this program statement be another if statement, as in the following statement:

```
if ( gameIsOver == 0 )
    if ( playerToMove == YOU )
        printf ("Your Move\n");
```

If the value of gameIsOver is 0, the following statement is executed, which is another if state-ment. This if statement compares the value of playerToMove against YOU. If the two values are equal, the message "Your Move" is displayed at the terminal. Therefore, the printf state-ment is executed only if gameIsOver equals 0 *and* playerToMove equals YOU. In fact, this state-ment could have been equivalently formulated using compound relationals as follows:

```
if ( gameIsOver == 0  &&  playerToMove == YOU )
     printf ("Your Move\n");
```

A more practical example of "nested" if statements is if you added an else clause to the previous example, as follows:

```
if ( gameIsOver == 0 )
    if ( playerToMove == YOU )
         printf ("Your Move\n");
    else
         printf ("My Move\n");
```

Execution of this statement proceeds as described previously. However, if gameIsOver equals 0 and the value of playerToMove is not equal to YOU, then the else clause is executed. This displays the message "My Move" at the terminal. If gameIsOver does not equal 0, the entire if statement that follows, including its associated else clause, is skipped.

Notice how the else clause is associated with the if statement that tests the value of playerToMove, and not with the if statement that tests the value of gameIsOver. The general rule is that an else clause is always associated with the last if statement that does not contain an else.

You can go one step further and add an else clause to the outermost if statement in the preceding example. This else clause is executed if the value of gameIsOver is not 0.

```
if ( gameIsOver == 0 )
    if ( playerToMove == YOU )
         printf ("Your Move\n");
    else
         printf ("My Move\n");
else
    printf ("The game is over\n");
```

The proper use of indentation goes a long way toward aiding your understanding of the logic of complex statements.

Of course, even if you use indentation to indicate the way you think a statement will be inter-preted in the C language, it might not always coincide with the way that the compiler actually interprets the statement. For instance, removing the first else clause from the previous example

```
if ( gameIsOver == 0 )
    if ( playerToMove == YOU )
         printf ("Your Move\n");
else
    printf ("The game is over\n");
```

does *not* result in the statement being interpreted as indicated by its format. Instead, this statement is interpreted as

```
if ( gameIsOver == 0 )
    if ( playerToMove == YOU )
        printf ("Your Move\n");
    else
        printf ("The game is over\n");
```

because the `else` clause is associated with the last un-elsed `if`. You can use braces to force a different association in those cases in which an innermost `if` does not contain an `else`, but an outer `if` does. The braces have the effect of "closing off" the `if` statement. Thus,

```
if ( gameIsOver == 0 ) {
    if ( playerToMove == YOU )
        printf ("Your Move\n");
}
else
    printf ("The game is over\n");
```

achieves the desired effect, with the message "The game is over" being displayed if the value of `gameIsOver` is not 0.

The `else if` Construct

You've seen how the `else` statement comes into play when you have a test against two possible conditions—either the number is even, else it is odd; either the year is a leap year, else it is not. However, programming decisions that you have to make are not always so black-and-white. Consider the task of writing a program that displays –1 if a number typed in by a user is less than zero, 0 if the number typed in is equal to zero, and 1 if the number is greater than zero. (This is actually an implementation of what is commonly called the *sign* function.) Obviously, you must make three tests in this case—to determine if the number that is keyed in is negative, zero, or positive. Our simple `if`-`else` construct does not work. Of course, in this case, you could always resort to three separate `if` statements, but this solution does not always work in general—especially if the tests that are made are not mutually exclusive.

You can handle the situation just described by adding an `if` statement to your `else` clause. Because the statement that followed an `else` can be any valid C program statement, it seems logical that it can be another `if`. Thus, in the general case, you could write

```
if ( expression 1 )
    program statement 1
else
    if ( expression 2 )
        program statement 2
    else
        program statement 3
```

which effectively extends the if statement from a two-valued logic decision to a three-valued logic decision. You can continue to add if statements to the else clauses, in the manner just shown, to effectively extend the decision to an *n*-valued logic decision.

The preceding construct is so frequently used that it is generally referred to as an else if construct and is usually formatted differently from that shown previously as

```
if ( expression 1 )
     program statement 1
else if ( expression 2 )
     program statement 2
else
     program statement 3
```

This latter method of formatting improves the readability of the statement and makes it clearer that a three-way decision is being made.

Program 5.6 illustrates the use of the else if construct by implementing the sign function discussed earlier.

Program 5.6 **Implementing the Sign Function**

```c
// Program to implement the sign function

#include <stdio.h>

int main (void)
{
    int  number, sign;

    printf ("Please type in a number: ");
    scanf ("%i", &number);

    if ( number < 0 )
        sign = -1;
    else if ( number == 0 )
        sign = 0;
    else            // Must be positive
        sign = 1;

    printf ("Sign = %i\n", sign);

    return 0;
}
```

Program 5.6 **Output**

```
Please type in a number: 1121
Sign = 1
```

Program 5.6   **Output (Rerun)**

```
Please type in a number: -158
Sign = -1
```

Program 5.6   **Output (Second Rerun)**

```
Please type in a number: 0
Sign = 0
```

If the number that is entered is less than zero, sign is assigned the value -1; if the number is equal to zero, sign is assigned the value 0; otherwise, the number must be greater than zero, so sign is assigned the value 1.

Program 5.7 analyzes a character that is typed in from the terminal and classifies it as either an alphabetic character (*a–z* or *A–Z*), a digit (*0–9*), or a special character (anything else). To read a single character from the terminal, the format characters %c are used in the scanf () call.

Program 5.7   **Categorizing a Single Character Entered at the Terminal**

```c
// Program to categorize a single character that is entered at the terminal

#include <stdio.h>

int main (void)
{
    char  c;

    printf ("Enter a single character:\n");
    scanf ("%c", &c);

    if ( (c >= 'a'  &&  c <= 'z')  || (c >= 'A'  &&  c <= 'Z') )
        printf ("It's an alphabetic character.\n");
    else if  ( c >= '0'  &&  c <= '9' )
        printf ("It's a digit.\n");
    else
        printf ("It's a special character.\n");

    return 0;
}
```

Program 5.7   **Output**

```
Enter a single character:
&
It's a special character.
```

Program 5.7   **Output (Rerun)**

```
Enter a single character:
8
It's a digit.
```

Program 5.7   **Output (Second Rerun)**

```
Enter a single character:
B
It's an alphabetic character.
```

The first test that is made after the character is read in determines whether the `char` variable `c` is an alphabetic character. This is done by testing if the character is either a lowercase letter or an uppercase letter. The former test is made by the expression

```
( c >= 'a'  &&  c <= 'z' )
```

which is TRUE if `c` is within the range of characters `'a'` through `'z'`; that is, if `c` is a lowercase letter. The latter test is made by the expression

```
( c >= 'A'  &&  c <= 'Z' )
```

which is TRUE if `c` is within the range of characters `'A'` through `'Z'`; that is, if `c` is an uppercase letter. These tests work on all computer systems that store characters inside the machine in a format known as ASCII format.[1]

If the variable `c` is an alphabetic character, the first `if` test succeeds and the message `It's an alphabetic character.` is displayed. If the test fails, the `else if` clause is executed. This clause determines if the character is a digit. Note that this test compares the character `c` against the *characters* `'0'` and `'9'` and *not* the *integers* 0 and 9. This is because a character was read in from the terminal, and the characters `'0'` to `'9'` are not the same as the numbers 0–9. In fact, on a computer system that uses the ASCII format mentioned previously, the character `'0'` is actually represented internally as the number 48, the character `'1'` as the number 49, and so on.

If `c` is a digit character, the phrase `It's a digit.` is displayed. Otherwise, if `c` is not alphabetic and is not a digit, the final `else` clause is executed and displays the phrase "It's a special character." Execution of the program is then complete.

You should note that even though `scanf()` is used here to read just a single character, the Enter (or Return) key must still be pressed after the character is typed to send the input to the program. In general, whenever you're reading data from the terminal, the program doesn't see any of the data typed on the line until the Enter key is pressed.

---

1. *It's better to use routines in the standard library called* `islower()` *and* `isupper()` *and avoid the internal representation issue entirely. To do that, you need to include the line* `#include <ctype.h>` *in your program. However, we've put this here for illustrative purposes only.*

For your next example, suppose you want to write a program that allows the user to type in simple expressions of the form

```
number   operator   number
```

The program evaluates the expression and displays the results at the terminal, to two decimal places of accuracy. The operators that you want to have recognized are the normal operators for addition, subtraction, multiplication, and division. Program 5.8 makes use of a large `if` statement with many `else if` clauses to determine which operation is to be performed.

Program 5.8   **Evaluating Simple Expressions**

```
/* Program to evaluate simple expressions of the form
            number  operator  number                    */

#include <stdio.h>

int main (void)
{
    float   value1, value2;
    char    operator;

    printf ("Type in your expression.\n");
    scanf ("%f %c %f", &value1, &operator, &value2);

    if ( operator == '+' )
        printf ("%.2f\n", value1 + value2);
    else if ( operator == '-' )
        printf ("%.2f\n", value1 - value2);
    else if ( operator == '*' )
        printf ("%.2f\n", value1 * value2);
    else if ( operator == '/' )
        printf ("%.2f\n", value1 / value2);

    return 0;
}
```

Program 5.8   **Output**

```
Type in your expression.
123.5 + 59.3
182.80
```

Program 5.8   **Output (Rerun)**

```
Type in your expression.
198.7 / 26
7.64
```

Program 5.8   **Output (Second Rerun)**

```
Type in your expression.
89.3 * 2.5
223.25
```

The scanf() call specifies that three values are to be read into the variables value1, operator, and value2. A floating value can be read in with the %f format characters, the same characters used for the output of floating values. This is the format used to read in the value of the variable value1, which is the first operand of your expression.

Next, you want to read in the operator. Because the operator is a character ('+', '-', '*', or '/') and not a number, you read it into the character variable operator. The %c format characters tell the system to read in the next character from the terminal. The blank spaces inside the format string indicate that an arbitrary number of blank spaces are to be permitted on the input. This enables you to separate the operands from the operator with blank spaces when you type in these values. If you had specified the format string "%f%c%f" instead, no spaces would have been permitted after typing in the first number and before typing in the operator. This is because when the scanf() function is reading a character with the %c format characters, the next character on the input, *even if it is a blank space*, is the character that is read. However, it should be noted that, in general, the scanf() function *always* ignores leading spaces when it is reading in either a decimal or floating-point number. Therefore, the format string "%f %c%f" would have worked just as well in the preceding program.

After the second operand has been keyed in and stored in the variable value2, the program proceeds to test the value of operator against the four permissible operators. When a correct match is made, the corresponding printf() statement is executed to display the results of the calculation. Execution of the program is then complete.

A few words about program thoroughness are in order at this point. While the preceding program does accomplish the task that it was set to perform, the program is not really complete because it does not account for mistakes made by the user. For example, what happens if the user types in a ? for the operator by mistake? The program simply "falls through" the if statement and no messages ever appear at the terminal to alert the user that he incorrectly typed in his expression.

Another case that is overlooked is when the user types in a division operation with zero as the divisor. You know by now that you should never attempt to divide a number by zero in C. The program should check for this case.

Trying to predict the ways that a program can fail or produce unwanted results and then taking preventive measures to account for such situations is a necessary part of producing good, reliable programs. Running a sufficient number of test cases against a program often points the finger to portions of the program that do not account for certain cases. But it goes further than that. It must become a matter of self-discipline while coding a program to always say "What would happen if ..." and to insert the necessary program statements to handle the situation properly.

Program 5.8A, a modified version of Program 5.8, accounts for division by zero and the keying in of an unknown operator.

Program 5.8A   Revising the Program to Evaluate Simple Expressions

```
/* Program to evaluate simple expressions of the form
                value   operator   value                    */

#include <stdio.h>

int main (void)
{
    float   value1, value2;
    char    operator;

    printf ("Type in your expression.\n");
    scanf ("%f %c %f", &value1, &operator, &value2);

    if ( operator == '+' )
        printf ("%.2f\n", value1 + value2);
    else if ( operator == '-' )
        printf ("%.2f\n", value1 - value2);
    else if ( operator == '*' )
        printf ("%.2f\n", value1 * value2);
    else if ( operator == '/' )
        if ( value2 == 0 )
            printf ("Division by zero.\n");
        else
            printf ("%.2f\n", value1 / value2);
    else
        printf ("Unknown operator.\n");

    return 0;
}
```

Program 5.8A   Output

```
Type in your expression.
123.5 + 59.3
182.80
```

Program 5.8A   Output (Rerun)

```
Type in your expression.
198.7 / 0
Division by zero.
```

Program 5.8A   **Output (Second Rerun)**

```
Type in your expression.
125 $ 28
Unknown operator.
```

When the operator that is typed in is the slash, for division, another test is made to determine if `value2` is `0`. If it is, an appropriate message is displayed at the terminal. Otherwise, the division operation is carried out and the results are displayed. Pay careful attention to the nesting of the `if` statements and the associated `else` clauses in this case.

The `else` clause at the end of the program catches any "fall throughs." Therefore, any value of `operator` that does not match any of the four characters tested causes this `else` clause to be executed, resulting in the display of "Unknown operator."

The `switch` Statement

The type of `if-else` statement chain that you encountered in the last program example—in which the value of a variable is successively compared against different values—is so commonly used when developing programs that a special program statement exists in the C language for performing precisely this function. The name of the statement is the `switch` statement, and its general format is

```
switch ( expression )
{
    case value1:
                program statement
                program statement
                    . . .
                break;
    case value2:
                program statement
                program statement
                    . . .
                break;
        . . .
    case valuen:
                program statement
                program statement
                    . . .
                break;
    default:
                program statement
                program statement
                    . . .
                break;
}
```

The *expression* enclosed within parentheses is successively compared against the values *value1, value2, ..., valuen*, which must be simple constants or constant expressions. If a case is found whose value is equal to the value of *expression*, the program statements that follow the case are executed. Note that when more than one such program statement is included, they do *not* have to be enclosed within braces.

The break statement signals the end of a particular case and causes execution of the switch statement to be terminated. Remember to include the break statement at the end of every case. Forgetting to do so for a particular case causes program execution to continue into the next case whenever that case gets executed.

The special optional case called default is executed if the value of *expression* does not match any of the case values. This is conceptually equivalent to the "fall through" else that you used in the previous example. In fact, the general form of the switch statement can be equivalently expressed as an if statement as follows:

```
if ( expression == value1 )
{
    program statement
    program statement
        . . .
}
else if ( expression == value2 )
{
    program statement
    program statement
        . . .
}
    . . .
else if ( expression == valuen )
{
    program statement
    program statement
        . . .
}
else
{
    program statement
    program statement
        . . .
}
```

Bearing this mind, you can translate the big if statement from Program 5.8A into an equivalent switch statement, as shown in Program 5.9.

Program 5.9   **Revising the Program to Evaluate Simple Expressions, Version 2**

```c
/* Program to evaluate simple expressions of the form
            value  operator  value                  */

#include <stdio.h>

int main (void)
{
    float  value1, value2;
    char   operator;

    printf ("Type in your expression.\n");
    scanf ("%f %c %f", &value1, &operator, &value2);

    switch (operator)
    {
        case '+':
            printf ("%.2f\n", value1 + value2);
            break;
        case '-':
            printf ("%.2f\n", value1 - value2);
            break;
        case '*':
            printf ("%.2f\n", value1 * value2);
            break;
        case '/':
            if ( value2 == 0 )
                printf ("Division by zero.\n");
            else
                printf ("%.2f\n", value1 / value2);
            break;
        default:
            printf ("Unknown operator.\n");
            break;
    }

    return 0;
}
```

Program 5.9   **Output**

```
Type in your expression.
178.99 - 326.8
-147.81
```

After the expression has been read in, the value of operator is successively compared against the values as specified by each case. When a match is found, the statements contained inside the case are executed. The break statement then sends execution out of the switch statement, where execution of the program is complete. If none of the cases match the value of operator, the default case, which displays Unknown operator. is executed.

The break statement in the default case is actually unnecessary in the preceding program because no statements follow this case inside the switch. Nevertheless, it is a good programming habit to remember to include the break at the end of every case.

When writing a switch statement, bear in mind that no two case values can be the same. However, you can associate more than one case value with a particular set of program statements. This is done simply by listing the multiple case values (with the keyword case before the value and the colon after the value in each case) before the common statements that are to be executed. As an example, in the following switch statement, the printf statement, which multiples value1 by value2, is executed if operator is equal to an asterisk or to the lowercase letter x.

```
switch (operator)
{
            ...

    case '*':
    case 'x':
            printf ("%.2f\n", value1 * value2);
            break;
            ...

}
```

Boolean Variables

Many new programmers soon find themselves with the task of having to write a program to generate a table of *prime numbers*. To refresh your memory, a positive integer *p* is a prime number if it is not evenly divisible by any other integers, other than 1 and itself. The first prime integer is defined to be 2. The next prime is 3, because it is not evenly divisible by any integers other than 1 and 3, and 4 is *not* prime because it *is* evenly divisible by 2.

There are several approaches that you can take to generate a table of prime numbers. If you have the task of generating all prime numbers up to 50, for example, the most straightforward (and simplest) algorithm to generate such a table is simply to test each integer *p* for divisibility by all integers from 2 through p-1. If any such integer is evenly divided by *p*, then *p* is not prime; otherwise, it is a prime number. Program 5.10 illustrates the program to generate a table of prime numbers.

Program 5.10   **Generating a Table of Prime Numbers**

```
// Program to generate a table of prime numbers

#include <stdio.h>
```

```
int main (void)
{
    int     p, d;
    _Bool   isPrime;

    for ( p = 2;  p <= 50;  ++p ) {
        isPrime = 1;

        for ( d = 2;  d < p;  ++d )
            if ( p % d  ==  0 )
                isPrime = 0;

            if ( isPrime != 0 )
                printf ("%i  ", p);
    }


    printf ("\n");
    return 0;
}
```

Program 5.10   **Output**

2   3   5   7   11   13   17   19   23   29   31   37   41   43   47

Several points are worth noting about the program in Program 5.10. The outermost for statement sets up a loop to cycle through the integers 2 through 50. The loop variable p represents the value you are currently testing to see if it is prime. The first statement in the loop assigns the value 1 to the variable isPrime. The use of this variable will become apparent shortly.

A second loop is set up to divide p by the integers from 2 through p-1. Inside the loop, a test is made to see if the remainder of p divided by d is 0. If it is, you know that p cannot be prime because an integer other than 1 and itself can evenly divide it. To signal that p is no longer a candidate as a prime number, the value of the variable isPrime is set equal to 0.

When the innermost loop finishes execution, the value of isPrime is tested. If its value is not equal to zero, no integer was found that evenly divides p; therefore, p must be a prime number, and its value is displayed.

You might have noticed that the variable isPrime takes on either the value 0 or 1, and no other values. That's why you declared it to be a _Bool variable. Its value is 1 as long as p still qualifies as a prime number. But as soon as a single even divisor is found, its value is set to 0 to indicate that p no longer satisfies the criteria for being prime. Often, variables that are used in such a manner are referred to as *flags*. A flag typically assumes only one of two different values. Furthermore, the value of a flag is usually tested at least once in the program to see if it is "on" (TRUE) or "off" (FALSE), and some particular action is taken based upon the results of the test.

In C, the notion of a flag being TRUE or FALSE is most naturally translated into the values 1 and 0, respectively. So in the Program 5.10, when you set the value of isPrime to 1 inside the loop, you are effectively setting it as TRUE to indicate that p "is prime." If during the course of execution of the inner for loop an even divisor is found, the value of isPrime is set to FALSE to indicate that p no longer "is prime."

It is no coincidence that the value 1 is typically used to represent the TRUE or "on" state and 0 to represent the FALSE or "off" state. This representation corresponds to the notion of a single bit inside a computer. When the bit is "on," its value is 1; when it is "off," its value is 0. But in C, there is an even more convincing argument in favor of these logic values. It has to do with the way the C language treats the concept of TRUE and FALSE.

Recall from the beginning of this chapter that if the conditions specified inside the if state-ment are "satisfied," the program statement that immediately follows executes. But what exactly does "satisfied" mean? In the C language, satisfied means nonzero, and nothing more. So the statement

```
if ( 100 )
    printf ("This will always be printed.\n");
```

results in execution of the printf() statement because the condition in the if statement (in this case, simply the value 100) is nonzero and, therefore, is satisfied.

In each of the programs in this chapter, the notions of "nonzero means satisfied" and "zero means not satisfied" are used. This is because whenever a relational expression is evaluated in C, it is given the value 1 if the expression is satisfied and 0 if the expression is not satisfied. So evaluation of the statement

```
if  ( number < 0 )
    number = -number;
```

actually proceeds as follows:

1. The relational expression number < 0 is evaluated. If the condition is satisfied, that is, if number is less than zero, the value of the expression is 1; otherwise, its value is 0.

2. The if statement tests the result of the expression evaluation. If the result is nonzero, the statement that immediately follows is executed; otherwise, the statement is skipped.

The preceding discussion also applies to evaluation of conditions inside the for, while, and do statements. Evaluation of compound relational expressions such as in the statement

```
while  ( char != 'e'  &&  count != 80 )
```

also proceeds as outlined previously. If both specified conditions are valid, the result is 1; but if either condition is not valid, the result of the evaluation is 0. The results of the evaluation are then checked. If the result is 0, the while loop terminates; otherwise it continues.

Returning to Program 5.10 and the notion of flags, it is perfectly valid in C to test if the value of a flag is TRUE by an expression such as

```
if ( isPrime )
```

rather than with the equivalent expression

```
if ( isPrime != 0 )
```

To easily test if the value of a flag is FALSE, you can use the *logical negation* operator, !. In the expression

```
if ( ! isPrime )
```

the logical negation operator is used to test if the value of `isPrime` is FALSE (read this statement as "if not `isPrime`"). In general, an expression such as

```
! expression
```

negates the logical value of `expression`. So if `expression` is zero, the logical negation operator produces a 1. And if the result of the evaluation of `expression` is nonzero, the negation operator yields a 0.

The logical negation operator can be used to easily "flip" the value of a flag, such as in the expression

```
myMove = ! myMove;
```

As you might expect, this operator has the same precedence as the unary minus operator, which means that it has higher precedence than all binary arithmetic operators and all relational operators. So to test if the value of a variable x is not less than the value of a variable y, such as in

```
! ( x < y )
```

the parentheses are required to ensure proper evaluation of the expression. Of course, you could have equivalently expressed the previous expression as

```
x >= y
```

In Chapter 3, "Variables, Data Types, and Arithmetic Expressions," you learned about some special values that are defined in the language which you can use when working with Boolean values. These are the type `bool`, and the values `true` and `false`. To use these, you need to include the header file `<stdbool.h>` inside your program. Program 5.10A is a rewrite of Program 5.10, which takes advantage of this data type and values.

Program 5.10A   Revising the Program to Generate a Table of Prime Numbers

```
//  Program to generate a table of prime numbers

#include <stdio.h>
#include <stdbool.h>

int main (void)
{
    int   p, d;
```

```
    bool  isPrime;

    for ( p = 2;  p <= 50;  ++p ) {
        isPrime = true;

        for ( d = 2;  d < p;  ++d )
            if ( p % d  ==  0 )
                isPrime = false;

        if ( isPrime != false )
            printf ("%i  ", p);
    }


    printf ("\n");
    return 0;
}
```

Program 5.10A   **Output**

```
2   3   5   7   11   13   17   19   23   29   31   37   41   43   47
```

As you can see, by including `<stdbool.h>` in your program, you can declare variables to be of type `bool` instead of `_Bool`. This is strictly for cosmetic purposes because the former is easier to read and type than the latter, and it fits in more with the style of the other basic C data types, such as `int`, `float`, and `char`.

The Conditional Operator

Perhaps the most unusual operator in the C language is one called the *conditional* operator. Unlike all other operators in C—which are either unary or binary operators—the conditional operator is a *ternary* operator; that is, it takes three operands. The two symbols that are used to denote this operator are the question mark (?) and the colon (:). The first operand is placed before the ?, the second between the ? and the :, and the third after the :.

The general format of the conditional operator is

```
condition  ?  expression1  :  expression2
```

where `condition` is an expression, usually a relational expression, that is evaluated first whenever the conditional operator is encountered. If the result of the evaluation of `condition` is TRUE (that is, nonzero), then `expression1` is evaluated and the result of the evaluation becomes the result of the operation. If `condition` evaluates FALSE (that is, zero), then `expression2` is evaluated and its result becomes the result of the operation.

The conditional operator is most often used to assign one of two values to a variable depending upon some condition. For example, suppose you have an integer variable x and another integer variable s. If you want to assign -1 to s if x were less than zero, and the value of x^2 to s otherwise, the following statement could be written:

```
s = ( x < 0 ) ? -1 : x * x;
```

The condition x < 0 is first tested when the preceding statement is executed. Parentheses are generally placed around the condition expression to aid in the statement's readability. This is usually not required because the precedence of the conditional operator is very low—lower, in fact, than all other operators besides the assignment operators and the comma operator.

If the value of x is less than zero, the expression immediately following the ? is evaluated. This expression is simply the constant integer value -1, which is assigned to the variable s if x is less than zero.

If the value of x is not less than zero, the expression immediately following the : is evaluated and assigned to s. So if x is greater than or equal to zero, the value of x * x, or $x2$, is assigned to s.

As another example of the use of the conditional operator, the following statement assigns to the variable maxValue the maximum of a and b:

```
maxValue = ( a > b ) ? a : b;
```

If the expression that is used after the : (the "else" part) consists of another conditional operator, you can achieve the effects of an "else if" clause. For example, the *sign* function that was implemented in Program 5.6 can be written in one program line using two conditional operators as follows:

```
sign = ( number < 0 ) ? -1 : (( number == 0 ) ? 0 : 1);
```

If number is less than zero, sign is assigned the value -1; else if number is equal to zero, sign is assigned the value 0; else it is assigned the value 1. The parentheses around the "else" part of the preceding expression are actually unnecessary. This is because the conditional operator associates from right to left, meaning that multiple uses of this operator in a single expression, such as in

```
e1 ? e2 : e3 ? e4 : e5
```

group from right to left and, therefore, are evaluated as

```
e1 ? e2 : ( e3 ? e4 : e5 )
```

It is not necessary that the conditional operator be used on the right-hand side of an assignment—it can be used in any situation in which an expression could be used. This means that you could display the sign of the variable number, without first assigning it to a variable, using a printf statement as shown:

```
printf ("Sign = %i\n", ( number < 0 ) ? -1 : ( number == 0 ) ? 0 : 1);
```

The conditional operator is very handy when writing preprocessor *macros* in C. This is seen in detail in Chapter 12, "The Preprocessor."

This concludes the discussions on making decisions. In Chapter 6, "Working with Arrays," you get your first look at more sophisticated data types. The *array* is a powerful concept that will find its way into many programs that you will develop in C. Before moving on, test your understanding of the material covered in this chapter by completing the following exercises.

Exercises

1. Type in and run the 12 programs presented in this chapter. Compare the output produced by each program with the output presented after each program in the text. Try experimenting with each program by keying in values other than those shown.

2. Write a program that asks the user to type in two integer values at the terminal. Test these two numbers to determine if the first is evenly divisible by the second, and then display an appropriate message at the terminal.

3. Write a program that accepts two integer values typed in by the user. Display the result of dividing the first integer by the second, to three-decimal-place accuracy. Remember to have the program check for division by zero.

4. Write a program that acts as a simple "printing" calculator. The program should allow the user to type in expressions of the form

   ```
   number    operator
   ```

   The following operators should be recognized by the program:

   ```
   +    -    *    /    S    E
   ```

   The S operator tells the program to set the "accumulator" to the typed-in number. The E operator tells the program that execution is to end. The arithmetic operations are performed on the contents of the accumulator with the number that was keyed in acting as the second operand. The following is a "sample run" showing how the program should operate:

   ```
   Begin Calculations
   10 S           Set Accumulator to 10
   = 10.000000    Contents of Accumulator
   2 /            Divide by 2
   = 5.000000     Contents of Accumulator
   55 -           Subtract 55
   -50.000000
   100.25 S       Set Accumulator to 100.25
   = 100.250000
   4 *            Multiply by 4
   = 401.000000
   0 E            End of program
   = 401.000000
   End of Calculations.
   ```

   Make certain that the program detects division by zero and also checks for unknown operators.

5. You developed Program 4.9 to reverse the digits of an integer typed in from the terminal. However, this program does not function well if you type in a negative number. Find out what happens in such a case and then modify the program so that negative numbers are correctly handled. For example, if the number –8645 is typed in, the output of the program should be 5468–.

6. Write a program that takes an integer keyed in from the terminal and extracts and displays each digit of the integer in English. So, if the user types in 932, the program should display

   `nine three two`

   Remember to display "zero" if the user types in just a 0. (*Note:* This exercise is a hard one!)

7. Program 5.10 has several inefficiencies. One inefficiency results from checking even numbers. Because it is obvious that any even number greater than 2 cannot be prime, the program could simply skip all even numbers as possible primes *and* as possible divisors. The inner `for` loop is also inefficient because the value of p is *always* divided by all values of d from 2 through p-1. This inefficiency could be avoided by adding a test for the value of `isPrime` in the conditions of the `for` loop. In this manner, the `for` loop could be set up to continue as long as no divisor was found and the value of d was less than p. Modify Program 5.10 to incorporate these two changes. Then run the program to verify its operation. (*Note:* In Chapter 6, you discover even more efficient ways of generating prime numbers.)

6

Working with Arrays

The C language provides a capability that enables you to define a set of ordered data items known as an array. This chapter describes how arrays can be defined and manipulated. In later chapters, you learn more about arrays to illustrate how well they work together with program functions, structures, character strings, and pointers. But before you get to those topics, you first need to cover the basics of arrays, including

- Setting up simple arrays
- Initializing arrays
- Working with character arrays
- Using the const keyword
- Implementing multidimensional arrays
- Creating variable-length arrays

Suppose you have a set of grades that you want to read into the computer, and suppose that you want to perform some operations on these grades, such as rank them in ascending order, compute their average, or find their median. In Program 5.2, you were able to calculate the average of a set of grades by simply adding each grade into a cumulative total as each grade was entered. However, if you want to rank the grades into ascending order, for example, you need to do something further. If you think about the process of ranking a set of grades, you quickly realize that you cannot perform such an operation until each and every grade has been entered. Therefore, using the techniques described previously, you would read in each grade and store it into a unique variable, perhaps with a sequence of statements such as the following:

```
printf ("Enter grade 1\n");
scanf ("%i", &grade1);
printf ("Enter grade 2\n");
scanf ("%i", &grade2);
    . . .
```

After the grades have been entered, you can then proceed to rank them. This can be done by setting up a series of if statements to compare each of the values to determine the smallest grade, the next smallest grade, and so on, until the maximum grade has been determined. If you sit down and try to write a program to perform precisely this task, you soon realize that for any reasonably sized list of grades (where reasonably sized is probably only about 10), the resulting program is quite large and complex. All is not lost, however, as this is one instance in which the array comes to the rescue.

Defining an Array

You can define a variable called grades, which represents not a *single* value of a grade, but an entire *set of grades*. Each element of the set can then be referenced by means of a number called an *index* number or *subscript*. Whereas in mathematics a subscripted variable, x_i, refers to the *i*th element *x* in a set, in C the equivalent notation is as follows:

x[i]

So the expression

grades[5]

(read as "grades sub 5") refers to element number 5 in the array called grades. Array elements begin with the number zero, so

grades[0]

actually refers to the first element of the array. (For this reason, it is easier to think of it as referring to element number zero, rather than as referring to the first element.)

An individual array element can be used anywhere that a normal variable can be used. For example, you can assign an array value to another variable with a statement such as the following:

g = grades[50];

This statement takes the value contained in grades[50] and assigns it to g. More generally, if i is declared to be an integer variable, the statement

g = grades[i];

takes the value contained in element number i of the grades array and assigns it to g. So if i is equal to 7 when the preceding statement is executed, the value of grades[7] is assigned to g.

A value can be stored in an element of an array simply by specifying the array element on the left side of an equal sign. In the statement

grades[100] = 95;

the value 95 is stored in element number 100 of the grades array. The statement

grades[i] = g;

has the effect of storing the value of g in grades[i].

The capability to represent a collection of related data items by a single array enables you to develop concise and efficient programs. For example, you can easily sequence through the elements in the array by varying the value of a variable that is used as a subscript in the array. So the `for` loop

```
for ( i = 0;   i < 100;   ++i )
    sum += grades[i];
```

sequences through the first 100 elements of the array `grades` (elements 0 through 99) and adds the value of each grade into `sum`. When the `for` loop is finished, the variable `sum` then contains the total of the first 100 values of the `grades` array (assuming `sum` was set to zero before the loop was entered).

When working with arrays, remember that the first element of an array is indexed by zero, and the last element is indexed by the number of elements in the array minus one.

In addition to integer constants, integer-valued expressions can also be used inside the brackets to reference a particular element of an array. So if `low` and `high` are defined as integer variables, the statement

```
next_value = sorted_data[(low + high) / 2];
```

assigns the value indexed to the variable `next_value` by evaluating the expression `(low + high) / 2`. If `low` is equal to 1 and `high` is equal to 9, the value of `sorted_data[5]` is assigned to `next_value`. In addition, if `low` is equal to 1 and `high` is equal to 10, the value of `sorted_data[5]` is also referenced because you know that an integer division of 11 by 2 gives the result of 5.

Just as with variables, arrays must also be declared before they are used. The declaration of an array involves declaring the type of element that will be contained in the array—such as `int`, `float`, or `char`—as well as the maximum number of elements that will be stored inside the array. (The C compiler needs this latter information to determine how much of its memory space to reserve for the particular array.)

As an example, the declaration

```
int   grades[100];
```

declares `grades` to be an array containing 100 integer elements. Valid references to this array can be made by using subscripts from 0 through 99. But be careful to use valid subscripts because C does not do any checking of array bounds for you. So a reference to element number 150 of array `grades`, as previously declared, does not necessarily cause an error but does most likely cause unwanted, if not unpredictable, program results.

To declare an array called `averages` that contains 200 floating-point elements, the declaration

```
float   averages[200];
```

is used. This declaration causes enough space inside the computer's memory to be reserved to contain 200 floating-point numbers. Similarly, the declaration

```
int  values[10];
```

reserves enough space for an array called `values` that could hold up to 10 integer numbers. You can better conceptualize this reserved storage space by referring to Figure 6.1.

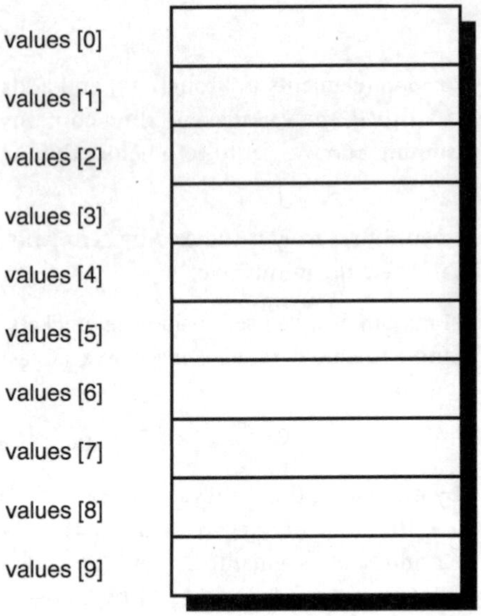

values [0]
values [1]
values [2]
values [3]
values [4]
values [5]
values [6]
values [7]
values [8]
values [9]

Figure 6.1   The array `values` in memory.

The elements of arrays declared to be of type `int`, `float`, or `char` can be manipulated in the same fashion as ordinary variables. You can assign values to them, display their values, add to them, subtract from them, and so on. So, if the following statements appear in a program, the array `values` would contain the numbers as shown in Figure 6.2.

```
int  values[10];

values[0]  = 197;
values[2]  = -100;
values[5]  = 350;
values[3]  = values[0] + values[5];
values[9]  = values[5] / 10;
--values[2];
```

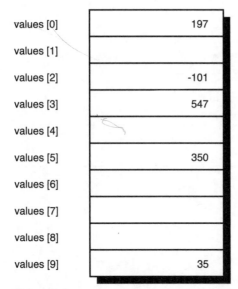

values [0]	197
values [1]	
values [2]	-101
values [3]	547
values [4]	
values [5]	350
values [6]	
values [7]	
values [8]	
values [9]	35

Figure 6.2   `values` with some initialized elements.

The first assignment statement has the effect of storing the value 197 in `values[0]`. In a similar fashion, the second and third assignment statements store –100 and 350 into `values[2]` and `values[5]`, respectively. The next statement adds the contents of `values[0]` (which is 197) to the contents of `values[5]` (which is 350) and stores the result of 547 in `values[3]`. In the following program statement, 350—the value contained in `values[5]`— is divided by 10 and the result is stored in `values[9]`. The last statement decrements the contents of `values[2]`, which has the effect of changing its value from –100 to –101.

The preceding program statements are incorporated into Program 6.1. The `for` loop sequences through each element of the array, displaying its value at the terminal in turn.

Program 6.1   **Working with an Array**

```
#include <stdio.h>

int main (void)
{
    int   values[10];
    int   index;

    values[0] = 197;
    values[2] = -100;
    values[5] = 350;
    values[3] = values[0] + values[5];
    values[9] =
```

```
        values[5] / 10;
        --values[2];

        for ( index = 0;  index < 10;  ++index )
            printf ("values[%i] = %i\n", index, values[index]);

        return 0;
}
```

Program 6.1   **Output**

```
values[0] = 197
values[1] = -2
values[2] = -101
values[3] = 547
values[4] = 4200224
values[5] = 350
values[6] = 4200326
values[7] = 4200224
values[8] = 8600872
values[9] = 35
```

The variable `index` assumes the `values` 0 through 9 as the last valid subscript of an array is always one less than the number of elements (due to that zeroth element). Because you never assigned values to five of the elements in the array—elements 1, 4, and 6 through 8—the `values` that are displayed for them are meaningless. You will probably see different values than what are displayed here. For this reason, no assumption should ever be made as to the value of an uninitialized variable or array element.

Using Array Elements as Counters

It's now time to consider a slightly more practical example. Suppose you took a telephone survey to discover how people felt about a particular television show and you asked each respondent to rate the show on a scale from 1 to 10, inclusive. After interviewing 5,000 people, you accumulated a list of 5,000 numbers. Now, you want to analyze the results. One of the first pieces of data you want to gather is a table showing the distribution of the ratings. In other words, you want to know how many people rated the show a 1, how many rated it a 2, and so on up to 10.

Although not an impossible chore, it would be a bit tedious to go through each response and manually count the number of responses in each rating category. In addition, if you have a response that could be answered in more than 10 ways (consider the task of categorizing the age of the respondent), this approach would be even more unreasonable. So, you want to develop a program to count the number of responses for each rating. The first impulse might be to set up 10 different counters, called perhaps `rating_1` through `rating_10`, and then to increment the appropriate counter each time the corresponding rating was entered. But once again, if you are dealing with more than 10 possible choices, this approach could become a bit tedious. And besides, an approach that uses an array provides the vehicle for implementing a much cleaner solution, even in this case.

You can set up an array of counters called `ratingCounters`, for example, and then you can increment the corresponding counter as each response is entered. To conserve space in this book, Program 6.2 assumes you are dealing with only 20 responses. In addition, it's always good practice to first get a program working on a smaller test case before proceeding with the full set of data because problems that are discovered in the program are much easier to isolate and debug if the amount of test data is small.

Program 6.2   **Demonstrating an Array of Counters**

```c
#include <stdio.h>

int main (void)
{
    int   ratingCounters[11], i, response;

    for ( i = 1;  i <= 10;  ++i )
        ratingCounters[i] = 0;

    printf ("Enter your responses\n");

    for ( i = 1;  i <= 20;  ++i ) {
        scanf ("%i", &response);

        if ( response < 1 || response > 10 )
            printf ("Bad response: %i\n", response);
        else
            ++ratingCounters[response];
    }

    printf ("\n\nRating   Number of Responses\n");
    printf ("------ -------------------\n");

    for ( i = 1;  i <= 10;  ++i )
        printf ("%4i%14i\n", i, ratingCounters[i]);

    return 0;
}
```

Program 6.2   **Output**

```
Enter your responses
6
5
```

```
8
3
9
6
5
7
15
Bad response: 15
5
5
1
7
4
10
5
5
6
8
9
```

```
Rating    Number of Responses
------    -------------------
1              1
2              0
3              1
4              1
5              6
6              3
7              2
8              2
9              2
10             1
```

The array ratingCounters is defined to contain 11 elements. A valid question you might ask is, "If there are only 10 possible responses to the survey, why is the array defined to contain 11 elements rather than 10?" The answer lies in the strategy for counting the responses in each particular rating category. Because each response can be a number from 1 to 10, the program keeps track of the responses for any one particular rating by simply incrementing the corresponding array element (after first checking to make certain that the user entered a valid response between 1 and 10). For example, if a rating of 5 is typed in, the value of rating-Counters[5] is incremented by one. By employing this technique, the total number of respondents who rated the TV show a 5 are contained in ratingCounters[5].

The reason for 11 elements versus 10 should now be clear. Because the highest rating number is a 10, you must set up your array to contain 11 elements to index ratingCounters[10], remembering that because of the zeroth element, the number of elements in an array is always one more than the highest index number. Because no response can have a value of zero, ratingCounters[0] is never used. In fact, in the for loops that initialize and display the contents of the array, note that the variable i starts at 1, and thereby bypasses the initialization and display of ratingCounters[0].

As a point of discussion, you could have developed your program to use an array containing precisely 10 elements. Then, when each response was keyed in by the user, you could have instead incremented ratingCounters[response - 1]. This way, ratingCounters[0] would have contained the number of respondents who rated the show a 1, ratingCounters[1] the number who rated the show a 2, and so on. This is a perfectly fine approach. The only reason it was not used is because storing the number of responses of value n inside ratingCounters[n] is a slightly more straightforward approach.

Generating Fibonacci Numbers

Study Program 6.3, which generates a table of the first 15 *Fibonacci* numbers, and try to predict its output. What relationship exists between each number in the table?

Program 6.3   **Generating Fibonacci Numbers**

```
// Program to generate the first 15 Fibonacci numbers
#include <stdio.h>

int main (void)
{
    int  Fibonacci[15], i;

    Fibonacci[0] = 0;    // by definition
    Fibonacci[1] = 1;    // ditto

    for ( i = 2;  i < 15;  ++i )
        Fibonacci[i] = Fibonacci[i-2] + Fibonacci[i-1];

    for ( i = 0;  i < 15;  ++i )
        printf ("%i\n", Fibonacci[i]);

    return 0;
}
```

Program 6.3   **Output**

```
0
1
1
2
3
```

```
5
8
13
21
34
55
89
144
233
377
```

The first two Fibonacci numbers, called F_0 and F_1, are defined to be 0 and 1, respectively. Thereafter, each successive Fibonacci number Fi is defined to be the sum of the two preceding Fibonacci numbers F_{i-2} and F_{i-1}. So F_2 is calculated by adding together the values of F_0 and F_1. In the preceding program, this corresponds directly to calculating Fibonacci[2] by adding the values Fibonacci[0] and Fibonacci[1]. This calculation is performed inside the for loop, which calculates the values of F_2 through F_{14} (or, equivalently, Fibonacci[2] through Fibonacci[14]).

Fibonacci numbers actually have many applications in the field of mathematics and in the study of computer algorithms. The sequence of Fibonacci numbers historically originated from the "rabbits problem": If you start with a pair of rabbits and assume that each pair of rabbits produces a new pair of rabbits each month, that each newly born pair of rabbits can produce offspring by the end of their second month, and that rabbits never die, how many pairs of rabbits will you have after the end of one year? The answer to this problem rests in the fact that at the end of the nth month, there will be a total of F_{n+2} rabbits. Therefore, according to the table from Program 6.3, at the end of the twelfth month, you will have a total of 377 pairs of rabbits.

Using an Array to Generate Prime Numbers

Now, it's time to return to the prime number program that you developed in Chapter 5, "Making Decisions," and see how the use of an array can help you to develop a more efficient program. In Program 5.10A, the criteria that you used for determining if a number was prime was to divide the prime candidate by all successive integers from 2 up to the number −1. In exercise 7 in Chapter 5, you noted two inefficiencies with this approach that could easily be corrected. But even with these changes, the approach used is still not efficient. Although such questions of efficiency might not be important when dealing with a table of prime numbers up to 50, these questions do become important, for example, when you start thinking about generating a table of prime numbers up to 100,000.

An improved method for generating prime numbers involves the notion that a number is prime if it is not evenly divisible by any other prime number. This stems from the fact that any nonprime integer can be expressed as a multiple of prime factors. (For example, 20 has the prime factors 2, 2, and 5.) You can use this added insight to develop a more efficient prime number program. The program can test if a given integer is prime by determining if it is evenly divisible by any other previously generated prime. By now the term "previously generated" should trigger in your mind the idea that an array must be involved here. You can use an array to store each prime number as it is generated.

As a further optimization of the prime number generator program, it can be readily demonstrated that any nonprime integer *n* must have as one of its factors an integer that is less than or equal to the square root of *n*. This means that it is only necessary to determine if a given integer is prime by testing it for even divisibility against all prime factors up to the square root of the integer.

Program 6.4 incorporates the previous discussions into a program to generate all prime numbers up to 50.

Program 6.4 Revising the Program to Generate Prime Numbers, Version 2

```
#include <stdio.h>
#include <stdbool.h>

// Modified program to generate prime numbers

int main (void)
{
    int   p, i, primes[50], primeIndex = 2;
    bool isPrime;

    primes[0] = 2;
    primes[1] = 3;

    for ( p = 5;  p <= 50;  p = p + 2 ) {
        isPrime = true;

        for ( i = 1;  isPrime  && p / primes[i] >= primes[i]; ++i )
            if ( p % primes[i] == 0 )
                isPrime = false;

        if ( isPrime == true ) {
            primes[primeIndex] = p;
            ++primeIndex;
        }
    }

    for ( i = 0;  i < primeIndex;  ++i )
        printf ("%i  ", primes[i]);

    printf ("\n");

    return 0;
}
```

Program 6.4   **Output**

---
2 3 5 7 11 13 17 19 23 29 31 37 41 43 47

The expression

```
p / primes[i] >= primes[i]
```

is used in the innermost `for` loop as a test to ensure that the value of `p` does not exceed the square root of `primes[i]`. This test comes directly from the discussions in the previous paragraph. (You might want to think about the math a bit.)

Program 6.4 starts by storing 2 and 3 as the first two primes in the array `primes`. This array has been defined to contain 50 elements, even though you obviously don't need that many locations for storing the prime numbers. The variable `primeIndex` is initially set to `2`, which is the next free slot in the `primes` array. A `for` loop is then set up to run through the odd integers from 5 to 50. After the Boolean variable `isPrime` is set to `true`, another `for` loop is entered. This loop successively divides the value of `p` by all of the previously generated prime numbers that are stored in the array `primes`. The index variable `i` starts at `1` because it is not necessary to test any values of `p` for divisibility by `primes[0]` (which is `2`). This is true because our program does not even consider even numbers as possible primes. Inside the loop, a test is made to see if the value of `p` is evenly divisible by `primes[i]`, and if it is, then `isPrime` is set `false`. The `for` loop continues execution so long as the value of `isPrime` is `true` *and* the value of `primes[i]` does not exceed the square root of `p`.

After exiting the `for` loop, a test of the `isPrime` flag determines whether to store the value of `p` as the next prime number inside the `primes` array.

After all values of `p` have been tried, the program displays each prime number that has been stored inside the `primes` array. The value of the index variable `i` varies from `0` through `primeIndex - 1` because `primeIndex` was always set pointing to the *next* free slot in the `primes` array.

Initializing Arrays

Just as you can assign initial values to variables when they are declared, so can you assign initial values to the elements of an array. This is done by simply listing the initial `values` of the array, starting from the first element. Values in the list are separated by commas and the entire list is enclosed in a pair of braces.

The statement

```
int  counters[5] = { 0, 0, 0, 0, 0 };
```

declares an array called `counters` to contain five integer values and initializes each of these elements to zero. In a similar fashion, the statement

```
int  integers[5] = { 0, 1, 2, 3, 4 };
```

sets the value of `integers[0]` to `0`, `integers[1]` to `1`, `integers[2]` to `2`, and so on.

Arrays of characters are initialized in a similar manner; thus the statement

```
char  letters[5] = { 'a', 'b', 'c', 'd', 'e' };
```

defines the character array `letters` and initializes the five elements to the characters `'a'`, `'b'`, `'c'`, `'d'`, and `'e'`, respectively.

It is not necessary to completely initialize an entire array. If fewer initial values are specified, only an equal number of elements are initialized. The remaining values in the array are set to zero. So the declaration

```
float  sample_data[500] = { 100.0, 300.0, 500.5 };
```

initializes the first three values of `sample_data` to `100.0`, `300.0`, and `500.5`, and sets the remaining 497 elements to zero.

By enclosing an element number in a pair of brackets, specific array elements can be initialized in any order. For example,

```
float sample_data[500] = { [2] = 500.5, [1] = 300.0, [0] = 100.0 };
```

initializes the `sample_data` array to the same values as shown in the previous example. And the statements

```
int  x = 1233;
int  a[10] =  { [9] = x + 1, [2] = 3, [1] = 2, [0] = 1 };
```

define a 10-element array and initialize the last element to the value of x + 1 (or to 1234), and the first three elements to 1, 2, and 3, respectively.

Unfortunately, C does not provide any shortcut mechanisms for initializing array elements. That is, there is no way to specify a repeat count, so if it were desired to initially set all 500 values of `sample_data` to 1, all 500 would have to be explicitly spelled out. In such a case, it is better to initialize the array inside the program using an appropriate `for` loop.

Program 6.5 illustrates two types of array-initialization techniques.

Program 6.5   Initializing Arrays

```
#include <stdio.h>

int main (void)
{
    int  array_values[10] = { 0, 1, 4, 9, 16 };
    int  i;

    for ( i = 5;  i < 10;  ++i )
     array_values[i] = i * i;

    for ( i = 0;  i < 10;  ++i )
```

```
        printf ("array_values[%i] = %i\n", i, array_values[i]);

    return 0;
}
```

Program 6.5 **Output**

```
array_values[0] = 0
array_values[1] = 1
array_values[2] = 4
array_values[3] = 9
array_values[4] = 16
array_values[5] = 25
array_values[6] = 36
array_values[7] = 49
array_values[8] = 64
array_values[9] = 81
```

In the declaration of the array array_values, the first five elements of the array are initialized to the square of their element number (for example, element number 3 is set equal to 3^2 or 9). The first for loop shows how this same type of initialization can be performed inside a loop. This loop sets each of the elements 5 through 9 to the square of its element number. The second for loop simply runs through all 10 elements to display their values at the terminal.

Character Arrays

The purpose of Program 6.6 is to simply illustrate how a character array can be used. However, one point is worthy of discussion. Can you spot it?

Program 6.6 **Introducing Character Arrays**

```
#include <stdio.h>

int main (void)
{
    char  word[] = { 'H', 'e', 'l', 'l', 'o', '!' };
    int   i;

    for ( i = 0;  i < 6;  ++i )
        printf ("%c", word[i]);

    printf ("\n");


    return 0;
}
```

Program 6.6 **Output**

```
Hello!
```

The most notable point in the preceding program is the declaration of the character array `word`. There is no mention of the number of elements in the array. The C language allows you to define an array without specifying the number of elements. If this is done, the size of the array is determined automatically based on the number of initialization elements. Because Program 6.6 has six initial values listed for the array `word`, the C language implicitly dimensions the array to six elements.

This approach works fine so long as you initialize every element in the array at the point that the array is defined. If this is not to be the case, you must explicitly dimension the array.

In the case of using index numbers in the initialization list, as in

```
float sample_data[] = { [0] = 1.0, [49] = 100.0, [99] = 200.0 };
```

the largest index number specified sets the size of the array. In this case, `sample_data` is set to contain 100 elements, based on the largest index value of 99 that is specified.

Base Conversion Using Arrays

The next program further illustrates the use of integer and character arrays. The task is to develop a program that converts a positive integer from its base 10 representation into its equivalent representation in another base up to base 16. As inputs to the program, you specify the number to be converted and also the base to which you want the number converted. The program then converts the keyed-in number to the appropriate base and displays the result.

The first step in developing such a program is to devise an algorithm to convert a number from base 10 to another base. An algorithm to generate the digits of the converted number can be informally stated as follows: A digit of the converted number is obtained by taking the modulo of the number by the base. The number is then divided by the base, with any fractional remainder discarded, and the process is repeated until the number reaches zero.

The outlined procedure generates the digits of the converted number starting from the right-most digit. See how this works in the following example. Suppose you want to convert the number 10 into base 2. Table 6.1 shows the steps that would be followed to arrive at the result.

Table 6.1 **Converting an Integer from Base 10 to Base 2**

Number	Number Modulo 2	Number / 2
10	0	5
5	1	2
2	0	1
1	1	0

The result of converting 10 to base 2 is, therefore, seen to be 1010, reading the digits of the "Number Modulo 2" column from the bottom to the top.

To write a program that performs the preceding conversion process, you must take a couple of things into account. First, the fact that the algorithm generates the digits of the converted number in reverse order is not very nice. You certainly can't expect the user to read the result from right to left, or from the bottom of the page upward. Therefore, you must correct this problem. Rather than simply displaying each digit as it is generated, you can have the program store each digit inside an array. Then, when you've finished converting the number, you can display the contents of the array in the correct order.

Second, you must realize that you specified for the program to handle conversion of numbers into bases up to 16. This means that any digits of the converted number that are between 10 and 15 must be displayed using the corresponding letters, A through F. This is where our character array enters the picture.

Examine Program 6.7 to see how these two issues are handled. This program also introduces the type qualifier const, which is used for variables whose value does not change in a program.

Program 6.7 Converting a Positive Integer to Another Base

```c
// Program to convert a positive integer to another base

#include <stdio.h>

int main (void)
{
    const char baseDigits[16] = {
            '0', '1', '2', '3', '4', '5', '6', '7',
            '8', '9', 'A', 'B', 'C', 'D', 'E', 'F' };
    int      convertedNumber[64];
    long int numberToConvert;
    int      nextDigit, base, index = 0;

    // get the number and the base

    printf ("Number to be converted? ");
    scanf ("%ld", &numberToConvert);
    printf ("Base? ");
    scanf ("%i", &base);

    // convert to the indicated base

    do {
        convertedNumber[index] = numberToConvert % base;
        ++index;
        numberToConvert = numberToConvert / base;
```

```
    }
    while  ( numberToConvert != 0 );


    // display the results in reverse order

    printf ("Converted number = ");

    for (--index;  index >= 0;  --index ) {
        nextDigit = convertedNumber[index];
        printf ("%c", baseDigits[nextDigit]);
    }

    printf ("\n");
    return 0;
}
```

Program 6.7   **Output**

```
Number to be converted? 10
Base?·2
Converted number = 1010
```

Program 6.7   **Output (Rerun)**

```
Number to be converted? 128362
Base? 16
Converted number = 1F56A
```

The `const` Qualifier

The compiler allows you to associate the `const` qualifier with variables whose values will not be changed by the program. That is, you can tell the compiler that the specified variables have a *const*ant value throughout the program's execution. If you try to assign a value to a `const` variable after initializing it, or try to increment or decrement it, the compiler might issue an error message, although it is not required to do so. One of the motivations for the `const` attribute in the language is that it allows the compiler to place your `const` variables into read-only memory. (Normally, the instructions of your program are also placed into read-only memory.)

As an example of the `const` attribute, the line

```
const  double  pi = 3.141592654;
```

declares the `const` variable `pi`. This tells the compiler that this variable will not be modified by the program. If you subsequently wrote a line like this in your program:

```
pi = pi / 2;
```

the gcc compiler would give you an error message similar to this:

```
foo.c:16: error: assignment of read-only variable 'pi'
```

Returning to Program 6.7, the character array baseDigits is set up to contain the 16 possible digits that will be displayed for the converted number. It is declared as a const array because its contents will not be changed after it is initialized. Note that this fact also aids in the program's readability.

The array convertedNumber is defined to contain a maximum of 64 digits, which holds the results of converting the largest possible long integer to the smallest possible base (base 2) on just about all machines. The variable numberToConvert is defined to be of type long int so that relatively large numbers can be converted if desired. Finally, the variables base (to contain the desired conversion base) and index (to index into the convertedNumber array) are both defined to be of type int.

After the user keys in the values of the number to be converted and the base—note that the scanf() call to read in a long integer value takes the format characters %ld—the program then enters a do loop to perform the conversion. The do was chosen so that at least one digit appears in the convertedNumber array even if the user keys in the number zero to be converted.

Inside the loop, the numberToConvert modulo the base is computed to determine the next digit. This digit is stored inside the convertedNumber array, and the index in the array is incremented by 1. After dividing the numberToConvert by the base, the conditions of the do loop are checked. If the value of numberToConvert is 0, the loop terminates; otherwise, the loop is repeated to determine the next digit of the converted number.

When the do loop is complete, the value of the variable index is the number of digits in the converted number. Because this variable is incremented one time too many inside the do loop, its value is initially decremented by 1 in the for loop. The purpose of this for loop is to display the converted number at the terminal. The for loop sequences through the convertedNumber array in *reverse* sequence to display the digits in the correct order.

Each digit from the convertedNumber array is in turn assigned to the variable nextDigit. For the numbers 10 through 15 to be correctly displayed using the letters A through F, a lookup is then made inside the array baseDigits, using the value of nextDigit as the index. For the digits 0 through 9, the corresponding location in the array baseDigits contains nothing more than the characters '0' through '9' (which as you recall *are* distinct from the integers 0 through 9). Locations 10 through 15 of the array contain the characters 'A' through 'F'. So, if the value of nextDigit is 10, for example, the character contained in baseDigits[10], or 'A', is displayed. And if the value of nextDigit is 8, the character '8' as contained in baseDigits[8] is displayed.

When the value of index becomes less than zero, the for loop is finished. At this point, the program displays a newline character, and program execution is terminated.

Incidentally, you might be interested in knowing that you could have easily avoided the intermediate step of assigning the value of convertedNumber[index] to nextDigit by directly specifying this expression as the subscript of the `baseDigits` array in the `printf()` call. In other words, the expression

`baseDigits[ convertedNumber[index] ]`

could have been supplied to the `printf()` routine with the same results achieved. Of course, this expression is a bit more cryptic than the two equivalent expressions used by the program.

It should be pointed out that the preceding program is a bit sloppy. No check was ever made to ensure that the value of `base` was between 2 and 16. If the user had entered 0 for the value of the base, the division inside the `do` loop would have been a division by zero. You should never allow this to happen. In addition, if the user had keyed in 1 as the value of the base, the program would enter an infinite loop because the value of `numberToConvert` would never reach zero. If the user had entered a base value that was greater than 16, you might have exceeded the bounds of the `baseDigits` array later in the program. That's another "gotcha" that you must avoid because the C system does not check this condition for us.

In Chapter 7, "Working with Functions," you rewrite this program and resolve these issues. But now, it's time to look at an interesting extension to the notion of an array.

Multidimensional Arrays

The types of arrays that you have been exposed to so far are all linear arrays—that is, they all dealt with a single dimension. The C language allows arrays of any dimension to be defined. In this section, you take a look at two-dimensional arrays.

One of the most natural applications for a two-dimensional array arises in the case of a matrix. Consider the 4 × 5 matrix shown in Table 6.2.

Table 6.2   **A 4 × 5 Matrix**

10	5	-3	17	82
9	0	0	8	-7
32	20	1	0	14
0	0	8	7	6

In mathematics, it is quite common to refer to an element of a matrix by use of a `double` subscript. So if you call the preceding matrix M, the notation $M_{i,j}$ refers to the element in the ith row, jth column, where i ranges from 1 to 4, and j ranges from 1 to 5. The notation $M_{3,2}$ refers to the value 20, which is found in the 3rd row, 2nd column of the matrix. In a similar fashion, $M_{4,5}$ refers to the element contained in the 4th row, 5th column: the value 6.

In C, you can use an analogous notation when referring to elements of a two-dimensional array. However, because C likes to start numbering things at zero, the 1st row of the matrix is actually row 0, and the 1st column of the matrix is column 0. The preceding matrix would then have row and column designations, as shown in Table 6.3.

Table 6.3   **A 4 × 5 Matrix in C**

Column (j)	0	1	2	3	4
Row (i)					
0	10	5	-3	17	82
1	9	0	0	8	-7
2	32	20	1	0	14
3	0	0	8	7	6

Whereas in mathematics the notation $M_{i,j}$ is used, in C the equivalent notation is

M[i][j]

Remember, the first index number refers to the row number, whereas the second index number references the column. So the statement

sum = M[0][2] + M[2][4];

adds the value contained in row 0, column 2—which is -3—to the value contained in row 2, column 4—which is 14—and assigns the result of 11 to the variable sum.

Two-dimensional arrays are declared the same way that one-dimensional arrays are; thus

int M[4][5];

declares the array M to be a two-dimensional array consisting of 4 rows and 5 columns, for a total of 20 elements. Each position in the array is defined to contain an integer value.

Two-dimensional arrays can be initialized in a manner analogous to their one-dimensional counterparts. When listing elements for initialization, the values are listed by row. Brace pairs are used to separate the list of initializers for one row from the next. So to define and initialize the array M to the elements listed in Table 6.3, a statement such as the following can be used:

```
int  M[4][5] = {
                { 10,  5, -3, 17, 82 },
                {  9,  0,  0,  8, -7 },
                { 32, 20,  1,  0, 14 },
                {  0,  0,  8,  7,  6 }
              };
```

Pay particular attention to the syntax of the preceding statement. Note that commas are required after each brace that closes off a row, except in the case of the final row. The use of the inner pairs of braces is actually optional. If not supplied, initialization proceeds by row. Thus, the preceding statement could also have been written as follows:

```
int  M[4][5] = { 10, 5, -3, 17, 82, 9, 0, 0, 8, -7, 32,
                 20, 1, 0, 14, 0, 0, 8, 7, 6 };
```

As with one-dimensional arrays, it is not required that the entire array be initialized. A statement such as

```
int  M[4][5] = {
                 { 10,  5, -3 },
                 {  9,  0,  0 },
                 { 32, 20,  1 },
                 {  0,  0,  8 }
               };
```

only initializes the first three elements of each row of the matrix to the indicated values. The remaining values are set to 0. Note that, in this case, the inner pairs of braces *are required* to force the correct initialization. Without them, the first two rows and the first two elements of the third row would have been initialized instead. (Verify to yourself that this is the case.)

Subscripts can also be used in the initialization list, in a like manner to single-dimensional arrays. So the declaration

```
int matrix[4][3] = {  [0][0] = 1,  [1][1] = 5,  [2][2] = 9 };
```

initializes the three indicated elements of `matrix` to the specified values. The unspecified elements are set to zero by default.

Variable Length Arrays[1]

This section discusses a feature in the language that enables you to work with arrays in your programs without having to give them a constant size.

In the examples in this chapter, you have seen how the size of an array is declared to be of a specific size. The C language allows you to declare arrays of a variable size. For example, Program 6.3 only calculates the first 15 Fibonacci numbers. But what if you want to calculate 100 or even 500 Fibonacci numbers? Or, what if you want to have the user specify the number of Fibonacci numbers to generate? Study Program 6.8 to see one method for resolving this problem.

---

1. *The ANSI C11 standard makes support for variable length arrays optional. Check your compiler documentation to see if in fact this feature is supported.*

Program 6.8   **Generating Fibonacci Numbers Using Variable Length Arrays**

```c
// Generate Fibonacci numbers using variable length arrays

#include <stdio.h>

int main (void)
{
    int i, numFibs;

    printf ("How many Fibonacci numbers do you want (between 1 and 75)? ");
    scanf ("%i", &numFibs);

    if (numFibs < 1 || numFibs > 75) {
        printf ("Bad number, sorry!\n");
        return 1;
    }

    unsigned long long int   Fibonacci[numFibs];

    Fibonacci[0] = 0;          // by definition
    Fibonacci[1] = 1;          // ditto

    for ( i = 2;  i < numFibs;  ++i )
        Fibonacci[i] = Fibonacci[i-2] + Fibonacci[i-1];

    for ( i = 0;  i < numFibs;  ++i )
        printf ("%llu  ", Fibonacci[i]);

    printf ("\n");

    return 0;
}
```

Program 6.8   **Output**

```
How many Fibonacci numbers do you want (between 1 and 75)? 50
0  1  1  2  3  5  8  13  21  34  55  89  144  233  377  610  987  1597  2584
4181  6765  10946  17711  28657  46368  75025  121393  196418  317811  514229
832040  1346269  2178309  3524578  5702887  9227465  14930352  24157817
39088169  63245986  102334155  165580141  267914296  433494437  701408733
1134903170  1836311903  2971215073  4807526976  7778742049
```

Program 6.8 has several points worth discussing. First, the variables i and numFibs are declared. The latter variable is used to store the requested number of Fibonacci numbers that the user wants to generate. Notice the range of the entered value is checked by the program, which is good programming practice. If the value is out of range (that is, less than 1 or greater than 75), the program displays a message and returns a value of 1. Executing the `return` statement at that point in the program causes the program to terminate immediately, and no further statements are executed. As noted in Chapter 2, "Compiling and Running Your First Program," the nonzero value that is returned indicates by convention that the program terminated with an error condition, and that fact could be tested by another program if desired.

After the number has been entered by the user, you see the statement

```
unsigned long long int    Fibonacci[numFibs];
```

The `Fibonacci` array is declared to contain `numFibs` elements. This is called a variable length array because the size of the array is specified by a variable and not by a constant expression. Also, as previously noted, a variable can be declared anywhere in a program, as long as the declaration occurs before the variable is first used. So although this declaration appears out of place, it's perfectly legitimate. It's not usually considered good programming style to do this, however, mainly because, by convention, the variable declarations are often grouped together so someone reading the program can see the variables and their types in one place.

Because Fibonacci numbers get large very quickly, the array is declared to contain the largest positive integer value you can specify, namely an `unsigned long long int`. As an exercise, you might want to determine the largest Fibonacci number that you can store inside an `unsigned long long int` variable on your computer.

The rest of the program is self-explanatory: The requested number of Fibonacci numbers are calculated and then displayed to the user. The execution of the program is then complete.

A technique known as *dynamic memory allocation* is also often used to allocate space for arrays while a program is executing. This involves using functions such as `malloc()` and `calloc()` that are in the standard C library. This topic is discussed in detail in Chapter 16, "Miscellaneous and Advanced Features."

You have seen how arrays are powerful constructs that are available in virtually all programming languages. A program example showing the use of multidimensional arrays is deferred to Chapter 7, which begins a detailed discussion of one of the most important concepts in the C language—the program *function*. Before proceeding to that chapter, however, try to work the following exercises.

Exercises

1. Type in and run the eight programs presented in this chapter. Compare the output produced by each program with the output presented after each program in the text.

2. Modify Program 6.1 so that the elements of the array `values` are initially set to 0. Use a `for` loop to perform the initialization.

3. Program 6.2 permits only 20 responses to be entered. Modify that program so that any number of responses can be entered. So that the user does not have to count the number of responses in the list, set up the program so that the value `999` can be keyed in by the user to indicate that the last response has been entered. (*Hint:* You can use the `break` statement here if you want to exit your loop.)

4. Write a program that calculates the average of an array of 10 floating-point values.

5. What output do you expect from the following program?

```
#include <stdio.h>

int main (void)
{
    int numbers[10] = { 1, 0, 0, 0, 0, 0, 0, 0, 0, 0 };
    int  i, j;

    for ( j = 0;  j < 10;  ++j )
        for ( i = 0;  i < j;  ++i )
            numbers[j]  +=  numbers[i];

    for ( j = 0;  j < 10;  ++j )
        printf ("%i ", numbers[j]);

    printf ("\n");

    return 0;
}
```

6. You don't need to use an array to generate Fibonacci numbers. You can simply use three variables: two to store the previous two Fibonacci numbers and one to store the current one. Rewrite Program 6.3 so that arrays are not used. Because you're no longer using an array, you need to display each Fibonacci number as you generate it.

7. Prime numbers can also be generated by an algorithm known as the *Sieve of Eratosthenes*. The algorithm for this procedure is presented here. Write a program that implements this algorithm. Have the program find all prime numbers up to n = 150. What can you say about this algorithm as compared to the ones used in the text for calculating prime numbers?

Sieve of Eratosthenes Algorithm

To Display All Prime Numbers Between 1 and n

Step 1: Define an array of integers P. Set all elements P_i to 0, $2 <= i <= n$.

Step 2: Set i to 2.

Step 3: If $i > n$, the algorithm terminates.

Step 4: If P_i is 0, then i is prime.

Step 5: For all positive integer values of j, such that $i \times j \le n$, set P_{ixj} to 1.

Step 6: Add 1 to i and go to step 3.

8. Find out if your compiler supports variable-length arrays. If it does, write a small program to test the feature out.

Working with Functions

Behind all well-written programs in the C programming language lies the same fundamental element—the function. You've used functions in every program that you've encountered so far. The `printf()` and `scanf()` routines are examples of functions. Indeed, each and every program also uses a function called `main()`. You may be wondering, "What's the big deal about functions?" When you start breaking down the your programming task into functions, your code will be easier to write, read, understand, debug, modify, and maintain. Obviously, anything that can accomplish all of these things is worthy of a bit of fanfare. As a result this is a chapter packed with important information, including

- Understanding the basics of functions.

- Explaining local, global, automatic, and static variables.

- Using single-dimensional and multi-dimensional arrays with functions.

- Returning data from functions

- Using functions to execute top-down programming

- Calling functions from within other functions, as well as recursive functions.

Defining a Function

First, you must understand what a function is, and then you can proceed to find out how it can be most effectively used in the development of programs. Go back to the very first program that you wrote (Program 2.1), which displayed the phrase "Programming is fun.":

```
#include <stdio.h>

int main (void)
{
    printf ("Programming is fun.\n");

    return 0;
}
```

Here is a function called printMessage() that does the same thing:

```
void printMessage (void)
{
    printf ("Programming is fun.\n");
}
```

The differences between printMessage() and the function main() from Program 2.1 is in the first and last line. The first line of a function definition tells the compiler (in order from left to right) four things about the function:

1. Who can call it (discussed in Chapter 14, "Working with Larger Programs")

2. The type of value it returns

3. Its name

4. The arguments it takes

The first line of the printMessage() function definition tells the compiler that the function returns no value (the first use of the keyword void), its name is printMessage, and that it takes no arguments (the second use of the keyword void). You learn more details about the void keyword shortly.

Obviously, choosing meaningful function names is just as important as choosing meaningful variable names—the choice of names greatly affects the program's readability.

Recall from discussions of Program 2.1 that main() is a specially recognized name in the C system that always indicates where the program is to begin execution. You must *always* have a main(). You can add a main() function to the preceding code to end up with a complete program, as shown in Program 7.1.

Program 7.1 **Writing a Function in C**

```
#include <stdio.h>

void printMessage (void)
{
    printf ("Programming is fun.\n");
}

int main (void)
{
    printMessage ();

    return 0;
}
```

Program 7.1 **Output**

```
Programming is fun.
```

Program 7.1 consists of *two* functions: `printMessage()` and `main()`. Program execution always begins with `main()`. Inside that function, the statement

```
printMessage ();
```

appears. This statement indicates that the function `printMessage()` is to be executed. The open and close parentheses are used to tell the compiler that `printMessage()` is a function and that no arguments or values are to be passed to this function (which is consistent with the way the function is defined in the program). When a function call is executed, program execution is transferred directly to the indicated function. Inside the `printMessage()` function, the `printf()` statement is executed to display the message "Programming is fun.". After the message has been displayed, the `printMessage()` routine is finished (as signaled by the closing brace) and the program *returns* to the `main()` routine, where program execution continues at the point where the function call was executed. By this time you may have noted that the terms *function* and *routine* are used interchangeably—the two terms basically mean the same thing.

Note that it is acceptable to insert a `return` statement at the end of `printMessage()` like this:

```
return;
```

Because `printMessage()` does not return a value, no value is specified for the `return`. This statement is optional because reaching the end of a function without executing a `return` has the effect of exiting the function anyway without returning a value. In other words, either with or without the `return` statement, the behavior on exit from `printMessage()` is identical.

As mentioned previously, the idea of calling a function is not new. The `printf()` and `scanf()` routines are both program functions. The main distinction here is that these routines did not have to be written by you because they are a part of the standard C library. When you use the `printf()` function to display a message or program results, execution is transferred to the `printf()` function, which performs the required tasks and then returns back to the program. In each case, execution is returned to the program statement that immediately follows the call to the function.

Now try to predict the output from Program 7.2.

Program 7.2 **Calling Functions**

```
#include <stdio.h>

void printMessage (void)
{
    printf ("Programming is fun.\n");
}
```

```
int main (void)
{
    printMessage ();
    printMessage ();

    return 0;
}
```

Program 7.2 **Output**

```
Programming is fun.
Programming is fun.
```

Execution of the preceding program starts at main(), which contains two calls to the print-Message() function. When the first call to the function is executed, control is sent directly to the printMessage() function, which displays the message "Programming is fun." and then returns to the main() routine. Upon return, another call to the printMessage() routine is encountered, which results in the execution of the same function a second time. After the return is made from the printMessage() function, execution is terminated.

As a final example of the printMessage() function, try to predict the output from Program 7.3

Program 7.3 **More on Calling Functions**

```
#include <stdio.h>

void printMessage (void)
{
    printf ("Programming is fun.\n");
}

int main (void)
{
    int  i;

    for ( i = 1;  i <= 5;  ++i )
        printMessage ();

    return 0;
}
```

Program 7.3 **Output**

```
Programming is fun.
Programming is fun.
Programming is fun.
Programming is fun.
Programming is fun.
```

Arguments and Local Variables

When the printf() function is called, you always supply one or more values to the function, the first value being the format string and the remaining values being the specific program results to be displayed. These values, called *arguments*, greatly increase the usefulness and flexibility of a function. Unlike your printMessage() routine, which displays the same message each time it is called, the printf() function displays whatever you tell it to display.

You can define a function that accepts arguments. In Chapter 4, "Program Looping," you developed an assortment of programs for calculating triangular numbers. Here, you define a function to generate a triangular number, called appropriately enough, calculateTriangularNumber(). As an argument to the function, you specify which triangular number to calculate. The function then calculates the desired number and displays the results at the terminal. Program 7.4 shows the function to accomplish this task and a main() routine to try it out.

Program 7.4 **Calculating the nth Triangular Number**

```
// Function to calculate the nth triangular number

#include <stdio.h>

void calculateTriangularNumber (int n)
{
    int   i, triangularNumber = 0;

    for ( i = 1;  i <= n;  ++i )
        triangularNumber += i;

    printf ("Triangular number %i is %i\n", n, triangularNumber);
}

int main (void)
{
    calculateTriangularNumber (10);
    calculateTriangularNumber (20);
    calculateTriangularNumber (50);

    return 0;
}
```

Program 7.4 **Output**

```
Triangular number 10 is 55
Triangular number 20 is 210
Triangular number 50 is 1275
```

Function Prototype Declaration

The function `calculateTriangularNumber()` requires a bit of explanation. The first line of the function:

```
void calculateTriangularNumber (int n)
```

is called the *function prototype declaration*. It tells the compiler that `calculateTriangularNumber()` is a function that returns no value (the keyword `void`) and that takes a single argument, called n, which is an `int`. The name that is chosen for an argument, called its *formal parameter name*, as well as the name of the function itself, can be any valid name formed by observing the naming rules outlined in Chapter 3, "Variables, Data Types, and Arithmetic Expressions," for forming variable names. For obvious reasons, you should choose meaningful names.

After the formal parameter name has been defined, it can be used to refer to the argument anywhere inside the body of the function.

The beginning of the function's definition is indicated by the opening curly brace. Because you want to calculate the nth triangular number, you have to set up a variable to store the value of the triangular number as it is being calculated. You also need a variable to act as your loop index. The variables `triangularNumber` and `i` are defined for these purposes and are declared to be of type `int`. These variables are defined and initialized in the same manner that you defined and initialized your variables inside the `main` routine in previous programs.

Automatic Local Variables

Variables defined inside a function are known as *automatic local* variables because they are automatically "created" each time the function is called, and because their values are local to the function. The value of a local variable can only be accessed by the function in which the variable is defined. Its value cannot be accessed by any other function. If an initial value is given to a variable inside a function, that initial value is assigned to the variable *each* time the function is called.

When defining a local variable inside a function, it is more precise in C to use the keyword `auto` before the definition of the variable. An example of this is as follows:

```
auto int  i, triangularNumber = 0;
```

Because the C compiler assumes by default that any variable defined inside a function is an automatic local variable, the keyword `auto` is seldom used, and for this reason it is not used in this book.

Returning to the program example, after the local variables have been defined, the function calculates the triangular number and displays the results. The closing brace then defines the end of the function.

Inside the `main()` routine, the value `10` is passed as the argument in the first call to `calculateTriangularNumber()`. Execution is then transferred directly to the function where the value `10` *becomes the value of the formal parameter* n inside the function. The function then proceeds to calculate the value of the 10th triangular number and display the result.

The next time that `calculateTriangularNumber()` is called, the argument 20 is passed. In a similar process, as described earlier, this value becomes the value of n inside the function. The function then proceeds to calculate the value of the 20th triangular number and display the answer at the terminal.

For an example of a function that takes more than one argument, rewrite the greatest common divisor program (Program 4.7) in function form. The two arguments to the function are the two numbers whose greatest common divisor (*gcd*) you want to calculate. See Program 7.5.

Program 7.5   Revising the Program to Find the Greatest Common Divisor

```
/* Function to find the greatest common divisor
        of two nonnegative integer values            */

#include <stdio.h>

void gcd (int u, int v)
{
    int  temp;

    printf ("The gcd of %i and %i is ", u, v);

    while ( v != 0 ) {
        temp = u % v;
        u = v;
        v = temp;
    }

    printf ("%i\n", u);
}


int main (void)
{
    gcd (150, 35);
    gcd (1026, 405);
    gcd (83, 240);

    return 0;
}
```

Program 7.5   Output

```
The gcd of 150 and 35 is 5
The gcd of 1026 and 405 is 27
The gcd of 83 and 240 is 1
```

The function gcd() is defined to take two integer arguments. The function refers to these arguments through their formal parameter names u and v. After declaring the variable temp to be of type int, the program displays the values of the arguments u and v, together with an appropriate message. The function then calculates and displays the greatest common divisor of the two integers.

You might be wondering why there are two printf() statements inside the function gcd. You must display the values of u and v *before* you enter the while loop because their values are changed inside the loop. If you wait until after the loop has finished, the values displayed for u and v do not at all resemble the original values that were passed to the routine. Another solution to this problem is to assign the values of u and v to two variables before entering the while loop. The values of these two variables can then be displayed together with the value of u (the greatest common divisor) using a single printf() statement after the while loop has completed.

Returning Function Results

The functions in Programs 7.4 and 7.5 perform some straightforward calculations and then display the results of the calculations at the terminal. However, you might not always want to have the results of your calculations displayed. The C language provides you with a convenient mechanism whereby the results of a function can be *returned* to the calling routine. This is not new to you because you've used it in all previous programs to return from main. The general syntax of this construct is straightforward enough:

```
return expression;
```

This statement indicates that the function is to return the value of *expression* to the calling routine. Parentheses are placed around *expression* by some programmers as a matter of programming style, but their use is optional.

An appropriate return statement is not enough. When the function declaration is made, you must also declare the *type of value the function returns*. This declaration is placed immediately *before* the function's name. Each of the previous examples in this book defined the function main() to return an integer value, which is why the keyword int is placed directly before the function name. On the other hand, a function declaration that starts like this:

```
float  kmh_to_mph (float  km_speed)
```

begins the definition of a function kmh_to_mph, which takes one float argument called km_speed and which *returns* a floating-point value. Similarly,

```
int  gcd (int  u, int  v)
```

defines a function gcd with integer arguments u and v that returns an integer value. In fact, you can modify Program 7.5 so that the greatest common divisor is not displayed by the function gcd but is instead returned to the main() routine, as shown in Program 7.6.

Program 7.6   **Finding the Greatest Common Divisor and Returning the Results**

```c
/* Function to find the greatest common divisor of two
      nonnegative integer values and to return the result    */

#include <stdio.h>

int  gcd (int u, int v)
{
    int  temp;

    while ( v != 0 ) {
        temp = u % v;
        u = v;
        v = temp;
    }

    return u;
}

int main (void)
{
    int  result;

    result = gcd (150, 35);
    printf ("The gcd of 150 and 35 is %i\n", result);

    result = gcd (1026, 405);
    printf ("The gcd of 1026 and 405 is %i\n", result);

    printf ("The gcd of 83 and 240 is %i\n", gcd (83, 240));

    return 0;
}
```

Program 7.6   **Output**

```
The gcd of 150 and 35 is 5
The gcd of 1026 and 405 is 27
The gcd of 83 and 240 is 1
```

After the value of the greatest common divisor has been calculated by the gcd() function, the statement

```c
return u;
```

is executed. This has the effect of returning the value of u, which is the value of the greatest common divisor, back to the calling routine.

You might be wondering what you can do with the value that is returned to the calling routine. As you can see from the `main()` routine, in the first two cases, the value that is returned is stored in the variable `result`. More precisely, the statement

```
result = gcd (150, 35);
```

says to call the function `gcd()` with the arguments 150 and 35 and to store the value that is returned by this function in the variable `result`.

The result that is returned by a function does not have to be assigned to a variable, as you can see by the last statement in the `main()` routine. In this case, the result returned by the call

```
gcd (83, 240)
```

is passed directly to the `printf()` function, where its value is displayed.

A C function can only return a single value in the manner just described. Unlike some other languages, C makes no distinction between subroutines (procedures) and functions. In C, there is only the function, which can optionally return a value. If the declaration of the type returned by a function is omitted, the C compiler assumes that the function returns an `int`—if it returns a value at all. Some C programmers take advantage of the fact that functions are assumed to return an `int` by default and omit the return type declaration. This is poor programming practice and should be avoided. When a function returns a value, make certain you declare the type of value returned in the function's header, if only for the sake of improving the program's readability. In this manner, you can always identify from the function header not only the function's name and the number and type of its arguments, but also if it returns a value and the returned value's type.

As noted earlier, a function declaration that is preceded by the keyword `void` explicitly informs the compiler that the function does not return a value. A subsequent attempt at using the function in an expression, as if a value were returned, results in a compiler error message. For example, because the `calculateTriangularNumber()` function of Program 7.4 did not return a value, you placed the keyword `void` before its name when defining the function. Subsequently attempting to use this function as if it returned a value, as in

```
number = calculateTriangularNumber (20);
```

results in a compiler error.

In a sense, the `void` data type is actually defining the *absence* of a data type. Therefore, a function declared to be of type `void` has no value and cannot be used as if it does have a value in an expression.

In Chapter 5, "Making Decisions," you wrote a program to calculate and display the absolute value of a number. Now, write a function that takes the absolute value of its argument and then returns the result. Instead of using integer values as you did in Program 5.1, write this function to take a floating value as an argument and to return the answer as type `float`, as shown in Program 7.7.

Program 7.7   **Calculating the Absolute Value**

```c
// Function to calculate the absolute value

#include <stdio.h>

float  absoluteValue (float x)
{
    if ( x < 0 )
      x = -x;

    return x;
}

int main (void)
{
    float   f1 = -15.5, f2 = 20.0, f3 = -5.0;
    int     i1 = -716;
    float   result;

    result = absoluteValue (f1);
    printf ("result = %.2f\n", result);
    printf ("f1 = %.2f\n", f1);

    result = absoluteValue (f2) + absoluteValue (f3);
    printf ("result = %.2f\n", result);

    result = absoluteValue ( (float) i1 );
    printf ("result = %.2f\n", result);

    result = absoluteValue (i1);
    printf ("result = %.2f\n", result);

    printf ("%.2f\n", absoluteValue (-6.0) / 4 );

    return 0;
}
```

Program 7.7   **Output**

```
result = 15.50
f1 = -15.50
result = 25.00
result = 716.00
result = 716.00
1.50
```

The `absoluteValue()` function is relatively straightforward. The formal parameter called x is tested against zero. If it is less than zero, the value is negated to take its absolute value. The result is then returned back to the calling routine with an appropriate `return` statement.

You should note some interesting points with respect to the `main()` routine that tests out the `absoluteValue()` function. In the first call to the function, the value of the variable f1, initially set to –15.5, is passed. Inside the function itself, this value is assigned to the variable x. Because the result of the `if` test is TRUE, the statement that negates the value of x is executed, thereby setting the value of x to 15.5. In the next statement, the value of x is returned to the `main()` routine where it is assigned to the variable `result` and is then displayed.

When the value of x is changed inside the `absoluteValue()` function, this in no way affects the value of the variable f1. When f1 was passed to the `absoluteValue()` function, its *value was automatically copied* into the formal parameter x by the system. Therefore, any changes made to the value of x inside the function affect only the value of x and not the value of f1. This is verified by the second `printf()` call, which displays the unchanged value of f1. Make certain you understand that it's not possible for a function to directly change the value of any of its arguments—it can only change copies of them.

The next two calls to the `absoluteValue()` function illustrate how the result returned by a function can be used in an arithmetic expression. The absolute value of f2 is added to the absolute value of f3 and the sum is assigned to the variable `result`.

The fourth call to the `absoluteValue()` function introduces the notion that the type of argument that is passed to a function should agree with the type of argument as declared inside the function. Because the function `absoluteValue()` expects a floating value as its argument, the integer variable i1 is first cast to type `float` before the call is made. If you omit the cast operation, the compiler does it for you anyway because it knows the `absoluteValue()` function is expecting a floating argument. (This is verified by the fifth call to the `absoluteValue()` function.) However, it's clearer what's going on if you do the casting yourself rather than relying on the system to do the conversion for you.

The final call to the `absoluteValue()` function shows that the rules for evaluation of arithmetic expressions also pertain to values returned by functions. Because the value returned by the `absoluteValue()` function is declared to be of type `float`, the compiler treats the division operation as the division of a floating-point number by an integer. As you recall, if one operand of a term is of type `float`, the operation is performed using floating arithmetic. In accordance with this rule, the division of the absolute value of –6.0 by 4 produces a result of 1.5.

Now that you've defined a function that computes the absolute value of a number, you can use it in any future programs in which you might need such a calculation performed. In fact, the next program (Program 7.8) is just such an example.

Functions Calling Functions Calling...

With most cell phones having calculator apps on them, it's usually no big deal to find the square root of a particular number should the need arise. But years ago, students were taught manual techniques that could be used to arrive at an approximation of the square root of a number. One such approximation method that lends itself most readily to solution by a computer is known as the *Newton-Raphson Iteration Technique*. In Program 7.8, you write a square root function that uses this technique to arrive at an approximation of the square root of a number.

The Newton-Raphson method can be easily described as follows. You begin by selecting a "guess" at the square root of the number. The closer that this guess is to the actual square root, the fewer the number of calculations that have to be performed to arrive at the square root. For the sake of argument, however, assume that you are not very good at guessing and, therefore, always make an initial guess of 1.

The number whose square root you want to obtain is divided by the initial guess and is then added to the value of guess. This intermediate result is then divided by 2. The result of this division becomes the new guess for another go-around with the formula. That is, the number whose square root you are calculating is divided by this new guess, added into this new guess, and then divided by 2. This result then becomes the new guess and another iteration is performed.

Because you don't want to continue this iterative process forever, you need some way of knowing when to stop. Because the successive guesses that are derived by repeated evaluation of the formula get closer and closer to the true value of the square root, you can set a limit that you can use for deciding when to terminate the process. The difference between the square of the guess and the number itself can then be compared against this limit—usually called epsilon (ε). If the difference is less than ε, the desired accuracy for the square root has been obtained and the iterative process can be terminated.

This procedure can be expressed in terms of an algorithm, as shown next.

Newton-Raphson Method to Compute the Square Root of *x*

Step 1. Set the value of guess to 1.

Step 2. If $|\text{guess}^2 - x| < \varepsilon$, proceed to step 4.

Step 3. Set the value of guess to $(x\ /\ \text{guess}\ +\ \text{guess})\ /\ 2$ and return to step 2.

Step 4. The guess is the approximation of the square root.

It is necessary to test the *absolute* difference of guess2 and x against ε in step 2 because the value of guess can approach the square root of x from either side.

Now that you have an algorithm for finding the square root at your disposal, it once again becomes a relatively straightforward task to develop a function to calculate the square root. For the value of ε in the following function, the value .00001 was arbitrarily chosen. See the example in Program 7.8.

Program 7.8 **Calculating the Square Root of a Number**

```
// Function to calculate the absolute value of a number

#include <stdio.h>
```

```
float  absoluteValue (float x)
{
    if ( x < 0 )
        x = -x;
    return (x);-
}


// Function to compute the square root of a number

float  squareRoot (float x)
{
    const float  epsilon = .00001;
    float        guess   = 1.0;

    while ( absoluteValue (guess * guess - x) >= epsilon )
        guess = ( x / guess + guess ) / 2.0;

    return guess;
}



int main (void)
{
    printf ("squareRoot (2.0) = %f\n", squareRoot (2.0));
    printf ("squareRoot (144.0) = %f\n", squareRoot (144.0));
    printf ("squareRoot (17.5) = %f\n", squareRoot (17.5));

    return 0;
}
```

Program 7.8 **Output**

```
squareRoot (2.0) = 1.414216
squareRoot (144.0) = 12.000000
squareRoot (17.5) = 4.183300
```

The actual values that are displayed by running this program on your computer system might differ slightly in the less significant digits.

The preceding program requires a detailed analysis. The absoluteValue() function is defined first. This is the same function that was used in Program 7.7.

Next, you find the squareRoot() function. This function takes one argument named x and returns a value of type float. Inside the body of the function, two local variables named epsilon and guess are defined. The value of epsilon, which is used to determine when to end the iteration process, is set to .00001. You can change epsilon to an even smaller value.

The smaller the value of epsilon, the more accurate the result will be, but a smaller value will also take more time to calculate the result. The value of your guess at the square root of the number is initially set to 1.0. These initial values are assigned to these two variables each time that the function is called.

After the local variables have been declared, a while loop is set up to perform the iterative calculations. The statement that immediately follows the while condition is repetitively executed as long as the absolute difference between $guess^2$ and x is greater than or equal to epsilon. The expression

```
guess * guess - x
```

is evaluated and the result of the evaluation is passed to the absoluteValue function. The result returned by the absoluteValue function is then compared against the value of epsilon. If the value is greater than or equal to epsilon, the desired accuracy of the square root has not yet been obtained. In that case, another iteration of the loop is performed to calculate the next value of guess.

Eventually, the value of guess is close enough to the true value of the square root, and the while loop terminates. At that point, the value of guess is returned to the calling program. Inside the main() function, this returned value is passed to the printf() function, where it is displayed.

You might have noticed that *both* the absoluteValue() function and the squareRoot() function have formal parameters named x. The C compiler doesn't get confused, however, and keeps these two values distinct.

In fact, a function always has its own set of formal parameters. So the formal parameter x used inside the absoluteValue() function is distinct from the formal parameter x used inside the squareRoot() function.

The same is true for local variables. You can declare local variables with the same name inside as many functions as you want. The C compiler does not confuse the usage of these variables because a local variable can only be accessed within the function it is defined. Another way of saying this is that the *scope* of a local variable is the function in which it is defined. (As you discover in Chapter 10, "Pointers," C does provide a mechanism for indirectly accessing a local variable from outside of a function.)

Based upon this discussion, you can understand that when the value of guess2 - x is passed to the absoluteValue() function and assigned to the formal parameter x, this assignment has absolutely *no* effect on the value of x inside the squareRoot() function.

Declaring Return Types and Argument Types

As mentioned previously, the C compiler assumes that a function returns a value of type int as the default case. More specifically, when a call is made to a function, the compiler assumes that the function returns a value of type int unless either of the following has occurred:

1. The function has been defined in the program before the function call is encountered.

2. The value returned by the function has been *declared* before the function call is encountered.

In Program 7.8, the `absoluteValue()` function is defined before the compiler encounters a call to this function from within the `squareRoot()` function. The compiler knows, therefore, that when this call is encountered, the `absoluteValue()` function will return a value of type `float`. Had the `absoluteValue()` function been defined *after* the `squareRoot()` function, then upon encountering the call to the `absoluteValue()` function, the compiler would have assumed that this function returned an integer value. Most C compilers catch this error and generate an appropriate diagnostic message.

To be able to define the `absoluteValue()` function *after* the `squareRoot()` function (or even in another file—see Chapter 14), you must *declare* the type of result returned by the `absoluteValue()` function *before* the function is called. The declaration can be made inside the `squareRoot()` function itself, or outside of any function. In the latter case, the declaration is usually made at the beginning of the program.

Not only is the function declaration used to declare the function's return type, but it is also used to tell the compiler how many arguments the function takes and what their types are.

To declare `absoluteValue()` as a function that returns a value of type `float` and that takes a single argument, also of type `float`, the following declaration is used:

```
float  absoluteValue (float);
```

As you can see, you just have to specify the argument type inside the parentheses, and not its name. You can optionally specify a "dummy" name after the type if you want:

```
float  absoluteValue (float  x);
```

This name doesn't have to be the same as the one used in the function definition—the compiler ignores it anyway.

A foolproof way to write a function declaration is to simply use your text editor to make a copy of the first line from the actual definition of the function. Remember to place a semicolon at the end.

If the function doesn't take an argument, use the keyword `void` between the parentheses. If the function doesn't return a value, this fact can also be declared to thwart any attempts at using the function as if it does:

```
void  calculateTriangularNumber (int  n);
```

If the function takes a variable number of arguments (such as is the case with `printf()` and `scanf()`), the compiler must be informed. The declaration

```
int printf (char *format, ...);
```

tells the compiler that `printf()` takes a character *pointer* as its first argument (more on that later), and is followed by any number of additional arguments (the use of the ...). The functions printf() and scanf() are declared in the special file stdio.h. This is why you have been placing the following line at the start of each of your programs:

```
#include <stdio.h>
```

Without this line, the compiler can assume printf() and scanf() take a fixed number of arguments, which could result in incorrect code being generated.

The compiler automatically converts your arguments to the appropriate types when a function is called, but only if you have placed the function's definition or have declared the function and its argument types before the call.

Here are some reminders and suggestions about functions:

1. Remember that, by default, the compiler assumes that a function returns an int.

2. When defining a function that returns an int, define it as such.

3. When defining a function that doesn't return a value, define it as void.

4. The compiler converts your arguments to agree with the ones the function expects only if you have previously defined or declared the function.

5. To play it safe, declare all functions in your program, even if they are defined before they are called. (You might decide later to move them somewhere else in your file or even to another file.)

Checking Function Arguments

The square root of a negative number takes you away from the realm of real numbers and into the area of imaginary numbers. So what happens if you pass a negative number to your squareRoot function? The fact is, the Newton-Raphson process would never converge; that is, the value of guess would not get closer to the correct value of the square root with each iteration of the loop. Therefore, the criteria set up for termination of the while loop would *never* be satisfied, and the program would enter an infinite loop. Execution of the program would have to be abnormally terminated by typing in some command or pressing a special key combination (such as Ctrl+C).

Obviously, you should modify the program to correctly account for this situation. You could put the burden on the calling routine and mandate that it never pass a negative argument to the squareRoot() function. Although this approach might seem reasonable, it does have its drawbacks. Eventually, you would develop a program that used the squareRoot() function but which forgot to check the argument before calling the function. If a negative number were then passed to the function, the program would go into an infinite loop as described and would have to be aborted.

A much wiser and safer solution to the problem is to place the onus of checking the value of the argument on the squareRoot() function itself. In that way, the function is "protected" from *any* program that uses it. A reasonable approach to take is to check the value of the argument x inside the function and then (optionally) display a message if the argument is negative. The function can then immediately return without performing its calculations. As an indication to the calling routine that the squareRoot() function did not work as expected, a value not normally returned by the function could be returned.[1]

The following is a modified squareRoot() function, which tests the value of its argument and which also includes a prototype declaration for the absoluteValue() function as described in the previous section.

```
/* Function to compute the square root of a number.
   If a negative argument is passed, then a message
   is displayed and -1.0 is returned.                    */

float   squareRoot (float x)
{
    const   float   epsilon = .00001;
    float   guess   = 1.0;
    float   absoluteValue (float  x);

    if ( x < 0 )
    {
        printf ("Negative argument to squareRoot.\n");
        return -1.0;
    }

    while  ( absoluteValue (guess * guess - x) >= epsilon )
           guess = ( x / guess + guess ) / 2.0;

    return guess;
}
```

If a negative argument is passed to the preceding function, an appropriate message is displayed, and the value –1.0 is immediately returned to the calling routine. If the argument is not negative, calculation of the square root proceeds as previously described.

As you can see from the modified squareRoot() function (and as you also saw in the last example from Chapter 6, "Working with Arrays"), you can have more than one return statement in a function. Whenever a return is executed, control is immediately sent back to the calling function; any program statements in the function that appear after the return are not executed. This fact also makes the return statement ideal for use by a function that does not return a value. In such a case, as noted earlier in this chapter, the return statement takes the simpler form

```
return;
```

---

1. The square root routine in the standard C library is called sqrt () and it returns a domain error if a negative argument is supplied. The actual value that is returned is implementation-defined. On some systems, if you try to display such a value, it displays as nan, which means not a number.

because no value is to be returned. Obviously, if the function *is* supposed to return a value, this form cannot be used to return from the function.

Top-Down Programming

The notion of functions that call functions that in turn call functions, and so on, forms the basis for producing good, structured programs. In the `main()` routine of Program 7.8, the `squareRoot()` function is called several times. All the details concerned with the actual calculation of the square root are contained within the `squareRoot()` function itself, and not within `main()`. Thus, you can write a call to this function before you even write the instructions of the function itself, as long as you specify the arguments that the function takes and the value that it returns.

Later, when proceeding to write the code for the `squareRoot()` function, this same type of *top-down programming* technique can be applied: You can write a call to the `absoluteValue()` function without concerning yourself at that time with the details of operation of that function. All you need to know is that you *can* develop a function to take the absolute value of a number.

The same programming technique that makes programs easier to write also makes them easier to read. Thus, the reader of Program 7.8 can easily determine upon examination of the `main()` routine that the program is simply calculating and displaying the square root of three numbers. She need not sift through all of the details of how the square root is actually calculated to glean this information. If she wants to get more involved in the details, she can study the specific code associated with the `squareRoot()` function. Inside that function, the same discussion applies to the `absoluteValue()` function. She does not need to know how the absolute value of a number is calculated to understand the operation of the `squareRoot()` function. Such details are relegated to the `absoluteValue()` function itself, which can be studied if a more detailed knowledge of its operation is desired.

Functions and Arrays

As with ordinary variables and values, it is also possible to pass the value of an array element and even an entire array as an argument to a function. To pass a single array element to a function (which is what you did in Chapter 6 when you used the `printf()` function to display the elements of an array), the array element is specified as an argument to the function in the normal fashion. So, to take the square root of `averages[i]` and assign the result to a variable called `sq_root_result`, a statement such as

```
sq_root_result = squareRoot (averages[i]);
```

does the trick.

Inside the `squareRoot()` function itself, nothing special has to be done to handle single array elements passed as arguments. In the same manner as with a simple variable, the value of the array element is copied into the value of the corresponding formal parameter when the function is called.

Passing an entire array to a function is an entirely new ball game. To pass an array to a function, it is only necessary to list the name of the array, *without any subscripts*, inside the call to the function. As an example, if you assume that gradeScores has been declared as an array containing 100 elements, the expression

```
minimum (gradeScores)
```

in effect passes the entire 100 elements contained in the array gradeScores to the function called minimum(). Naturally, on the other side of the coin, the minimum() function must be expecting an entire array to be passed as an argument and must make the appropriate formal parameter declaration. So the minimum() function might look something like this:

```
int  minimum (int  values[100])
{
    ...
    return minValue;
}
```

The declaration defines the function minimum() as returning a value of type int and as taking as its argument an array containing 100 integer elements. References made to the formal parameter array values reference the appropriate elements inside the array that was passed to the function. Based upon the function call previously shown and the corresponding function declaration, a reference made to values[4], for example, would actually reference the value of gradeScores[4].

For your first program that illustrates a function that takes an array as an argument, you can write a function minimum to find the minimum value in an array of 10 integers. This function, together with a main() routine to set up the initial values in the array, is shown in Program 7.9.

Program 7.9   **Finding the Minimum Value in an Array**

```
// Function to find the minimum value in an array

#include <stdio.h>

int  minimum (int  values[10])
{
    int  minValue, i;

    minValue = values[0];

    for ( i = 1;  i < 10;  ++i )
        if ( values[i] < minValue )
            minValue = values[i];

    return minValue;
}
```

```
int main (void)          .
{
    int   scores[10], i, minScore;
    int   minimum (int   values[10]);

    printf ("Enter 10 scores\n");

    for ( i = 0;  i < 10;  ++i )
        scanf ("%i", &scores[i]);

    minScore = minimum (scores);
    printf ("\nMinimum score is %i\n", minScore);

    return 0;
}
```

Program 7.9 **Output**

```
Enter 10 scores
69
97
65
87
69
86
78
67
92
90

Minimum score is 65
```

The first thing that catches your eye inside main() is the prototype declaration for the minimum() function. This tells the compiler that minimum() returns an int and takes an array of 10 integers. Remember, it's not necessary to make this declaration here because the minimum() function is defined before it's called from inside main(). However, play it safe throughout the rest of this text and declare all functions that are used.

After the array scores is defined, the user is prompted to enter 10 values. The scanf() call places each number as it is keyed in into scores[i], where i ranges from 0 through 9. After all the values have been entered, the minimum() function is called with the array scores as an argument.

The formal parameter name values is used to reference the elements of the array inside the function. It is declared to be an array of 10 integer values. The local variable minValue is used to store the minimum value in the array and is initially set to values[0], the first value in the array. The for loop sequences through the remaining elements of the array, comparing each element in turn against the value of minValue. If the value of values[i] is less than minValue, a new minimum in the array has been found. In such a case, the value of minValue is reassigned to this new minimum value and the scan through the array continues.

When the for loop has completed execution, minValue is returned to the calling routine, where it is assigned to the variable minScore and is then displayed.

With your general-purpose minimum() function in hand, you can use it to find the minimum of *any* array containing 10 integers. If you had five different arrays containing 10 integers each, you could simply call the minimum() function five separate times to find the minimum value of each array. In addition, you can just as easily define other functions to perform tasks, such as finding the maximum value, the median value, the mean (average) value, and so on.

By defining small, independent functions that perform well-defined tasks, you can build upon these functions to accomplish more sophisticated tasks and also make use of them for other related programming applications. For example, you could define a function statistics(), which takes an array as an argument and perhaps, in turn, calls a mean() function, a standardDeviation() function, and so on, to accumulate statistics about an array. This type of program methodology is the key to the development of programs that are easy to write, understand, modify, and maintain.

Of course, your general-purpose minimum() function is not so general purpose in the sense that it only works on an array of precisely 10 elements. But this problem is relatively easy to rectify. You can extend the versatility of this function by having it take the number of elements in the array as an argument. In the function declaration, you can then omit the specification of the number of elements contained in the formal parameter array. The C compiler actually ignores this part of the declaration anyway; all the compiler is concerned with is the fact that an array is expected as an argument to the function and not how many elements are in it.

Program 7.10 is a revised version of Program 7.9 in which the minimum() function finds the minimum value in an integer array of arbitrary length.

Program 7.10   **Revising the Function to Find the Minimum Value in an Array**

```
// Function to find the minimum value in an array

#include <stdio.h>

int  minimum (int  values[], int  numberOfElements)
{
    int  minValue, i;

    minValue = values[0];

    for ( i = 1;  i < numberOfElements;  ++i )
        if ( values[i] < minValue )
            minValue = values[i];
```

```
        return minValue;
}

int main (void)
{
    int   array1[5] = { 157, -28, -37, 26, 10 };
    int   array2[7] = { 12, 45, 1, 10, 5, 3, 22 };
    int   minimum (int  values[], int  numberOfElements);

    printf ("array1 minimum: %i\n", minimum (array1, 5));
    printf ("array2 minimum: %i\n", minimum (array2, 7));

    return 0;
}
```

Program 7.10 **Output**

```
array1 minimum: -37
array2 minimum: 1
```

This time, the function `minimum()` is defined to take two arguments: first, the array whose minimum you want to find and second, the number of elements in the array. The open and close brackets that immediately follow `values` in the function header serve to inform the C compiler that `values` is an array of integers. As stated previously, the compiler really doesn't need to know how large it is.

The formal parameter `numberOfElements` replaces the constant `10` as the upper limit inside the `for` statement. So the `for` statement sequences through the array from `values[1]` through the last element of the array, which is `values[numberOfElements - 1]`.

In the `main()` routine, two arrays called `array1` and `array2` are defined to contain five and seven elements, respectively.

Inside the first `printf()` call, a call is made to the `minimum()` function with the arguments `array1` and `5`. This second argument specifies the number of elements contained in `array1`. The `minimum()` function finds the minimum value in the array and the returned result of –37 is then displayed. The second time the `minimum()` function is called, `array2` is passed, together with the number of elements in that array. The result of 1 as returned by the function is then passed to the `printf()` function to be displayed.

Assignment Operators

Study Program 7.11 and try to guess the output *before* looking at the actual program results.

Program 7.11   **Changing Array Elements in Functions**

```c
#include <stdio.h>

void multiplyBy2 (float  array[], int  n)
{
    int  i;

    for ( i = 0;  i < n;  ++i )
        array[i] *= 2;
}

int main (void)
{

    float   floatVals[4] = { 1.2f, -3.7f, 6.2f, 8.55f };
    int     i;
    void    multiplyBy2 (float  array[], int  n);

    multiplyBy2 (floatVals, 4);

    for ( i = 0;  i < 4;  ++i )
        printf ("%.2f   ", floatVals[i]);

    printf ("\n");

    return 0;
}
```

Program 7.11   **Output**

```
2.40    -7.40   12.40    17.10
```

When you were examining Program 7.11, your attention surely must have been drawn to the following statement:

```c
array[i] *= 2;
```

The effect of the "times equals" operator (*=) is to multiply the expression on the left side of the operator by the expression on the right side of the operator and *to store the result back into the variable on the left side of the operator*. So, the previous expression is equivalent to the following statement:

```c
array[i] = array[i] * 2;
```

Getting back to the main point to be made about the preceding program, you might have realized by now that the function multiplyBy2() actually *changes* values inside the floatVals array. Isn't this a contradiction to what you learned before about a function not being able to change the value of its arguments? Not really.

This program example points out one major distinction that must always be kept in mind when dealing with array arguments: if a function changes the value of an array element, that change is made to the original array that was passed to the function. This change remains in effect even after the function has completed execution and has returned to the calling routine.

The reason an array behaves differently from a simple variable or an array element—whose value *cannot* be changed by a function—is worthy of explanation. As mentioned previously, when a function is called, the values that are passed as arguments to the function are copied into the corresponding formal parameters. This statement is still valid. However, when dealing with arrays, the entire contents of the array are *not* copied into the formal parameter array. Instead, the function gets passed information describing *where* in the computer's memory the array is located. Any changes made to the formal parameter array by the function are actually made to the original array passed to the function, and not to a copy of the array. Therefore, when the function returns, these changes still remain in effect.

Remember, the discussion about changing array values in a function applies only to entire arrays that are passed as arguments, and not to individual elements, whose values are copied into the corresponding formal parameters and, therefore, cannot be permanently changed by the function. Chapter 10 discusses this concept in greater detail.

Sorting Arrays

To further illustrate the idea that a function can change values in an array passed as an argument, you will develop a function to sort (rank) an array of integers. The process of sorting has always received much attention by computer scientists, probably because sorting is an operation that is so commonly performed. Many sophisticated algorithms have been developed to sort a set of information in the least amount of time, using as little of the computer's memory as possible. Because the purpose of this book is not to teach such sophisticated algorithms, you develop a sort() function that uses a fairly straightforward algorithm to sort an array into *ascending order*. Sorting an array into ascending order means rearranging the values in the array so that the elements progressively increase in value from the smallest to the largest. By the end of such a sort, the minimum value is contained in the first location of the array, whereas the maximum value is found in the last location of the array, with values that progressively increase in between.

If you want to sort an array of *n* elements into ascending order, you can do so by performing a successive comparison of each of the elements of the array. You can begin by comparing the first element in the array against the second. If the first element is greater in value than the second, you simply "swap" the two values in the array; that is, exchange the values contained in these two locations.

Next, compare the first element in the array (which you now know is less than the second) against the third element in the array. Once again, if the first value is greater than the third, you exchange these two values. Otherwise, you leave them alone. Now, you have the smallest of the first three elements contained in the first location of the array.

If you repeat the previous process for the remaining elements in the array—comparing the first element against each successive element and exchanging their values if the former is larger than the latter—the smallest value of the entire array is contained in the first location of the array by the end of the process.

If you now did the same thing with the second element of the array, that is, compare it against the third element, then against the fourth, and so on; and if you exchange any values that are out of order, you end up with the next smallest value contained in the second location of the array when the process is complete.

It should now be clear how you can go about sorting the array by performing these successive comparisons and exchanges as needed. The process stops after you have compared the next-to-last element of the array against the last and have interchanged their values if required. At that point, the entire array has been sorted into ascending order.

The following algorithm gives a more concise description of the preceding sorting process. This algorithm assumes that you are sorting an array a of n elements.

Simple Exchange Sort Algorithm

> **Step 1.** Set i to 0.
>
> **Step 2.** Set j to $i + 1$.
>
> **Step 3.** If $a[i] > a[j]$, exchange their values.
>
> **Step 4.** Set j to $j + 1$. If $j < n$, go to step 3.
>
> **Step 5.** Set i to $i + 1$. If $i < n - 1$, go to step 2.
>
> **Step 6.** a is now sorted in ascending order.

Program 7.12 implements the preceding algorithm in a function called sort, which takes two arguments: the array to be sorted and the number of elements in the array.

Program 7.12   **Sorting an Array of Integers into Ascending Order**

```
// Program to sort an array of integers into ascending order

#include <stdio.h>

void  sort (int  a[], int  n)
{
    int  i, j, temp;

    for ( i = 0;  i < n - 1;  ++i )
        for ( j = i + 1;  j < n;  ++j )
            if ( a[i] > a[j] ) {
                temp = a[i];
                a[i] = a[j];
                a[j] = temp;
```

```
            }
    }

int main (void)
{
    int   i;
    int   array[16] = { 34, -5, 6, 0, 12, 100, 56, 22,
                        44, -3, -9, 12, 17, 22, 6, 11 };
    void sort (int  a[], int  n);

    printf ("The array before the sort:\n");

    for ( i = 0;  i < 16;  ++i )
        printf ("%i ", array[i]);

    sort (array, 16);

    printf ("\n\nThe array after the sort:\n");

    for ( i = 0;  i < 16;  ++i )
        printf ("%i ", array[i]);

    printf ("\n");

    return 0;
}
```

Program 7.12 **Output**

```
The array before the sort:
34 -5 6 0 12 100 56 22 44 -3 -9 12 17 22 6 11

The array after the sort:
-9 -5 -3 0 6 6 11 12 12 17 22 22 34 44 56 100
```

The sort() function implements the algorithm as a set of nested for loops. The outermost loop sequences through the array from the first element through the next-to-last element (a[n-2]). For each such element, a second for loop is entered, which starts from the element after the one currently selected by the outer loop and ranges through the last element of the array.

If the elements are out of order (that is, if a[i] is greater than a[j]), the elements are switched. The variable temp is used as a temporary storage place while the switch is being made.

When both for loops are finished, the array has been sorted into ascending order. Execution of the function is then complete.

In the main() routine, array is defined and initialized to 16 integer values. The program then displays the values of the array at the terminal and proceeds to call the sort() function, passing as arguments `array` and `16`, the number of elements in `array`. After the function returns, the program once again displays the values contained in `array`. As you can see from the output, the function successfully sorted the array into ascending order.

The `sort()` function shown in Program 7.12 is fairly simple. The price that must be paid for such a simplistic approach is one of execution time. If you have to sort an extremely large array of values (arrays containing thousands of elements, for example), the `sort()` routine as you have implemented it here could take a considerable amount of execution time. If this happened, you would have to resort to one of the more sophisticated algorithms. *The Art of Computer Programming, Volume 3, Sorting and Searching* (Donald E. Knuth, Addison-Wesley) is a classic reference source for such algorithms.[2]

Multidimensional Arrays

A multidimensional array element can be passed to a function just as any ordinary variable or single-dimensional array element can. So the statement

```
squareRoot (matrix[i][j]);
```

calls the `squareRoot()` function, passing the value contained in `matrix[i][j]` as the argument.

An entire multidimensional array can be passed to a function in the same way that a single-dimensional array can: You simply list the name of the array. For example, if the matrix `measured_values` is declared to be a two-dimensional array of integers, the C statement

```
scalarMultiply (measured_values, constant);
```

can be used to invoke a function that multiplies each element in the matrix by the value of `constant`. This implies, of course, that the function itself can change the values contained inside the `measured_values` array. The discussion of this topic for single-dimensional arrays also applies here: An assignment made to any element of the formal parameter array inside the function makes a permanent change to the array that was passed to the function.

When declaring a single-dimensional array as a formal parameter inside a function, you learned that the actual dimension of the array is not needed; simply use a pair of empty brackets to inform the C compiler that the parameter is, in fact, an array. This does not totally apply in the case of multidimensional arrays. For a two-dimensional array, the number of rows in the array can be omitted, but the declaration *must* contain the number of columns in the array. So the declarations

```
int   array_values[100][50]
```

and

```
int   array_values[][50]
```

---

2. There is also a function called `qsort ()` in the standard C library that can be used to sort an array containing any data type. However, before you use it, you need to understand pointers to functions, which are discussed in Chapter 10.

are both valid declarations for a formal parameter array called `array_values` containing 100 rows by 50 columns; but the declarations

```
int   array_values[100][]
```

and

```
int   array_values[][]
```

are not because the number of columns in the array *must* be specified.

In Program 7.13, you define a function `scalarMultiply()`, which multiplies a two-dimensional integer array by a scalar integer value. Assume for purposes of this example that the array is dimensioned 3 × 5. The `main()` routine calls the `scalarMultiply()` routine twice. After each call, the array is passed to the `displayMatrix()` routine to display the contents of the array. Pay careful attention to the nested `for` loops that are used in both `scalarMultiply()` and `displayMatrix()` to sequence through each element of the two-dimensional array.

Program 7.13   **Using Multidimensional Arrays and Functions**

```c
#include <stdio.h>

int main (void)
{
    void   scalarMultiply (int  matrix[3][5], int  scalar);
    void   displayMatrix (int  matrix[3][5]);
    int    sampleMatrix[3][5] =
            {
                {  7, 16, 55, 13, 12 },
                { 12, 10, 52,  0,  7 },
                { -2,  1,  2,  4,  9 }
            };

    printf ("Original matrix:\n");
    displayMatrix (sampleMatrix);

    scalarMultiply (sampleMatrix, 2);

    printf ("\nMultiplied by 2:\n");
    displayMatrix (sampleMatrix);

    scalarMultiply (sampleMatrix, -1);

    printf ("\nThen multiplied by -1:\n");
    displayMatrix (sampleMatrix);

    return 0;
```

```
}


// Function to multiply a 3 x 5 array by a scalar

void  scalarMultiply (int  matrix[3][5], int  scalar)
{
    int  row, column;

    for ( row = 0;  row < 3;  ++row )
        for ( column = 0;  column < 5;  ++column )
            matrix[row][column]  *=  scalar;
}



void  displayMatrix (int  matrix[3][5])
{
    int   row, column;

    for ( row = 0;  row < 3;  ++row) {
        for ( column = 0;  column < 5;  ++column )
            printf ("%5i", matrix[row][column]);

        printf ("\n");
    }
}
```

Program 7.13 **Output**

```
Original matrix:
    7   16   55   13   12
   12   10   52    0    7
   -2    1    2    4    9

Multiplied by 2:
   14   32  110   26   24
   24   20  104    0   14
   -4    2    4    8   18

Then multiplied by -1:
  -14  -32 -110  -26  -24
  -24  -20 -104    0  -14
    4   -2   -4   -8  -18
```

The main() routine defines the matrix sampleValues and then calls the displayMatrix()
function to display its initial values at the terminal. Inside the displayMatrix() routine,
notice the nested for statements. The first or outermost for statement sequences through each

row in the matrix, so the value of the variable row varies from 0 through 2. For each value of row, the innermost for statement is executed. This for statement sequences through each column of the particular row, so the value of the variable column ranges from 0 through 4.

The printf() statement displays the value contained in the specified row and column using the format characters %5i to ensure that the elements line up in the display. After the innermost for loop has finished execution—meaning that an entire row of the matrix has been displayed—a newline character is displayed so that the next row of the matrix is displayed on the next line.

The first call to the scalarMultiply() function specifies that the sampleMatrix array is to be multiplied by 2. Inside the function, a simple set of nested for loops is set up to sequence through each element in the array. The element contained in matrix[row][column] is multiplied by the value of scalar in accordance with the use of the assignment operator *=. After the function returns to the main() routine, the displayMatrix() function is once again called to display the contents of the sampleMatrix() array. The program's output verifies that each element in the array has, in fact, been multiplied by 2.

The scalarMultiply() function is called a second time to multiply the now modified elements of the sampleMatrix array by –1. The modified array is then displayed by a final call to the displayMatrix() function, and program execution is then complete.

Multidimensional Variable-Length Arrays and Functions

You can take advantage of the variable-length array feature in the C language and write functions that can take multidimensional arrays of varying sizes. For example, Program 7.13 can be rewritten so that the scalarMultiply() and displayMatrix() functions can accept matrices containing any number of rows and columns, which can be passed as arguments to the functions. See Program 7.14.

Program 7.14   **Multidimensional Variable-Length Arrays**

```
#include <stdio.h>

int main (void)
{

    void   scalarMultiply (int nRows, int nCols,
                          int  matrix[nRows][nCols], int  scalar);
    void   displayMatrix (int nRows, int nCols, int  matrix[nRows][nCols]);
    int    sampleMatrix[3][5] =
           {
               {  7, 16, 55, 13, 12 },
               { 12, 10, 52,  0,  7 },
               { -2,  1,  2,  4,  9 }
           };
```

```
    printf ("Original matrix:\n");
    displayMatrix (3, 5, sampleMatrix);

    scalarMultiply (3, 5, sampleMatrix, 2);
    printf ("\nMultiplied by 2:\n");
    displayMatrix (3, 5, sampleMatrix);

    scalarMultiply (3, 5, sampleMatrix, -1);
    printf ("\nThen multiplied by -1:\n");
    displayMatrix (3, 5, sampleMatrix);

    return 0;
}

// Function to multiply a matrix by a scalar

void  scalarMultiply (int nRows, int nCols,
                      int  matrix[nRows][nCols], int  scalar)
{
    int  row, column;

    for ( row = 0;  row < nRows;  ++row )
        for ( column = 0;  column < nCols;  ++column )
            matrix[row][column]  *=  scalar;
}


void  displayMatrix (int nRows, int nCols, int  matrix[nRows][nCols])
{
    int   row, column;

    for ( row = 0;  row < nRows;  ++row) {
        for ( column = 0;  column < nCols;  ++column )
            printf ("%5i", matrix[row][column]);

        printf ("\n");
    }
}
```

Program 7.14 **Output**

```
Original matrix:
    7   16   55   13   12
   12   10   52    0    7
   -2    1    2    4    9
```

```
Multiplied by 2:
    14   32  110   26   24
    24   20  104    0   14
    -4    2    4    8   18

Then multiplied by -1:
   -14  -32 -110  -26  -24
   -24  -20 -104    0  -14
     4   -2   -4   -8  -18
```

The function declaration for scalarMultiply() looks like this:

```
void  scalarMultiply (int nRows, int nCols, int matrix[nRows][nCols], int  scalar)
```

The rows and columns in the matrix, nRows, and nCols, must be listed as arguments *before* the matrix itself so that the compiler knows about these parameters before it encounters the declaration of matrix in the argument list. If you try it this way instead:

```
void  scalarMultiply (int matrix[nRows][nCols], int nRows, int nCols, int  scalar)
```

you get an error from the compiler because it doesn't know about nRows and nCols when it sees them listed in the declaration of matrix.

As you can see, the output shown in Program 7.14 matches that shown in Program 7.13. Now, you have two functions (scalarMultiply() and displayMatrix()) that you can use with matrices of any size. This is one of the advantages of using variable-length arrays.

Global Variables

It is now time to tie together many of the principles you have learned in this chapter, as well as learn some new ones. Take Program 6.7, which converted a positive integer to another base, and rewrite it in function form. To do this, you must conceptually divide the program into logical segments. If you glance back at that program, you see that this is readily accomplished simply by looking at the three comment statements inside main(). They suggest the three primary functions that the program is performing: getting the number and base from the user, converting the number to the desired base, and displaying the results.

You can define three functions to perform an analogous task. The first function you call is getNumberAndBase(). This function prompts the user to enter the number to be converted and the base, and reads these values. Here, you make a slight improvement over what was done in Program 6.7. If the user types in a value of base that is less than 2 or greater than 16, the program displays an appropriate message at the terminal and sets the value of the base to 10. In this manner, the program ends up redisplaying the original number to the user. (Another approach might be to let the user reenter a new value for the base, but this is left as an exercise.)

The second function you call is `convertNumber()`. This function takes the value as typed in by the user and converts it to the desired base, storing the digits resulting from the conversion process inside the `convertedNumber` array.

The third and final function you call is `displayConvertedNumber()`. This function takes the digits contained inside the `convertedNumber` array and displays them to the user in the correct order. For each digit to be displayed, a lookup is made inside the `baseDigits` array so that the correct character is displayed for the corresponding digit.

The three functions that you define communicate with each other by means of *global variables*. As noted previously, one of the fundamental properties of a local variable is that its value can be accessed only by the function in which the variable is defined. As you might expect, this restriction does not apply to global variables. That is, a global variable's value can be accessed by *any* function in the program.

The distinguishing quality of a global variable declaration versus a local variable declaration is that the former is made *outside* of any function. This indicates its global nature—it does not belong to any particular function. *Any* function in the program can then access the value of that variable and can change its value if desired.

In Program 7.15, four global variables are defined. Each of these variables is used by at least two functions in the program. Because the baseDigits array and the variable nextDigit are used exclusively by the function `displayConvertedNumber()`, they are not defined as global variables. Instead, these variables are locally defined within the function `displayConvertedNumber()`.

The global variables are defined first in the program. Because they are not defined within any particular function, these variables are global, which means that they can now be referenced by any function in the program.

Program 7.15   **Converting a Positive Integer to Another Base**

```
// Program to convert a positive integer to another base

#include <stdio.h>

int        convertedNumber[64];
long int   numberToConvert;
int        base;
int        digit = 0;

void  getNumberAndBase (void)
{
    printf ("Number to be converted? ");
    scanf ("%li", &numberToConvert);

    printf ("Base? ");
    scanf ("%i", &base);
```

```c
    if ( base < 2  ||  base > 16 ) {
        printf ("Bad base - must be between 2 and 16\n");
        base = 10;
    }
}

void  convertNumber (void)
{
    do {

        convertedNumber[digit] = numberToConvert % base;
        ++digit;
        numberToConvert /= base;
    }
    while ( numberToConvert != 0 );
}

void  displayConvertedNumber (void)
{
    const char  baseDigits[16] =
            { '0', '1', '2', '3', '4', '5', '6', '7',
              '8', '9', 'A', 'B', 'C', 'D', 'E', 'F' };
    int    nextDigit;

    printf ("Converted number = ");

    for (--digit;  digit >= 0; --digit ) {
        nextDigit = convertedNumber[digit];
        printf ("%c", baseDigits[nextDigit]);
    }

    printf ("\n");
}

int main (void)
{
    void  getNumberAndBase (void), convertNumber (void),
          displayConvertedNumber (void);

    getNumberAndBase ();
    convertNumber ();
    displayConvertedNumber ();

    return 0;
}
```

Program 7.15 **Output**

```
Number to be converted? 100
Base? 8
Converted number = 144
```

Program 7.15 **Output (Rerun)**

```
Number to be converted? 1983
Base? 0
Bad base - must be between 2 and 16
Converted number = 1983
```

Notice how the wise choice of function names makes the operation of Program 7.15 clear. Spelled out directly in the `main()` routine is the function of the program: to get a number and a base, convert the number, and then display the converted number. The much-improved readability of this program over the equivalent one from Chapter 6 is a direct result of the structuring of the program into separate functions that perform small, well-defined tasks. Note that you do not even need comment statements inside the `main()` routine to describe what the program is doing—the function names speak for themselves.

The primary use of global variables is in programs in which many functions must access the value of the same variable. Rather than having to pass the value of the variable to each individual function as an argument, the function can explicitly reference the variable instead. There is a drawback with this approach. Because the function explicitly references a particular global variable, the generality of the function is somewhat reduced. So, every time that function is to be used, you must ensure that the global variable exists, by its particular name.

For example, the `convertNumber()` function of Program 7.15 succeeds in converting only a number that is stored in the variable `numberToConvert` to a base as specified by the value of the variable `base`. Furthermore, the variable `digit` and the array `convertedNumber` must be defined. A far more flexible version of this function would allow the arguments to be passed to the function.

Although the use of global variables can reduce the number of arguments that need to be passed to a function, the price that must be paid is reduced function generality and, in some cases, reduced program readability. This issue of program readability stems from the fact that if you use global variables, the variables that are used by a particular function are not evident simply by examining the function's header. Also, a call to the particular function does not indicate to the reader what types of parameters the function needs as inputs or produces as outputs.

Some programmers adopt the convention of prefixing all global variable names with the letter "g". For example, their variable declarations for Program 7.15 might look like this:

```
int        gConvertedNumber[64];
long int   gNumberToConvert;
int        gBase;
int        gDigit = 0;
```

The reason for adopting such a convention is that it becomes easier to pick out a global variable from a local one when reading through a program. For example, the statement

```
nextMove = gCurrentMove + 1;
```

implies that `nextMove` is a local variable and `gCurrentMove` is a global one. This tells the reader of this line about the scope of these variables and where to look for their declarations.

One final thing about global variables. They do have default initial values: zero. So, in the global declaration

```
int  gData[100];
```

all 100 elements of the `gData` array are set to zero when the program begins execution.

So remember that although global variables have default initial values of zero, local variables have no default initial value and so must be explicitly initialized by the program.

Automatic and Static Variables

When you normally declare a local variable inside a function, as in the declaration of the variables `guess` and `epsilon` in your `squareRoot()` function

```
float   squareRoot (float  x)
{
    const float  epsilon = .00001;
    float  guess   = 1.0;
        . . .
}
```

you are declaring *automatic* local variables. Recall that the keyword `auto` can, in fact, precede the declaration of such variables, but is optional because it is the default case. An automatic variable is, in a sense, actually created each time the function is called. In the preceding example, the local variables `epsilon` and `guess` are created whenever the `squareRoot()` function is called. As soon as the `squareRoot()` function is finished, these local variables "disappear." This process happens automatically, hence the name automatic variables.

Automatic local variables can be given initial values, as is done with the values of `epsilon` and `guess`, previously. In fact, any valid C expression can be specified as the initial value for a simple automatic variable. The value of the expression is calculated and assigned to the automatic local variable *each* time the function is called. And because an automatic variable disappears after the function completes execution, the value of that variable disappears along with it. In other words, the value an automatic variable has when a function finishes execution is *guaranteed* not to exist the next time the function is called.

If you place the word `static` in front of a variable declaration, you are in an entirely new ballgame. The word `static` in C refers not to an electric charge, but rather to the notion of something that has no movement. This is the key to the concept of a static variable—it does *not* come and go as the function is called and returns. This implies that the value a static variable has upon leaving a function is the same value that variable will have the next time the function is called.

Static variables also differ with respect to their initialization. A static, local variable is initialized only *once* at the start of overall program execution—and not each time that the function is called. Furthermore, the initial value specified for a static variable *must* be a simple constant or constant expression. Static variables also have default initial values of zero, unlike automatic variables, which have no default initial value.

In the function `auto_static()`, which is defined as follows:

```
void auto_static (void)
{
    static int  staticVar = 100;


          .

          .

          .

}
```

the value of `staticVar` is initialized to 100 only once when program execution begins. To set its value to 100 each time the function is executed, an explicit assignment statement is needed, as in

```
void auto_static (void)
{
    static int  staticVar;

    staticVar = 100;

          .

          .

          .

}
```

Of course, reinitializing `staticVar` this way defeats the purpose of using a `static` variable in the first place.

Program 7.16 should help make the concepts of automatic and static variables a bit clearer.

Program 7.16 Illustrating Static and Automatic Variables

```
// Program to illustrate static and automatic variables

#include <stdio.h>

void  auto_static (void)
{
    int         autoVar = 1;
    static int  staticVar = 1;
```

```
    printf ("automatic = %i, static = %i\n", autoVar, staticVar);

    ++autoVar;
    ++staticVar;
}


int main (void)
{
    int    i;
    void   auto_static (void);

    for ( i = 0;  i < 5;  ++i )
         auto_static ();

    return 0;
}
```

Program 7.16 **Output**

```
automatic = 1, static = 1
automatic = 1, static = 2
automatic = 1, static = 3
automatic = 1, static = 4
automatic = 1, static = 5
```

Inside the auto_static() function, two local variables are declared. The first variable, called autoVar, is an automatic variable of type int with an initial value of 1. The second variable, called staticVar, is a static variable, also of type int and also with an initial value of 1. The function calls the printf() routine to display the values of these two variables. After this, the variables are each incremented by 1, and execution of the function is then complete.

The main() routine sets up a loop to call the auto_static() function five times. The output from Program 7.16 points out the difference between the two variable types. The value of the automatic variable is listed as 1 for each line of the display. This is because its value is set to 1 each time the function is called. On the other hand, the output shows the value of the static variable steadily increasing from 1 through 5. This is because its value is set equal to 1 only once—when program execution begins—and because its value is retained from one function call to the next.

The choice of whether to use a static variable or automatic variable depends upon the intended use of the variable. If you want the variable to retain its value from one function call to the next (for example, consider a function that counts the number of times that it is called), use a static variable. Also, if your function uses a variable whose value is set once and then never changes, you might want to declare the variable static, as it saves the inefficiency of having the variable reinitialized each time that the function is called. This efficiency consideration is even more important when dealing with arrays.

From the other direction, if the value of a local variable must be initialized at the beginning of each function call, an automatic variable seems the logical choice.

Recursive Functions

The C language supports a capability known as *recursive* function. Recursive functions can be effectively used to succinctly and efficiently solve problems. They are commonly used in applications in which the solution to a problem can be expressed in terms of successively applying the same solution to subsets of the problem. One example might be in the evaluation of expressions containing nested sets of parenthesized expressions. Other common applications involve the searching and sorting of data structures called *trees* and *lists*.

Recursive functions are most commonly illustrated by an example that calculates the factorial of a number. Recall that the factorial of a positive integer *n*, written *n!*, is simply the product of the successive integers 1 through *n*. The factorial of 0 is a special case and is defined equal to 1. So 5! is calculated as follows:

```
5!    =  5 x 4 x 3 x 2 x 1
      =  120
```

And 6! is calculated like so:

```
6!    =  6 x 5 x 4 x 3 x 2 x 1
      =  720
```

Comparing the calculation of 6! to the calculation of 5!, observe that the former is equal to 6 times the latter; that is, $6! = 6 \times 5!$. In the general case, the factorial of any positive integer *n* greater than zero is equal to *n* multiplied by the factorial of *n* - 1:

```
n! = n x (n - 1)!
```

The expression of the value of *n!* in terms of the value of *(n-1)!* is called a *recursive* definition because the definition of the value of a factorial is based on the value of another factorial. In fact, you can develop a function that calculates the factorial of an integer n according to this recursive definition. Such a function is illustrated in Program 7.17.

Program 7.17 **Calculating Factorials Recursively**

```c
#include <stdio.h>

int main (void)
{
    unsigned int  j;
    unsigned long int  factorial (unsigned int  n);

    for ( j = 0;  j < 11;  ++j )
        printf ("%2u! = %lu\n", j, factorial (j));
```

```
    return 0;
}

// Recursive function to calculate the factorial of a positive integer

unsigned long int  factorial (unsigned int  n)
{
    unsigned long int  result;

    if  ( n == 0 )
        result = 1;
    else
        result = n * factorial (n - 1);

    return result;
}
```

Program 7.17 **Output**

```
 0! = 1
 1! = 1
 2! = 2
 3! = 6
 4! = 24
 5! = 120
 6! = 720
 7! = 5040
 8! = 40320
 9! = 362880
10! = 3628800
```

The fact that the factorial() function includes a call to itself makes this function recursive. When the function is called to calculate the factorial of 3, the value of the formal parameter n is set to 3. Because this value is not zero, the following program statement

```
result = n * factorial (n - 1);
```

is executed, which, given the value of n, is evaluated as

```
result = 3 * factorial (2);
```

This expression specifies that the factorial() function is to be called, this time to calculate the factorial of 2. Therefore, the multiplication of 3 by this value is left pending while factorial (2) is calculated.

Even though you are again calling the same function, you should conceptualize this as a call to a separate function. Each time any function is called in C—be it recursive or not—the function gets its own set of local variables and formal parameters with which to work. Therefore, the local variable `result` and the formal parameter n that exist when the `factorial()` function is called to calculate the factorial of 3 are distinct from the variable `result` and the parameter n when the function is called to calculate the factorial of 2.

With the value of n equal to 2, the `factorial()` function executes the statement

```
result = n * factorial (n - 1);
```

which is evaluated as

```
result = 2 * factorial (1);
```

Once again, the multiplication of 2 by the factorial of 1 is left pending while the `factorial()` function is called to calculate the factorial of 1.

With the value of n equal to 1, the `factorial()` function once again executes the statement

```
result = n * factorial (n - 1);
```

which is evaluated as

```
result = 1 * factorial (0);
```

When the `factorial()` function is called to calculate the factorial of 0, the function sets the value of `result` to 1 and *return*, thus initiating the evaluation of all of the pending expressions. So the value of `factorial (0)`, or 1, is returned to the calling function (which happens to be the `factorial()` function), multiplied by 1, and assigned to `result`. This value of 1, which represents the value of `factorial (1)`, is then returned back to the calling function (once again the `factorial()` function) where it is multiplied by 2, stored into `result`, and returned as the value of `factorial (2)`. Finally, the returned value of 2 is multiplied by 3, thus completing the pending calculation of `factorial (3)`. The resulting value of 6 is returned as the final result of the call to the `factorial()` function, to be displayed by the `printf()` function.

In summary, the sequence of operations that is performed in the evaluation of `factorial (3)` can be conceptualized as follows:

```
factorial (3) = 3 * factorial (2)
              = 3 * 2 * factorial (1)
              = 3 * 2 * 1 * factorial (0)
              = 3 * 2 * 1 * 1
              = 6
```

It might be a good idea for you to trace through the operation of the `factorial()` function with a pencil and paper. Assume that the function is initially called to calculate the factorial of 4. List the values of n and `result` at each call to the `factorial()` function.

This discussion concludes this chapter on functions and variables. The program function is a powerful tool in the C programming language. Enough cannot be said about the critical importance of structuring a program in terms of small, well-defined functions. Functions are used heavily throughout the remainder of this book. At this point, you should review any topics covered in this chapter that still seem unclear. Working through the following exercises will also help reinforce the topics that have been discussed.

Exercises

1. Type in and run the 17 programs presented in this chapter. Compare the output produced by each program with the output presented after each program in the text.

2. Modify Program 7.4 so the value of `triangularNumber` is returned by the function. Then go back to Program 4.5 and change that program so that it calls the new version of the `calculateTriangularNumber()` function.

3. Modify Program 7.8 so that the value of `epsilon` is passed as an argument to the function. Try experimenting with different values of `epsilon` to see the effect that it has on the value of the square root.

4. Modify Program 7.8 so that the value of `guess` is printed each time through the `while` loop. Notice how quickly the value of `guess` converges to the square root. What conclusions can you reach about the number of iterations through the loop, the number whose square root is being calculated, and the value of the initial guess?

5. The criteria used for termination of the loop in the `squareRoot()` function of Program 7.8 is not suitable for use when computing the square root of very large or very small numbers. Rather than comparing the *difference* between the value of x and the value of `guess`^{2}, the program should compare the *ratio* of the two values to 1. The closer this ratio gets to 1, the more accurate the approximation of the square root.

   Modify Program 7.8 so this new termination criteria is used.

6. Modify Program 7.8 so that the `squareRoot()` function accepts a double precision argument and returns the result as a double precision value. Be certain to change the value of the variable `epsilon` to reflect the fact that double precision variables are now being used.

7. Write a function that raises an integer to a positive integer power. Call the function `x_to_the_n()` taking two integer arguments x and n. Have the function return a `long int`, which represents the results of calculating x^n.

8. An equation of the form

   ```
   ax² + bx + c = 0
   ```

   is known as a *quadratic* equation. The values of *a*, *b*, and *c* in the preceding example represent constant values. So

   ```
   4x² - 17x - 15 = 0
   ```

   represents a quadratic equation where $a = 4$, $b = -17$, and $c = -15$. The values of *x* that satisfy a particular quadratic equation, known as the *roots* of the equation, can be calculated by substituting the values of *a*, *b*, and *c* into the following two formulas:

   $$x = \frac{-b \pm \sqrt{b^2 - 4ac}}{2a}$$

If the value of b^2-4ac, called the *discriminant*, is less than zero, the roots of the equation, x_1 and x_2, are imaginary numbers.

Write a program to solve a quadratic equation. The program should allow the user to enter the values for *a*, *b*, and *c*. If the discriminant is less than zero, a message should be displayed that the roots are imaginary; otherwise, the program should then proceed to calculate and display the two roots of the equation. (*Note:* Be certain to make use of the squareRoot() function that you developed in this chapter.)

9. The least common multiple (*lcm*) of two positive integers *u* and *v* is the smallest positive integer that is evenly divisible by both *u* and *v*. Thus, the *lcm* of 15 and 10, written *lcm* (15, 10), is 30 because 30 is the smallest integer divisible by both 15 and 10. Write a function lcm() that takes two integer arguments and returns their *lcm*. The lcm() function should calculate the least common multiple by calling the gcd() function from Program 7.6 in accordance with the following identity:

    lcm (u, v) = uv / gcd (u, v)   u, v >= 0

10. Write a function prime() that returns 1 if its argument is a prime number and returns 0 otherwise.

11. Write a function called arraySum() that takes two arguments: an integer array and the number of elements in the array. Have the function return as its result the sum of the elements in the array.

12. A matrix *M* with *i* rows, *j* columns can be *transposed* into a matrix *N* having *j* rows and *i* columns by simply setting the value of $N_{a,b}$ equal to the value of $M_{b,a}$ for all relevant values of *a* and *b*.

    a. Write a function transposeMatrix() that takes as an argument a 4 × 5 matrix and a 5 × 4 matrix. Have the function transpose the 4 × 5 matrix and store the results in the 5 × 4 matrix. Also write a main() routine to test the function.

    b. Using variable-length arrays, rewrite the transposeMatrix() function developed in exercise 12a to take the number of rows and columns as arguments, and to transpose the matrix of the specified dimensions.

13. Modify the sort() function from Program 7.12 to take a third argument indicating whether the array is to be sorted in ascending or descending order. Then modify the sort() algorithm to correctly sort the array into the indicated order.

14. Rewrite the functions developed in the last four exercises to use global variables instead of arguments. For example, the preceding exercise should now sort a globally defined array.

15. Modify Program 7.14 so that the user is asked again to type in the value of the base if an invalid base is entered. The modified program should continue to ask for the value of the base until a valid response is given.

16. Modify Program 7.14 so that the user can convert any number of integers. Make provision for the program to terminate when a zero is typed in as the value of the number to be converted.

8

Working with Structures

Chapter 6, "Working with Arrays," introduced the array that permits you to group elements of the same type into a single logical entity. To reference an element in the array, all that is necessary is that the name of the array be given together with the appropriate subscript.

The C language provides another tool for grouping elements together. This falls under the name of *structures* and forms the basis for the discussions in this chapter. As you will see, the structure is a powerful concept that you will use in many C programs that you develop.

This chapter will introduce several key aspects of structures, including

- Defining structures

- Passing structures to functions

- Arrays of structures

- Structures of arrays

The Basics of Structures

Suppose you want to store a date—for example 9/25/15—inside a program, perhaps to be used for the heading of some program output, or even for computational purposes. A natural method for storing the date is to simply assign the month to an integer variable called month, the day to an integer variable called day, and the year to an integer variable called year. So the statements

```
int  month = 9, day = 25, year = 2015;
```

work just fine. This is a totally acceptable approach. But suppose your program also needs to store the date of purchase of a particular item, for example. You can go about the same procedure of defining three more variables such as purchaseMonth, purchaseDay, and purchaseYear. Whenever you need to use the purchase date, these three variables could then be explicitly accessed.

Using this method, you must keep track of three separate variables for each date that you use in the program—variables that are logically related. It would be much better if you could somehow group these sets of three variables together. This is precisely what the structure in C allows you to do.

A Structure for Storing the Date

You can define a structure called `date` in the C language that consists of three components that represent the month, day, and year. The syntax for such a definition is rather straightforward, as follows:

```
struct  date
{
    int  month;
    int  day;
    int  year;
};
```

The `date` structure just defined contains three integer *members* called `month`, `day`, and `year`. The definition of `date` in a sense defines a new type in the language in that variables can subsequently be declared to be of type `struct date`, as in the declaration

```
struct date  today;
```

You can also declare a variable `purchaseDate` to be of the same type by a separate declaration, such as

```
struct date  purchaseDate;
```

Or, you can simply include the two declarations on the same line, as in

```
struct date  today, purchaseDate;
```

Unlike variables of type `int`, `float`, or `char`, a special syntax is needed when dealing with structure variables. A member of a structure is accessed by specifying the variable name, followed by a period, and then the member name. For example, to set the value of the `day` in the variable `today` to `25`, you write

```
today.day = 25;
```

Note that there are no spaces permitted between the variable name, the period, and the member name. To set the `year` in `today` to `2015`, the expression

```
today.year = 2015;
```

can be used. Finally, to test the value of `month` to see if it is equal to `12`, a statement such as

```
if  ( today.month == 12 )
    nextMonth = 1;
```

does the trick.

Try to determine the effect of the following statement.

```
if  ( today.month == 1  &&  today.day == 1 )
  printf ("Happy New Year!!!\n");
```

Program 8.1 incorporates the preceding discussions into an actual C program.

Program 8.1   **Illustrating a Structure**

```
// Program to illustrate a structure

#include <stdio.h>

int main (void)
{
    struct   date
    {
        int   month;
        int   day;
        int   year;
    };

    struct date   today;

    today.month = 9;
    today.day = 25;
    today.year = 2015;

    printf ("Today's date is %i/%i/%.2i.\n", today.month, today.day,
            today.year % 100);

    return 0;
}
```

Program 8.1   **Output**

```
Today's date is 9/25/15.
```

The first statement inside main() defines the structure called date to consist of three integer members called month, day, and year. In the second statement, the variable today is declared to be of type struct date. The first statement simply defines what a date structure looks like to the C compiler and causes no storage to be reserved inside the computer. The second statement declares a variable to be of type struct date and, therefore, *does* cause memory to be reserved for storing the three integer values of the variable today. Be certain you understand the difference between defining a structure and declaring variables of the particular structure type.

After today has been declared, the program then proceeds to assign values to each of the three members of today, as depicted in Figure 8.1.

```
today.month = 9;
today.day = 25;
today.year = 2015;
```

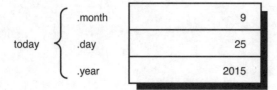

Figure 8.1   Assigning values to a structure variable.

After the assignments have been made, the values contained inside the structure are displayed by an appropriate printf() call. The remainder of today.year divided by 100 is calculated prior to being passed to the printf() function so that just 15 is displayed for the year. Recall that the format characters %.2i are used to specify that two integer digits are to be displayed with zero fill. This ensures that you would see the proper display for the last two digits of the year if you had a year ending between 01 and 09.

Using Structures in Expressions

When it comes to the evaluation of expressions, structure members follow the same rules as ordinary variables do in the C language. So division of an integer structure member by another integer is performed as an integer division, as in

```
century = today.year / 100 + 1;
```

Suppose you want to write a simple program that accepts today's date as input and displays tomorrow's date to the user. Now, at first glance, this seems a perfectly simple task to perform. You can ask the user to enter today's date and then proceed to calculate tomorrow's date by a series of statements, such as

```
tomorrow.month = today.month;
tomorrow.day   = today.day + 1;
tomorrow.year  = today.year;
```

Of course, the preceding statements work just fine for the majority of dates, but the following two cases are not properly handled:

1. If today's date falls at the end of a month.

2. If today's date falls at the end of a year (that is, if today's date is December 31).

One way to determine easily if today's date falls at the end of a month is to set up an array of integers that corresponds to the number of days in each month. A lookup inside the array for a particular month then gives the number of days in that month. So the statement

```
int  daysPerMonth[12] = { 31, 28, 31, 30, 31, 30, 31, 31, 30, 31, 30, 31 };
```

defines an array called daysPerMonth containing 12 integer elements. For each month i, the value contained in daysPerMonth[i - 1] corresponds to the number of days in that particular month. Therefore, the number of days in April, which is the fourth month of the year, is given by daysPerMonth[3], which is equal to 30. (You could define the array to contain 13 elements, with daysPerMonth[i] corresponding to the number of days in month i. Access into the array could then be made directly based on the month number, rather than on the month number minus 1. The decision of whether to use 12 or 13 elements in this case is strictly a matter of personal preference.)

If it is determined that today's date falls at the end of the month, you can calculate tomorrow's date by simply adding 1 to the month number and setting the value of the day equal to 1.

To solve the second problem mentioned earlier, you must determine if today's date is at the end of a month and if the month is 12. If this is the case, then tomorrow's day and month must be set equal to 1 and the year appropriately incremented by 1.

Program 8.2 asks the user to enter today's date, calculates tomorrow's date, and displays the results.

Program 8.2   **Determining Tomorrow's Date**

```
// Program to determine tomorrow's date

#include <stdio.h>

int main (void)
{
    struct  date
    {
        int  month;
        int  day;
        int  year;
    };

    struct date  today, tomorrow;

    const int  daysPerMonth[12] = { 31, 28, 31, 30, 31, 30,
                                    31, 31, 30, 31, 30, 31 };

    printf ("Enter today's date (mm dd yyyy): ");
    scanf ("%i%i%i", &today.month, &today.day, &today.year);
```

```
    if ( today.day != daysPerMonth[today.month - 1] ) {
        tomorrow.day = today.day + 1;
        tomorrow.month = today.month;
        tomorrow.year = today.year;
    }
    else if ( today.month == 12 ) {     // end of year
        tomorrow.day = 1;
        tomorrow.month = 1;
        tomorrow.year = today.year + 1;
    }
    else {                              // end of month
        tomorrow.day = 1;
        tomorrow.month = today.month + 1;
        tomorrow.year = today.year;
    }

    printf ("Tomorrow's date is %i/%i/%.2i.\n", tomorrow.month,
        tomorrow.day, tomorrow.year % 100);

    return 0;
}
```

Program 8.2 **Output**

```
Enter today's date (mm dd yyyy): 12 17 2013
Tomorrow's date is 12/18/13.
```

Program 8.2 **Output (Rerun)**

```
Enter today's date (mm dd yyyy): 12 31 2014
Tomorrow's date is 1/1/15.
```

Program 8.2 **Output (Second Rerun)**

```
Enter today's date (mm dd yyyy): 2 28 2012
Tomorrow's date is 3/1/12.
```

If you look at the program's output, you quickly notice that there seems to be a mistake somewhere: The day after February 28, 2012 is listed as March 1, 2012 and *not* as February 29, 2012. The program forgot about leap years! You fix this problem in the following section. First, you need to analyze the program and its logic.

After the date structure is defined, two variables of type struct date, today and tomorrow, are declared. The program then asks the user to enter today's date. The three integer values that are entered are stored into today.month, today.day, and today.year, respectively. Next, a test is made to determine if the day is at the end of the month, by comparing today.day to daysPerMonth[today.month - 1]. If it is not the end of the month, tomorrow's date is calculated by simply adding 1 to the day and setting tomorrow's month and year equal to today's month and year.

If today's date does fall at the end of the month, another test is made to determine if it is the end of the year. If the month equals 12, meaning that today's date is December 31, tomorrow's date is set equal to January 1 of the next year. If the month does not equal 12, tomorrow's date is set to the first day of the following month (of the same year).

After tomorrow's date has been calculated, the values are displayed to the user with an appropriate printf() statement call, and program execution is complete.

Functions and Structures

Now, you can return to the problem that was discovered in the previous program. Your program thinks that February always has 28 days, so naturally when you ask it for the day after February 28, it always displays March 1 as the answer. You need to make a special test for the case of a leap year. If the year is a leap year, and the month is February, the number of days in that month is 29. Otherwise, the normal lookup inside the daysPerMonth array can be made.

A good way to incorporate the required changes into Program 8.2 is to develop a function called numberOfDays() to determine the number of days in a month. The function would perform the leap year test and the lookup inside the daysPerMonth array as required. Inside the main() routine, all that has to be changed is the if statement, which compares the value of today.day to daysPerMonth[today.month - 1]. Instead, you could now compare the value of today.day to the value returned by your numberOfDays() function.

Study Program 8.3 carefully to determine what is being passed to the numberOfDays() function as an argument.

Program 8.3   **Revising the Program to Determine Tomorrow's Date**

```
// Program to determine tomorrow's date

#include <stdio.h>
#include <stdbool.h>

struct   date
{
    int   month;
    int   day;
    int   year;
};

int main (void)
{
    struct date   today, tomorrow;
```

```
    int  numberOfDays (struct date d);

    printf ("Enter today's date (mm dd yyyy): ");
    scanf ("%i%i%i", &today.month, &today.day, &today.year);

    if  ( today.day != numberOfDays (today) ) {
        tomorrow.day = today.day + 1;
        tomorrow.month = today.month;
        tomorrow.year = today.year;
    }
    else if ( today.month == 12 ) {     // end of year
        tomorrow.day = 1;
        tomorrow.month = 1;
        tomorrow.year = today.year + 1;
    }
    else {                              // end of month
        tomorrow.day = 1;
        tomorrow.month = today.month + 1;
        tomorrow.year = today.year;
    }

    printf ("Tomorrow's date is %i/%i/%.2i.\n",tomorrow.month,
                tomorrow.day, tomorrow.year % 100);

    return 0;
}

// Function to find the number of days in a month

int  numberOfDays  (struct date  d)
{
    int    days;
    bool   isLeapYear (struct date  d);
    const int    daysPerMonth[12] =
        { 31, 28, 31, 30, 31, 30, 31, 31, 30, 31, 30, 31 };

    if ( isLeapYear (d) == true &&  d.month == 2 )
        days = 29;
    else
        days = daysPerMonth[d.month - 1];

    return days;
}

// Function to determine if it's a leap year

bool  isLeapYear (struct date  d)
```

```
{
    bool  leapYearFlag;

    if ( (d.year % 4 == 0  && d.year % 100 != 0)  ||
                d.year % 400 == 0 )
        leapYearFlag = true;    // It's a leap year
    else
        leapYearFlag = false;   // Not a leap year

    return leapYearFlag;
}
```

Program 8.3   **Output**

```
Enter today's date (mm dd yyyy): 2 28 2016
Tomorrow's date is 2/29/16.
```

Program 8.3   **Output (Rerun)**

```
Enter today's date (mm dd yyyy): 2 28 2014
Tomorrow's date is 3/1/14.
```

The first thing that catches your eye in the preceding program is the fact that the definition of the date structure appears first and outside of any function. This makes the definition known throughout the file. Structure definitions behave very much like variables—if a structure is defined within a particular function, only that function knows of its existence. This is a *local* structure definition. If you define the structure outside of any function, that definition is *global*. A global structure definition allows any variables that are subsequently defined in the program (either inside or outside of a function) to be declared to be of that structure type.

Inside the main() routine, the prototype declaration

```
int  numberOfDays (struct date d);
```

informs the C compiler that the numberOfDays() function returns an integer value and takes a single argument of type struct date.

Instead of comparing the value of today.day against the value daysPerMonth[today.month - 1], as was done in the preceding example, the statement

```
if  ( today.day != numberOfDays (today) )
```

is used. As you can see from the function call, you are specifying that the structure today is to be passed as an argument. Inside the numberOfDays() function, the appropriate declaration must be made to inform the system that a structure is expected as an argument:

```
int  numberOfDays  (struct date  d)
```

As with ordinary variables, and unlike arrays, any changes made by the function to the values contained in a structure argument have no effect on the original structure. They affect only the copy of the structure that is created when the function is called.

The `numberOfDays()` function begins by determining if it is a leap year and if the month is February. The former determination is made by calling another function called `isLeapYear()`. You learn about this function shortly. From reading the `if` statement

```
if ( isLeapYear (d) == true   && d.month == 2 )
```

you can assume that the `isLeapYear()` function returns `true` if it is a leap year and returns `false` if it is not a leap year. This is directly in line with our discussions of Boolean variables in Chapter 5, "Making Decisions." Recall that the standard header file `<stdbool.h>` defines the values `bool`, `true`, and `false` for you, which is why this file is included at the beginning of Program 8.3.

An interesting point to be made about the previous `if` statement concerns the choice of the function name `isLeapYear()`. This name makes the `if` statement extremely readable and implies that the function is returning some kind of yes/no answer.

Getting back to the program, if the determination is made that it is February of a leap year, the value of the variable `days` is set to 29; otherwise, the value of `days` is found by indexing the `daysPerMonth` array with the appropriate month. The value of `days` is then returned to the `main()` routine, where execution is continued as in Program 8.2.

The `isLeapYear()` function is straightforward enough—it simply tests the year contained in the `date` structure given as its argument and returns `true` if it is a leap year and `false` if it is not.

As an exercise in producing a better-structured program, take the entire process of determining tomorrow's date and relegate it to a separate function. You can call the new function `dateUpdate()` and have it take as its argument today's date. The function then calculates tomorrow's date and *returns* the new date back to us. Program 8.4 illustrates how this can be done in C.

Program 8.4   **Revising the Program to Determine Tomorrow's Date, Version 2**

```c
// Program to determine tomorrow's date

#include <stdio.h>
#include <stdbool.h>

struct  date
{
    int  month;
    int  day;
    int  year;
};

// Function to calculate tomorrow's date
```

```
struct date  dateUpdate (struct date  today)
{
    struct date  tomorrow;
    int  numberOfDays (struct date  d);

    if ( today.day != numberOfDays (today) ) {
        tomorrow.day = today.day + 1;
        tomorrow.month = today.month;
        tomorrow.year = today.year;
    }
    else if ( today.month == 12 )  {   // end of year
        tomorrow.day = 1;
        tomorrow.month = 1;
        tomorrow.year = today.year + 1;
    }
    else {                          // end of month
        tomorrow.day = 1;
        tomorrow.month = today.month + 1;
        tomorrow.year = today.year;
    }

    return tomorrow;
}

// Function to find the number of days in a month

int  numberOfDays  (struct date  d)
{
    int  days;
    bool isLeapYear (struct date  d);
    const int  daysPerMonth[12] =
      { 31, 28, 31, 30, 31, 30, 31, 31, 30, 31, 30, 31 };

    if ( isLeapYear (d)  &&  d.month == 2 )
        days = 29;
    else
        days = daysPerMonth[d.month - 1];

    return days;
}

// Function to determine if it's a leap year

bool  isLeapYear (struct date  d)
{
    bool  leapYearFlag;
```

```
        if ( (d.year % 4 == 0  &&  d.year % 100 != 0)  ||
                    d.year % 400 == 0 )
            leapYearFlag = true;    // It's a leap year
        else
            leapYearFlag = false;   // Not a leap year

        return leapYearFlag;
}

int main (void)
{
    struct date  dateUpdate (struct date  today);
    struct date  thisDay, nextDay;

    printf ("Enter today's date (mm dd yyyy): ");
    scanf ("%i%i%i", &thisDay.month, &thisDay.day,
                &thisDay.year);

    nextDay = dateUpdate (thisDay);

    printf ("Tomorrow's date is %i/%i/%.2i.\n",nextDay.month,
                nextDay.day, nextDay.year % 100);

    return 0;
}
```

Program 8.4 **Output**

```
Enter today's date (mm dd yyyy): 2 28 2016
Tomorrow's date is 2/29/16.
```

Program 8.4 **Output (Rerun)**

```
Enter today's date (mm dd yyyy): 2 22 2015
Tomorrow's date is 2/23/15.
```

Inside main(), the statement

```
next_date = dateUpdate (thisDay);
```

illustrates the ability to pass a structure to a function and to return one as well. The dateUp-
date() function has the appropriate declaration to indicate that the function returns a value
of type struct date. Inside the function is the same code that was included in the main()
routine of Program 8.3. The functions numberOfDays() and isLeapYear() remain unchanged
from that program.

Make certain that you understand the hierarchy of function calls in the preceding program: The `main()` function calls `dateUpdate()`, which in turn calls `numberOfDays()`, which itself calls the function `isLeapYear()`.

A Structure for Storing the Time

Suppose you have the need to store values inside a program that represents various times expressed as hours, minutes, and seconds. Because you have seen how useful our `date` structure has been in helping you to logically group the day, month, and year, it seems only natural to use a structure that you could call appropriately enough, `time`, to group the hours, minutes, and seconds. The structure definition is straightforward enough, as follows:

```
struct time
{
    int    hour;
    int    minutes;
    int    seconds;
};
```

Most computer installations choose to express the time in terms of a 24-hour clock, known as military time. This representation avoids the hassle of having to qualify a time with a.m. or p.m. The hour begins with 0 at 12 midnight and increases by 1 until it reaches 23, which represents 11:00 p.m. So, for example, 4:30 means 4:30 a.m., whereas 16:30 represents 4:30 p.m.; and 12:00 represents noon, whereas 00:01 represents 1 minute after midnight.

Virtually all computers have a clock inside in the system that is always running. This clock is used for such diversified purposes as informing the user of the current time, causing certain events to occur or programs to be executed at specific times, or recording the time that a particular event occurs. One or more computer programs are usually associated with the clock. One of these programs might be executed every second, for example, to update the current time that is stored somewhere in the computer's memory.

Suppose you want to mimic the function of the program described previously—namely, to develop a program that updates the time by one second. If you think about this for a second (pun intentional), you realize that this problem is quite analogous to the problem of updating the date by one day.

Just as finding the next day had some special requirements, so does the process of updating the time. In particular, these special cases must be handled:

1. If the number of seconds reaches 60, the seconds must be reset to 0 and the minutes increased by 1.

2. If the number of minutes reaches 60, the minutes must be reset to 0 and the hour increased by 1.

3. If the number of hours reaches 24, the hours, minutes, and seconds must be reset to 0.

Program 8.5 uses a function called timeUpdate(), which takes as its argument the current time and returns a time that is one second later.

Program 8.5   **Updating the Time by One Second**

```c
// Program to update the time by one second

#include <stdio.h>

struct time
{
    int   hour;
    int   minutes;
    int   seconds;
};

int main (void)
{
    struct time  timeUpdate (struct time  now);
    struct time  currentTime, nextTime;

    printf ("Enter the time (hh:mm:ss): ");
    scanf ("%i:%i:%i", &currentTime.hour,
            &currentTime.minutes, &currentTime.seconds);

    nextTime = timeUpdate (currentTime);

    printf ("Updated time is %.2i:%.2i:%.2i\n", nextTime.hour,
             nextTime.minutes, nextTime.seconds );

    return 0;
}

// Function to update the time by one second

struct time  timeUpdate (struct time  now)
{
    ++now.seconds;

    if ( now.seconds == 60 ) {      // next minute
       now.seconds = 0;
       ++now.minutes;

       if ( now.minutes == 60 ) {  // next hour
           now.minutes = 0;
           ++now.hour;
```

```
            if ( now.hour == 24 ) // midnight
                now.hour = 0;
        }
    }

    return now;
}
```

Program 8.5 **Output**

```
Enter the time (hh:mm:ss): 12:23:55
Updated time is 12:23:56
```

Program 8.5 **Output (Rerun)**

```
Enter the time (hh:mm:ss): 16:12:59
Updated time is 16:13:00
```

Program 8.5 **Output (Second Rerun)**

```
Enter the time (hh:mm:ss): 23:59:59
Updated time is 00:00:00
```

The main() routine asks the user to enter in the time. The scanf() call uses the format string
"%i:%i:%i"

to read the data. Specifying a nonformat character, such as ' : ', in a format string signals to the
scanf() function that the particular character is expected as input. Therefore, the format string
listed in Program 8.5 specifies that three integer values are to be input—the first separated from
the second by a colon, and the second separated from the third by a colon. In Chapter 15,
"Input and Output Operations in C," you learn how the scanf() function returns a value that
can be tested to determine if the values were entered in the correct format.

After the time has been entered, the program calls the timeUpdate() function, passing along
the currentTime() as the argument. The result returned by the function is assigned to the
struct time variable nextTime, which is then displayed with an appropriate printf() call.

The timeUpdate() function begins execution by "bumping" the time in now by one second.
A test is then made to determine if the number of seconds has reached 60. If it has, the
seconds are reset to 0 and the minutes are increased by 1. Another test is then made to see if
the number of minutes has now reached 60, and if it has, the minutes are reset to 0 and the
hour is increased by 1. Finally, if the two preceding conditions are satisfied, a test is then made
to see if the hour is equal to 24; that is, if it is precisely midnight. If it is, the hour is reset to
0. The function then returns the value of now, which contains the updated time, back to the
calling routine.

Initializing Structures

Initializing structures is similar to initializing arrays—the elements are simply listed inside a pair of braces, with each element separated by a comma.

To initialize the `date` structure variable `today` to July 2, 2015, the statement

```
struct date   today = { 7, 2, 2015 };
```

can be used. The statement

```
struct time  this_time = { 3, 29, 55 };
```

defines the `struct time` variable `this_time` and sets its value to 3:29:55 a.m. As with other variables, if `this_time` is a local structure variable, it is initialized each time the function is entered. If the structure variable is made static (by placing the keyword `static` in front of it), it is only initialized once at the start of program execution. In either case, the initial values listed inside the curly braces must be constant expressions.

As with the initialization of an array, fewer values might be listed than are contained in the structure. So the statement

```
struct time  time1 = { 12, 10 };
```

sets `time1.hour` to 12 and `time1.minutes` to 10 but gives no initial value to `time1.seconds`. In such a case, its default initial value is undefined.

You can also specify the member names in the initialization list. In that case, the general format is

```
.member = value
```

This method enables you to initialize the members in any order, or to only initialize specified members. For example,

```
struct time time1 = { .hour = 12, .minutes = 10 };
```

sets the `time1` variable to the same initial values as shown in the previous example. The statement

```
struct date today = { .year = 2015 };
```

sets just the `year` member of the `date` structure variable `today` to 2015.

Compound Literals

You can assign one or more values to a structure in a single statement using what is known as *compound literals*. For example, assuming that `today` has been previously declared as a `struct date` variable, the assignment of the members of `today` as shown in Program 8.1 can also be done in a single statement as follows:

```
today = (struct date) { 9, 25, 2015 };
```

Note that this statement can appear anywhere in the program; it is not a declaration statement. The type cast operator is used to tell the compiler the type of the expression, which in this case is struct date, and is followed by the list of values that are to be assigned to the members of the structure, in order. These values are listed in the same way as if you were initializing a structure variable.

You can also specify values using the .*member* notation like this:

```
today = (struct date) { .month = 9, .day = 25, .year = 2015 };
```

The advantage of using this approach is that the arguments can appear in any order. Without explicitly specifying the member names, they must be supplied in the order in which they are defined in the structure.

The following example shows the dateUpdate() function from Program 8.4 rewritten to take advantage of compound literals:

```
// Function to calculate tomorrow's date - using compound literals

struct date  dateUpdate (struct date  today)
{
    struct date  tomorrow;
    int  numberOfDays (struct date  d);

    if ( today.day != numberOfDays (today) )
        tomorrow = (struct date) { today.month, today.day + 1, today.year };
    else if ( today.month == 12 )        // end of year
        tomorrow = (struct date) { 1, 1, today.year + 1 };
    else                                 // end of month
        tomorrow = (struct date) { today.month + 1, 1, today.year };


    return tomorrow;
}
```

Whether you decide to use compound literals in your programs is up to you. In this case, the use of compound literals makes the dateUpdate() function easier to read.

Compound literals can be used in other places where a valid structure expression is allowed. This is a perfectly valid, albeit totally impractical example of such a use:

```
nextDay =  dateUpdate ((struct date) { 5, 11, 2004} );
```

The dateUpdate() function expects an argument of type struct date, which is precisely the type of compound literal that is supplied as the argument to the function.

Arrays of Structures

You have seen how useful the structure is in enabling you to logically group related elements together. With the time structure, for instance, it is only necessary to keep track of one variable, instead of three, for each time that is used by the program. So, to handle 10 different times in a program, you only have to keep track of 10 different variables, instead of 30.

An even better method for handling the 10 different times involves the combination of two powerful features of the C programming language: structures and arrays. C does not limit you to storing simple data types inside an array; it is perfectly valid to define an *array of structures*. For example,

```
struct time  experiments[10];
```

defines an array called experiments, which consists of 10 elements. Each element inside the array is defined to be of type struct time. Similarly, the definition

```
struct date  birthdays[15];
```

defines the array birthdays to contain 15 elements of type struct date. Referencing a particular structure element inside the array is quite natural. To set the second birthday inside the birthdays array to August 8, 1986, the sequence of statements

```
birthdays[1].month = 8;
birthdays[1].day   = 8;
birthdays[1].year  = 1986;
```

works just fine. To pass the entire time structure contained in experiments[4] to a function called checkTime(), the array element is specified:

```
checkTime (experiments[4]);
```

As is to be expected, the checkTime function declaration must specify that an argument of type struct time is expected:

```
void checkTime (struct time  t0)
{
    .
    .
    .
}
```

Initialization of arrays containing structures is similar to initialization of multidimensional arrays. So the statement

```
struct time  runTime [5] =
    {  {12, 0, 0},  {12, 30, 0},  {13, 15, 0} };
```

sets the first three times in the array runTime to 12:00:00, 12:30:00, and 13:15:00. The inner pairs of braces are optional, meaning that the preceding statement can be equivalently expressed as

```
struct time  runTime[5] =
    { 12, 0, 0, 12, 30, 0, 13, 15, 0 };
```

The following statement

```
struct time runTime[5] =
    { [2] = {12, 0, 0} };
```

initializes just the third element of the array to the specified value, whereas the statement

```
static struct time runTime[5] = { [1].hour = 12, [1].minutes = 30 };
```

sets just the hours and minutes of the second element of the runTime array to 12 and 30, respectively.

Program 8.6 sets up an array of time structures called testTimes. The program then calls your timeUpdate function from Program 8.5.

In Program 8.6, an array called testTimes is defined to contain five different times. The elements in this array are assigned initial values that represent the times 11:59:59, 12:00:00, 1:29:59, 23:59:59, and 19:12:27, respectively. Figure 8.2 can help you to understand what the testTimes array actually looks like inside the computer's memory. A particular time structure stored in the testTimes array is accessed by using the appropriate index number 0–4. A particular member (hour, minutes, or seconds) is then accessed by appending a period followed by the member name.

For each element in the testTimes array, Program 8.6 displays the time as represented by that element, calls the timeUpdate() function from Program 8.5, and then displays the updated time.

Program 8.6   Illustrating Arrays of Structures

```
//  Program to illustrate arrays of structures

#include <stdio.h>

struct  time
{
    int  hour;
    int  minutes;
    int  seconds;
};

int main (void)
{
    struct time  timeUpdate (struct time  now);
    struct time  testTimes[5] =
        { { 11, 59, 59 }, { 12, 0, 0 }, { 1, 29, 59 },
          { 23, 59, 59 }, { 19, 12, 27 }};
```

```
    int  i;

    for ( i = 0;  i < 5;  ++i ) {
        printf ("Time is %.2i:%.2i:%.2i", testTimes[i].hour,
            testTimes[i].minutes, testTimes[i].seconds);

        testTimes[i] = timeUpdate (testTimes[i]);

        printf (" ...one second later it's %.2i:%.2i:%.2i\n",
            testTimes[i].hour, testTimes[i].minutes, testTimes[i].seconds);
    }

    return 0;
}

struct time  timeUpdate (struct time  now)
{
    ++now.seconds;

    if ( now.seconds == 60 ) {       // next minute
        now.seconds = 0;
        ++now.minutes;

        if ( now.minutes == 60 ) { // next hour
            now.minutes = 0;
            ++now.hour;

            if ( now.hour == 24 ) // midnight
                now.hour = 0;
        }
    }

    return now;
}
```

Program 8.6   Output

```
Time is 11:59:59 ...one second later it's 12:00:00
Time is 12:00:00 ...one second later it's 12:00:01
Time is 01:29:59 ...one second later it's 01:30:00
Time is 23:59:59 ...one second later it's 00:00:00
Time is 19:12:27 ...one second later it's 19:12:28
```

The concept of an array of structures is a very powerful and important one in C. Make certain you understand it fully before you move on.

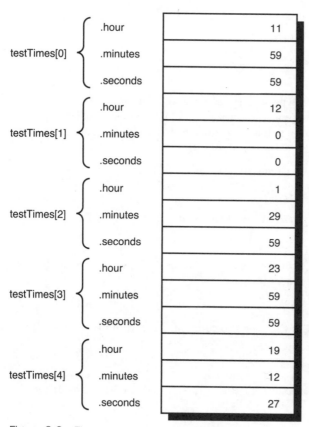

Figure 8.2   The array `testTimes` in memory.

Structures Containing Structures

C provides you with an enormous amount of flexibility in defining structures. For instance, you can define a structure that itself contains other structures as one or more of its members, or you can define structures that contain arrays.

You have seen how it is possible to logically group the month, day, and year into a structure called `date` and how to group the hour, minutes, and seconds into a structure called `time`. In some applications, you might have the need to logically group both a date and a time together. For example, you might need to set up a list of events that are to occur at a particular date and time.

What the preceding discussion implies is that you want to have a convenient means for associating *both* the date and the time together. You can do this in C by defining a new structure, called, for example, `dateAndTime`, which contains as its members two elements: the date and the time.

```
struct dateAndTime
{
    struct date    sdate;
    struct time    stime;
};
```

The first member of this structure is of type struct date and is called sdate. The second member of the dateAndTime structure is of type struct time and is called stime. This definition of a dateAndTime structure requires that a date structure and a time structure have been previously defined to the compiler.

Variables can now be defined to be of type struct dateAndTime, as in

```
struct dateAndTime  event;
```

To reference the date structure of the variable event, the syntax is the same:

```
event.sdate
```

So, you could call your dateUpdate() function with this date as the argument and assign the result back to the same place by a statement such as

```
event.sdate = dateUpdate (event.sdate);
```

You can do the same type of thing with the time structure contained within your dateAnd-Time structure:

```
event.stime = timeUpdate (event.stime);
```

To reference a particular member *inside* one of these structures, a period followed by the member name is tacked on the end:

```
event.sdate.month = 10;
```

This statement sets the month of the date structure contained within event to October, and the statement

```
++event.stime.seconds;
```

adds one to the seconds contained within the time structure.

The event variable can be initialized in the expected manner:

```
struct dateAndTime  event =
        { { 2, 1, 2015 }, { 3, 30, 0 } };
```

This sets the date in the variable event to February 1, 2015, and sets the time to 3:30:00.

Of course, you can use members' names in the initialization, as in

```
struct dateAndTime event =
        { { .month = 2, .day = 1, .year = 2015 },
          { .hour = 3, .minutes = 30, .seconds = 0 }
        };
```

Naturally, it is possible to set up an array of `dateAndTime` structures, as is done with the following declaration:

```
struct dateAndTime  events[100];
```

The array `events` is declared to contain 100 elements of type `struct dateAndTime`. The fourth `dateAndTime` contained within the array is referenced in the usual way as `events[3]`, and the *i*th date in the array can be sent to your `dateUpdate()` function as follows:

```
events[i].sdate = dateUpdate (events[i].sdate);
```

To set the first time in the array to noon, the series of statements

```
events[0].stime.hour    = 12;
events[0].stime.minutes = 0;
events[0].stime.seconds = 0;
```

can be used.

Structures Containing Arrays

As the heading of this section implies, it is possible to define structures that contain arrays as members. One of the most common applications of this type is setting up an array of characters inside a structure. For example, suppose you want to define a structure called `month` that contains as its members the number of days in the month as well as a three-character abbreviation for the month name. The following definition does the job:

```
struct  month
{
    int     numberOfDays;
    char    name[3];
};
```

This sets up a `month` structure that contains an integer member called `numberOfDays` and a character member called `name`. The member `name` is actually an array of three characters. You can now define a variable to be of type `struct  month` in the normal fashion:

```
struct month  aMonth;
```

You can set the proper fields inside `aMonth` for January with the following sequence of statements:

```
aMonth.numberOfDays = 31;
aMonth.name[0] = 'J';
aMonth.name[1] = 'a';
aMonth.name[2] = 'n';
```

Or, you can initialize this variable to the same values with the following statement:

```
struct month  aMonth = { 31, { 'J', 'a', 'n' } };
```

To go one step further, you can set up 12-month structures inside an array to represent each month of the year:

```
struct month  months[12];
```

Program 8.7 illustrates the `months` array. Its purpose is simply to set up the initial values inside the array and then display these values at the terminal.

It might be easier for you to conceptualize the notation that is used to reference particular elements of the `months` array as defined in the program by examining Figure 8.3.

Program 8.7   Illustrating Structures and Arrays

```c
// Program to illustrate structures and arrays

#include <stdio.h>

int main (void)
{
    int  i;

    struct  month
    {
        int    numberOfDays;
        char   name[3];
    };

    const struct month  months[12] =
        { { 31, {'J', 'a', 'n'} },  { 28, {'F', 'e', 'b'} },
          { 31, {'M', 'a', 'r'} },  { 30, {'A', 'p', 'r'} },
          { 31, {'M', 'a', 'y'} },  { 30, {'J', 'u', 'n'} },
          { 31, {'J', 'u', 'l'} },  { 31, {'A', 'u', 'g'} },
          { 30, {'S', 'e', 'p'} },  { 31, {'O', 'c', 't'} },
          { 30, {'N', 'o', 'v'} },  { 31, {'D', 'e', 'c'} } };

    printf ("Month    Number of Days\n");
    printf ("-----    --------------\n");

    for ( i = 0;  i < 12;  ++i )
        printf (" %c%c%c           %i\n",
              months[i].name[0], months[i].name[1],
              months[i].name[2], months[i].numberOfDays);

    return 0;
}
```

Program 8.7   **Output**

Month	Number of Days
-----	---------------
Jan	31
Feb	28
Mar	31
Apr	30
May	31
Jun	30
Jul	31
Aug	31
Sep	30
Oct	31
Nov	30
Dec	31

As you can see in Figure 8.3, the notation

```
months[0]
```

refers to the *entire* month structure contained in the first location of the months array. The type of this expression is struct month. Therefore, when passing months[0] to a function as an argument, the corresponding formal parameter inside the function must be declared to be of type struct month.

Going one step further, the expression

```
months[0].numberOfDays
```

refers to the numberOfDays member of the month structure contained in months[0]. The type of this expression is int. The expression

```
months[0].name
```

references the three-character array called name inside the month structure of months[0]. If passing this expression as an argument to a function, the corresponding formal parameter is declared to be an array of type char.

Finally, the expression

```
months[0].name[0]
```

references the first character of the name array contained in months[0] (the character 'J').

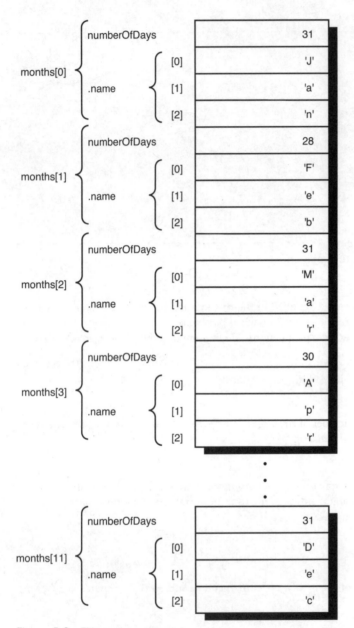

Figure 8.3   The array months.

Structure Variants

You do have some flexibility in defining a structure. First, it is valid to declare a variable to be of a particular structure type at the same time that the structure is defined. This is done simply by including the variable name (or names) before the terminating semicolon of the structure definition. For example, the statement

```
struct  date
{
    int  month;
    int  day;
    int  year;
} todaysDate, purchaseDate;
```

defines the structure `date` *and* also declares the variables `todaysDate` and `purchaseDate` to be of this type. You can also assign initial values to the variables in the normal fashion. Thus,

```
struct  date
{
    int  month;
    int  day;
    int  year;
} todaysDate = { 1, 11, 2005 };
```

defines the structure `date` and the variable `todaysDate` with initial values as indicated.

If all of the variables of a particular structure type are defined when the structure is defined, the structure name can be omitted. So the statement

```
struct
{
    int  month;
    int  day;
    int  year;
}  dates[100];
```

defines an array called `dates` to consist of 100 elements. Each element is a structure containing three integer members: `month`, `day`, and `year`. Because you did not supply a name to the structure, the only way to subsequently declare variables of the same type is by explicitly defining the structure again.

You have seen how structures can be used to conveniently reference groups of data under a single label. You've also seen in this chapter how easily you can define arrays of structures and work with them with functions. In the next chapter, you learn how to work with arrays of characters, also known as character strings. Before going on, try the following exercises.

Exercises

1. Type in and run the seven programs presented in this chapter. Compare the output produced by each program with the output presented after each program in the text.

2. In certain applications, particularly in the financial area, it is often necessary to calculate the number of elapsed days between two dates. For example, the number of days between July 2, 2015, and July 16, 2015, is obviously 14. But how many days are there between August 8, 2014, and February 22, 2015? This calculation requires a bit more thought.

   Luckily, a formula can be used to calculate the number of days between two dates. This is affected by computing the value of N for each of the two dates and then taking the difference, where N is calculated as follows:

   ```
   N = 1461 x f(year, month) / 4 + 153 x g(month) / 5  + day
   ```

   where:

   ```
   f(year, month)    =    year - 1        if  month <= 2
                          year            otherwise
   ```

   ```
   g(month)   =      month + 13      if month <= 2
                     month + 1       otherwise
   ```

   As an example of applying the formula, to calculate the number of days between August 8, 2004, and February 22, 2005, you can calculate the values of N^1 and N^2 by substituting the appropriate values into the preceding formula as shown:

   ```
   N¹    = 1461 x f(2004, 8) / 4   +   153 x g(8) / 5   +   3
         = (1461 x 2004) / 4   +   (153 x 9) / 5   +   3
         = 2,927,844 / 4   +   1,377 / 5   +   3
         = 731,961 + 275 + 3
         = 732,239


   N²    = 1461 x f(2005, 2) / 4   +   153 x g(2) / 5   +   21
         = (1461 x 2004) / 4   +   (153 x 15) / 5   +   21
         = 2,927,844 / 4   +   2295 / 5   +   21
         = 731,961 + 459 + 21
         = 732,441
   ```

   Number of elapsed days   = N^2 - N^1

                                = 732,441 – 732,239

                                = 202

   So the number of days between the two dates is shown to be 202. The preceding formula is applicable for any dates after March 1, 1900 (1 must be added to N for dates from

March 1, 1800, to February 28, 1900, and 2 must be added for dates between March 1, 1700, and February 28, 1800).

Write a program that permits the user to type in two dates and then calculates the number of elapsed days between the two dates. Try to structure the program logically into separate functions. For example, you should have a function that accepts as an argument a date structure and returns the value of N computed as shown previously. This function can then be called twice, once for each date, and the difference taken to determine the number of elapsed days.

3. Write a function elapsed_time that takes as its arguments two time structures and returns a time structure that represents the elapsed time (in hours, minutes, and seconds) between the two times. So the call

   elapsed_time (time1, time2)

   where time1 represents 3:45:15 and time2 represents 9:44:03, should return a time structure that represents 5 hours, 58 minutes, and 48 seconds. Be careful with times that cross midnight.

4. If you take the value of N as computed in exercise 2, subtract 621,049 from it, and then take that result modulo 7, you get a number from 0 to 6 that represents the day of the week (Sunday through Saturday, respectively) on which the particular day falls. For example, the value of N computed for August 8, 2004, is 732,239 as derived previously. 732,239 − 621,049 gives 111,190, and 111,190 % 7 gives 2, indicating that this date falls on a Tuesday.

   Use the functions developed in the previous exercise to develop a program that displays the day of the week on which a particular date falls. Make certain that the program displays the day of the week in English (such as "Monday").

5. Write a function called clockKeeper() that takes as its argument a dateAndTime structure as defined in this chapter. The function should call the timeUpdate() function, and if the time reaches midnight, the function should call the dateUpdate function to switch over to the next day. Have the function return the updated dateAndTime structure.

6. Replace the dateUpdate() function from Program 8.4 with the modified one that uses compound literals as presented in the text. Run the program to verify its proper operation.

9

Character Strings

Now, you are ready to take a look at character strings in more detail. Data manipulation is the single-most important function your programs will perform. Numbers, in their various data formats, only cover half the story. You also need to deal with words, characters, and alphanumeric combinations of the two. Although the C language does not have a string data type like many other languages, you've already seen that a combination of the `char` data type and arrays can cover what you need. In addition, there are both library functions as well as routines you can write to manipulate string data. This chapter covers the basics, including

- Understanding character arrays
- Employing variable-length character arrays
- Using escape characters
- Adding character arrays to structures
- Performing data operations on strings

Revisiting the Basics of Strings

You were first introduced to character strings in Chapter 2, "Compiling and Running Your First Program," when you wrote your first C program. In the statement

```
printf ("Programming in C is fun.\n");
```

the argument that is passed to the `printf()` function is the character string

```
"Programming in C is fun.\n"
```

The double quotation marks are used to delimit the character string, which can contain any combinations of letters, numbers, or special characters, other than a double quotation mark. But as you shall see shortly, it is even possible to include a double quotation mark inside a character string.

When introduced to the data type char, you learned that a variable that is declared to be of this type can contain only a *single* character. To assign a single character to such a variable, the character is enclosed within a pair of single quotation marks. Thus, the assignment

```
plusSign = '+';
```

has the effect of assigning the character '+' to the variable plusSign, assuming it has been appropriately declared. In addition, you learned that there *is* a distinction made between the single quotation and double quotation marks, and that if plusSign is declared to be of type char, then the statement

```
plusSign = "+";
```

is incorrect. Be certain you remember that single quotation and double quotation marks are used to create two different types of constants in C.

Arrays of Characters

If you want to be able to deal with variables that can hold more than a single character[1], this is precisely where the array of characters comes into play.

In Program 6.6, you defined an array of characters called word as follows:

```
char  word [] = { 'H', 'e', 'l', 'l', 'o', '!' };
```

Remembering that in the absence of a particular array size, the C compiler automatically computes the number of elements in the array based upon the number of initializers, this statement reserves space in memory for exactly six characters, as shown in Figure 9.1.

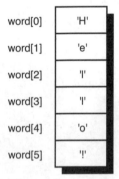

Figure 9.1   The array word in memory.

---

1. *Recall that the type* wchar_t *can be used for representing so-called wide characters, but that's for handling a single character from an international character set. The discussion here is about storing sequences of multiple characters.*

To print out the contents of the array word, you ran through each element in the array and displayed it using the %c format characters.

With this technique, you can begin to build an assortment of useful functions for dealing with character strings. Some of the more commonly performed operations on character strings include combining two character strings together (concatenation), copying one character string to another, extracting a portion of a character string (substring), and determining if two character strings are equal (that is, if they contain the same characters). Take the first mentioned operation, concatenation, and develop a function to perform this task. You can define a call to your concat() function as follows:

```
concat (result, str1, n1, str2, n2);
```

where str1 and str2 represent the two character arrays that are to be concatenated and n1 and n2 represent the number of characters in the respective arrays. This makes the function flexible enough so that you can concatenate two character arrays of arbitrary length. The argument result represents the character array that is to be the destination of the concatenated character arrays str1 followed by str2. See Program 9.1.

Program 9.1 Concatenating Character Arrays

```
// Function to concatenate two character arrays

#include <stdio.h>

void  concat (char   result[], const char   str1[], int   n1,
                     const char   str2[], int   n2)
{
    int  i, j;

    // copy str1 to result

    for ( i = 0;  i < n1;  ++i )
        result[i] = str1[i];

    // copy str2 to result

    for ( j = 0;  j < n2;  ++j )
        result[n1 + j] = str2[j];
}

int main (void)
{
    void    concat (char   result[], const char   str1[], int   n1,
                       const char   str2[], int   n2);
    const   char   s1[5] = { 'T', 'e', 's', 't', ' ' };
    const   char   s2[6] = { 'w', 'o', 'r', 'k', 's', '.' };
```

```
char    s3[11];
int     i;

concat (s3, s1, 5, s2, 6);

for ( i = 0;  i < 11;  ++i )
    printf ("%c", s3[i]);

printf ("\n");

return 0;
}
```

Program 9.1   **Output**

Test works.

The first `for` loop inside the `concat()` function copies the characters from the `str1` array into the `result` array. This loop is executed `n1` times, which is the number of characters contained inside the `str1` array.

The second `for` loop copies `str2` into the `result` array. Because `str1` was `n1` characters long, copying into `result` begins at `result[n1]`—the position immediately following the one occupied by the last character of `str1`. After this `for` loop is done, the `result` array contains the `n1+n2` characters representing `str2` concatenated to the end of `str1`.

Inside the `main()` routine, two `const character` arrays, `s1` and `s2`, are defined. The first array is initialized to the characters `'T'`, `'e'`, `'s'`, `'t'`, and `' '`. This last character represents a blank space and is a perfectly valid character constant. The second array is initially set to the characters `'w'`, `'o'`, `'r'`, `'k'`, `'s'`, and `'.'`. A third character array, `s3`, is defined with enough space to hold `s1` concatenated to `s2`, or 11 characters. It is not declared as a `const` array because its contents will be changed.

The function call

```
concat (s3, s1, 5, s2, 6);
```

calls the `concat()` function to concatenate the character arrays `s1` and `s2`, with the destination array `s3`. The arguments 5 and 6 are passed to the function to indicate the number of characters in `s1` and `s2`, respectively.

After the `concat()` function has completed execution and returns to `main()`, a `for` loop is set up to display the results of the function call. The 11 elements of `s3` are displayed, and as you can see from the program's output, the `concat()` function seems to be working properly. In the preceding program example, it is assumed that the first argument to the `concat()` function—the result array—contains enough space to hold the resulting concatenated character arrays. Failure to do so can produce unpredictable results when the program is run.

Variable-Length Character Strings

You can adopt a similar approach to that used by the concat() function for defining other functions to deal with character arrays. That is, you can develop a set of routines, each of which has as its arguments one or more character arrays plus the number of characters contained in each such array. Unfortunately, after working with these functions for a while, you will find that it gets a bit tedious trying to keep track of the number of characters contained in each character array that you are using in your program—especially if you are using your arrays to store character strings of varying sizes. What you need is a method for dealing with character arrays without having to worry about precisely how many characters you have stored in them.

There is such a method, and it is based upon the idea of placing a special character at the end of every character string. In this manner, the function can then determine for itself when it has reached the end of a character string after it encounters this special character. By developing all of your functions to deal with character strings in this fashion, you can eliminate the need to specify the number of characters that are contained inside a character string.

In the C language, the special character that is used to signal the end of a string is known as the *null* character and is written as '\0'. So, the statement

```
const char  word [] = { 'H', 'e', 'l', 'l', 'o', '!', '\0' };
```

defines a character array called word that contains *seven* characters, the last of which is the null character. (Recall that the backslash character [\] is a special character in the C language and does not count as a separate character; therefore, '\0' represents a single character in C.) The array word is depicted in Figure 9.2.

word[0]	'H'
word[1]	'e'
word[2]	'l'
word[3]	'l'
word[4]	'o'
word[5]	'!'
word[6]	'\0'

Figure 9.2   The array word with a terminating null character.

To begin with an illustration of how these *variable-length* character strings are used, write a function that counts the number of characters in a character string, as shown in Program 9.2. Call the function stringLength() and have it take as its argument a character array that is

terminated by the null character. The function determines the number of characters in the
array and returns this value back to the calling routine. Define the number of characters in the
array as the number of characters up to, but not including, the terminating null character. So,
the function call

```
stringLength (characterString)
```

should return the value 3 if characterString is defined as follows:

```
char  characterString[] = { 'c', 'a', 't', '\0' };
```

Program 9.2   **Counting the Characters in a String**

```
// Function to count the number of characters in a string

#include <stdio.h>

int  stringLength (const char  string[])
{
    int  count = 0;

    while ( string[count] != '\0' )
        ++count;

    return count;
}

int main (void)
{
    int    stringLength (const char  string[]);
    const char  word1[] = { 'a', 's', 't', 'e', 'r', '\0' };
    const char  word2[] = { 'a', 't', '\0' };
    const char  word3[] = { 'a', 'w', 'e', '\0' };

    printf ("%i   %i   %i\n", stringLength (word1),
            stringLength (word2), stringLength (word3));

    return 0;
}
```

Program 9.2   **Output**

```
5    2    3
```

The stringLength() function declares its argument as a const array of characters because it is
not making any changes to the array, merely counting its size.

Inside the `stringLength()` function, the variable `count` is defined and its value set to `0`. The program then enters a `while` loop to sequence through the `string` array until the null character is reached. When the function finally hits upon this character, signaling the end of the character string, the `while` loop is exited and the value of `count` is returned. This value represents the number of characters in the string, excluding the null character. You might want to trace through the operation of this loop on a small character array to verify that the value of `count` when the loop is exited is in fact equal to the number of characters in the array, excluding the null character.

In the `main()` routine, three character arrays, `word1`, `word2`, and `word3`, are defined. The `printf()` function call displays the results of calling the `stringLength()` function for each of these three character arrays.

Initializing and Displaying Character Strings

Now, it is time to go back to the `concat()` function developed in Program 9.1 and rewrite it to work with variable-length character strings. Obviously, the function must be changed somewhat because you no longer want to pass as arguments the number of characters in the two arrays. The function now takes only three arguments: the two character arrays to be concatenated and the character array in which to place the result.

Before delving into this program, you should first learn about two nice features that C provides for dealing with character strings.

The first feature involves the initialization of character arrays. C permits a character array to be initialized by simply specifying a constant character string rather than a list of individual characters. So, for example, the statement

```
char  word[] = { "Hello!" };
```

can be used to set up an array of characters called `word` with the initial characters 'H', 'e', 'l', 'l', 'o', '!', and '\0', respectively. You can also omit the braces when initializing character arrays in this manner. So, the statement

```
char word[] =  "Hello!";
```

is perfectly valid. Either statement is equivalent to the statement

```
char  word[] = { 'H', 'e', 'l', 'l', 'o', '!', '\0' };
```

If you're explicitly specifying the size of the array, make certain you leave enough space for the terminating null character. So, in

```
char  word[7] = { "Hello!" };
```

the compiler has enough room in the array to place the terminating null character. However, in

```
char  word[6] = { "Hello!" };
```

the compiler can't fit a terminating null character at the end of the array, and so it doesn't put one there (and it doesn't complain about it either).

In general, wherever they appear in your program, character-string constants in the C language are automatically terminated by the null character. This fact helps functions such as `printf()` determine when the end of a character string has been reached. So, in the call

```
printf ("Programming in C is fun.\n");
```

the null character is automatically placed after the newline character in the character string, thereby enabling the `printf()` function to determine when it has reached the end of the format string.

The other feature to be mentioned here involves the display of character strings. The special format characters `%s` inside a `printf()` format string can be used to display an array of characters that is terminated by the null character. So, if `word` is a null-terminated array of characters, the `printf()` call

```
printf ("%s\n", word);
```

can be used to display the entire contents of the `word` array at the terminal. The `printf()` function assumes when it encounters the `%s` format characters that the corresponding argument is a character string that is terminated by a null character.

The two features just described were incorporated into the `main()` routine of Program 9.3, which illustrates your revised `concat()` function. Because you are no longer passing the number of characters in each string as arguments to the function, the function must determine when the end of each string is reached by testing for the null character. Also, when `str1` is copied into the `result` array, you want to be certain *not* to also copy the null character because this ends the string in the `result` array right there. You do need, however, to place a null character into the `result` array *after* `str2` has been copied so as to signal the end of the newly created string.

Program 9.3   **Concatenating Character Strings**

```
#include <stdio.h>

int main (void)
{
    void  concat (char  result[], const char  str1[], const char  str2[]);
    const char  s1[] = { "Test " };
    const char  s2[] = { "works." };
    char  s3[20];

    concat (s3, s1, s2);

    printf ("%s\n", s3);

    return 0;
}
```

```
// Function to concatenate two character strings

void concat (char  result[], const char  str1[], const char  str2[])
{
    int  i, j;

    // copy str1 to result

    for ( i = 0;  str1[i] != '\0';  ++i )
        result[i] = str1[i];

    // copy str2 to result

    for ( j = 0;  str2[j] != '\0';  ++j )
        result[i + j] = str2[j];

    // Terminate the concatenated string with a null character

    result [i + j] = '\0';
}
```

Program 9.3   **Output**

Test works.

In the first for loop of the concat() function, the characters contained inside str1 are copied into the result array until the null character is reached. Because the for loop terminates as soon as the null character is matched, it does not get copied into the result array.

In the second loop, the characters from str2 are copied into the result array directly after the final character from str1. This loop makes use of the fact that when the previous for loop finished execution, the value of i was equal to the number of characters in str1, excluding the null character. Therefore, the assignment statement

result[i + j] = str2[j];

is used to copy the characters from str2 into the proper locations of result.

After the second loop is completed, the concat() function puts a null character at the end of the string. Study the function to ensure that you understand the use of i and j. Many program errors when dealing with character strings involve the use of an index number that is off by 1 in either direction.

Remember, to reference the first character of an array, an index number of 0 is used. In addition, if a character array string contains n characters, excluding the null byte, then string[n - 1] references the last (nonnull) character in the string, whereas string[n] references the null character. Furthermore, string must be defined to contain at least n + 1 characters, bearing in mind that the null character occupies a location in the array.

Returning to the program, the main() routine defines two char arrays, s1 and s2, and sets their values using the new initialization technique previously described. The array s3 is defined to contain 20 characters, thus ensuring that sufficient space is reserved for the concatenated character string and saving you from the trouble of having to precisely calculate its size.

The concat function is then called with the three strings s1, s2, and s3 as arguments. The result, as contained in s3 after the concat function returns, is displayed using the %s format characters. Although s3 is defined to contain 20 characters, the printf() function only displays characters from the array up to the null character.

Testing Two Character Strings for Equality

You cannot directly test two strings to see if they are equal with a statement such as

```
if ( string1 == string2 )
    . . .
```

because the equality operator can only be applied to simple variable types, such as floats, ints, or chars, and not to more sophisticated types, such as structures or arrays.

To determine if two strings are equal, you must explicitly compare the two character strings character by character. If you reach the end of both character strings at the same time, and if all of the characters up to that point are identical, the two strings are equal; otherwise, they are not.

It might be a good idea to develop a function that can be used to compare two character strings, as shown in Program 9.4. You can call the function equalStrings() and have it take as arguments the two character strings to be compared. Because you are only interested in determining whether the two character strings are equal, you can have the function return a bool value of true (or nonzero) if the two strings are identical, and false (or zero) if they are not. In this way, the function can be used directly inside test statements, such as in

```
if   ( equalStrings (string1, string2) )
    . . .
```

Program 9.4   **Testing Strings for Equality**

```
// Function to determine if two strings are equal

#include <stdio.h>
#include <stdbool.h>

bool equalStrings (const char   s1[], const char   s2[])
{
    int  i = 0;
    bool areEqual;

    while ( s1[i] == s2 [i]  &&
                s1[i] != '\0' &&  s2[i] != '\0' )
```

```
        ++i;

    if ( s1[i] == '\0'  &&  s2[i] == '\0' )
        areEqual = true;
    else
        areEqual = false;

    return areEqual;
}


int main (void)
{
    bool  equalStrings (const char  s1[], const char  s2[]);
    const char  stra[] = "string compare test";
    const char  strb[] = "string";

    printf ("%i\n", equalStrings (stra, strb));
    printf ("%i\n", equalStrings (stra, stra));
    printf ("%i\n", equalStrings (strb, "string"));

    return 0;
}
```

Program 9.4 **Output**

```
0
1
1
```

The `equalStrings()` function uses a `while` loop to sequence through the character strings `s1` and `s2`. The loop is executed so long as the two character strings are equal (`s1[i] == s2[i]`) and so long as the end of either string is not reached (`s1[i] != '\0' && s2[i] != '\0'`). The variable `i`, which is used as the index number for both arrays, is incremented each time through the `while` loop.

The `if` statement that executes after the `while` loop has terminated determines if you have simultaneously reached the end of both strings `s1` and `s2`. You could have used the statement

```
if ( s1[i] == s2[i] )
    . . .
```

instead to achieve the same results. If you *are* at the end of both strings, the strings must be identical, in which case `areEqual` is set to `true` and returned to the calling routine. Otherwise, the strings are not identical and `areEqual` is set to `false` and returned.

In `main()`, two character arrays `stra` and `strb` are set up and assigned the indicated initial values. The first call to the `equalStrings()` function passes these two character arrays as arguments. Because these two strings are not equal, the function correctly returns a value of false, or 0.

The second call to the equalStrings() function passes the string stra twice. The function correctly returns a true value to indicate that the two strings are equal, as verified by the program's output.

The third call to the equalStrings() function is a bit more interesting. As you can see from this example, you can pass a constant character string to a function that is expecting an array of characters as an argument. In Chapter 10, "Pointers," you see how this works. The equal-Strings() function compares the character string contained in strb to the character string "string" and returns true to indicate that the two strings are equal.

Inputting Character Strings

By now, you are used to the idea of displaying a character string using the %s format characters. But what about reading in a character string from your window (or your "terminal window")? Well, on your system, there are several library functions that you can use to input character strings. The scanf() function can be used with the %s format characters to read in a string of characters up to a blank space, tab character, or the end of the line, whichever occurs first. So, the statements

```
char  string[81];

scanf ("%s", string);
```

have the effect of reading in a character string typed into your terminal window and storing it inside the character array string. Note that unlike previous scanf() calls, in the case of reading strings, the & is *not* placed before the array name (the reason for this is also explained in Chapter 10).

If the preceding scanf() call is executed, and the following characters are entered:

```
Gravity
```

the string "Gravity" is read in by the scanf() function and is stored inside the string array. If the following line of text is typed instead:

```
iTunes playlist
```

just the string "iTunes" is stored inside the string array because the blank space after the word scanf() terminates the string. If the scanf() call is executed again, this time the string "playlist" is stored inside the string array because the scanf() function always continues scanning from the most recent character that was read in.

The scanf() function automatically terminates the string that is read in with a null character. So, execution of the preceding scanf() call with the line of text

```
abcdefghijklmnopqrstuvwxyz
```

causes the entire lowercase alphabet to be stored in the first 26 locations of the string array, with string[26] automatically set to the null character.

If s1, s2, and s3 are defined to be character arrays of appropriate sizes, execution of the statement

```
scanf ("%s%s%s", s1, s2, s3);
```

with the line of text

```
mobile app development
```

results in the assignment of the string "mobile" to s1, "app" to s2, and "development" to s3. If the following line of text is typed instead:

```
tablet computer
```

it results in the assignment of the string "tablet" to s1, and "computer" to s2. Because no further characters appear on the line, the scanf() function then waits for more input to be entered.

In Program 9.5, scanf() is used to read three character strings.

Program 9.5   **Reading Strings with** scanf()

```
//   Program to illustrate the %s scanf format characters

#include <stdio.h>

int main (void)
{
    char   s1[81], s2[81], s3[81];

    printf ("Enter text:\n");

    scanf ("%s%s%s", s1, s2, s3);

    printf ("\ns1 = %s\ns2 = %s\ns3 = %s\n", s1, s2, s3);
    return 0;
}
```

Program 9.5   **Output**

```
Enter text:
smart phone
apps

s1 = smart
s2 = phone
s3 = apps
```

In the preceding program, the scanf() function is called to read in three character strings: s1, s2, and s3. Because the first line of text contains only two character strings—where the definition of a character string to scanf() is a sequence of characters up to a space, tab, or the end of the line—the program waits for more text to be entered. After this is done, the printf() call is used to verify that the strings "smart", "phone", and "apps" are correctly stored inside the string arrays s1, s2, and s3, respectively.

If you type in more than 80 consecutive characters to the preceding program without pressing the spacebar, the tab key, or the Enter (or Return) key, scanf() overflows one of the character arrays. This might cause the program to terminate abnormally or cause unpredictable things to happen. Unfortunately, scanf() has no way of knowing how large your character arrays are. When handed a %s format, it simply continues to read and store characters until one of the noted terminator characters is reached.

If you place a number after the % in the scanf format string, this tells scanf the maximum number of characters to read. So, if you used the following scanf call:

```
scanf ("%80s%80s%80s", s1, s2, s3);
```

instead of the one shown in Program 9.5, scanf knows that no more than 80 characters are to be read and stored into either s1, s2, or s3. (You still have to leave room for the terminating null character that scanf stores at the end of the array. That's why %80s is used instead of %81s.)

Single-Character Input

The standard library provides several functions for the express purposes of reading and writing single characters and entire character strings. A function called getchar() can be used to read in a single character from the terminal. Repeated calls to the getchar() function return successive single characters from the input. When the end of the line is reached, the function returns the newline character '\n'. So, if the characters "abc" are typed, followed immediately by the Enter (or Return) key, the first call to the getchar() function returns the character 'a', the second call returns the character 'b', the third call returns 'c', and the fourth call returns the newline character '\n'. A fifth call to this function causes the program to wait for more input to be entered from the terminal.

You might be wondering why you need the getchar() function when you already know how to read in a single character with the %c format characters of the scanf() function. Using the scanf() function for this purpose is a perfectly valid approach; however, the getchar() function is a more direct approach because its sole purpose is for reading in single characters, and, therefore, it does not require any arguments. The function returns a single character that might be assigned to a variable or used as desired by the program.

In many text-processing applications, you need to read in an entire line of text. This line of text is frequently stored in a single place—generally called a "buffer"—where it is processed further. Using the scanf() call with the %s format characters does not work in such a case because the string is terminated as soon as a space is encountered in the input.

Also available from the function library is a function called gets(). The sole purpose of this function—you guessed it—is to read in a single line of text. As an interesting program exercise, Program 9.6 shows how a function similar to the gets() function—called readLine() here—can be developed using the getchar() function. The function takes a single argument: a character array in which the line of text is to be stored. Characters read from the terminal window up to, but not including, the newline character are stored in this array by the function.

Program 9.6   **Reading Lines of Data**

```c
#include <stdio.h>

int main (void)
{
    int    i;
    char   line[81];
    void   readLine (char  buffer[]);

    for ( i = 0; i < 3; ++i )
    {
        readLine (line);
        printf ("%s\n\n", line);
    }

    return 0;
}


// Function to read a line of text from the terminal

void  readLine (char  buffer[])
{
    char   character;
    int    i = 0;

    do
    {
        character = getchar ();
        buffer[i] = character;
        ++i;
    }
    while ( character != '\n' );

    buffer[i - 1] = '\0';
}
```

Program 9.6   **Output**

This is a sample line of text.
This is a sample line of text.

abcdefghijklmnopqrstuvwxyz
abcdefghijklmnopqrstuvwxyz

runtime library routines
runtime library routines

The do loop in the readLine() function is used to build up the input line inside the character array buffer. Each character that is returned by the getchar() function is stored in the next location of the array. When the newline character is reached—signaling the end of the line—the loop is exited. The null character is then stored inside the array to terminate the character string, replacing the newline character that was stored there the last time that the loop was executed. The index number i − 1 indexes the correct position in the array because the index number was incremented one extra time inside the loop the last time it was executed.

The main() routine defines a character array called line with enough space reserved to hold 81 characters. This ensures that an entire line (80 characters has historically been used as the line length of a "standard terminal") plus the null character can be stored inside the array. However, even in windows that display 80 or fewer characters per line, you are still in danger of overflowing the array if you continue typing past the end of the line without pressing the Enter (or Return) key. It is a good idea to extend the readLine() function to accept as a second argument the size of the buffer. In this way, the function can ensure that the capacity of the buffer is not exceeded.

Another good idea for this program is to improve the user interactivity by adding a prompt line that informs the user what the program is looking for. Adding the following line before the do...while loop in the readLine() function makes things more clear for the program's user:

```
printf("Enter a line of text, up to 80 characters. Hit enter when done:\n");
```

A line like this can also specify the format you are looking for in a data point, like a dollar sign ($) before a money amount, or a colon (:) between the hours and minutes of a time entry. Cues like this are another way to minimize data-entry errors.

The program then enters a for loop, which simply calls the readLine() function three times. Each time that this function is called, a new line of text is read from the terminal. This line is simply echoed back at the terminal to verify proper operation of the function. After the third line of text has been displayed, execution of Program 9.6 is complete.

For your next program example (see Program 9.7), consider a practical text-processing application: counting the number of words in a portion of text. This program develops a function called countWords(), which takes as its argument a character string and which returns the number of words contained in that string. For the sake of simplicity, assume here that a word is defined as a sequence of one or more alphabetic characters. The function can scan the character string for the occurrence of the first alphabetic character and considers all subsequent characters up to the first nonalphabetic character as part of the same word. Then, the function can continue scanning the string for the next alphabetic character, which identifies the start of a new word.

Program 9.7 **Counting Words**

```
// Function to determine if a character is alphabetic

#include <stdio.h>
#include <stdbool.h>

bool alphabetic (const char  c)
{
    if  ( (c >= 'a'  &&  c <= 'z') || (c >= 'A'  &&  c <= 'Z') )
        return true;
    else
        return false;
}

/* Function to count the number of words in a string */

int  countWords (const char  string[])
{
    int    i, wordCount = 0;
    bool  lookingForWord = true, alphabetic (const char  c);

    for ( i = 0;  string[i] != '\0';  ++i )
        if ( alphabetic(string[i]) )
        {
            if ( lookingForWord )
            {
                ++wordCount;
                lookingForWord = false;
            }
        }
        else
            lookingForWord = true;

    return wordCount;
}

int main (void)
{
    const char  text1[] = "Well, here goes.";
    const char  text2[] = "And here we go... again.";
    int    countWords (const char  string[]);
```

```
        printf ("%s - words = %i\n", text1, countWords (text1));
        printf ("%s - words = %i\n", text2, countWords (text2));

        return 0;
}
```

Program 9.7   **Output**

```
Well, here goes. - words = 3
And here we go... again. - words = 5
```

The alphabetic() function is straightforward enough—it simply tests the value of the character passed to it to determine if it is either a lowercase or uppercase letter. If it is either, the function returns true, indicating that the character is alphabetic; otherwise, the function returns false.

The countWords() function is not as straightforward. The integer variable i is used as an index number to sequence through each character in the string. The integer variable looking-ForWord is used as a flag to indicate whether you are currently in the process of looking for the start of a new word. At the beginning of the execution of the function, you obviously *are* looking for the start of a new word, so this flag is set to true. The local variable wordCount is used for the obvious purpose of counting the number of words in the character string.

For each character inside the character string, a call to the alphabetic() function is made to determine whether the character is alphabetic. If the character is alphabetic, the lookingForWord flag is tested to determine if you are in the process of looking for a new word. If you are, the value of wordCount is incremented by 1, and the lookingForWord flag is set to false, indicating that you are no longer looking for the start of a new word.

If the character is alphabetic and the lookingForWord flag is false, this means that you are currently scanning *inside* a word. In such a case, the for loop is continued with the next character in the string.

If the character is not alphabetic—meaning either that you have reached the end of a word or that you have still not found the beginning of the next word—the flag lookingForWord is set to true (even though it might already be true).

When all of the characters inside the character string have been examined, the function returns the value of wordCount to indicate the number of words that were found in the character string.

It is helpful to present a table of the values of the various variables in the countWords function to see how the algorithm works. Table 9.1 shows such a table, with the first call to the countWords function from the preceding program as an example. The first line of Table 9.1 shows the initial value of the variables wordCount and lookingForWord before the for loop is entered. Subsequent lines depict the values of the indicated variables each time through the for loop. So, the second line of the table shows that the value of wordCount has been set to 1 and the lookingForWord flag set to false (0) after the first time through the loop (after the

'W' has been processed). The last line of the table shows the final values of the variables when the end of the string is reached. You should spend some time studying this table, verifying the values of the indicated variables against the logic of the countWords() function. After this has been accomplished, you should then feel comfortable with the algorithm that is used by the function to count the number of words in a string.

Table 9.1   **Execution of the** countWords() **Function**

i	string[i]	wordCount	lookingForWord
		0	true
0	'W'	1	false
1	'e'	1	false
2	'l'	1	false
3	'l'	1	false
4	','	1	true
5	' '	1	true
6	'h'	2	false
7	'e'	2	false
8	'r'	2	false
9	'e'	2	false
10	' '	2	true
11	'g'	3	false
12	'o'	3	false
13	'e'	3	false
14	's'	3	false
15	'.'	3	true
16	'\0'	3	true

The Null String

Now consider a slightly more practical example of the use of the countWords() function. This time, you make use of your readLine() function to allow the user to type in multiple lines of text. The program then counts the total number of words in the text and displays the result.

To make the program more flexible, you do not limit or specify the number of lines of text that are entered. Therefore, you must have a way for the user to "tell" the program when he is done entering text. One way to do this is to have the user simply press the Enter (or Return) key an extra time after the last line of text has been entered. When the readLine() function is called to read in such a line, the function immediately encounters the newline character and, as a result, stores the null character as the first (and only) character in the buffer. Your program can check for this special case and can know that the last line of text has been entered after a line containing no characters has been read.

A character string that contains no characters other than the null character has a special name in the C language; it is called the *null string*. When you think about it, the use of the null string is still perfectly consistent with all of the functions that you have defined so far in this chapter. The `stringLength()` function correctly returns 0 as the size of the null string; your `concat()` function also properly concatenates "nothing" onto the end of another string; even your `equalStrings()` function works correctly if either or both strings are null (and in the latter case, the function correctly calls these strings equal).

Always remember that the null string does, in fact, have a character in it, albeit a null one.

Sometimes, it becomes desirable to set the value of a character string to the null string. In C, the null string is denoted by an adjacent pair of double quotation marks. So, the statement

```
char  buffer[100] = "";
```

defines a character array called `buffer` and sets its value to the null string. Note that the character string `""` is *not* the same as the character string `" "` because the second string contains a single blank character. (If you are doubtful, send both strings to the `equalStrings()` function and see what result comes back.)

Program 9.8 uses the `readLine()`, `alphabetic()`, and `countWords()` functions from previous programs..

Program 9.8 **Counting Words in a Piece of Text**

```
#include <stdio.h>
#include <stdbool.h>

bool alphabetic (const char  c)
{
    if ( (c >= 'a'  && c <= 'z') || (c >= 'A'  && c <= 'Z') )
        return true;
    else
        return false;
}


void  readLine (char  buffer[])
{
    char  character;
    int   i = 0;

    do
    {
```

```
            character = getchar ();
            buffer[i] = character;
            ++i;
        }
    while ( character != '\n' );

    buffer[i - 1] = '\0';
}


int   countWords (const char   string[])
{
    int    i, wordCount = 0;
    bool   lookingForWord = true, alphabetic (const char   c);

    for ( i = 0;  string[i] != '\0';  ++i )
        if ( alphabetic(string[i]) )
        {
            if ( lookingForWord )
            {
                ++wordCount;
                lookingForWord = false;
            }
        }
        else
            lookingForWord = true;

    return wordCount;
}


int main (void)
{
    char   text[81];
    int    totalWords = 0;
    int    countWords (const char   string[]);
    void   readLine (char   buffer[]);
    bool   endOfText = false;

    printf ("Type in your text.\n");
    printf ("When you are done, press 'RETURN'.\n\n");

    while ( ! endOfText )
    {
        readLine (text);

        if ( text[0] == '\0' )
            endOfText = true;
        else
```

```
            totalWords += countWords (text);
    }

    printf ("\nThere are %i words in the above text.\n",  totalWords);

    return 0;
}
```

Program 9.8   **Output**

```
Type in your text.
When you are done, press 'RETURN'.

Wendy glanced up at the ceiling where the mound of lasagna loomed
like a mottled mountain range. Within seconds, she was crowned with
ricotta ringlets and a tomato sauce tiara. Bits of beef formed meaty
moles on her forehead. After the second thud, her culinary coronation
was complete.
Return
There are 48 words in the above text.
```

The line labeled *Return* indicates the pressing of the Enter or Return key.

The `endOfText` variable is used as a flag to indicate when the end of the input text has been reached. The `while` loop is executed as long as this flag is `false`. Inside this loop, the program calls the `readLine()` function to read a line of text. The `if` statement then tests the input line that is stored inside the `text` array to see if just the Enter (or Return) key was pressed. If so, then the buffer contains the null string, in which case the `endOfText` flag is set to `true` to signal that all of the text has been entered.

If the buffer does contain some text, the `countWords()` function is called to count the number of words in the `text` array. The value that is returned by this function is added into the value of `totalWords`, which contains the cumulative number of words from all lines of text entered thus far.

After the `while` loop is exited, the program displays the value of `totalWords`, along with some informative text.

It might seem that the preceding program does not help to reduce your work efforts much because you still have to manually enter all of the text at the terminal. But as you will see in Chapter 15, "Input and Output Operations in C," this same program can also be used to count the number of words contained in a file stored on a disk, for example. So, an author using a computer system for the preparation of a manuscript might find this program extremely valuable as it can be used to quickly determine the number of words contained in the manuscript (assuming the file is stored as a normal text file and not in some word processor format like Microsoft Word).

Escape Characters

As alluded to previously, the backslash character has a special significance that extends beyond its use in forming the newline and null characters. Just as the backslash and the letter n, when used in combination, cause subsequent printing to begin on a new line, so can other characters be combined with the backslash character to perform special functions. These various backslash characters, often referred to as *escape characters*, are summarized in Table 9.2.

Table 9.2   **Escape Characters**

Escape Character	Name
\a	Audible alert
\b	Backspace
\f	Form feed
\n	Newline
\r	Carriage return
\t	Horizontal tab
\v	Vertical tab
\\	Backslash
\"	Double quotation mark
\'	Single quotation mark
\?	Question mark
\nnn	Octal character value *nnn*
\unnnn	Universal character name
\Unnnnnnnn	Universal character name
\xnn	Hexadecimal character value *nn*

The first seven characters listed in Table 9.2 perform the indicated function on most output devices when they are displayed. The *audible alert* character, \a, sounds a "bell." So, the printf() call

```
printf ("\aSYSTEM SHUT DOWN IN 5 MINUTES!!\n");
```

sounds an alert and displays the indicated message.

Including the backspace character '\b' inside a character string causes the terminal to backspace one character at the point at which the character appears in the string, provided that it is supported. Similarly, the function call

```
printf ("%i\t%i\t%i\n", a, b, c);
```

displays the value of a, space over to the next tab setting (typically set to every eight columns by default), displays the value of b, space over to the next tab setting, and then displays the value of c. The horizontal tab character is particularly useful for lining up data in columns.

To include the backslash character itself inside a character string, two backslash characters are necessary, so the printf() call

```
printf ("\\t is the horizontal tab character.\n");
```

displays the following:

```
\t is the horizontal tab character.
```

Note that because the \\ is encountered first in the string, a tab is not displayed in this case.

To include a double quotation character inside a character string, it must be preceded by a backslash. So, the printf() call

```
printf ("\"Hello,\" he said.\n");
```

results in the display of the message

```
"Hello," he said.
```

To assign a single quotation character to a character variable, the backslash character must be placed before the quotation mark. If c is declared to be a variable of type char, the statement

```
c = '\'';
```

assigns a single quotation character to c.

The backslash character, followed immediately by a ?, is used to represent a ? character. This is sometimes necessary when dealing with *trigraphs* in non-ASCII character sets. For more details, consult Appendix A, "C Language Summary."

The final four entries in Table 9.2 enable *any* character to be included in a character string. In the escape character '\nnn', nnn is a one- to three-digit *octal* number. In the escape character '\xnn', nn is a hexadecimal number. These numbers represent the internal *code* of the character. This enables characters that might not be directly available from the keyboard to be coded into a character string. For example, to include an ASCII escape character, which has the value octal 33, you could include the sequence \033 or \x1b inside your string.

The null character '\0' is a special case of the escape character sequence described in the preceding paragraph. It represents the character that has a value of 0. In fact, because the value of the null character *is* 0, this knowledge is frequently used by programmers in tests and loops dealing with variable-length character strings. For example, the loop to count the length of a character string in the function stringLength() from Program 9.2 can also be equivalently coded as follows:

```
while ( string[count] )
    ++count;
```

The value of `string[count]` is nonzero until the null character is reached, at which point the `while` loop is exited.

It should once again be pointed out that these escape characters are only considered a single character inside a string. So, the character string `"\033\"Hello\"\n"` actually consists of nine characters (not counting the terminating null): the character `'\033'`, the double quotation character `'\"'`, the five characters in the word `Hello`, the double quotation character once again, and the newline character. Try passing the preceding character string to the `string-Length()` function to verify that nine is indeed the number of characters in the string (again, excluding the terminating null).

A *universal character name* is formed by the characters \u followed by four hexadecimal numbers or the characters \U followed by eight hexadecimal numbers. It is used for specifying characters from extended character sets; that is, character sets that require more than the standard eight bits for internal representation. The universal character name escape sequence can be used to form identifier names from extended character sets, as well as to specify 16-bit and 32-bit characters inside wide character string and character string constants. For more information, refer to Appendix A.

More on Constant Strings

If you place a backslash character at the very end of the line and follow it immediately by a carriage return, it tells the C compiler to ignore the end of the line. This line continuation technique is used primarily for continuing long constant character strings onto the next line and, as you see in Chapter 12, "The Preprocessor," for continuing a *macro* definition onto the next line.

Without the line continuation character, your C compiler generates an error message if you attempt to initialize a character string across multiple lines; for example:

```
        char  letters[] =
            { "abcdefghijklmnopqrstuvwxyz
ABCDEFGHIJKLMNOPQRSTUVWXYZ" };
```

By placing a backslash character at the end of each line to be continued, a character string constant can be written over multiple lines:

```
        char  letters[] =
            { "abcdefghijklmnopqrstuvwxyz\
ABCDEFGHIJKLMNOPQRSTUVWXYZ" };
```

It is necessary to begin the continuation of the character string constant at the *beginning* of the next line because, otherwise, the leading blank spaces on the line get stored in the character string. The preceding statement, therefore, has the net result of defining the character array `letters` and of initializing its elements to the character string

```
"abcdefghijklmnopqrstuvwxyzABCDEFGHIJKLMNOPQRSTUVWXYZ"
```

Another way to break up long character strings is to divide them into two or more adjacent strings. Adjacent strings are constant strings separated by zero or more spaces, tabs, or newlines. The compiler automatically concatenates adjacent strings together. Therefore, writing the strings

```
"one"  "two"  "three"
```

is syntactically equivalent to writing the single string

```
"onetwothree"
```

So, the `letters` array can also be set to the letters of the alphabet by writing

```
char  letters[] =
    { "abcdefghijklmnopqrstuvwxyz"
      "ABCDEFGHIJKLMNOPQRSTUVWXYZ" };
```

Finally, the three `printf()` calls

```
printf ("Programming in C is fun\n");
printf ("Programming"  " in C is fun\n");
printf ("Programming"  " in C"  " is fun\n");
```

all pass a *single* argument to `printf()` because the compiler concatenates the strings together in the second and third calls.

Character Strings, Structures, and Arrays

You can combine the basic elements of the C programming language to form very powerful programming constructs in many ways. In Chapter 8, "Working with Structures," for example, you saw how you could easily define an array of structures. Program 9.9 further illustrates the notion of arrays of structures, combined with the variable-length character string.

Suppose you want to write a computer program that acts like a dictionary. If you had such a program, you could use it whenever you came across a word whose meaning was not clear. You could type the word into the program, and the program could then automatically "look up" the word inside the dictionary and tell you its definition.

If you contemplate developing such a program, one of the first thoughts that comes to mind is the representation of the word and its definition inside the computer. Obviously, because the word and its definition are logically related, the notion of a structure comes immediately to mind. You can define a structure called `entry`, for example, to hold the word and its definition:

```
struct  entry
{
    char  word[15];
    char  definition[50];
};
```

In the preceding structure definition, you have defined enough space for a 14-letter word (remember, you are dealing with variable-length character strings, so you need to leave room for the null character) plus a 49-character definition. The following is an example of a variable defined to be of type `struct entry` that is initialized to contain the word "blob" and its definition.

```
struct entry  word1 = { "blob", "an amorphous mass" };
```

Because you want to provide for many words inside your dictionary, it seems logical to define an array of `entry` structures, such as in

```
struct entry  dictionary[100];
```

which allows for a dictionary of 100 words. Obviously, this is far from sufficient if you are interested in setting up an English language dictionary, which requires at least 100,000 entries to be of any value. In that case, you would probably adopt a more sophisticated approach, one that would typically involve storing the dictionary on the computer's disk, as opposed to storing its entire contents in memory.

Having defined the structure of your dictionary, you should now think a bit about its organization. Most dictionaries are organized alphabetically. It makes sense to organize yours the same way. For now, assume that this is because it makes the dictionary easier to read. Later, you see the real motivation for such an organization.

Now, it's time to think about the development of the program. It is convenient to define a function to look up a word inside the dictionary. If the word is found, the function could return the entry number of the word inside the dictionary; otherwise, the function could return −1 to indicate that the word was not found in the dictionary. So, a typical call to this function, which you can call `lookup()`, might appear as follows:

```
entry = lookup (dictionary, word, entries);
```

In this case, the `lookup()` function searches `dictionary` for the word as contained in the character string `word`. The third argument, `entries`, represents the number of entries in the dictionary. The function searches the dictionary for the specified word and returns the entry number in the dictionary if the word is found, or returns −1 if the word is not found.

In Program 9.9, the `lookup()` function uses the `equalStrings()` function defined in Program 9.4 to determine if the specified word matches an entry in the dictionary.

Program 9.9   Using the Dictionary Lookup Program

```
// Program to use the dictionary lookup program

#include <stdio.h>
#include <stdbool.h>

struct  entry
{
```

```
        char    word[15];
        char    definition[50];
};

bool equalStrings (const char  s1[], const char  s2[])
{
        int  i = 0;
        bool areEqual;

        while ( s1[i] == s2 [i]  &&
                    s1[i] != '\0' && s2[i] != '\0' )
            ++i;

        if ( s1[i] == '\0'  && s2[i] == '\0' )
            areEqual = true;
        else
            areEqual = false;

        return areEqual;
}

// function to look up a word inside a dictionary

int  lookup (const struct entry  dictionary[], const char  search[],
            const int  entries)
{
        int  i;
        bool equalStrings (const char s1[], const char s2[]);

        for ( i = 0;  i < entries;  ++i )
            if ( equalStrings (search, dictionary[i].word) )
                return i;

        return -1;
}

int main (void)
{
        const struct entry  dictionary[100] =
          { { "aardvark", "a burrowing African mammal"      },
            { "abyss",    "a bottomless pit"                },
            { "acumen",   "mentally sharp; keen"            },
            { "addle",    "to become confused"              },
            { "aerie",    "a high nest"                     },
            { "affix",    "to append; attach"               },
            { "agar",     "a jelly made from seaweed"       },
            { "ahoy",     "a nautical call of greeting"     },
```

```
        { "aigrette", "an ornamental cluster of feathers" },
        { "ajar",     "partially opened"                 } };

    char  word[10];
    int   entries = 10;
    int   entry;
    int   lookup (const struct entry  dictionary[], const char  search[],
                  const int  entries);

    printf ("Enter word: ");
    scanf ("%14s", word);
    entry = lookup (dictionary, word, entries);

    if ( entry != -1 )
        printf ("%s\n", dictionary[entry].definition);
    else
        printf ("Sorry, the word %s is not in my dictionary.\n", word);

    return 0;
}
```

Program 9.9 **Output**

```
Enter word: agar
a jelly made from seaweed
```

Program 9.9 **Output (Rerun)**

```
Enter word: accede
Sorry, the word accede is not in my dictionary.
```

The lookup() function sequences through each entry in the dictionary. For each such entry, the function calls the equalStrings() function to determine if the character string search matches the word member of the particular dictionary entry. If it does match, the function returns the value of the variable i, which is the entry number of the word that was found in the dictionary. The function is exited immediately upon execution of the return statement, despite the fact that the function is in the middle of executing a for loop.

If the lookup() function exhausts all the entries in the dictionary without finding a match, the return statement after the for loop is executed to return the "not found" indication (–1) back to the caller.

A Better Search Method

The method used by the lookup() function to search for a particular word in the dictionary is straightforward enough; the function simply performs a sequential search through all the entries in the dictionary until either a match is made or the end of the dictionary is reached.

For a small-sized dictionary like the one in your program, this approach is perfectly fine. However, if you start dealing with large dictionaries containing hundreds or perhaps even thousands of entries, this approach might no longer be sufficient because of the time it takes to sequentially search through all of the entries. The time required can be considerable—even though considerable in this case could mean only a fraction of a second. One of the prime considerations that must be given to any sort of information retrieval program is that of speed. Because the searching process is one that is so frequently used in computer applications, much attention has been given by computer scientists to developing efficient algorithms for searching (about as much attention as has been given to the process of sorting).

You can make use of the fact that your dictionary is in alphabetical order to develop a more efficient `lookup()` function. The first obvious optimization that comes to mind is in the case that the word you are looking for does not exist in the dictionary. You can make your `lookup()` function "intelligent" enough to recognize when it has gone too far in its search. For example, if you look up the word "active" in the dictionary defined in Program 9.9, as soon as you reach the word "acumen," you can conclude that "active" is not there because, if it was, it would have appeared in the dictionary *before* the word "acumen."

As was mentioned, the preceding optimization strategy does help to reduce your search time somewhat, but only when a particular word is *not* present in the dictionary. What you are really looking for is an algorithm that reduces the search time in most cases, not just in one particular case. Such an algorithm exists under the name of the *binary search*.

The strategy behind the binary search is relatively simple to understand. To illustrate how this algorithm works, take an analogous situation of a simple guessing game. Suppose I pick a number from 1 to 99 and then tell you to try to guess the number in the fewest number of guesses. For each guess that you make, I can tell you if you are too low, too high, or if your guess is correct. After a few tries at the game, you will probably realize that a good way to narrow in on the answer is by using a halving process. For example, if you take 50 as your first guess, an answer of either "too high" or "too low" narrows the possibilities down from 100 to 49. If the answer was "too high," the number must be from 1 to 49, inclusive; if the answer was "too low," the number must be from 51 to 99, inclusive.

You can now repeat the halving process with the remaining 49 numbers. So if the first answer was "too low," the next guess should be halfway between 51 and 99, which is 75. This process can be continued until you finally narrow in on the answer. On the average, this procedure takes far less time to arrive at the answer than any other search method.

The preceding discussion describes precisely how the binary search algorithm works. The following provides a formal description of the algorithm. In this algorithm, you are looking for an element *x* inside an array *M*, which contains *n* elements. The algorithm assumes that the array *M* is sorted in ascending order.

Binary Search Algorithm

  Step 1: Set *low* to 0, *high* to $n - 1$.

  Step 2: If *low* > *high*, *x* does not exist in *M* and the algorithm terminates.

Step 3: Set *mid* to (*low* + *high*) / 2.

Step 4: If M[*mid*] < *x*, set *low* to *mid* + 1 and go to step 2.

Step 5: If M[*mid*] > *x*, set *high* to *mid* − 1 and go to step 2.

Step 6: M[*mid*] equals *x* and the algorithm terminates.

The division performed in step 3 is an integer division, so if *low* is 0 and *high* is 49, the value of *mid* is 24.

Now that you have the algorithm for performing a binary search, you can rewrite your lookup() function to use this new search strategy. Because the binary search must be able to determine if one value is less than, greater than, or equal to another value, you might want to replace your equalStrings() function with another function that makes this type of determination for two character strings. Call the function compareStrings() and have it return the value –1 if the first string is lexicographically less than the second string, 0 if the two strings are equal, and 1 if the first string is lexicographically greater than the second string. So, the function call

```
compareStrings ("alpha", "altered")
```

returns the value –1 because the first string is lexicographically less than the second string (think of this to mean that the first string occurs *before* the second string in a dictionary). And, the function call

```
compareStrings ("zioty", "yucca");
```

returns the value 1 because "zioty" is lexicographically greater than "yucca."

In Program 9.10, the new compareStrings() function is presented. The lookup function now uses the binary search method to scan through the dictionary. The main() routine remains unchanged from the previous program.

Program 9.10 **Modifying the Dictionary Lookup Using Binary Search**

```
// Dictionary lookup program

#include <stdio.h>

struct  entry
{
    char  word[15];
    char  definition[50];
};

// Function to compare two character strings

int  compareStrings (const char  s1[], const char  s2[])
{
```

```
    int  i = 0, answer;

    while ( s1[i] == s2[i] && s1[i] != '\0'&& s2[i] != '\0' )
        ++i;

    if ( s1[i] < s2[i] )
        answer = -1;                /* s1 < s2 */
    else if ( s1[i] == s2[i] )
        answer = 0;                 /* s1 == s2 */
    else
        answer = 1;                 /* s1 > s2 */

    return answer;
}

// Function to look up a word inside a dictionary

int  lookup (const struct entry  dictionary[], const char  search[],
             const int  entries)
{
    int  low = 0;
    int  high = entries - 1;
    int  mid, result;
    int  compareStrings (const char  s1[], const char  s2[]);

    while  ( low <= high )
    {
        mid = (low + high) / 2;
        result = compareStrings (dictionary[mid].word, search);

        if ( result == -1 )
            low = mid + 1;
        else if ( result == 1 )
            high = mid - 1;
        else
            return mid;    /* found it */
    }

    return -1;             /* not found */
}

int main (void)
{
    const struct entry  dictionary[100] =
        { { "aardvark", "a burrowing African mammal"       },
          { "abyss",    "a bottomless pit"                 },
          { "acumen",   "mentally sharp; keen"             },
```

```
          { "addle",    "to become confused"             },
          { "aerie",    "a high nest"                    },
          { "affix",    "to append; attach"              },
          { "agar",     "a jelly made from seaweed"      },
          { "ahoy",     "a nautical call of greeting"    },
          { "aigrette", "an ornamental cluster of feathers" },
          { "ajar",     "partially opened"               } };

    int   entries = 10;
    char  word[15];
    int   entry;
    int   lookup (const struct entry  dictionary[], const char  search[],
                  const int  entries);

    printf ("Enter word: ");
    scanf ("%14s", word);

    entry = lookup (dictionary, word, entries);

    if ( entry != -1 )
        printf ("%s\n", dictionary[entry].definition);
    else
        printf ("Sorry, the word %s is not in my dictionary.\n", word);

    return 0;
}
```

Program 9.10 **Output**

```
Enter word: aigrette
an ornamental cluster of feathers
```

Program 9.10 **Output (Rerun)**

```
Enter word: acerb
Sorry, that word is not in my dictionary.
```

The compareStrings() function is identical to the equalStrings() function up through the end of the while loop. When the while loop is exited, the function analyzes the two characters that resulted in the termination of the while loop. If s1[i] is less than s2[i], s1 must be lexicographically less than s2. In such a case, -1 is returned. If s1[i] is equal to s2[i], the two strings are equal so 0 is returned. If neither is true, s1 must be lexicographically greater than s2, in which case 1 is returned.

The lookup() function defines int variables low and high and assigns them initial values defined by the binary search algorithm. The while loop executes as long as low does not exceed high. Inside the loop, the value mid is calculated by adding low and high and dividing the result by 2. The `compareStrings()` function is then called with the word contained in `dictionary[mid]` and the word you are searching for as arguments. The returned value is assigned to the variable `result`.

If `compareStrings()` returns a value of –1—indicating that `dictionary[mid].word` is less than `search`—`lookup()` sets the value of `low` to `mid + 1`. If `compareStrings()` returns 1—indicating that `dictionary[mid].search` is greater than `search`—`lookup()` sets the value of `high` to `mid – 1`. If neither –1 nor 1 is returned, the two strings must be equal, and, in that case, `lookup()` returns the value of `mid`, which is the entry number of the word in the dictionary.

If `low` eventually exceeds `high`, the word is not in the dictionary. In that case, `lookup()` returns –1 to indicate this "not found" condition.

Character Operations

Character variables and constants are frequently used in relational and arithmetic expressions. To properly use characters in such situations, it is necessary for you to understand how they are handled by the C compiler.

Whenever a character constant or variable is used in an expression in C, it is automatically converted to, and subsequently treated as, an integer value.

In Chapter 5, "Making Decisions," you saw how the expression

```
c >= 'a'  &&  c <= 'z'
```

could be used to determine if the character variable `c` contained a lowercase letter. As mentioned there, such an expression could be used on systems that used an ASCII character representation because the lowercase letters are represented sequentially in ASCII, with no other characters in-between. The first part of the preceding expression, which compares the value of `c` against the value of the character constant `'a'`, is actually comparing the value of `c` against the internal representation of the character `'a'`. In ASCII, the character `'a'` has the value 97, the character `'b'` has the value 98, and so on. Therefore, the expression `c >= 'a'` is TRUE (nonzero) for any lowercase character contained in `c` because it has a value that is greater than or equal to 97. However, because there are characters other than the lowercase letters whose ASCII values are greater than 97 (such as the open and close braces), the test must be bounded on the other end to ensure that the result of the expression is TRUE for lowercase characters only. For this reason, `c` is compared against the character `'z'`, which, in ASCII, has the value 122.

Because comparing the value of `c` against the characters `'a'` and `'z'` in the preceding expression actually compares `c` to the numerical representations of `'a'` and `'z'`, the expression

```
c >= 97  &&  c <= 122
```

could be equivalently used to determine if `c` is a lowercase letter. The first expression is preferred, however, because it does not require the knowledge of the specific numerical values of the characters `'a'` and `'z'`, and because its intentions are less obscure.

The printf() call

```
printf ("%i\n", c);
```

can be used to print out the value that is used to internally represent the character stored inside c. If your system uses ASCII, the statement

```
printf ("%i\n", 'a');
```

displays 97, for example.

Try to predict what the following two statements would produce:

```
c = 'a' + 1;
printf ("%c\n", c);
```

Because the value of 'a' is 97 in ASCII, the effect of the first statement is to assign the value 98 to the character variable c. Because this value represents the character 'b' in ASCII, this is the character that is displayed by the printf() call.

Although adding one to a character constant hardly seems practical, the preceding example gives way to an important technique that is used to convert the characters '0' through '9' into their corresponding numerical values 0 through 9. Recall that the character '0' is not the same as the integer 0, the character '1' is not the same as the integer 1, and so on. In fact, the character '0' has the numerical value 48 in ASCII, which is what is displayed by the following printf() call:

```
printf ("%i\n", '0');
```

Suppose the character variable c contains one of the characters '0' through '9' and that you want to convert this value into the corresponding integer 0 through 9. Because the digits of virtually all character sets are represented by sequential integer values, you can easily convert c into its integer equivalent by subtracting the character constant '0' from it. Therefore, if i is defined as an integer variable, the statement

```
i = c - '0';
```

has the effect of converting the character digit contained in c into its equivalent integer value. Suppose c contained the character '5', which, in ASCII, is the number 53. The ASCII value of '0' is 48, so execution of the preceding statement results in the integer subtraction of 48 from 53, which results in the integer value 5 being assigned to i. On a machine that uses a character set other than ASCII, the same result would most likely be obtained, even though the internal representations of '5' and '0' might differ.

The preceding technique can be extended to convert a character string consisting of digits into its equivalent numerical representation. This has been done in Program 9.11 in which a function called strToInt() is presented to convert the character string passed as its argument into an integer value. The function ends its scan of the character string after a non-digit character is encountered and returns the result back to the calling routine. It is assumed that an int variable is large enough to hold the value of the converted number.

Program 9.11   **Converting a String to its Integer Equivalent**

```c
// Function to convert a string to an integer

#include <stdio.h>

int  strToInt (const char  string[])
{
    int  i, intValue, result = 0;

    for  ( i = 0; string[i] >= '0' && string[i] <= '9'; ++i )
    {
        intValue = string[i] - '0';
        result = result * 10 + intValue;
    }

    return result;
}

int main (void)
{
    int  strToInt (const char  string[]);

    printf ("%i\n", strToInt("245"));
    printf ("%i\n", strToInt("100") + 25);
    printf ("%i\n", strToInt("13x5"));

    return 0;
}
```

Program 9.11   **Output**

```
245
125
13
```

The for loop is executed as long as the character contained in string[i] is a digit character. Each time through the loop, the character contained in string[i] is converted into its equivalent integer value and is then added into the value of result multiplied by 10. To see how this technique works, consider execution of this loop when the function is called with the character string "245" as an argument: The first time through the loop, intValue is assigned the value of string[0] - '0'. Because string[0] contains the character '2', this results in the value 2 being assigned to intValue. Because the value of result is 0 the first time through the loop, multiplying it by 10 produces 0, which is added to intValue and stored back in result. So, by the end of the first pass through the loop, result contains the value 2.

The second time through the loop, intValue is set equal to 4, as calculated by subtracting '0' from '4'. Multiplying result by 10 produces 20, which is added to the value of intValue, producing 24 as the value stored in result.

The third time through the loop, intValue is equal to '5' – '0', or 5, which is added into the value of result multiplied by 10 (240). Thus, the value 245 is the value of result after the loop has been executed for the third time.

Upon encountering the terminating null character, the for loop is exited and the value of result, 245, is returned to the calling routine.

The strToInt() function could be improved in two ways. First, it doesn't handle negative numbers. Second, it doesn't let you know whether the string contained *any* valid digit characters at all. For example, strToInt ("xxx") returns 0. These improvements are left as an exercise.

This discussion concludes this chapter on character strings. As you can see, C provides capabilities that enable character strings to be efficiently and easily manipulated. The library actually contains a wide variety of library functions for performing operations on strings. For example, it offers the function strlen() to calculate the length of a character string; strcmp() to compare two strings; strcat() to concatenate two strings; strcpy() to copy one string to another; atoi() to convert a string to an integer; and isupper(), islower(), isalpha(), and isdigit() to test whether a character is uppercase, lowercase, alphabetic, or a digit. A good exercise is to rewrite the examples from this chapter to make use of these routines. Consult Appendix B, "The Standard C Library," which lists many of the functions available from the library.

Exercises

1. Type in and run the 11 programs presented in this chapter. Compare the output produced by each program with the output presented after each program in the text.

2. Why could you have replaced the while statement of the equalStrings() function of Program 9.4 with the statement

   ```
   while ( s1[i] == s2[i]  &&  s1[i] != '\0' )
   ```

   to achieve the same results?

3. The countWords() function from Programs 9.7 and 9.8 incorrectly counts a word that contains an apostrophe as two separate words. Modify this function to correctly handle this situation. Also, extend the function to count a sequence of positive or negative numbers, including any embedded commas and periods, as a single word.

4. Write a function called substring() to extract a portion of a character string. The function should be called as follows:

   ```
   substring (source, start, count, result);
   ```

where `source` is the character string from which you are extracting the substring, `start` is an index number into `source` indicating the first character of the `substring`, `count` is the number of characters to be extracted from the `source` string, and `result` is an array of characters that is to contain the extracted substring. For example, the call

```
substring ("character", 4, 3, result);
```

extracts the substring `"act"` (three characters starting with character number 4) from the string `"character"` and places the result in `result`.

Be certain the function inserts a null character at the end of the substring in the result array. Also, have the function check that the requested number of characters does, in fact, exist in the string. If this is not the case, have the function end the substring when it reaches the end of the source string. So, for example, a call such as

```
substring ("two words", 4, 20, result);
```

should just place the string "words" inside the result array, even though 20 characters were requested by the call.

5. Write a function called `findString()` to determine if one character string exists inside another string. The first argument to the function should be the character string that is to be searched and the second argument is the string you are interested in finding. If the function finds the specified string, have it return the location in the source string where the string was found. If the function does not find the string, have it return –1. So, for example, the call

```
index = findString ("a chatterbox", "hat");
```

searches the string `"a chatterbox"` for the string `"hat"`. Because `"hat"` does exist inside the source string, the function returns 3 to indicate the starting position inside the source string where `"hat"` was found.

6. Write a function called `removeString()` to remove a specified number of characters from a character string. The function should take three arguments: the source string, the starting index number in the source string, and the number of characters to remove. So, if the character array `text` contains the string `"the wrong son"`, the call

```
removeString (text, 4, 6);
```

has the effect of removing the characters "wrong" (the word "wrong" plus the space that follows) from the array `text`. The resulting string inside `text` is then `"the son"`.

7. Write a function called `insertString()` to insert one character string into another string. The arguments to the function should consist of the source string, the string to be inserted, and the position in the source string where the string is to be inserted. So, the call

```
insertString (text, "per", 10);
```

with `text` as originally defined in the previous exercise, results in the character string `"per"` being inserted inside `text`, beginning at `text[10]`. Therefore, the character string `"the wrong person"` is stored inside the `text` array after the function returned.

8. Using the `findString()`, `removeString()`, and `insertString()` functions from preceding exercises, write a function called `replaceString()` that takes three character string arguments as follows

```
replaceString (source, s1, s2);
```

and that replaces s1 inside source with the character string s2. The function should call the `findString()` function to locate s1 inside source, then call the `removeString()` function to remove s1 from source, and finally call the `insertString()` function to insert s2 into source at the proper location.

So, the function call

```
replaceString (text, "1", "one");
```

replaces the first occurrence of the character string "1" inside the character string text, if it exists, with the string "one". Similarly, the function call

```
replaceString (text, "*", "");
```

has the effect of removing the first asterisk inside the text array because the replacement string is the null string.

9. You can extend even further the usefulness of the `replaceString()` function from the preceding exercise if you have it return a value that indicates whether the replacement succeeded, which means that the string to be replaced was found inside the source string. So, if the function returns `true` if the replacement succeeds and `false` if it does not, the loop

```
do
    stillFound = replaceString (text, " ", "");
while ( stillFound );
```

could be used to remove *all* blank spaces from text, for example.

Incorporate this change into the `replaceString()` function and try it with various character strings to ensure that it works properly.

10. Write a function called `dictionarySort()` that sorts a dictionary, as defined in Programs 9.9 and 9.10, into alphabetical order.

11. Extend the `strToInt()` function from Program 9.11 so that if the first character of the string is a minus sign, the value that follows is taken as a negative number.

12. Write a function called `strToFloat()` that converts a character string into a floating-point value. Have the function accept an optional leading minus sign. So, the call

```
strToFloat ("-867.6921");
```

should return the value -867.6921.

13. If c is a lowercase character, the expression

```
c - 'a' + 'A'
```

produces the uppercase equivalent of c, assuming an ASCII character set.

Write a function called uppercase() that converts all lowercase characters in a string into their uppercase equivalents.

14. Write a function called intToStr() that converts an integer value into a character string. Be certain the function handles negative integers properly.

10

Pointers

In this chapter, you examine one of the most sophisticated features of the C programming language: pointers. In fact, the power and flexibility that C provides in dealing with pointers serve to set it apart from many other programming languages. Pointers enable you to effectively represent complex data structures, to change values passed as arguments to functions, to work with memory that has been allocated "dynamically" (see Chapter 16, "Miscellaneous and Advanced Features"), and to more concisely and efficiently deal with arrays.

As you become a more proficient C programmer, you will find yourself using pointers in all aspects of the development process, so this chapter covers a wide range of ways to implement and use pointers including

- Defining simple pointers
- Using pointers in common C expressions
- Implementing pointers to structures, arrays, and functions
- Using pointers to create linked lists
- Applying the `const` keyword to pointers
- Passing pointers as arguments to functions

Again, while this is some of the most challenging topics you will cover in your C programming learning process, once you gain a fundamental understanding of these topics, your programs will gain significant elegance and power.

Pointers and Indirection

To understand the way in which pointers operate, it is first necessary to understand the concept of *indirection*. You are familiar with this concept from your everyday life. For example, suppose you need to buy a new ink cartridge for your printer. In the company that you work for, all purchases are handled by the Purchasing department. So, you call Jim in Purchasing and ask him to order the new cartridge for you. Jim, in turn, calls the local supply store to order the cartridge. This approach to obtain your new cartridge is actually an indirect one because you are not ordering the cartridge directly from the supply store yourself.

This same notion of indirection applies to the way pointers work in C. A pointer provides an indirect means of accessing the value of a particular data item. And just as there are reasons why it makes sense to go through the Purchasing department to order new cartridges (you don't have to know which particular store the cartridges are being ordered from, for example), so are there good reasons why, at times, it makes sense to use pointers in C.

Defining a Pointer Variable

But enough talk—it's time to see how pointers actually work. Suppose you define a variable called count as follows:

```
int   count = 10;
```

You can define another variable, called int_pointer, that can be used to enable you to indirectly access the value of count by the declaration

```
int   *int_pointer;
```

The asterisk defines to the C system that the variable int_pointer is of type *pointer to* int. This means that int_pointer is used in the program to indirectly access the value of one or more integer values.

You have seen how the & operator was used in the scanf() calls of previous programs. This unary operator, known as the *address* operator, is used to make a pointer to an object in C. So, if x is a variable of a particular type, the expression &x is a pointer to that variable. The expression &x can be assigned to any pointer variable, if desired, that has been declared to be a pointer to the same type as x.

Therefore, with the definitions of count and int_pointer as given, you can write a statement such as

```
int_pointer = &count;
```

to set up the indirect reference between int_pointer and count. The address operator has the effect of assigning to the variable int_pointer, not the value of count, but a *pointer* to the variable count. The link that has been made between int_pointer and count is conceptualized in Figure 10.1. The directed line illustrates the idea that int_pointer does not directly contain the value of count, but a pointer to the variable count.

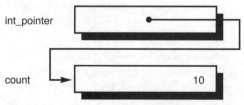

Figure 10.1   Pointer to an integer.

To reference the contents of count through the pointer variable int_pointer, you use the *indirection* operator, which is the asterisk *. So, if x is defined as type int, the statement

```
x = *int_pointer;
```

assigns the value that is indirectly referenced through int_pointer to the variable x. Because int_pointer was previously set pointing to count, this statement has the effect of assigning the value contained in the variable count—which is 10—to the variable x.

The previous statements have been incorporated into Program 10.1, which illustrates the two fundamental pointer operators: the address operator, &, and the indirection operator, *.

Program 10.1   **Illustrating Pointers**

```
#include <stdio.h>

int main (void)
{
    int    count = 10, x;
    int    *int_pointer;

    int_pointer = &count;
    x = *int_pointer;

    printf ("count = %i, x = %i\n", count, x);

    return 0;
}
```

Program 10.1   **Output**

```
count = 10, x = 10
```

The variables count and x are declared to be integer variables in the normal fashion. On the next line, the variable int_pointer is declared to be of type "pointer to int." Note that the two lines of declarations could have been combined into the single line

```
int  count = 10, x, *int_pointer;
```

Next, the address operator is applied to the variable count. This has the effect of creating a pointer to this variable, which is then assigned by the program to the variable int_pointer.

Execution of the next statement in the program,

```
x = *int_pointer;
```

proceeds as follows: The indirection operator tells the C system to treat the variable int_pointer as containing a pointer to another data item. This pointer is then used to access the desired data item, whose type is specified by the declaration of the pointer variable. Because you told the compiler that `int_pointer` points to integers when you declared the variable, the compiler knows that the value referenced by the expression `*int_pointer` is an integer. And because you set `int_pointer` to point to the integer variable `count` in the previous program statement, it is the value of `count` that is indirectly accessed by this expression.

You should realize that Program 10.1 is a manufactured example of the use of pointers and does not show a practical use for them in a program. Such motivation is presented shortly, after you have become familiar with the basic ways in which pointers can be defined and manipulated in a program.

Program 10.2 illustrates some interesting properties of pointer variables. Here, a pointer to a character is used.

Program 10.2   **More Pointer Basics**

```
#include <stdio.h>

int main (void)
{
    char   c = 'Q';
    char   *char_pointer = &c;

    printf ("%c %c\n", c, *char_pointer);

    c = '/';
    printf ("%c %c\n", c, *char_pointer);

    *char_pointer = '(';
    printf ("%c %c\n", c, *char_pointer);

    return 0;
}
```

Program 10.2   **Output**

```
Q Q
/ /
( (
```

The character variable `c` is defined and initialized to the character `'Q'`. In the next line of the program, the variable `char_pointer` is defined to be of type "pointer to `char`," meaning that whatever value is stored inside this variable should be treated as an indirect reference (pointer) to a character. Notice that you can assign an initial value to this variable in the normal fashion. The value that you assign to `char_pointer` in the program is a pointer to the variable `c`, which is obtained by applying the address operator to the variable `c`. (Note that this initialization generates a compiler error if `c` had been defined *after* this statement because a variable must always be declared *before* its value can be referenced in an expression.)

The declaration of the variable `char_pointer` and the assignment of its initial value could have been equivalently expressed in two separate statements as

```
char   *char_pointer;
char_pointer = &c;
```

(and *not* by the statements

```
char   *char_pointer;
*char_pointer = &c;
```

as might be implied from the single-line declaration).

Always remember, that the value of a pointer in C is meaningless until it is set pointing to something.

The first `printf()` call simply displays the contents of the variable `c` and the contents of the variable that is referenced by `char_pointer`. Because you set `char_pointer` to point to the variable `c`, the value that is displayed is the contents of `c`, as verified by the first line of the program's output.

In the next line of the program, the character `'/'` is assigned to the character variable `c`. Because `char_pointer` still points to the variable `c`, displaying the value of `*char_pointer` in the subsequent `printf()` call correctly displays this new value of `c` at the terminal. This is an important concept. Unless the value of `char_pointer` is changed, the expression `*char_pointer` *always* accesses the value of `c`. So, as the value of `c` changes, so does the value of `*char_pointer`.

The previous discussion can help you to understand how the program statement that appears next in the program works. Unless `char_pointer` is changed, the expression `*char_pointer` always references the value of `c`. Therefore, in the expression

```
*char_pointer = '(';
```

you are assigning the left parenthesis character to `c`. More formally, the character `'('` is assigned to the variable that is pointed to by `char_pointer`. You know that this variable is `c` because you placed a pointer to `c` in `char_pointer` at the beginning of the program.

The preceding concepts are the key to your understanding of the operation of pointers. Please review them at this point if they still seem a bit unclear.

Using Pointers in Expressions

In Program 10.3, two integer pointers, `p1` and `p2`, are defined. Notice how the value referenced by a pointer can be used in an arithmetic expression. If `p1` is defined to be of type "pointer to integer," what conclusion do you think can be made about the use of `*p1` in an expression?

Program 10.3 **Using Pointers in Expressions**

```
// More on pointers

#include <stdio.h>

int main (void)
{
    int  i1, i2;
    int  *p1, *p2;

    i1 = 5;
    p1 = &i1;
    i2 = *p1 / 2 + 10;
    p2 = p1;

    printf ("i1 = %i, i2 = %i, *p1 = %i, *p2 = %i\n", i1, i2, *p1, *p2);

    return 0;
}
```

Program 10.3 **Output**

```
i1 = 5, i2 = 12, *p1 = 5, *p2 = 5
```

After defining the integer variables i1 and i2 and the integer pointer variables p1 and p2, the program then assigns the value 5 to i1 and stores a pointer to i1 inside p1. Next, the value of i2 is calculated with the following expression:

```
i2 = *p1 / 2 + 10;
```

As implied from the discussions of Program 10.2, if a pointer px points to a variable x, and px has been defined to be a pointer to the same data type as is x, then use of *px in an expression is, in all respects, identical to the use of x in the same expression.

Because in Program 10.3 the variable p1 is defined to be an integer pointer, the preceding expression is evaluated using the rules of integer arithmetic. And because the value of *p1 is 5 (p1 points to i1), the final result of the evaluation of the preceding expression is 12, which is the value that is assigned to i2. (The pointer reference operator * has higher precedence than the arithmetic operation of division. In fact, this operator, as well as the address operator &, has higher precedence than *all* binary operators in C.)

In the next statement, the value of the pointer p1 is assigned to p2. This assignment is perfectly valid and has the effect of setting p2 to point to the same data item to which p1 points. Because p1 points to i1, after the assignment statement has been executed, p2 *also* points to i1 (and you can have as many pointers to the same item as you want in C).

The printf() call verifies that the values of i1, *p1, and *p2 are all the same (5) and that the value of i2 was set to 12 by the program.

Working with Pointers and Structures

You have seen how a pointer can be defined to point to a basic data type, such as an `int` or a `char`. But pointers can also be defined to point to structures. In Chapter 8, "Working with Structures," you defined your `date` structure as follows:

```
struct date
{
    int  month;
    int  day;
    int  year;
};
```

Just as you defined variables to be of type `struct date`, as in

```
struct date    todaysDate;
```

so can you define a variable to be a pointer to a `struct date` variable:

```
struct date  *datePtr;
```

The variable `datePtr`, as just defined, then can be used in the expected fashion. For example, you can set it to point to `todaysDate` with the assignment statement

```
datePtr = &todaysDate;
```

After such an assignment has been made, you then can indirectly access any of the members of the `date` structure pointed to by `datePtr` in the following way:

```
(*datePtr).day = 21;
```

This statement has the effect of setting the day of the `date` structure pointed to by `datePtr` to 21. The parentheses are required because the structure member operator . has higher precedence than the indirection operator `*`.

To test the value of `month` stored in the `date` structure pointed to by `datePtr`, a statement such as

```
if  ( (*datePtr).month == 12  )
        . . .
```

can be used.

Pointers to structures are so often used in C that a special operator exists in the language. The structure pointer operator `->`, which is the dash followed by the greater than sign, permits expressions that would otherwise be written as

```
(*x).y
```

to be more clearly expressed as

```
x->y
```

So, the previous `if` statement can be conveniently written as

```
if  ( datePtr->month == 12 )
    ...
```

Program 8.1, the first program that illustrated structures, was rewritten using the concept of structure pointers, as shown in Program 10.4.

Program 10.4 **Using Pointers to Structures**

```
//  Program to illustrate structure pointers

#include <stdio.h>

int main (void)
{
    struct date
    {
        int   month;
        int   day;
        int   year;
    };

    struct date  today, *datePtr;

    datePtr = &today;

    datePtr->month = 9;
    datePtr->day = 25;
    datePtr->year = 2015;

    printf ("Today's date is %i/%i/%.2i.\n",
            datePtr->month, datePtr->day, datePtr->year % 100);

    return 0;
}
```

Program 10.4 **Output**

```
Today's date is 9/25/15.
```

Figure 10.2 depicts how the variables `today` and `datePtr` would look after all of the assignment statements from the preceding program have been executed.

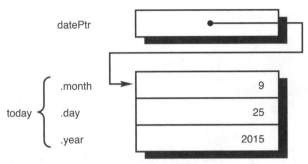

Figure 10.2   Pointer to a structure.

Once again, it should be pointed out that there is no real motivation shown here as to why you should even bother using a structure pointer when it seems as though you can get along just fine without it (as you did in Program 8.1). You will discover the motivation shortly.

Structures Containing Pointers

Naturally, a pointer also can be a member of a structure. In the structure definition

```
struct  intPtrs
{
    int  *p1;
    int  *p2;
};
```

a structure called `intPtrs` is defined to contain two integer pointers, the first one called `p1` and the second one `p2`. You can define a variable of type `struct  intPtrs` in the usual way:

```
struct intPtrs  pointers;
```

The variable `pointers` can now be used in the normal fashion, remembering that `pointers` itself is *not* a pointer, but a structure variable that has two pointers as its members.

Program 10.5 shows how the `intPtrs` structure can be handled in a C program.

Program 10.5   **Using Structures Containing Pointers**

```
// Function to use structures containing pointers

#include <stdio.h>

int main (void)
{
    struct  intPtrs
    {
        int  *p1;
```

```
        int  *p2;
    };

    struct intPtrs  pointers;
    int  i1 = 100, i2;

    pointers.p1 = &i1;
    pointers.p2 = &i2;
    *pointers.p2 = -97;

    printf ("i1 = %i, *pointers.p1 = %i\n", i1, *pointers.p1);
    printf ("i2 = %i, *pointers.p2 = %i\n", i2, *pointers.p2);
    return 0;
}
```

Program 10.5 **Output**

```
i1 = 100, *pointers.p1 = 100
i2 = -97, *pointers.p2 = -97
```

After the variables have been defined, the assignment statement

```
pointers.p1 = &i1;
```

sets the p1 member of pointers pointing to the integer variable i1, whereas the next statement

```
pointers.p2 = &i2;
```

sets the p2 member pointing to i2. Next, -97 is assigned to the variable that is pointed to by pointers.p2. Because you just set this to point to i2, -97 is stored in i2. No parentheses are needed in this assignment statement because, as mentioned previously, the structure member operator . has higher precedence than the indirection operator. Therefore, the pointer is correctly referenced from the structure *before* the indirection operator is applied. Of course, parentheses could have been used just to play it safe, as at times it can be difficult to try to remember which of two operators has higher precedence.

The two printf() calls that follow each other in the preceding program verify that the correct assignments were made.

Figure 10.3 has been provided to help you understand the relationship between the variables i1, i2, and pointers after the assignment statements from Program 10.5 have been executed. As you can see in Figure 10.3, the p1 member points to the variable i1, which contains the value 100, whereas the p2 member points to the variable i2, which contains the value -97.

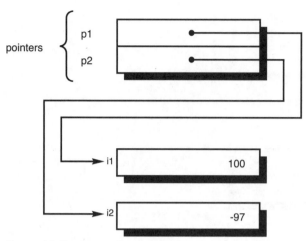

Figure 10.3   Structure containing pointers.

Linked Lists

The concepts of pointers to structures and structures containing pointers are very powerful ones in C, for they enable you to create sophisticated data structures, such as *linked lists*, *doubly linked lists*, and *trees*.

Suppose you define a structure as follows:

```
struct entry
{
    int           value;
    struct entry  *next;
};
```

This defines a structure called `entry`, which contains two members. The first member of the structure is a simple integer called `value`. The second member of the structure is a member called `next`, which is a *pointer to an* `entry` *structure*. Think about this for a moment. Contained inside an `entry` structure is a pointer to another `entry` structure. This is a perfectly valid concept in the C language. Now suppose you define two variables to be of type `struct entry` as follows:

```
struct entry  n1, n2;
```

You set the next pointer of structure `n1` to point to structure `n2` by executing the following statement:

```
n1.next = &n2;
```

This statement effectively makes a link between `n1` and `n2`, as depicted in Figure 10.4.

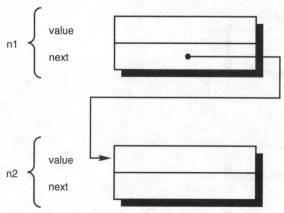

Figure 10.4   Linked structures.

Assuming a variable n3 were also defined to be of type struct entry, you could add another link with the following statement:

```
n2.next = &n3;
```

This resulting chain of linked entries, known more formally as a *linked list*, is illustrated in Figure 10.5. Program 10.6 illustrates this linked list.

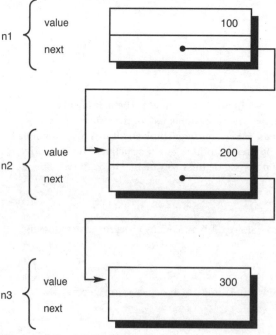

Figure 10.5   A linked list.

Program 10.6   **Using Linked Lists**

```c
// Function to use linked lists

#include <stdio.h>

int main (void)
{
    struct   entry
    {
        int             value;
        struct entry  *next;
    };

    struct entry n1, n2, n3;
    int            i;

    n1.value = 100;
    n2.value = 200;
    n3.value = 300;

    n1.next = &n2;
    n2.next = &n3;

    i = n1.next->value;
    printf ("%i  ", i);

    printf ("%i\n", n2.next->value);

    return 0;
}
```

Program 10.6   **Output**

```
200   300
```

The structures n1, n2, and n3 are defined to be of type struct entry, which consists of an integer member called value and a pointer to an entry structure called next. The program then assigns the values 100, 200, and 300 to the value members of n1, n2, and n3, respectively.

The next two statements in the program

```c
n1.next = &n2;
n2.next = &n3;
```

set up the linked list, with the next member of n1 pointing to n2 and the next member of n2 pointing to n3.

Execution of the statement

```
i = n1.next->value;
```

proceeds as follows: The `value` member of the `entry` structure pointed to by `n1.next` is accessed and assigned to the integer variable `i`. Because you set `n1.next` to point to `n2`, the `value` member of `n2` is accessed by this statement. Therefore, this statement has the net result of assigning 200 to `i`, as verified by the `printf` call that follows in the program. You might want to verify that the expression `n1.next->value` is the correct one to use and not `n1.next.value`, because the `n1.next` field contains a pointer to a structure, and not the structure itself. This distinction is important and can quickly lead to programming errors if it is not fully understood.

The structure member operator `.` and the structure pointer operator `->` have the same precedence in the C language. In expressions such as the preceding one, where both operators are used, the operators are evaluated from left to right. Therefore, the expression is evaluated as

```
i = (n1.next)->value;
```

which is what was intended.

The second `printf()` call in Program 10.6 displays the `value` member that is pointed to by `n2.next`. Because you set `n2.next` to point to `n3`, the contents of `n3.value` are displayed by the program.

As mentioned, the concept of a linked list is a very powerful one in programming. Linked lists greatly simplify operations such as the insertion and removal of elements from large lists of sorted items.

For example, if `n1`, `n2`, and `n3` are as defined previously, you can easily remove `n2` from the list simply by setting the `next` field of `n1` to point to whatever `n2` is pointing to:

```
n1.next = n2.next;
```

This statement has the effect of copying the pointer contained in `n2.next` into `n1.next`, and, because `n2.next` was set to point to `n3`, `n1.next` is now pointing to `n3`. Furthermore, because `n1` no longer points to `n2`, you have effectively removed it from your list. Figure 10.6 depicts this situation after the preceding statement is executed. Of course, you could have set `n1` pointing to `n3` directly with the statement

```
n1.next = &n3;
```

but this latter statement is not as general because you must know in advance that `n2` is pointing to `n3`.

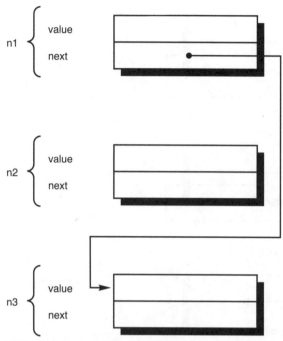

Figure 10.6   Removing an entry from a linked list.

Inserting an element into a list is just as straightforward. If you want to insert a `struct entry` called n2_3 after n2 in the list, you can simply set `n2_3.next` to point to whatever `n2.next` was pointing to, and then set `n2.next` to point to n2_3. So, the sequence of statements

```
n2_3.next = n2.next;
n2.next = &n2_3;
```

inserts n2_3 into the list, immediately after entry n2. Note that the sequence of the preceding statements is important because executing the second statement first overwrites the pointer stored in `n2.next` before it has a chance to be assigned to `n2_3.next`. The inserted element n2_3 is depicted in Figure 10.7. Notice that n2_3 is not shown between n1 and n3. This is to emphasize that n2_3 can be anywhere in memory and does not have to physically occur after n1 and before n3. This is one of the main motivations for the use of a linked list approach for storing information: Entries of the list do not have to be stored sequentially in memory, as is the case with elements in an array.

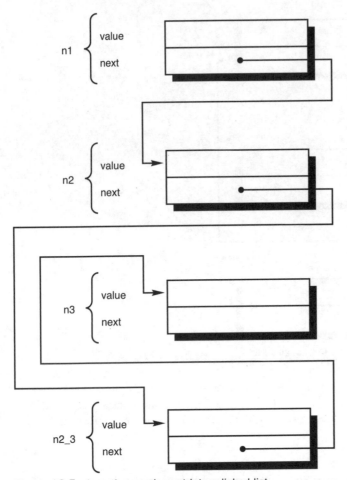

Figure 10.7   Inserting an element into a linked list.

Before developing some functions to work with linked lists, two more issues must be discussed. Usually associated with a linked list is at least one pointer to the list. Often, a pointer to the start of the list is kept. So, for your original three-element list, which consisted of n1, n2, and n3, you can define a variable called list_pointer and set it to point to the beginning of the list with the statement

```
struct entry *list_pointer = &n1;
```

assuming that n1 has been previously defined. A pointer to a list is useful for sequencing through the entries in the list, as you see shortly.

The second issue to be discussed involves the idea of having some way to identify the end of the list. This is needed so that a procedure that searches through the list, for example, can tell when it has reached the final element in the list. By convention, a constant value of 0 is used for such a purpose and is known as the *null* pointer. You can use the null pointer to mark the end of a list by storing this value in the pointer field of the last entry of the list.[1]

In your three-entry list, you can mark its end by storing the null pointer in n3.next:

```
n3.next = (struct entry *) 0;
```

You see in Chapter 12, "The Preprocessor," how this assignment statement can be made a bit more readable.

The type cast operator is used to cast the constant 0 to the appropriate type ("pointer to struct entry"). It's not required, but makes the statement more readable.

Figure 10.8 depicts the linked list from Program 10.6, with a struct entry pointer called list_pointer pointing to the start of the list and the n3.next field set to the null pointer.

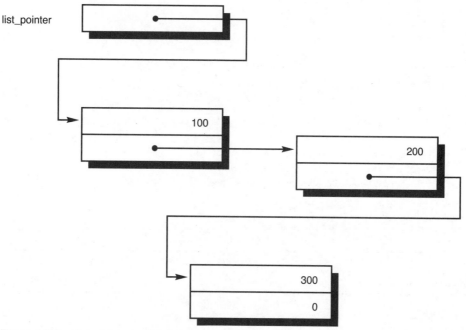

Figure 10.8   Linked list showing list pointer and terminating null.

Program 10.7 incorporates the concepts just described. The program uses a while loop to sequence through the list and display the value member of each entry in the list.

---

1. *A null pointer is not necessarily internally represented as the value 0. However, the compiler must recognize assignment of the constant 0 to a pointer as assigning the null pointer. This also applies to comparing a pointer against the constant 0: The compiler interprets it as a test to see if the pointer is null.*

Program 10.7   Traversing a Linked List

```c
// Program to traverse a linked list

#include <stdio.h>

int main (void)
{
    struct entry
    {
        int             value;
        struct entry    *next;
    };

    struct entry    n1, n2, n3;
    struct entry    *list_pointer = &n1;

    n1.value = 100;
    n1.next  = &n2;

    n2.value = 200;
    n2.next  = &n3;

    n3.value = 300;
    n3.next  = (struct entry *) 0;    // Mark list end with null pointer

    while ( list_pointer != (struct entry *) 0 ) {
        printf ("%i\n", list_pointer->value);
        list_pointer = list_pointer->next;
    }

    return 0;
}
```

Program 10.7   Output

```
100
200
300
```

The program defines the variables n1, n2, and n3 and the pointer variable list_pointer, which is initially set to point to n1, the first entry in the list. The next program statements link together the three elements of the list, with the next member of n3 set to the null pointer to mark the end of the list.

A while loop is then set up to sequence through each element of the list. This loop is executed as long as the value of list_pointer is not equal to the null pointer. The printf() call inside the while loop displays the value member of the entry currently pointed to by list_pointer.

The statement that follows the `printf()` call,

```
list_pointer = list_pointer->next;
```

has the effect of taking the pointer from the `next` member of the structure pointed to by `list_pointer` and assigning it to `list_pointer`. So, the first time through the loop, this statement takes the pointer contained in `n1.next` (remember, `list_pointer` was initially set pointing to `n1`) and assigns it to `list_pointer`. Because this value is not null—it's a pointer to the `entry` structure `n2`—the `while` loop is repeated.

The second time through, the `while` loop results in the display of `n2.value`, which is `200`. The `next` member of `n2` is then copied into `list_pointer`, and because you set this value to point to `n3`, `list_pointer` points to `n3` by the end of the second pass through the loop.

When the `while` loop is executed the third time, the `printf` call displays the value of `300` as contained in `n3.value`. At that point, `list_pointer->next` (which is actually `n3.next`) is copied into `list_pointer`, and, because you set this member to the null pointer, the `while` loop terminates after it has been executed three times.

Trace through the operation of the `while` loop just discussed, using a pencil and paper, if necessary, to keep track of the values of the various variables. Understanding the operation of this loop is the key to your understanding the operation of pointers in C. Incidentally, it should be noted that this same `while` loop can be used to sequence through the elements of a list of *any* size, provided the end of the list is marked by the null pointer.

When working with actual linked lists in a program, you will not normally link together list entries that have been explicitly defined like in the program examples in this section. You did that here just to illustrate the mechanics of working with a linked list. In actual practice, you will typically ask the system to give you memory for each new list entry and you will link it into the list while the program is executing. This is done with a mechanism known as *dynamic memory allocation*, and is covered in Chapter 16.

The Keyword `const` and Pointers

You have seen how a variable or an array can be declared as `const` to alert the compiler as well as the reader that the contents of a variable or an array will not be changed by the program. With pointers, there are two things to consider: whether the pointer will be changed, and whether the value that the pointer points to will be changed. Think about that for a second. Assume the following declarations:

```
char c = 'X';
char *charPtr = &c;
```

The pointer variable `charPtr` is set pointing to the variable `c`. If the pointer variable is always set pointing to `c`, it can be declared as a `const` pointer as follows:

```
char * const charPtr = &c;
```

(Read this as "charPtr is a constant pointer to a character.") So, a statement like this:

```
charPtr = &d;    // not valid
```

causes the GNU C compiler to give a message like this:[2]

```
foo.c:10: warning: assignment of read-only variable 'charPtr'
```

Now if, instead, the location pointed to by charPtr will not change *through the pointer variable charPtr*, that can be noted with a declaration as follows:

```
const char *charPtr = &c;
```

(Read this as "charPtr points to a constant character.") Now of course, that doesn't mean that the value cannot be changed by the variable c, which is what charPtr is set pointing to. It means, however, that it won't be changed with a subsequent statement like this:

```
*charPtr = 'Y';    // not valid
```

which causes the GNU C compiler to issue a message like this:

```
foo.c:11: warning: assignment of read-only location
```

In the case in which both the pointer variable and the location it points to will not be changed through the pointer, the following declaration can be used:

```
const char * const *charPtr = &c;
```

The first use of const says the contents of the location the pointer references will not be changed. The second use says that the pointer itself will not be changed. Admittedly, this looks a little confusing, but it's worth noting at this point in the text.[3]

Pointers and Functions

Pointers and functions get along quite well together. That is, you can pass a pointer as an argument to a function in the normal fashion, and you can also have a function return a pointer as its result.

The first case cited previously, passing pointer arguments, is straightforward enough: The pointer is simply included in the list of arguments to the function in the normal fashion. So, to pass the pointer list_pointer from the previous program to a function called print_list(), you can write

```
print_list (list_pointer);
```

---

2. *Your compiler may give a different warning message, or no message at all.*

3. *The keyword* const *is not used in every program example where it can be employed; only in selected examples. Until you are familiar with reading expressions such as previously shown, it can make understanding the examples more difficult.*

Inside the print_list() routine, the formal parameter must be declared to be a pointer to the appropriate type:

```
void print_list  (struct entry  *pointer)
{
    ...
}
```

The formal parameter pointer can then be used in the same way as a normal pointer variable. One thing worth remembering when dealing with pointers that are sent to functions as arguments: The value of the pointer is copied into the formal parameter when the function is called. Therefore, any change made to the formal parameter by the function does *not* affect the pointer that was passed to the function. But here's the catch: Although the pointer cannot be changed by the function, the data elements that the pointer references *can* be changed! Program 10.8 helps clarify this point.

Program 10.8   **Using Pointers and Functions**

```
// Program to illustrate using pointers and functions

#include <stdio.h>

void test (int  *int_pointer)
{
    *int_pointer = 100;
}

int main (void)
{
    void test (int  *int_pointer);
    int  i = 50, *p = &i;

    printf ("Before the call to test i = %i\n", i);

    test (p);
    printf ("After the call to test i = %i\n", i);

    return 0;
}
```

Program 10.8   **Output**

```
Before the call to test i = 50
After the call to test i = 100
```

The function test() is defined to take as its argument a pointer to an integer. Inside the function, a single statement is executed to set the integer pointed to by int_pointer to the value 100.

The main() routine defines an integer variable i with an initial value of 50 and a pointer to an integer called p that is set to point to i. The program then displays the value of i and calls the test() function, passing the pointer p as the argument. As you can see from the second line of the program's output, the test() function did, in fact, change the value of i to 100.

Now consider Program 10.9.

Program 10.9   Using Pointers to Exchange Values

```
// More on pointers and functions

#include <stdio.h>

void  exchange (int * const pint1, int * const pint2)
{
    int   temp;

    temp = *pint1;
    *pint1 = *pint2;
    *pint2 = temp;
}

int main (void)
{
    void  exchange (int * const pint1, int * const pint2);
    int   i1 = -5, i2 = 66, *p1 = &i1, *p2 = &i2;

    printf ("i1 = %i, i2 = %i\n", i1, i2);

    exchange (p1, p2);
    printf ("i1 = %i, i2 = %i\n", i1, i2);

    exchange (&i1, &i2);
    printf ("i1 = %i, i2 = %i\n", i1, i2);

    return 0;
}
```

Program 10.9   Output

```
i1 = -5, i2 = 66
i1 = 66, i2 = -5
i1 = -5, i2 = 66
```

The purpose of the exchange() function is to interchange the two integer values pointed to by its two arguments. The function header

```
void  exchange (int * const pint1, int * const pint2)
```

says that the exchange () function takes two integer pointers as arguments, and that the pointers will not be changed by the function (the use of the keyword const).

The local integer variable temp is used to hold one of the integer values while the exchange is made. Its value is set equal to the integer that is pointed to by pint1. The integer pointed to by pint2 is then copied into the integer pointed to by pint1, and the value of temp is then stored in the integer pointed to by pint2, thus making the exchange complete.

The main () routine defines integers i1 and i2 with values of -5 and 66, respectively. Two integer pointers, p1 and p2, are then defined and are set to point to i1 and i2, respectively. The program then displays the values of i1 and i2 and calls the exchange () function, passing the two pointers, p1 and p2, as arguments. The exchange () function exchanges the value contained in the integer pointed to by p1 with the value contained in the integer pointed to by p2. Because p1 points to i1, and p2 to i2, the values of i1 and i2 end up getting exchanged by the function. The output from the second printf () call verifies that the exchange worked properly.

The second call to exchange () is a bit more interesting. This time, the arguments that are passed to the function are pointers to i1 and i2 that are manufactured right on the spot by applying the address operator to these two variables. Because the expression &i1 produces a pointer to the integer variable i1, this is right in line with the type of argument that your function expects for the first argument (a pointer to an integer). The same applies for the second argument as well. And as can be seen from the program's output, the exchange () function did its job and switched the values of i1 and i2 back to their original values.

You should realize that without the use of pointers, you could not have written your exchange () function to exchange the value of two integers because you are limited to returning only a single value from a function and because a function cannot permanently change the value of its arguments. Study Program 10.9 in detail. It illustrates with a small example the key concepts to be understood when dealing with pointers in C.

Program 10.10 shows how a function can return a pointer. The program defines a function called findEntry () whose purpose is to search through a linked list to find a specified value. When the specified value is found, the program returns a pointer to the entry in the list. If the desired value is not found, the program returns the null pointer.

Program 10.10 Returning a Pointer from a Function

```
#include <stdio.h>

struct entry
{
    int   value;
    struct entry   *next;
};

struct entry  *findEntry (struct entry  *listPtr, int match)
```

```
{
    while ( listPtr != (struct entry *) 0 )
        if ( listPtr->value == match )
            return (listPtr);
        else
            listPtr = listPtr->next;

    return (struct entry *) 0;
}

int main (void)
{
    struct entry  *findEntry (struct entry  *listPtr, int match);
    struct entry  n1, n2, n3;
    struct entry  *listPtr, *listStart = &n1;

    int search;

    n1.value = 100;
    n1.next =  &n2;

    n2.value = 200;
    n2.next =  &n3;

    n3.value = 300;
    n3.next =  0;

    printf ("Enter value to locate: ");
    scanf ("%i", &search);

    listPtr = findEntry (listStart, search);

    if ( listPtr != (struct entry *) 0 )
        printf ("Found %i.\n", listPtr->value);
    else
        printf ("Not found.\n");

    return 0;
}
```

Program 10.10   **Output**

```
Enter value to locate: 200
Found 200.
```

Program 10.10   **Output (Rerun)**

```
Enter value to locate: 400
Not found.
```

Program 10.10   **Output (Second Rerun)**

```
Enter value to locate: 300
Found 300.
```

The function header

```
struct entry  *findEntry (struct entry  *listPtr, int match)
```

specifies that the function `findEntry()` returns a pointer to an `entry` structure and that it takes such a pointer as its first argument and an integer as its second. The function begins by entering a `while` loop to sequence through the elements of the list. This loop is executed until either `match` is found equal to one of the `value` entries in the list (in which case the value of `listPtr` is immediately returned) or until the null pointer is reached (in which case the `while` loop is exited and a null pointer is returned).

After setting up the list as in previous programs, the `main()` routine asks the user for a value to locate in the list and then calls the `findEntry()` function with a pointer to the start of the list (`listStart`) and the value entered by the user (`search`) as arguments. The pointer that is returned by `findEntry()` is assigned to the `struct entry` pointer variable `listPtr`. If `listPtr` is not null, the `value` member pointed to by `listPtr` is displayed. This should be the same as the value entered by the user. If `listPtr` is null, then a "Not found." message is displayed.

The program's output verifies that the values 200 and 300 were correctly located in the list, and the value 400 was not found because it did not, in fact, exist in the list.

The pointer that is returned by the `findEntry()` function in the program does not seem to serve any useful purpose. However, in more practical situations, this pointer might be used to access other elements contained in the particular entry of the list. For example, you could have a linked list of your dictionary entries from Chapter 9, "Character Strings." Then, you could call the `findEntry()` function (or rename it `lookup()` as it was called in that chapter) to search the linked list of dictionary entries for the given word. The pointer returned by the `lookup()` function could then be used to access the `definition` member of the entry.

Organizing the dictionary as a linked list has several advantages. Inserting a new word into the dictionary is easy: After determining where in the list the new entry is to be inserted, it can be done by simply adjusting some pointers, as illustrated earlier in this chapter. Removing an entry from the dictionary is also simple. Finally, as you learn in Chapter 16, this approach also provides the framework that enables you to dynamically expand the size of the dictionary.

However, the linked list approach for the organization of the dictionary does suffer from one major drawback: You cannot apply your fast binary search algorithm to such a list. This algorithm only works with an array of elements that can be directly indexed. Unfortunately, there is no faster way to search your linked list other than by a straight, sequential search because each entry in the list can only be accessed from the previous one.

One way to glean the benefits of easy insertion and removal of elements, as well as fast search time, is by using a different type of data structure known as a *tree*. Other approaches, such as using *hash tables*, are also feasible. The reader is respectfully referred elsewhere—such as to *The Art of Computer Programming, Volume 3, Sorting and Searching* (Donald E. Knuth, Addison-Wesley)—for discussion of these types of data structures, which can be easily implemented in C with the techniques already described.

Pointers and Arrays

One of the most common uses of pointers in C is as pointers to arrays. The main reasons for using pointers to arrays are ones of notational convenience and of program efficiency. Pointers to arrays generally result in code that uses less memory and executes faster. The reason for this will become apparent through our discussions in this section.

If you have an array of 100 integers called `values`, you can define a pointer called `valuesPtr`, which can be used to access the integers contained in this array with the statement

```
int   *valuesPtr;
```

When you define a pointer that is used to point to the elements of an array, you don't designate the pointer as type "pointer to array"; rather, you designate the pointer as pointing to the type of element that is contained in the array.

If you have an array of characters called `text`, you could similarly define a pointer to be used to point to elements in `text` with the statement

```
char   *textPtr;
```

To set `valuesPtr` to point to the first element in the `values` array, you simply write

```
valuesPtr = values;
```

The address operator is not used in this case because the C compiler treats the appearance of an array name without a subscript as a pointer to the array. Therefore, simply specifying `values` without a subscript has the effect of producing a pointer to the first element of `values` (see Figure 10.9).

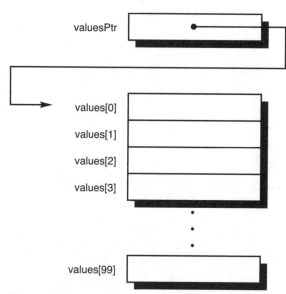

Figure 10.9   Pointer to an array element.

An equivalent way of producing a pointer to the start of `values` is to apply the address operator to the first element of the array. Thus, the statement

```
valuesPtr = &values[0];
```

can be used to serve the same purpose as placing a pointer to the first element of `values` in the pointer variable `valuesPtr`.

To set `textPtr` to point to the first character inside the `text` array, either the statement

```
textPtr = text;
```

or

```
textPtr = &text[0];
```

can be used. Whichever statement you choose to use is strictly a matter of taste.

The real power of using pointers to arrays comes into play when you want to sequence through the elements of an array. If `valuesPtr` is as previously defined and is set pointing to the first element of `values`, the expression

```
*valuesPtr
```

can be used to access the first integer of the `values` array, that is, `values[0]`. To reference `values[3]` through the `valuesPtr` variable, you can add 3 to `valuesPtr` and then apply the indirection operator:

```
*(valuesPtr + 3)
```

In general, the expression

```
*(valuesPtr + i)
```

can be used to access the value contained in `values[i]`.

So, to set `values[10]` to 27, you could obviously write the expression

```
values[10] = 27;
```

or, using `valuesPtr`, you could write

```
*(valuesPtr + 10) = 27;
```

To set `valuesPtr` to point to the second element of the `values` array, you can apply the address operator to `values[1]` and assign the result to `valuesPtr`:

```
valuesPtr = &values[1];
```

If `valuesPtr` points to `values[0]`, you can set it to point to `values[1]` by simply adding 1 to the value of `valuesPtr`:

```
valuesPtr += 1;
```

This is a perfectly valid expression in C and can be used for pointers to *any* data type.

So, in general, if a is an array of elements of type x, px is of type "pointer to x," and i and n are integer constants or variables, the statement

```
px = a;
```

sets px to point to the first element of a, and the expression

```
*(px + i)
```

subsequently references the value contained in `a[i]`. Furthermore, the statement

```
px += n;
```

sets px to point n elements farther in the array, *no matter what type of element is contained in the array.*

The increment and decrement operators `++` and `--` are particularly handy when dealing with pointers. Applying the increment operator to a pointer has the same effect as adding one to the pointer, while applying the decrement operator has the same effect as subtracting one from the pointer. So, if `textPtr` is defined as a `char` pointer and is set pointing to the beginning of an array of `chars` called `text`, the statement

```
++textPtr;
```

sets `textPtr` pointing to the next character in `text`, which is `text[1]`. In a similar fashion, the statement

```
--textPtr;
```

sets textPtr pointing to the previous character in text, assuming, of course, that textPtr was not pointing to the beginning of text prior to the execution of this statement.

It is perfectly valid to compare two pointer variables in C. This is particularly useful when comparing two pointers in the same array. For example, you can test the pointer valuesPtr to see if it points past the end of an array containing 100 elements by comparing it to a pointer to the last element in the array. So, the expression

```
valuesPtr > &values[99]
```

is TRUE (nonzero) if valuesPtr is pointing past the last element in the values array, and is FALSE (zero) otherwise. Recall from previous discussions that you can replace the preceding expression with its equivalent

```
valuesPtr > values + 99
```

because values used without a subscript is a pointer to the beginning of the values array. (Remember, it's the same as writing &values[0].)

Program 10.11 illustrates pointers to arrays. The arraySum function calculates the sum of the elements contained in an array of integers.

Program 10.11   **Working with Pointers to Arrays**

```c
// Function to sum the elements of an integer array

#include <stdio.h>

int  arraySum (int  array[], const int  n)
{
    int   sum = 0, *ptr;
    int  * const arrayEnd = array + n;

    for ( ptr = array;  ptr < arrayEnd;  ++ptr )
        sum += *ptr;

    return sum;
}


int main (void)
{
    int  arraySum (int  array[], const int  n);
    int  values[10] = { 3, 7, -9, 3, 6, -1, 7, 9, 1, -5 };

    printf ("The sum is %i\n", arraySum (values, 10));

    return 0;
}
```

Program 10.11   **Output**

The sum is 21

Inside the `arraySum()` function, the constant integer pointer `arrayEnd` is defined and set pointing immediately after the last element of `array`. A `for` loop is then set up to sequence through the elements of `array`. The value of `ptr` is set to point to the beginning of `array` when the loop is entered. Each time through the loop, the element of `array` pointed to by `ptr` is added into `sum`. The value of `ptr` is then incremented by the `for` loop to set it pointing to the next element in `array`. When `ptr` points past the end of `array`, the `for` loop is exited, and the value of `sum` is returned to the calling routine.

A Slight Digression About Program Optimization

It is pointed out that the local variable `arrayEnd` was not actually needed by the function because you could have explicitly compared the value of `ptr` to the end of the array inside the `for` loop:

```
for ( ...; pointer <= array + n; ... )
```

The sole motivation for using `arrayEnd` was one of optimization. Each time through the `for` loop, the looping conditions are evaluated. Because the expression `array + n` is never changed from within the loop, its value is constant throughout the execution of the `for` loop. By evaluating it once *before* the loop is entered, you save the time that would otherwise be spent reevaluating this expression each time through the loop. Although there is virtually no savings in time for a 10-element array, especially if the `arraySum()` function is called only once by the program, there could be a more substantial savings if this function were heavily used by a program for summing large-sized arrays, for example.

The other issue to be discussed about program optimization concerns the very use of pointers themselves in a program. In the `arraySum()` function discussed earlier, the expression `*ptr` is used inside the `for` loop to access the elements in the array. Formerly, you would have written your `arraySum()` function with a `for` loop that used an index variable, such as `i`, and then would have added the value of `array[i]` into `sum` inside the loop. In general, the process of indexing an array takes more time to execute than does the process of accessing the contents of a pointer. In fact, this is one of the main reasons why pointers are used to access the elements of an array—the code that is generated is generally more efficient. Of course, if access to the array is not generally sequential, pointers accomplish nothing, as far as this issue is concerned, because the expression `*(pointer + j)` takes just as long to execute as does the expression `array[j]`.

Is It an Array or Is It a Pointer?

Recall that to pass an array to a function, you simply specify the name of the array, as you did previously with the call to the `arraySum()` function. You should also remember that to produce a pointer to an array, you need only specify the name of the array. This implies that in the call to the `arraySum()` function, what was passed to the function was actually a *pointer* to the array `values`. This is precisely the case and explains why you are able to change the elements of an array from within a function.

But if it is indeed the case that a pointer to the array is passed to the function, then you might wonder why the formal parameter inside the function isn't declared to be a pointer. In other words, in the declaration of `array` in the `arraySum` function, why isn't the declaration

```
int  *array;
```

used? Shouldn't all references to an array from within a function be made using pointer variables?

To answer these questions, recall the previous discussion about pointers and arrays. As mentioned, if `valuesPtr` points to the same type of element as contained in an array called `values`, the expression `*(valuesPtr + i)` is in all ways equivalent to the expression `values[i]`, assuming that `valuesPtr` has been set to point to the beginning of `values`. What follows from this is that you also can use the expression `*(values + i)` to reference the ith element of the array `values`, and, in general, if `x` is an array of any type, the expression `x[i]` can always be equivalently expressed in C as `*(x + i)`.

As you can see, pointers and arrays are intimately related in C, and this is why you can declare `array` to be of type "array of ints" inside the `arraySum` function *or* to be of type "pointer to int." Either declaration works just fine in the preceding program—try it and see.

If you are going to be using index numbers to reference the elements of an array that is passed to a function, declare the corresponding formal parameter to be an array. This more correctly reflects the use of the array by the function. Similarly, if you are using the argument as a pointer to the array, declare it to be of type pointer.

Realizing now that you could have declared `array` to be an `int` pointer in the preceding program example, and then could have subsequently used it as such, you can eliminate the variable `ptr` from the function and use `array` instead, as shown in Program 10.12.

Program 10.12 Summing the Elements of an Array

```
// Function to sum the elements of an integer array  Ver. 2

#include <stdio.h>

int  arraySum (int  *array, const int  n)
{
    int  sum = 0;
    int  * const arrayEnd = array + n;

    for (  ; array < arrayEnd;  ++array )
        sum += *array;
```

```
    return sum;
}



int main (void)
{
    int  arraySum (int  *array, const int  n);
    int  values[10] = { 3,  7,  -9,  3,  6,  -1,  7,  9,  1,  -5 };

    printf ("The sum is %i\n", arraySum (values, 10));

    return 0;
}
```

Program 10.12   **Output**

The sum is 21

The program is fairly self-explanatory. The first expression inside the for loop was omitted because no value had to be initialized before the loop was started. One point worth repeating is that when the arraySum() function is called, a pointer to the values array is passed, where it is called array inside the function. Changes to the value of array (as opposed to the values referenced by array) do not in any way affect the contents of the values array. So, the increment operator that is applied to array is just incrementing a pointer to the array values, and not affecting its contents. (Of course, you know that you *can* change values in the array if you want to, simply by assigning values to the elements referenced by the pointer.)

Pointers to Character Strings

One of the most common applications of using a pointer to an array is as a pointer to a character string. The reasons are ones of notational convenience and efficiency. To show how easily pointers to character strings can be used, write a function called copyString() to copy one string into another. If you write this function using normal array indexing methods, the function might be coded as follows:

```
void copyString (char  to[], char  from[])
{
    int  i;

    for ( i = 0;  from[i] != '\0';  ++i )
        to[i] = from[i];

    to[i] = '\0';
}
```

The for loop is exited before the null character is copied into the to array, thus explaining the need for the last statement in the function.

If you write copyString() using pointers, you no longer need the index variable i. A pointer version is shown in Program 10.13.

Program 10.13   **Pointer Version of** copyString()

```
#include <stdio.h>

void copyString (char  *to, char  *from)
{
    for (  ;  *from != '\0';   ++from, ++to )
        *to = *from;

    *to = '\0';
}

int main (void)
{
    void  copyString (char  *to, char  *from);
    char  string1[] = "A string to be copied.";
    char  string2[50];

    copyString (string2, string1);
    printf ("%s\n", string2);

    copyString (string2, "So is this.");
    printf ("%s\n", string2);

    return 0;
}
```

Program 10.13   **Output**

```
A string to be copied.
So is this.
```

The copyString() function defines the two formal parameters to and from as character pointers and not as character arrays as was done in the previous version of copyString(). This reflects how these two variables are used by the function.

A for loop is then entered (with no initial conditions) to copy the string pointed to by from into the string pointed to by to. Each time through the loop, the from and to pointers are each incremented by one. This sets the from pointer pointing to the next character that is to be copied from the source string and sets the to pointer pointing to the location in the destination string where the next character is to be stored.

When the `from` pointer points to the null character, the `for` loop is exited. The function then places the null character at the end of the destination string.

In the `main()` routine, the `copyString()` function is called twice, the first time to copy the contents of `string1` into `string2`, and the second time to copy the contents of the constant character string `"So is this."` into `string2`.

Constant Character Strings and Pointers

The fact that the call

```
copyString (string2, "So is this.");
```

works in the previous program implies that when a constant character string is passed as an argument to a function, what is actually passed is a pointer to that character string. Not only is this true in this case, but it also can be generalized by saying that *whenever* a constant character string is used in C, it is a pointer to that character string that is produced. So, if `textPtr` is declared to be a character pointer, as in

```
char   *textPtr;
```

then the statement

```
textPtr = "A character string.";
```

assigns to `textPtr` a *pointer* to the constant character string `"A character string."` Be careful to make the distinction here between character pointers and character arrays, as the type of assignment just shown is *not* valid with a character array. So, for example, if `text` is defined instead to be an array of `chars`, with a statement such as

```
char   text[80];
```

then you *could not* write a statement such as

```
text = "This is not valid.";
```

The *only* time that C lets you get away with performing this type of assignment to a character array is when initializing it, as in

```
char   text[80] =  "This is okay.";
```

Initializing the `text` array in this manner does not have the effect of storing a pointer to the character string `"This is okay."` inside `text`, but rather the actual characters themselves inside corresponding elements of the `text` array.

If `text` is a character pointer, initializing `text` with the statement

```
char   *text =  "This is okay.";
```

assigns to it a pointer to the character string `"This is okay."`

As another example of the distinction between character strings and character string pointers, the following sets up an array called days, which contains *pointers* to the names of the days of the week.

```
char *days[] =
    { "Sunday", "Monday", "Tuesday", "Wednesday", "Thursday", "Friday", "Saturday" };
```

The array days is defined to contain seven entries, each a pointer to a character string. So days[0] contains a pointer to the character string "Sunday", days[1] contains a pointer to the string "Monday", and so on (see Figure 10.10). You could display the name of the third weekday, for example, with the following statement:

```
printf ("%s\n", days[3]);
```

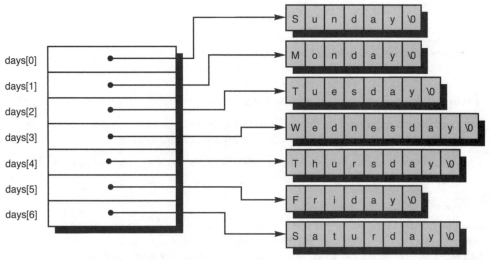

Figure 10.10   Array of pointers.

The Increment and Decrement Operators Revisited

Up to this point, whenever you used the increment or decrement operator, it was the only operator that appeared in the expression. When you write the expression ++x, you know that this has the effect of adding 1 to the value of the variable x. And as you have just seen, if x is a pointer to an array, this has the effect of setting x to point to the next element of the array.

The increment and decrement operators can be used in expressions in which other operators also appear. In such cases, it becomes important to know more precisely how these operators work.

So far, when you used the increment and decrement operators, you always placed them *before* the variables that were being incremented or decremented. So, to increment a variable i, you simply wrote

```
++i;
```

Actually, it also is perfectly valid to place the increment operator *after* the variable, as follows:

```
i++;
```

Both expressions are perfectly valid and both achieve the same result—namely, of incrementing the value of i. In the first case, where the ++ is placed before its operand, the increment operation is more precisely identified as a *preincrement*. In the second case, where the ++ is placed after its operand, the operation is identified as a *postincrement*.

The same discussion applies to the decrement operator. So the statement

```
--i;
```

technically performs a *predecrement* of i, whereas the statement

```
i--;
```

performs a *postdecrement* of i. Both have the same net result of subtracting 1 from the value of i.

It is when the increment and decrement operators are used in more complex expressions that the distinction between the *pre-* and *post-* nature of these operators is realized.

Suppose you have two integers called i and j. If you set the value of i to 0 and then write the statement

```
j = ++i;
```

the value that gets assigned to j is 1, and not 0 as you might expect. In the case of the preincrement operator, the variable is incremented *before* its value is used in the expression. So, in the preceding expression, the value of i is first incremented from 0 to 1 and then its value is assigned to j, as if the following two statements had been written instead:

```
++i;
j = i;
```

If you instead use the postincrement operator in the statement

```
j = i++;
```

then i is incremented *after* its value has been assigned to j. So, if i is 0 before the preceding statement is executed, 0 is assigned to j and *then* i is incremented by 1, as if the statements

```
j = i;
++i;
```

were used instead. As another example, if i is equal to 1, then the statement

```
x = a[--i];
```

has the effect of assigning the value of a[0] to x because the variable i is decremented before its value is used to index into a. The statement

```
x = a[i--];
```

used instead has the effect of assigning the value of a[1] to x because i is decremented after its value has been used to index into a.

As a third example of the distinction between the pre- and post- increment and decrement operators, the function call

```
printf ("%i\n", ++i);
```

increments i and then sends its value to the printf() function, whereas the call

```
printf ("%i\n", i++);
```

increments i after its value has been sent to the function. So, if i is equal to 100, the first printf() call displays 101, whereas the second printf() call displays 100. In either case, the value of i is equal to 101 after the statement has executed.

As a final example on this topic before presenting Program 10.14, if textPtr is a character pointer, the expression

```
*(++textPtr)
```

first increments textPtr and then fetches the character it points to, whereas the expression

```
*(textPtr++)
```

fetches the character pointed to by textPtr before its value is incremented. In either case, the parentheses are not required because the * and ++ operators have equal precedence but associate from right to left.

Now go back to the copyString() function from Program 10.13 and rewrite it to incorporate the increment operations directly into the assignment statement.

Because the to and from pointers are incremented each time after the assignment statement inside the for loop is executed, they should be incorporated into the assignment statement as post-increment operations. The revised for loop of Program 10.13 then becomes

```
for (  ;  *from != '\0';  )
    *to++ = *from++;
```

Execution of the assignment statement inside the loop proceeds as follows. The character pointed to by from is retrieved and then from is incremented to point to the next character in the source string. The referenced character is then stored inside the location pointed to by to, and then to is incremented to point to the next location in the destination string.

Study the preceding assignment statement until you fully understand its operation. Statements of this type are so commonly used in C programs, it's important that you understand it completely before continuing.

The preceding for statement hardly seems worthwhile because it has no initial expression and
no looping expression. In fact, the logic would be better served when expressed in the form of
a while loop. This has been done in Program 10.14. This program presents your new version
of the copyString() function. The while loop uses the fact that the null character is equal to
the value 0, as is commonly done by experienced C programmers.

Program 10.14 Revised Version of the copyString() Function

```
// Function to copy one string to another. Pointer Ver. 2

#include <stdio.h>

void  copyString (char  *to, char  *from)
{
    while ( *from )
        *to++ = *from++;

    *to = '\0';
}



int main (void)
{
    void  copyString (char  *to, char  *from);
    char  string1[] = "A string to be copied.";
    char  string2[50];

    copyString (string2, string1);
    printf ("%s\n", string2);

    copyString (string2, "So is this.");
    printf ("%s\n", string2);

    return 0;
}
```

Program 10.14 Output

```
A string to be copied.
So is this.
```

Operations on Pointers

As you have seen in this chapter, you can add or subtract integer values from pointers. Furthermore, you can compare two pointers to see if they are equal or not, or if one pointer is less than or greater than another pointer. The only other operation that is permitted on pointers is the subtraction of two pointers of the same type. The result of subtracting two pointers in C is the number of elements contained between the two pointers. So, if a points to an array of elements of any type and b points to another element somewhere farther along in the same array, the expression b – a represents the number of elements between these two pointers. For example, if p points to some element in an array x, the statement

```
n = p - x;
```

has the effect of assigning to the variable n (assumed here to be an integer variable) the index number of the element inside x to which p points.[4] Therefore, if p is set pointing to the hundredth element in x by a statement such as

```
p = &x[99];
```

the value of n after the previous subtraction is performed is 99.

As a practical application of this newly learned fact about pointer subtraction, take a look at a new version of the stringLength() function from Chapter 9.

In Program 10.15, the character pointer cptr is used to sequence through the characters pointed to by string until the null character is reached. At that point, string is subtracted from cptr to obtain the number of elements (characters) contained in the string. The program's output verifies that the function is working correctly.

Program 10.15   **Using Pointers to Find the Length of a String**

```
// Function to count the characters in a string - Pointer version

#include <stdio.h>

int  stringLength (const char  *string)
{
    const char  *cptr = string;

    while ( *cptr )
        ++cptr;
    return  cptr - string;
}

int main (void)
{
```

---

4. *The actual type of signed integer that is produced by subtracting two pointers (for example,* int, long int, *or* long long int) *is* ptrdiff_t, *which is defined in the standard header file* <stddef.h>.

```
        int  stringLength (const char  *string);

        printf ("%i  ", stringLength ("stringLength test"));
        printf ("%i  ", stringLength (""));
        printf ("%i\n", stringLength ("complete"));

        return 0;
}
```

Program 10.15   **Output**

```
17   0   8
```

Pointers to Functions

Of a slightly more advanced nature, but presented here for the sake of completeness, is the notion of a pointer to a function. When working with pointers to functions, the C compiler needs to know not only that the pointer variable points to a function, but also the type of value returned by that function as well as the number and types of its arguments. To declare a variable fnPtr to be of type "pointer to function that returns an int and that takes no arguments," the declaration

```
int  (*fnPtr) (void);
```

can be written. The parentheses around *fnPtr are required because otherwise the C compiler treats the preceding statement as the declaration of a function called fnPtr that returns a pointer to an int (because the function call operator () has higher precedence than the pointer indirection operator *).

To set your function pointer pointing to a specific function, you simply assign the name of the function to it. So, if lookup is a function that returns an int and that takes no arguments, the statement

```
fnPtr = lookup;
```

stores a pointer to this function inside the function pointer variable fnPtr. Writing a function name without a subsequent set of parentheses is treated in an analogous way to writing an array name without a subscript. The C compiler automatically produces a pointer to the specified function. An ampersand is permitted in front of the function name, but it's not required.

If the lookup() function has not been previously defined in the program, it is necessary to declare the function before the preceding assignment can be made. So, a statement such as

```
int  lookup (void);
```

is needed before a pointer to this function can be assigned to the variable fnPtr.

You can call the function that is indirectly referenced through a pointer variable by applying the function call operator to the pointer, listing any arguments to the function inside the parentheses. For example,

```
entry = fnPtr ();
```

calls the function pointed to by `fnPtr`, storing the returned value inside the variable `entry`.

One common application for pointers to functions is in passing them as arguments to other functions. The standard C library uses this, for example, in the function `qsort`, which performs a "quicksort" on an array of data elements. This function takes as one of its arguments a pointer to a function that is called whenever `qsort` needs to compare two elements in the array being sorted. In this manner, `qsort` can be used to sort arrays of any type, as the actual comparison of any two elements in the array is made by a user-supplied function, and not by the `qsort` function itself. Appendix B, "The Standard C Library," goes into more detail about `qsort` and contains an actual example of its use.

Another common application for function pointers is to create what is known as *dispatch* tables. You can't store functions themselves inside the elements of an array. However, it is valid to store function *pointers* inside an array. Given this, you can create tables that contain pointers to functions to be called. For example, you might create a table for processing different commands that will be entered by a user. Each entry in the table could contain both the command name and a pointer to a function to call to process that particular command. Now, whenever the user enters a command, you can look up the command inside the table and invoke the corresponding function to handle it.

Pointers and Memory Addresses

Before ending this discussion of pointers in C, you should note the details of how they are actually implemented. A computer's memory can be conceptualized as a sequential collection of storage cells. Each cell of the computer's memory has a number, called an *address*, associated with it. Typically, the first address of a computer's memory is numbered 0. On most computer systems, a "cell" is called a *byte*.

The computer uses memory for storing the instructions of your computer program, and also for storing the values of the variables that are associated with a program. So, if you declare a variable called `count` to be of type `int`, the system assigns location(s) in memory to hold the value of `count` while the program is executing. This location might be at address 500, for example, inside the computer's memory.

Luckily, one of the advantages of higher-level programming languages such as C is that you don't need to concern yourself with the particular memory addresses that are assigned to variables—they are automatically handled by the system. However, the knowledge that a unique memory address is associated with each variable will help you to understand the way pointers operate.

When you apply the address operator to a variable in C, the value that is generated is the actual address of that variable inside the computer's memory. (Obviously, this is where the address operator gets its name.) So, the statement

```
intPtr = &count;
```

assigns to `intPtr` the address in the computer's memory that has been assigned to the variable count. So, if `count` is located at address 500 and contains the value 10, this statement assigns the value 500 to `intPtr`, as depicted in Figure 10.11.

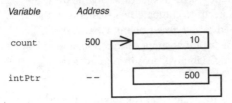

Variable   *Address*

count   500

intPtr   --

Figure 10.11   Pointers and memory addresses.

The address of `intPtr` is shown in Figure 10.11 as -- because its actual value is irrelevant for this example.

Applying the indirection operator to a pointer variable, as in the expression

```
*intPtr
```

has the effect of treating the value contained in the pointer variable as a memory address. The value stored at that memory address is then fetched and interpreted in accordance with the type declared for the pointer variable. So, if `intPtr` is of type pointer to int, the value stored in the memory address given by `*intPtr` is interpreted as an integer by the system. In our example, the value stored at memory address 500 is fetched and interpreted as an integer. The result of the expression is 10, and is of type `int`.

Storing a value in a location reference by a pointer, as in

```
*intPtr = 20;
```

proceeds in a like manner. The contents of `intPtr` is fetched and treated as a memory address. The specified integer value is then stored at that address. In the preceding statement, the integer value of 20 is, therefore, stored at memory address 500.

At times, system programmers must access particular locations inside the computer's memory. In such cases, this knowledge of the way that pointer variables operate proves helpful.

As you can see from this chapter, the pointer is a very powerful construct in C. The flexibility in defining pointer variables extends beyond those illustrated in this chapter. For example, you can define a pointer to a pointer, and even a pointer to a pointer to a pointer. These types of constructs are beyond the scope of this book, although they are simply logical extensions of everything you've learned about pointers in this chapter.

The topic of pointers is probably the hardest for novices to grasp. You should reread any sections of this chapter that still seem unclear before proceeding. Solving the exercises that follow will also help you to understand the material.

Exercises

1. Type in and run the 15 programs presented in this chapter. Compare the output produced by each program with the output presented after each program in the text.

2. Write a function called `insertEntry()` to insert a new entry into a linked list. Have the procedure take as arguments a pointer to the list entry to be inserted (of type `struct entry` as defined in this chapter), and a pointer to an element in the list *after* which the new `entry` is to be inserted.

3. The function developed in exercise 2 only inserts an element after an existing element in the list, thereby preventing you from inserting a new entry at the front of the list. How can you use this same function and yet overcome this problem? (*Hint:* Think about setting up a special structure to point to the beginning of the list.)

4. Write a function called `removeEntry()` to remove an `entry` from a linked list. The sole argument to the procedure should be a pointer to the list. Have the function remove the entry *after* the one pointed to by the argument. (Why can't you remove the entry pointed to by the argument?) You need to use the special structure you set up in exercise 3 to handle the special case of removing the first element from the list.

5. A *doubly linked list* is a list in which each entry contains a pointer to the preceding entry in the list as well as a pointer to the next entry in the list. Define the appropriate structure definition for a doubly linked list entry and then write a small program that implements a small doubly linked list and prints out the elements of the list.

6. Develop `insertEntry()` and `removeEntry()` functions for a doubly linked list that are similar in function to those developed in previous exercises for a singly linked list. Why can your `removeEntry()` function now take as its argument a direct pointer to the entry to be removed from the list?

7. Write a pointer version of the `sort()` function from Chapter 7, "Working with Functions." Be certain that pointers are exclusively used by the function, including index variables in the loops.

8. Write a function called `sort3()` to sort three integers into ascending order. (This function is not to be implemented with arrays.)

9. Rewrite the `readLine()` function from Chapter 9 so that it uses a character pointer rather than an array.

10. Rewrite the `compareStrings()` function from Chapter 9 to use character pointers instead of arrays.

11. Given the definition of a date structure as defined in this chapter, write a function called dateUpdate() that takes a pointer to a date structure as its argument and that updates the structure to the following day (see Program 8.4).

12. Given the following declarations:

```
char  *message = "Programming in C is fun\n";
char  message2[] = "You said it\n";
char  *format  = "x = %i\n";
int   x = 100;
```

determine whether each printf() call from the following sets is valid and produces the same output as other calls from the set.

```
/*** set 1 ***/
printf ("Programming in C is fun\n");
printf ("%s", "Programming in C is fun\n");
printf ("%s", message);
printf (message);

/*** set 2 ***/
printf ("You said it\n");
printf ("%s", message2);
printf (message2);
printf ("%s", &message2[0]);

/*** set 3 ***/
printf ("said it\n");
printf (message2 + 4);
printf ("%s", message2 + 4);
printf ("%s", &message2[4]);

/*** set 4 ***/
printf ("x = %i\n", x);
printf (format, x);
```

## 11

Operations on Bits

As mentioned on previous occasions, the C language was developed with systems programming applications in mind. Pointers are the perfect case in point because they give the programmer an enormous amount of control over and access into the computer's memory. Along these same lines, systems programmers frequently must get in and "twiddle with the bits" of particular computer words. You will learn how to manipulate bits with C-programming operators, including

- The bitwise AND operator
- The bitwise inclusive OR operator
- The bitwise exclusive OR operator
- The ones complement operator
- The left shift operator
- The right shift operator
- Bit fields

The Basics of Bits

Recall from the discussions in the previous chapter the concept of a *byte*. On most computer systems, a byte consists of eight smaller units called *bits*. A bit can assume either of two values: 1 or 0. So a byte stored at address 1000 in a computer's memory, for example, might be conceptualized as a string of eight binary digits as shown:

```
01100100
```

The rightmost bit of a byte is known as the *least significant* or *low-order* bit, whereas the leftmost bit is known as the *most significant* or *high-order* bit. If you treat the string of bits as an integer, the rightmost bit of the preceding byte represents 2^0 or 1, the bit immediately to its left represents 2^1 or 2, the next bit 2^2 or 4, and so on. Therefore, the preceding binary number represents the value $2^2 + 2^5 + 2^6 = 4 + 32 + 64 = 100$ decimal.

The representation of negative numbers is handled slightly differently. Most computers represent such numbers using a so-called "twos complement" notation. Using this notation, the leftmost bit represents the *sign* bit. If this bit is 1, the number is negative; otherwise, the bit is 0 and the number is positive. The remaining bits represent the value of the number. In twos complement notation, the value −1 is represented by all bits being equal to 1:

11111111

A convenient way to convert a negative number from decimal to binary is to first add 1 to the value, express the absolute value of the result in binary, and then "complement" all the bits; that is, change all 1s to 0s and 0s to 1s. So, for example, to convert -5 to binary, 1 is added, which gives -4; 4 expressed in binary is 00000100, and complementing the bits produces 11111011.

To convert a negative number from binary back to decimal, first complement all of the bits, convert the result to decimal, change the sign of the result, and then subtract 1.

Given this discussion about twos complement representation, the largest positive number that can be stored into n bits is $2^{n-1}-1$. So in eight bits, you can store a value up to $2^7 - 1$, or 127. Similarly, the smallest negative number that can be stored into n bits is -2^{n-1}, which in an eight-bit byte comes to −128. (Can you figure out why the largest positive and smallest negative values are not of the same magnitude?)

On most of today's processors, integers occupy four contiguous bytes, or 32 bits, in the computer's memory. The largest positive value that can, therefore, be stored into such an integer is $2^{31}-1$ or 2,147,483,647, whereas the smallest negative number that can be stored is −2,147,483,648.

In Chapter 3, "Variables, Data Types, and Arithmetic Expressions," you were introduced to the unsigned modifier and learned that it could be used to effectively increase the range of a variable. This is because the leftmost bit is no longer needed to store the sign of the number because you are only dealing with positive integers. This "extra" bit is used to increase the magnitude of the value stored in that variable by a factor of 2. More precisely, n bits can now be used to store values up to 2^n-1. On a machine that stores integers in 32 bits, this means that unsigned integers can range in value from 0 through 4,294,967,296.

Bit Operators

Now that you have learned some preliminaries, it's time to discuss the various bit operators that are available. Table 11.1 lists the C operators you can use to manipulate bits.

Table 11.1 **Bit operators**

Symbol	Operation
&	Bitwise AND
|	Bitwise Inclusive-OR

Symbol	Operation
^	Bitwise Exclusive-OR
~	Ones complement
<<	Left shift
>>	Right shift

All the operators listed in Table 11.1, with the exception of the ones complement operator ~, are binary operators and as such take two operands. Bit operations can be performed on any type of integer value in C—be it int, short, long, long long, and signed or unsigned—and on characters, but cannot be performed on floating-point values.

The Bitwise AND Operator

When two values are ANDed in C, the binary representations of the values are compared bit by bit. Each corresponding bit that is a 1 in the first value *and* a 1 in the second value produces a 1 in the corresponding bit position of the result; anything else produces a 0. If *b1* and *b2* represent corresponding bits of the two operands, then the following table, called a *truth table*, shows the result of *b1* ANDed with *b2* for all possible values of *b1* and *b2*.

b1	b2	b1 & b2
0	0	0
0	1	0
1	0	0
1	1	1

So, for example, if w1 and w2 are defined as short ints, and w1 is set equal to 25 and w2 is set equal to 77, then the C statement

```
w3 = w1 & w2;
```

assigns the value 9 to w3. This can be more easily seen by treating the values of w1, w2, and w3 as binary numbers. Assume that you are dealing with a short int size of 16 bits.

```
w1   0000000000011001    25
w2   0000000001001101   & 77
     -------------------------
w3   0000000000001001    9
```

If you think about the way the logical AND operator && works (true only if both operands are true), you will be able to more easily remember the way the bitwise AND operator works. Incidentally, make sure that you don't get these two operators confused! The logical AND operator && is used in logical expressions for producing a true/false result; it does not perform a bitwise AND.

Bitwise ANDing is frequently used for masking operations. That is, this operator can be used to easily set specific bits of a data item to 0. For example, the statement

```
w3 = w1 & 3;
```

assigns to w3 the value of w1 bitwise ANDed with the constant 3. This has the effect of setting all of the bits in w3, other than the rightmost two bits, to 0, and of preserving the rightmost two bits from w1.

As with all binary arithmetic operators in C, the binary bit operators can also be used as assignment operators by tacking on an equal sign. So the statement

```
word &= 15;
```

performs the same function as

```
word = word & 15;
```

and has the effect of setting all but the rightmost four bits of word to 0.

When using constants in performing bitwise operations, it is usually more convenient to express the constants in either octal or hexadecimal notation. The choice as to which to use is usually influenced by the size of the data with which you are dealing. For example, when dealing with 32-bit computers, hexadecimal notation is often used because 32 is an even multiple of 4 (the number of bits in a hexadecimal digit).

Program 11.1 is presented to illustrate the bitwise AND operator. Because you are dealing with only positive values in this program, all integers have been declared as unsigned int variables.

Program 11.1 The Bitwise AND Operator

```
// Program to demonstrate the bitwise AND operator
#include <stdio.h>

int main (void)
{
    unsigned int  word1 = 077u, word2 = 0150u, word3 = 0210u;

    printf ("%o  ", word1 & word2);
    printf ("%o  ", word1 & word1);
    printf ("%o  ", word1 & word2 & word3);
    printf ("%o\n", word1 & 1);

    return 0;
}
```

Program 11.1 Output

```
50  77  10  1
```

Recall that if an integer constant has a leading 0, it represents an octal (base 8) constant in C. Therefore, the three unsigned ints, word1, word2, and word3, are given initial *octal* values of 077, 0150, and 0210, respectively. Recall also from Chapter 3 that if a u or U follows an integer constant, it is treated as unsigned.

The first printf call displays octal 50 as the result of bitwise ANDing word1 with word2. The following depicts how this value was calculated:

```
word1    ... 000  111  111      077
word2    ... 001  101  000   & 0150
         -----------------------------
         ... 000  101  000      050
```

Only the rightmost nine bits of the previous values are shown because all bits to the left are 0. The binary numbers have been arranged in groups of three bits to make it easier to translate back and forth between binary and octal.

The second printf() call results in the display of octal 77, which is the result of ANDing word1 with itself. By definition, any quantity *x*, when ANDed with itself, produces *x*.

The third printf() call displays the result of ANDing word1, word2, and word3 together. The operation of bitwise ANDing is such that it makes no difference whether an expression such as a & b & c is evaluated as (a & b) & c or as a & (b & c), but for the record, evaluation proceeds from left to right. It is left as an exercise to you to verify that the displayed result of octal 10 is the correct result of ANDing word1 with word2 with word3.

The final printf() call has the effect of extracting the rightmost bit of word1. This is actually another way of testing if an integer is even or odd because that rightmost bit of any odd integer is 1 and of any even integer is 0. Therefore when the if statement

```
if  ( word1 & 1 )
    . . .
```

is executed, the expression is true if word1 is odd (because the result of the AND operation is 1) and false if it is even (because the result of the AND operation is 0). (*Note:* On machines that use a ones complement representation for numbers, this does not work for negative integers.)

The Bitwise Inclusive-OR Operator

When two values are bitwise Inclusive-ORed in C, the binary representation of the two values are once again compared bit by bit. This time, each bit that is a 1 in the first value *or* a 1 in the second value produces a 1 in the corresponding bit of the result. The truth table for the Inclusive-OR operator is shown next.

b1	b2	b1 | b2
0	0	0
0	1	1
1	0	1
1	1	1

So, if w1 is an unsigned int equal to octal 0431 and w2 is an unsigned int equal to octal 0152, then a bitwise Inclusive-OR of w1 and w2 produces a result of octal 0573 as shown:

```
w1   ... 100  011  001       0431
w2   ... 001  101  010   |   0152
     -----------------------------
     ... 101  111  011       0573
```

As was pointed out with the bitwise AND operator, be sure to not confuse the operation of bitwise ORing (|) with that of logical ORing (||), the latter operation being used to determine if either of two logical values is true.

Bitwise Inclusive-ORing, frequently called just bitwise ORing, is used to set some specified bits of a word to 1. For example, the statement

```
w1 = w1 | 07;
```

sets the three rightmost bits of w1 to 1, regardless of the state of these bits before the operation was performed. Of course, you could have used a special assignment operator in the statement, as follows:

```
w1 |= 07;
```

Presentation of a program example illustrating the use of the Inclusive-OR operator is deferred until later in this chapter.

The Bitwise Exclusive-OR Operator

The bitwise Exclusive-OR operator, which is often called the XOR operator, works as follows: For corresponding bits of the two operands, if either bit is a 1—but not both—the corresponding bit of the result is a 1; otherwise it is a 0. The truth table for this operator is as shown.

b1	b2	b1 ^ b2
0	0	0
0	1	1
1	0	1
1	1	0

If w1 and w2 were set equal to octal 0536 and octal 0266, respectively, then the result of w1 Exclusive-ORed with w2 would be octal 0750, as illustrated:

```
w1   ... 101  011  110       0536
w2   ... 010  110  110   ^   0266
     -----------------------------
     ... 111  101  000       0750
```

One interesting property of the Exclusive-OR operator is that any value Exclusive-ORed with itself produces 0. Historically, this trick was often used by assembly language programmers as a fast way to set a value to 0 or to compare two values to see if they were equal. This method is not recommended for use in C programs, however, as it doesn't save time and most likely makes the program more obscure.

Another interesting application of the Exclusive-OR operator is that it can be used to effectively exchange two values without the need for an extra memory location. You know that you would normally interchange two integers called i1 and i2 with a sequence of statements such as

```
temp = i1;
i1 = i2;
i2 = temp;
```

Using the Exclusive-OR operator, you can exchange values without the need of the temporary storage location:

```
i1 ^= i2;
i2 ^= i1;
i1 ^= i2;
```

It is left as an exercise to you to verify that the previous statements do in fact succeed in inter-changing the values of i1 and i2.

The Ones Complement Operator

The ones complement operator is a unary operator, and its effect is to simply "flip" the bits of its operand. Each bit of the operand that is a 1 is changed to a 0, and each bit that is a 0 is changed to a 1. The truth table is shown next simply for the sake of completeness.

b1	~b1
0	1
1	0

If w1 is a short int that is 16 bits long, and is set equal to octal 0122457, then taking the ones complement of this value produces a result of octal 0055320:

```
w1    1  010  010  100  101  111     0122457
~w1   0  101  101  011  010  000     0055320
```

The ones complement operator (~) should not be confused with the arithmetic minus operator (–) or with the logical negation operator (!). So if w1 is defined as an int, and set equal to 0, then –w1 still results in 0. If you apply the ones complement operator to w1, you end up with w1 being set to all ones, which is –1 when treated as a signed value in twos complement nota-tion. Finally, applying the logical negation operator to w1 produces the result true (1) because w1 is false (0).

The ones complement operator is useful when you don't know the precise bit size of the quantity that you are dealing with in an operation. Its use can help make a program more portable—in other words, less dependent on the particular computer on which the program is running and, therefore, easier to get running on a different machine. For example, to set the low-order bit of an int called w1 to 0, you can AND w1 with an int consisting of all 1s except for a single 0 in the rightmost bit. So a statement in C such as

```
w1 &= 0xFFFFFFFE;
```

works fine on machines in which an integer is represented by 32 bits.

If you replace the preceding statement with

```
w1 &= ~1;
```

w1 gets ANDed with the correct value on any machine because the ones complement of 1 is calculated and consists of as many leftmost one bits as are necessary to fill the size of an int (31 leftmost bits on a 32-bit integer system).

Program 11.2 summarizes the various bitwise operators presented thus far. Before proceeding, however, it is important to mention the precedences of the various operators. The AND, OR, and Exclusive-OR operators each have lower precedence than any of the arithmetic or relational operators, but higher precedence than the logical AND and logical OR operators. The bitwise AND is higher in precedence than the bitwise Exclusive-OR, which in turn is higher in precedence than the bitwise OR. The unary ones complement operator has higher precedence than *any* binary operator. For a summary of these operator precedences, see Appendix A, "C Language Summary."

Program 11.2   **Illustrate Bitwise Operators**

```
/* Program to illustrate bitwise operators */

#include <stdio.h>

int main (void)
{
    unsigned int  w1 = 0525u, w2 = 0707u, w3 = 0122u;

    printf ("%o    %o    %o\n", w1 & w2, w1 | w2, w1 ^ w2);
    printf ("%o    %o    %o\n", ~w1, ~w2, ~w3);
    printf ("%o    %o    %o\n", w1 ^ w1, w1 & ~w2, w1 | w2 | w3);
    printf ("%o    %o\n", w1 | w2 & w3, w1 | w2 & ~w3);
    printf ("%o    %o\n", ~(~w1 & ~w2), ~(~w1 | ~w2));

    w1 ^= w2;
    w2 ^= w1;
    w1 ^= w2;
    printf ("w1 = %o, w2 = %o\n", w1, w2);

    return 0;
}
```

Program 11.2 **Output**

```
505    727    222
37777777252    37777777070    37777777655
0    20    727
527    725
727    505
w1 = 707, w2 = 525
```

You should work out each of the operations from Program 11.2 with a paper and pencil to verify that you understand how the results were obtained. The program was run on a computer that uses 32 bits to represent an int.

In the fourth printf() call, it is important to remember that the bitwise AND operator has higher precedence than the bitwise OR, because this fact influences the resulting value of the expression.

The fifth printf() call illustrates DeMorgan's rule, namely that ~(~a & ~b) is equal to a | b and that ~(~a | ~b) is equal to a & b. The sequence of statements that follow next in the program verifies that the exchange operation works as discussed in "The Bitwise Exclusive-OR Operator" section.

The Left Shift Operator

When a left shift operation is performed on a value, the bits contained in the value are literally shifted to the left. Associated with this operation is the number of places (bits) that the value is to be shifted. Bits that are shifted out through the high-order bit of the data item are lost, and 0s are always shifted in through the low-order bit of the value. So if w1 is equal to 3, then the expression

```
w1 = w1 << 1;
```

which can also be expressed as

```
w1 <<= 1;
```

results in 3 being shifted one place to the left, which results in 6 being assigned to w1:

```
w1         ... 000 011    03
w1 << 1    ... 000 110    06
```

The operand on the left of the << operator is the value to be shifted, whereas the operand on the right is the number of bit positions by which the value is to be shifted. If you shift w1 one more place to the left, you end up with octal 014 as the value of w1:

```
w1         ... 000 110    06
w1 << 1    ... 001 100    014
```

Left shifting actually has the effect of multiplying the value that is shifted by two. In fact, some C compilers automatically perform multiplication by a power of two by left shifting the value the appropriate number of places because shifting is a much faster operation than multiplication on most computers.

A program example illustrating the left shift operator is presented after the right shift operator has been described.

The Right Shift Operator

As implied from its name, the right shift operator >> shifts the bits of a value to the right. Bits shifted out of the low-order bit of the value are lost. Right shifting an unsigned value always results in 0s being shifted in on the left; that is, through the high-order bits. What is shifted in on the left for signed values depends on the sign of the value that is being shifted and also on how this operation is implemented on your computer system. If the sign bit is 0 (meaning the value is positive), 0s are shifted in regardless of which machine you are running. However, if the sign bit is 1, on some machines 1s are shifted in, and on others 0s are shifted in. This former type of operation is known as an *arithmetic* right shift, whereas the latter is known as a *logical* right shift.

Never make any assumptions about whether a system implements an arithmetic or a logical right shift. A program that shifts signed values right might work correctly on one system but fail on another due to this type of assumption.

If w1 is an unsigned int, which is represented in 32 bits, and w1 is set equal to hexadecimal F777EE22, then shifting w1 one place to the right with the statement

```
w1 >>= 1;
```

sets w1 equal to hexadecimal 7BBBF711.

```
w1          1111 0111 0111 0111 1110 1110 0010 0010    F777EE22
w1 >> 1     0111 1011 1011 1011 1111 0111 0001 0001    7BBBF711
```

If w1 were declared to be a (signed) short int, the same result would be produced on some computers; on others, the result would be FBBBF711 if the operation were performed as an arithmetic right shift.

It should be noted that the C language does not produce a defined result if an attempt is made to shift a value to the left or right by an amount that is greater than or equal to the number of bits in the size of the data item. So, on a machine that represents integers in 32 bits, for example, shifting an integer to the left or right by 32 or more bits is not guaranteed to produce a defined result in your program. You should also note that if you shift a value by a negative amount, the result is also undefined.

A Shift Function

Now, it's time to put the left and right shift operators to work in an actual program example, as shown in Program 11.3. Some computers have a single machine instruction to shift a value to the left if the shift count is positive and to the right if the shift count is negative. Now, write a function in C to mimic this type of operation. You can have the function take two arguments: the value to be shifted and the shift count. If the shift count is positive, the value is shifted left the designated number of places; otherwise, the value is shifted right the number of places as specified by the absolute value of the shift count.

Program 11.3 **Implementing a Shift Function**

```
// Function to shift an unsigned int left if
// the count is positive, and right if negative

#include <stdio.h>

unsigned int  shift (unsigned int  value, int  n)
{
    if ( n > 0 )      // left shift
        value <<= n;
    else              // right shift
        value >>= -n;

    return value;
}

int main (void)
{
    unsigned int  w1 = 0177777u, w2 = 0444u;
    unsigned int  shift (unsigned int  value, int  n);

    printf ("%o\t%o\n", shift (w1, 5), w1 << 5);
    printf ("%o\t%o\n", shift (w1, -6), w1 >> 6);
    printf ("%o\t%o\n", shift (w2, 0), w2 >> 0);
    printf ("%o\n", shift (shift (w1, -3), 3));

    return 0;
}
```

Program 11.3 **Output**

```
7777740 7777740
1777    1777
444     444
177770
```

The shift() function shown in Program 11.3 declares the type of the argument value to be unsigned int, thus ensuring that a right shift of value will be zero filled; in other words, performed as a logical right shift.

If the value of n, which is the shift count, is greater than zero, the function shifts value left n bits. If n is negative (or zero), the function performs a right shift, where the number of places that value is shifted is obtained by negating the value of n.

The first call to the shift() function from the main() routine specifies that the value of w1 is to be left shifted five bits. The printf() call that displays the result of the call to the shift() function also displays the result of directly shifting w1 left five places so that these values can be compared.

The second call to the shift() function has the effect of shifting w1 six places to the right. The result returned by the function is identical to the result obtained by directly shifting w1 to the right six places, as verified by the program's output.

In the third call to shift(), a shift count of zero is specified. In this case, the shift function performs a right shift of value by zero bits, which, as you can see from the program's output, has no effect on the value.

The final printf() call illustrates nested function calls to the shift() function. The inner-most call to shift() is executed first. This call specifies that w1 is to be shifted right three places. The result of this function call, which is 0017777, is then passed to the shift() function to be shifted to the left three places. As you can see from the program's output, this has the net effect of setting the low-order three bits of w1 to 0. (Of course, you know by now that this could also have been done by simply ANDing w1 with ~7.)

Rotating Bits

For the next program example, which ties together some of the bit operations presented in this chapter, you will develop a function to rotate a value to the left or right. The process of rotation is similar to shifting, except that when a value is rotated to the left, the bits that are shifted out of the high-order bits are shifted back into the low-order bits. When a value is rotated to the right, the bits that are shifted out of the low-order bits of the value are shifted back into the high-order bits. So, if you are dealing with 32-bit unsigned integers, the value hexadecimal 80000000 rotated to the left by one bit produces hexadecimal 00000001 because the 1 from the sign bit that is normally lost by a left shift of one bit is brought around and shifted back into the low-order bit.

Your function takes two arguments: the first, the value to be rotated, and the second, the number of bits by which the object is to be rotated. If this second argument is positive, you rotate the value to the left; otherwise, you rotate the value to the right.

You can adopt a fairly straightforward approach to implementing your rotate function. For example, to compute the result of rotating x to the left by n bits, where x is of type int and n ranges from 0 to the number of bits in an int minus 1, you can extract the leftmost n bits of x, shift x to the left by n bits, and then put the extracted bits back into x at the right. A similar algorithm also can be used to implement the right rotate function.

Program 11.4 implements the rotate() function using the algorithm described previously. This function makes the assumption that an int uses 32 bits on the computer. Exercises at the end of the chapter show one way to write this function so that this assumption does not have to be made.

Program 11.4   **Implementing a Rotate Function**

```c
// Program to illustrate rotation of integers

#include <stdio.h>

int main (void)
{
    unsigned int  w1 = 0xabcdef00u, w2 = 0xffff1122u;
    unsigned int  rotate (unsigned int  value, int  n);

    printf ("%x\n", rotate (w1, 8));
    printf ("%x\n", rotate (w1, -16));
    printf ("%x\n", rotate (w2, 4));
    printf ("%x\n", rotate (w2, -2));
    printf ("%x\n", rotate (w1, 0));
    printf ("%x\n", rotate (w1, 44));

    return 0;
}

// Function to rotate an unsigned int left or right

unsigned int  rotate (unsigned int  value, int  n)
{
    unsigned int  result, bits;

    // scale down the shift count to a defined range

    if  ( n > 0 )
        n = n % 32;
    else
        n = -(-n % 32);

    if  ( n == 0 )
        result = value;
    else if ( n > 0 ) {     // left rotate
        bits = value >> (32 - n);
        result = value << n  |  bits;
    }
    else  {                 // right rotate
        n = -n;
        bits = value << (32 - n);
        result = value >> n  |  bits;
```

```
    }

    return result;
}
```

Program 11.4 **Output**

```
cdef00ab
ef00abcd
fff1122f
bfffc448
abcdef00
def00abc
```

The function first ensures that the shift count, n, is valid. The code

```
if  ( n > 0 )
    n = n % 32;
else
    n = -(-n % 32);
```

checks first to see if n is positive. If it is, the value of n modulo the size of an int (assumed to be 32 in this example) is calculated and stored back inside n. This places the shift count in the range of 0 through 31. If n is negative, its value is negated before the modulus operator is applied. This is done because C does not define the sign of the result of applying the modulus operator to a negative value. Your machine can produce either a positive or negative result. By negating the value first, you ensure the result is positive. You then apply the unary minus operator to the result to turn it negative again; that is, within the range of values –31 through 0.

If the adjusted shift count is 0, the function simply assigns value to result. Otherwise, it proceeds with the rotation.

An n-bit rotation to the left is divided into three steps by the function. First, the n leftmost bits of value are extracted and shifted to the right. This is done by shifting value to the right by the size of an int (in our case, 32) minus n. Next, value is shifted n bits to the left, and finally, the extracted bits are ORed back in. A similar procedure is followed to rotate value to the right.

In the main() routine, note the use of hexadecimal notation for a change. The first call to the rotate() function specifies that the value of w1 is to be rotated eight bits to the left. As can be seen from the program's output, the hexadecimal value cdef00ab is returned by the rotate() function, which is in fact abcdef00 rotated to the left eight bits.

The second call to the rotate() function has the effect of rotating the value of w1 16 bits to the right.

The next two calls to the rotate() function do similar things with the value of w2 and are fairly self-explanatory. The next-to-last call to rotate() specifies a rotate count of 0. The program's output verifies that in such a case the function simply returns the value unchanged.

The final call to `rotate()` specifies a left rotate 44 places. This has the net effect of rotating the value left 12 bits (44 % 32 is 12).

Bit Fields

With the bit operators discussed previously, you can proceed to perform all sorts of sophisticated operations on bits. Bit operations are frequently performed on data items that contain packed information. Just as a `short int` can be used to conserve memory space on some computers, so can you pack information into the bits of a byte or word if you do not need to use the entire byte or word to represent the data. For example, flags that are used for a Boolean true or false condition can be represented in a single bit on a computer. Declaring a `char` variable that will be used as a flag uses eight bits (one byte) on most computers, and a `_Bool` variable is likely to use eight bits as well. In addition, if you need to store many flags inside a large table, the amount of memory that is wasted could become significant.

Two methods are available in C that can be used to pack information together to make better use of memory. One way is to simply represent the data inside a normal `int`, for example, and then access the desired bits of the `int` using the bit operators described in the previous sections. Another way is to define a structure of packed information using a C construct known as a *bit field*.

To illustrate how the first method can be used, suppose you want to pack five data values into a word because you have to maintain a very large table of these values in memory. Assume that three of these data values are flags, which you call `f1`, `f2`, and `f3`; the fourth value is an integer called `type`, which ranges from `1` to `255`; and the final value is an integer called `index`, which ranges from `0` to `100,000`.

Storing the values of the flags `f1`, `f2`, and `f3` only requires three bits of storage, one bit for the true/false value of each flag. Storing the value of the integer `type`, which ranges from `1` to `255`, requires eight bits of storage. Finally, storing the value of the integer `index`, which can assume a value from `0` to `100,000`, requires 18 bits. Therefore, the total amount of storage needed to store the five data values, `f1`, `f2`, `f3`, `type`, and `index`, is 29 bits. You could define an integer variable that could be used to contain all five of these values, as in

```
unsigned int  packed_data;
```

and could then arbitrarily assign specific bits or *fields* inside `packed_data` to be used to store the five data values. One such assignment is depicted in Figure 11.1, which assumes that the size of `packed_data` is 32 bits.

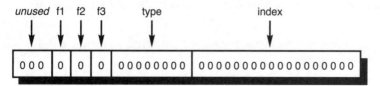

Figure 11.1   Bit field assignments in `packed_data`.

Note that packed_data has three unused bits. You can now apply the correct sequence of bit operations to packed_data to set and retrieve values to and from the various fields of the integer. For example, you can set the type field of packed_data to 7 by shifting the value 7 the appropriate number of places to the left and then ORing it into packed_data:

```
packed_data |= 7 << 18;
```

or you can set the type field to the value n, where n is between 0 and 255, by the statement

```
packed_data |= n << 18;
```

To ensure that n is between 0 and 255, you can AND it with 0xff before it is shifted.

Of course, the preceding statements only work if you know that the type field is zero; otherwise, you must zero it first by ANDing it with a value (frequently called a mask) that consists of 0s in the eight bit locations of the type field and 1s everywhere else:

```
packed_data &= 0xfc03ffff;
```

To save yourself the bother of having to explicitly calculate the preceding mask, and also to make the operation independent of the size of an integer, you could instead use the following statement to set the type field to zero:

```
packed_data &= ~(0xff << 18);
```

Combining the statements described previously, you can set the type field of packed_data to the value contained in the eight low-order bits of n, irrespective of any value previously stored in this field, with the following statement:

```
packed_data = (packed_data & ~(0xff << 18)) | ((n & 0xff) << 18);
```

In the preceding code, some of the parentheses are superfluous but were added to aid readability.

You can see how complex the preceding expression is for accomplishing the relatively simple task of setting the bits in the type field to a specified value. Extracting a value from one of these fields is not as bad: The field can be shifted into the low-order bits of the word and then ANDed with a mask of the appropriate bit length. So, to extract the type field of packed_data and assign it to n, the statement

```
n = (packed_data >> 18) & 0xff;
```

does the trick.

The C language does provide a more convenient way of dealing with bit fields. This method uses a special syntax in the structure definition that allows you to define a field of bits and assign a name to that field. Whenever the term "bit fields" is applied to C, it is this approach that is referenced.

To define the bit field assignments previously mentioned, you can define a structure called packed_struct, for example, as follows:

```
struct  packed_struct
{
    unsigned int  :3;
    unsigned int  f1:1;
    unsigned int  f2:1;
    unsigned int  f3:1;
    unsigned int  type:8;
    unsigned int  index:18;
};
```

The structure `packed_struct` is defined to contain six members. The first member is not named. The `:3` specifies three unnamed bits. The second member, called `f1`, is also an `unsigned int`. The `:1` that immediately follows the member name specifies that this member is to be stored in one bit. The flags `f2` and `f3` are similarly defined as being a single bit in length. The member `type` is defined to occupy eight bits, whereas the member `index` is defined as being 18 bits `long`.

The C compiler automatically packs the preceding bit field definitions together. The nice thing about this approach is that the fields of a variable defined to be of type `packed_struct` can now be referenced in the same convenient way normal structure members are referenced. So, if you declare a variable called `packed_data` as follows:

```
struct packed_struct  packed_data;
```

you could easily set the `type` field of `packed_data` to `7` with the simple statement

```
packed_data.type = 7;
```

or you could set this field to the value of n with the similar statement

```
packed_data.type = n;
```

In this last case, you need not worry about whether the value of n is too large to fit into the `type` field; only the low-order eight bits of n will be assigned to `packed_data.type`.

Extraction of the value from a bit field is also automatically handled, so the statement

```
n = packed_data.type;
```

extracts the `type` field from `packed_data` (automatically shifting it into the low-order bits as required) and assigns it to n.

Bit fields can be used in normal expressions and are automatically converted to integers. So the statement

```
i = packed_data.index / 5 + 1;
```

is perfectly valid, as is

```
if  ( packed_data.f2 )
    ...
```

which tests if flag f2 is true or false. One thing worth noting about bit fields is that there is no guarantee whether the fields are internally assigned from left to right or from right to left. This should not present a problem unless you are dealing with data that was created by a different program or by a different machine. In such cases, you must know how the bit fields are assigned and make the declarations appropriately. You could have defined the structure packed_struct as

```
struct   packed_struct
{
    unsigned int   index:9;
    unsigned int   type:4;
    unsigned int   f3:1;
    unsigned int   f2:1;
    unsigned int   f1:1;
    unsigned int   :3;
};
```

to achieve the same representation on a machine that assigns fields from right to left as depicted in Figure 11.1. Never make any assumptions about how structure members—whether they contain bit field members or not—are stored.

You can also include normal data types within a structure that contains bit fields. So if you want to define a structure that contained an int, a char, and two one-bit flags, the following definition is valid:

```
struct   table_entry
{
    int            count;
    char           c;
    unsigned int   f1:1;
    unsigned int   f2:1;
};
```

Certain points are worth mentioning with respect to bit fields. They can only be declared to be of integer or _Bool type. If just int is used in the declaration, it's implementation dependent whether this is interpreted as a signed or unsigned value. To play it safe, use the explicit declarations signed int or unsigned int. A bit field cannot be dimensioned; that is, you cannot have an array of fields, such as flag:1[5]. Finally, you cannot take the address of a bit field, and, therefore, there is obviously no such thing as a type "pointer to bit field."

Bit fields are packed into *units* as they appear in the structure definition, where the size of a *unit* is defined by the implementation and is most likely a word.

The C compiler does *not* rearrange the bit field definitions to try to optimize storage space.

A final point concerning the specification of fields concerns the special case of an unnamed field of length 0. This can be used to force alignment of the next field in the structure at the start of a unit boundary.

This concludes the discussion of bit operations in C. You can see how much power and flexibility the C language provides for the efficient manipulation of bits. Operators are conveniently provided in the language for performing bitwise AND, Inclusive-OR, Exclusive-OR, ones complement, and left and right shift operations. A special bit field format enables you to allocate a specified number of bits for a data item and to easily set and retrieve its value without having to use masking and shifting.

See Chapter 13, "Extending Data Types with the Enumerated Data Type, Type Definitions, and Data Type Conversions," for a discussion on what happens when you perform bitwise operations between two values of differing integral types, for example between an `unsigned long int` and a `short int`.

Before proceeding to the next chapter, try the following exercises to test your understanding of bit operations in C.

Exercises

1. Type in and run the four programs presented in this chapter. Compare the output produced by each program with the output presented after each program in the text.

2. Write a program that determines whether your particular computer performs an arithmetic or a logical right shift.

3. Given that the expression `~0` produces an integer that contains all 1s, write a function called `int_size()` that returns the number of bits contained in an `int` on your particular machine.

4. Using the result obtained in exercise 3, modify the `rotate()` function from Program 11.4 so that it no longer makes any assumptions about the size of an `int`.

5. Write a function called `bit_test()` that takes two arguments: an `unsigned int` and a bit number n. Have the function return 1 bit number n if it is on inside the word, and 0 if it is off. Assume that bit number 0 references the leftmost bit inside the integer. Also write a corresponding function called `bit_set()` that takes two arguments: an `unsigned int` and a bit number n. Have the function return the result of turning bit n on inside the integer.

6. Write a function called `bitpat_search()` that looks for the occurrence of a specified pattern of bits inside an `unsigned int`. The function should take three arguments and should be called as shown:

```
bitpat_search (source, pattern, n)
```

The function searches the integer `source`, starting at the leftmost bit, to see if the rightmost n bits of `pattern` occur in `source`. If the pattern is found, have the function return the number of the bit at which the pattern begins, where the leftmost bit is bit number 0. If the pattern is not found, then have the function return –1. So, for example, the call

```
index = bitpat_search (0xe1f4, 0x5, 3);
```

causes the `bitpat_search()` function to search the number 0xe1f4 (= 1110 0001 1111 0100 binary) for the occurrence of the three-bit pattern 0x5 (= 101 binary). The function returns 11 to indicate that the pattern was found in the source beginning with bit number 11.

Make certain that the function makes no assumptions about the size of an `int` (see exercise 3 in this chapter).

7. Write a function called `bitpat_get()` to extract a specified set of bits. Have it take three arguments: the first an `unsigned int`, the second an integer starting bit number, and the third a bit count. Using the convention that bit numbering starts at 0 with the leftmost bit, extract the specified number of bits from the first argument and return the result. So the call

    ```
    bitpat_get (x, 0, 3)
    ```

    extracts the three leftmost bits from x. The call

    ```
    bitpat_get (x, 3, 5)
    ```

    extracts five bits starting with the fourth bit in from the left.

8. Write a function called `bitpat_set()` to set a specified set of bits to a particular value. The function should take four arguments: a pointer to an `unsigned int` in which the specified bits are to be set; another `unsigned int` containing the value to which the specified bits are to be set, right adjusted in the `unsigned int`; a third `int` that specifies the starting bit number (with the leftmost bit numbered 0); and a fourth `int` specifying the size of the field. So the call

    ```
    bitpat_set (&x, 0, 2, 5);
    ```

    has the effect of setting the five bits contained in x, beginning with the third bit from the left (bit number 2), to 0. Similarly, the call

    ```
    bitpat_set (&x, 0x55u, 0, 8);
    ```

    sets the eight leftmost bits of x to hexadecimal 55.

    Make no assumptions about the particular size of an `int` (refer to exercise 3 in this chapter).

## 12

The Preprocessor

This chapter describes yet another unique feature of the C language that is not found in many other higher-level programming languages. The C preprocessor provides the tools that enable you to develop programs that are easier to develop, easier to read, easier to modify, and easier to port to different computer systems. You can also use the preprocessor to literally customize the C language to suit a particular programming application or to satisfy your own programming style. In this chapter, you cover

- Creating your own constants and macros with the `#define` statement
- Building your own library files with the `#include` statement
- Making more powerful programs with the conditional `#ifdef`, `#endif`, `#else`, and `#ifndef` Statements

The preprocessor is a part of the C compilation process that recognizes special statements that might be interspersed throughout a C program. As its name implies, the preprocessor actually analyzes these statements before analysis of the C program itself takes place. Preprocessor statements are identified by the presence of a pound sign, #, which must be the first nonspace character on the line. As you will see, preprocessor statements have a syntax that is slightly different from that of normal C statements. Almost every program you've written to this point has used preprocessor directive, specifically the `#include` directive. There's more you can do with that directive which will be covered later in this chapter, but you begin by examining the `#define` statement.

The `#define` Statement

One of the primary uses of the `#define` statement is to assign symbolic names to program constants. The preprocessor statement

```
#define   YES     1
```

defines the name `YES` and makes it equivalent to the value 1. The name `YES` can subsequently be used anywhere in the program where the constant 1 could be used. Whenever this name appears, its defined value of 1 is automatically substituted into the program by the preprocessor. For example, you might have the following C statement that uses the defined name `YES`:

```
gameOver = YES;
```

This statement assigns the value of YES to gameOver. You don't need to concern yourself with the actual value that you defined for YES, but because you do know that it is defined as 1, the preceding statement has the effect of assigning 1 to gameOver. The preprocessor statement

```
#define   NO    0
```

defines the name NO and makes its subsequent use in the program equivalent to specifying the value 0. Therefore, the statement

```
gameOver = NO;
```

assigns the value of NO to gameOver, and the statement

```
if ( gameOver == NO )
  . . .
```

compares the value of gameOver against the defined value of NO. Just about the only place that you *cannot* use a defined name is inside a character string; so the statement

```
char   *charPtr = "YES";
```

sets charPtr pointing to the string "YES" and not to the string "1".

A defined name is *not* a variable. Therefore, you cannot assign a value to it, unless the result of substituting the defined value is in fact a variable. Whenever a defined name is used in a program, whatever appears to the right of the defined name in the #define statement gets automatically substituted into the program by the preprocessor. It's analogous to doing a search and replace with a text editor; in this case, the preprocessor replaces all occurrences of the defined name with its associated text.

Notice that the #define statement has a special syntax: There is no equal sign used to assign the value 1 to YES. Furthermore, a semicolon does *not* appear at the end of the statement. Soon, you will understand why this special syntax exists. But first, take a look at a small program that uses the YES and NO defines as previously illustrated. The function isEven in Program 12.1 simply returns YES if its argument is even and NO if its argument is odd.

Program 12.1   **Introducing the** #define **Statement**

```
#include <stdio.h>

#define   YES    1
#define   NO     0

// Function to determine if an integer is even

int  isEven (int  number)
{
    int  answer;

    if ( number % 2 == 0 )
```

```
        answer = YES;
    else
        answer = NO;

    return answer;
}


int main (void)
{
    int  isEven (int  number);

    if ( isEven (17) == YES )
        printf ("yes ");
    else
        printf ("no ");

    if ( isEven (20) == YES )
        printf ("yes\n");
    else
        printf ("no\n");

    return 0;
}
```

Program 12.1 **Output**

no yes

The #define statements appear first in the program. This is not required; they can appear *anywhere* in the program. What is required is that a name be defined before it is referenced by the program. Defined names do not behave like variables: There is no such thing as a local define. After a name has been defined in a program, either inside or outside a function, it can subsequently be used *anywhere* in the program. Most programmers group their #define statements at the beginning of the program (or inside an *include* file[1]) where they can be quickly referenced and shared by more than one source file.

The defined name NULL is frequently used by programmers to represent the null pointer.[2]

By including a definition such as

```
#define  NULL  0
```

in a program, you can then write more readable statements, such as

```
while ( listPtr != NULL )
    ...
```

---

1. *Read on to learn how defines can be set up inside special files that you can include in your program.*
2. NULL *is already defined on your system inside a file named* <stddef.h>. *Again, include files are discussed in more detail shortly.*

to set up a `while` loop that will execute as long as the value of `listPtr` is not equal to the null pointer.

As another example of the use of a defined name, suppose you want to write three functions to find the area of a circle, the circumference of a circle, and the volume of a sphere of a given radius. Because all these functions need to use the constant π, which is not a particularly easy constant to remember, it makes sense to define the value of this constant once at the start of the program and then use this value where needed in each function.[3]

Program 12.2 shows how a definition for this constant can be set up and used in a program.

Program 12.2   More on Working with Defines

```
/* Function to calculate the area and circumference of a
   circle, and the volume of a sphere of a given radius  */

#include <stdio.h>

#define  PI        3.141592654

double  area (double  r)
{
    return PI * r * r;
}

double  circumference (double  r)
{
    return 2.0 * PI * r;
}

double  volume (double r)
{
    return 4.0 / 3.0  *  PI * r * r * r;
}

int main (void)
{
    double  area (double  r), circumference (double  r),
            volume (double r);

    printf ("radius = 1: %.4f   %.4f   %.4f\n",
            area(1.0), circumference(1.0), volume(1.0));

    printf ("radius = 4.98: %.4f   %.4f   %.4f\n",
```

---

3. The identifier M_PI is already defined for you in the header file <math.h>. By including that file in your program, you can use it directly in your programs.

```
        area(4.98), circumference(4.98), volume(4.98));

    return 0;
}
```

Program 12.2 **Output**

```
radius = 1: 3.1416    6.2832    4.1888
radius = 4.98: 77.9128    31.2903    517.3403
```

The symbolic name PI is defined as the value 3.141592654 at the beginning of the program. Subsequent use of the name PI inside the area(), circumference(), and volume() functions has the effect of causing its defined value to be automatically substituted at the appropriate point.

Assignment of a constant to a symbolic name frees you from having to remember the particular constant value every time you want to use it in a program. Furthermore, if you ever need to change the value of the constant (if, perhaps, you find out that you are using the wrong value, for example), you only have to change the value in one place in the program: in the #define statement. Without this approach, you would have to otherwise search throughout the program and explicitly change the value of the constant whenever it was used.

You might have realized that all the #define statements you have seen so far (YES, NO, NULL, and PI) have been written in capital letters. The reason this is done is to visually distinguish a defined value from a variable. Some programmers adopt the convention that all defined names be capitalized, so that it becomes easy to determine when a name represents a variable and when it represents a defined name. Another common convention is to prefix the defined value with the letter *k*. In that case, the following characters of the name are not capitalized. kMaximumValues and kSignificantDigits are two examples of defined names that adhere to this convention.

Program Extendability

Using a defined name for a constant value helps to make programs more readily extendable. For example, when you define an array, you must specify the number of elements in the array—either explicitly or implicitly (by specifying a list of initializers). Subsequent program statements will likely use the knowledge of the number of elements contained inside the array. For example, if the array dataValues is defined in a program as follows:

```
float   dataValues[1000];
```

there is a good chance that you will see statements in the program that use the fact that dataValues contains 1,000 elements. For instance, in a for loop

```
for ( i = 0;  i < 1000;  ++i )
    ...
```

you would use the value 1000 as an upper bound for sequencing through the elements of the array. A statement such as

```
if ( index  > 999 )
    ...
```

might also be used in the program to test if an index value exceeds the maximum size of the array.

Now suppose that you had to increase the size of the dataValues array from 1,000 to 2,000 elements. This would necessitate changing all statements that used the fact that dataValues contained 1,000 elements.

A better way of dealing with array bounds, which makes programs easier to extend, is to define a name for the upper array bound. So, if you define a name such as MAXIMUM_DATAVALUES with an appropriate #define statement:

```
#define  MAXIMUM_DATAVALUES    1000
```

you can subsequently define the dataValues array to contain MAXIMUM_DATAVALUES elements with the following program line:

```
float   dataValues[MAXIMUM_DATAVALUES];
```

Statements that use the upper array bound can also make use of this defined name. To sequence through the elements in dataValues, for example, the for statement

```
for ( i = 0;  i < MAXIMUM_DATAVALUES;  ++i )
    ...
```

could be used. To test if an index value is greater than the upper bound of the array, you could write

```
if  ( index > MAXIMUM_DATAVALUES - 1 )
    ...
```

and so on. The nicest thing about the preceding approach is that you can now easily change the size of the dataValues array to 2,000 elements by simply changing the definition:

```
#define  MAXIMUM_DATAVALUES    2000
```

And if the program is written to use MAXIMUM_DATAVALUES in all cases where the size of the array was used, the preceding definition could be the only statement in the program that would have to be changed.

Program Portability

Another nice use of the #define statement is that it helps to make programs more portable from one computer system to another. At times, it might be necessary to use constant values that are related to the particular computer on which the program is running. This might have to do with the use of a particular computer memory address, a filename, or the number of bits contained in a computer word, for example. You will recall that your `rotate()` function from Program 11.4 used the knowledge that an `int` contained 32 bits on the machine on which the program was executed.

If you want to execute this program on a different machine, on which an `int` contained 64 bits, the `rotate` function would not work correctly.[4] Study the following code. In situations in which the program *must* be written to make use of machine-dependent values, it makes sense to isolate such dependencies from the program as much as possible. The #define statement can help significantly in this respect. The new version of the `rotate` function would be easier to port to another machine, even though it is a rather simple case in point. Here's the new function:

```c
#include <stdio.h>

#define  kIntSize  32    // *** machine dependent !!! ***

// Function to rotate an unsigned int left or right

unsigned int  rotate (unsigned int  value, int  n)
{
    unsigned int  result, bits;

    /* scale down the shift count to a defined range */

    if  ( n > 0 )
        n = n % kIntSize;
    else
        n = -(-n % kIntSize);

    if  ( n == 0 )
        result = value;
    else if ( n > 0 )     /* left rotate */
    {
        bits = value >> (kIntSize - n);
        result = value << n  |  bits;
    }
    else                 /* right rotate */
    {
        n = -n;
        bits = value << (kIntSize - n) ;
        result = value >> n  |  bits;
    }

    return result;
}
```

---

4. Of course, you can write the `rotate` function so that it determines the number of bits in an `int` by itself and, therefore, is completely machine independent. Refer to exercises 3 and 4 at the end of Chapter 11, "Operations on Bits."

More Advanced Types of Definitions

A definition for a name can include more than a simple constant value. It can include an expression, and, as you will see shortly, just about anything else!

The following defines the name TWO_PI as the product of 2.0 and 3.141592654:

```
#define  TWO_PI    2.0 * 3.141592654
```

You can subsequently use this defined name anywhere in a program where the expression 2.0 × 3.141592654 would be valid. So you could have replaced the return statement of the circumference function from the previous program with the following statement, for example:

```
return  TWO_PI * r;
```

Whenever a defined name is encountered in a C program, *everything* that appears to the right of the defined name in the #define statement is literally substituted for the name at that point in the program. So, when the C preprocessor encounters the name TWO_PI in the return statement shown previously, it substitutes for this name whatever appeared in the #define statement for this name. Therefore, 2.0 × 3.141592654 is literally substituted by the preprocessor whenever the defined name TWO_PI occurs in the program.

The fact that the preprocessor performs a literal text substitution whenever the defined name occurs explains why you don't usually want to end your #define statement with a semicolon. If you did, then the semicolon would also be substituted into the program wherever the defined name appeared. If you had defined PI as

```
#define  PI        3.141592654;
```

and then written

```
return  2.0 * PI * r;
```

the preprocessor would replace the occurrence of the defined name PI with 3.141592654;. The compiler would therefore see this statement as

```
return  2.0 * 3.141592654; * r;
```

after the preprocessor had made its substitution, which would result in a syntax error.

A preprocessor definition does not have to be a valid C expression in its own right—just so long as wherever it is used the resulting expression is valid. For instance, the definition

```
#define  LEFT_SHIFT_8    << 8
```

is legitimate, even though what appears after LEFT_SHIFT_8 is not a syntactically valid expression. You can use your definition of LEFT_SHIFT_8 in a statement such as

```
x = y  LEFT_SHIFT_8;
```

to shift the contents of y to the left eight bits and assign the result to x. Of a much more practical nature, you can set up the definitions

```
#define  AND       &&
#define  OR        ||
```

and then write expressions such as

```
if ( x > 0  AND  x < 10 )
   . . .
```

and

```
if ( y == 0  OR  y == value )
   . . .
```

You can even include a #define statement for the equality test:

```
#define  EQUALS     ==
```

and then write the statement

```
if   ( y  EQUALS 0  OR  y EQUALS value )
   . . .
```

thus removing the very real possibility of mistakenly using a single equal sign for the equality test, as well as improving the statement's readability.

Although these examples illustrate the power of the #define, you should note that it is commonly considered poor programming practice to redefine the syntax of the underlying language in such a manner. Moreover, it can make it harder for someone else to understand your code.

To make things even more interesting, a defined value can itself reference another defined value. So the two defines

```
#define  PI         3.141592654
#define  TWO_PI      2.0 * PI
```

are perfectly valid. The name TWO_PI is defined in terms of the previously defined name PI, thus obviating the need to spell out the value 3.141592654 again.

Reversing the order of the defines, as in

```
#define  TWO_PI      2.0 * PI
#define  PI          3.141592654
```

is also valid. The rule is that you can reference other defined values in your definitions provided everything is defined at the time the defined name is *used* in the program. For readability, it is suggested that you don't use a defined term until it has been defined, though.

Good use of defines often reduces the need for comments within the program. Consider the following statement:

```
if ( year % 4 == 0  &&  year % 100 != 0  ||  year % 400 == 0 )
   . . .
```

You know from previous programs in this book that the preceding expression tests whether the variable year is a leap year. Now consider the following define and the subsequent if statement:

```
#define  IS_LEAP_YEAR    year % 4 == 0  &&  year % 100 != 0   \
                      || year % 400 == 0
    ...
if  ( IS_LEAP_YEAR )
    ...
```

Normally, the preprocessor assumes that a definition is contained on a single line of the program. If a second line is needed, the final character on the line must be a backslash character. This character signals a continuation to the preprocessor and is otherwise ignored. The same holds true for more than one continuation line; each line to be continued must be ended with a backslash character.

The preceding if statement is far easier to understand than the one shown directly before it. There is no need for a comment as the statement is self-explanatory. The purpose that the define IS_LEAP_YEAR serves is analogous to that served by a function. You could have used a call to a function named is_leap_year to achieve the same degree of readability. The choice of which to use in this case is completely subjective. Of course, the is_leap_year function could be made more general than the preceding define because it could be written to take an argument. This would enable you to test if the value of any variable were a leap year and not just the variable year to which the IS_LEAP_YEAR define restricts you. Actually, you *can* write a definition to take one or more arguments, which leads to our next point of discussion.

Arguments and Macros

IS_LEAP_YEAR can be defined to take an argument called y as follows:

```
#define  IS_LEAP_YEAR(y)    y % 4 == 0  &&  y % 100 != 0  \
                      || y % 400 == 0
```

Unlike a function, you do not define the type of the argument y here because you are merely performing a literal text substitution and not invoking a function.

Note that no spaces are permitted in the #define statement between the defined name and the left parenthesis of the argument list.

With the preceding definition, you can write a statement such as

```
if ( IS_LEAP_YEAR (year) )
    ...
```

to test whether the value of year were a leap year, or

```
if ( IS_LEAP_YEAR (next_year) )
    ...
```

to test whether the value of next_year were a leap year. In the preceding statement, the definition for IS_LEAP_YEAR would be directly substituted inside the if statement, with the argument next_year replacing y wherever it appeared in the definition. So the if statement would actually be seen by the compiler as

```
if ( next_year % 4 == 0  &&  next_year % 100 != 0   \
        || next_year % 400 == 0 )
    ...
```

In C, definitions are frequently called *macros*. This terminology is more often applied to definitions that take one or more arguments. An advantage of implementing something in C as a macro, as opposed to as a function, is that in a macro, the type of the argument is not important. For example, consider a macro called SQUARE that simply squares its argument. The definition

```
#define  SQUARE(x)   x * x
```

enables you to subsequently write statements, such as

```
y = SQUARE (v);
```

to assign the value of v^2 to y. The point to be made here is that v can be of type int, long, or float, for example, and the *same* macro can be used. If SQUARE were implemented as a function that took an int argument, for example, you couldn't use it to calculate the square of a double value. One consideration about macro definitions, which might be relevant to your application: Because macros are directly substituted into the program by the preprocessor, they inevitably use more memory space than an equivalently defined function. On the other hand, because a function takes time to call and to return, this overhead is avoided when a macro definition is used instead.

Although the macro definition for SQUARE is straightforward, there is an interesting pitfall to avoid when defining macros. As has been described, the statement

```
y = SQUARE (v);
```

assigns the value of v^2 to y. What do you think would happen in the case of the statement

```
y = SQUARE (v + 1);
```

This statement does *not* assign the value of (v + 1)2 to y as you would expect. Because the preprocessor performs a literal text substitution of the argument into the macro definition, the preceding expression would actually be evaluated as

```
y = v + 1 * v + 1;
```

which would obviously not produce the expected results. To handle this situation properly, parentheses are needed in the definition of the SQUARE macro:

```
#define  SQUARE(x)   ( (x) * (x) )
```

Even though the preceding definition might look strange, remember that it is the entire expression as given to the SQUARE macro that is literally substituted wherever x appears in the definition. With your new macro definition for SQUARE, the statement

```
y = SQUARE (v + 1);
```

is then correctly evaluated as

```
y = ( (v + 1) * (v + 1) );
```

The conditional expression operator can be particularly handy when defining macros. The following defines a macro called MAX that gives the maximum of two values:

```
#define  MAX(a,b)    ( ((a) > (b)) ? (a) : (b) )
```

This macro enables you to subsequently write statements such as

```
limit = MAX (x + y, minValue);
```

which would assign to limit the maximum of x + y and minValue. Parentheses were placed around the entire MAX definition to ensure that an expression such as

```
MAX (x, y) * 100
```

gets evaluated properly; and parentheses were individually placed around each argument to ensure that expressions such as

```
MAX (x & y, z)
```

get correctly evaluated. The bitwise AND operator has lower precedence than the > operator used in the macro. Without the parentheses in the macro definition, the > operator would be evaluated before the bitwise AND, producing the incorrect result.

The following macro tests if a character is a lowercase letter:

```
#define  IS_LOWER_CASE(x)   ( ((x) >= 'a') && ((x) <= 'z') )
```

and thereby permits expressions such as

```
if ( IS_LOWER_CASE (c)  )
    . . .
```

to be written. You can even use this macro in a subsequent macro definition to convert an ASCII character from lowercase to uppercase, leaving any nonlowercase character unchanged:

```
#define  TO_UPPER(x) ( IS_LOWER_CASE (x) ? (x) - 'a' + 'A' : (x) )
```

The program loop

```
while ( *string  != '\0' )
{
    *string = TO_UPPER (*string);
    ++string;
}
```

would sequence through the characters pointed to by `string`, converting any lowercase characters in the string to uppercase.[5]

Variable Number of Arguments to Macros

A macro can be defined to take an indeterminate or variable number of arguments. This is specified to the preprocessor by putting three dots at the end of the argument list. The remaining arguments in the list are collectively referenced in the macro definition by the special identifier `__VA_ARGS__`. As an example, the following defines a macro called `debugPrintf` to take a variable number of arguments:

```
#define debugPrintf(...)   printf ("DEBUG:" __VA_ARGS__);
```

Legitimate macro uses would include

```
debugPrintf ("Hello world!\n");
```

as well as

```
debugPrintf ("i = %i, j = %i\n", i, j);
```

In the first case, the output would be

```
DEBUG: Hello world!
```

And in the second case, if `i` had the value `100` and `j` the value `200`, the output would be

```
DEBUG: i = 100, j = 200
```

The `printf()` call in the first case gets expanded into

```
printf ("DEBGUG: " "Hello world\n");
```

by the preprocessor, which also concatenates the adjacent character string constants together. So the final `printf()` call looks like this:

```
printf ("DEBGUG: Hello world\n");
```

The # Operator

If you place a # in front of a parameter in a macro definition, the preprocessor creates a constant string out of the macro argument when the macro is invoked. For example, the definition

```
#define str(x)   # x
```

---

5. There are a host of functions in the library for doing character tests and conversions. For example, `islower` and `toupper` serve the same purpose as the macros `IS_LOWER_CASE` and `TO_UPPER`. For more details, consult Appendix B, "The Standard C Library."

causes the subsequent invocation

```
str (testing)
```

to be expanded into

```
"testing"
```

by the preprocessor. The `printf()` call

```
printf (str (Programming in C is fun.\n));
```

is therefore equivalent to

```
printf ("Programming in C is fun.\n");
```

The preprocessor literally inserts double quotation marks around the actual macro argument. Any double quotation marks or backslashes in the argument are preserved by the preprocessor. So

```
str ("hello")
```

produces

```
"\"hello\""
```

A more practical example of the use of the # operator might be in the following macro definition:

```
#define  printint(var)    printf (# var " = %i\n", var)
```

This macro is used to display the value of an integer variable. If `count` is an integer variable with a value of `100`, the statement

```
printint (count);
```

is expanded into

```
printf ("count" " = %i\n", count);
```

which, after string concatenation is performed on the two adjacent strings, becomes

```
printf ("count = %i\n", count);
```

So the # operator gives you a means to create a character string out of a macro argument. Incidentally, a space between the # and the parameter name is optional.

The ## Operator

This operator is used in macro definitions to join two *tokens* together. It is preceded (or followed) by the name of a parameter to the macro. The preprocessor takes the actual argument to the macro that is supplied when the macro is invoked and creates a single token out of that argument and whatever token follows (or precedes) the ##.

Suppose, for example, you have a list of variables x1 through x100. You can write a macro called printx that simply takes as its argument an integer value 1 through 100 and that displays the corresponding x variable as shown:

```
#define  printx(n)    printf ("%i\n", x ## n)
```

The portion of the define that reads

```
x ## n
```

says to take the tokens that occur before and after the ## (the letter x and the argument n, respectively) and make a single token out of them. So the call

```
printx (20);
```

is expanded into

```
printf ("%i\n", x20);
```

The printx macro can even use the previously defined printint macro to get the variable name as well as its value displayed:

```
#define  printx(n)    printint(x ## n)
```

The invocation

```
printx (10);
```

first expands into

```
printint (x10);
```

and then into

```
printf ("x10" " = %i\n", x10);
```

and finally into

```
printf ("x10 = %i\n", x10);
```

The #include Statement

After you have programmed in C for a while, you will find yourself developing your own set of macros and functions that you will want to use in each of your programs. But instead of having to type these macros into each new program you write, the preprocessor enables you to collect all your definitions into a separate file and then *include* the file and all its macros and user-defined functions in your program, using the #include statement. These files normally end with the characters .h and are referred to as *header* or *include* files.

Suppose you are writing a series of programs for performing various metric conversions. You might want to set up some defines for all of the constants that you need to perform your conversions:

```
#define  INCHES_PER_CENTIMETER    0.394
#define  CENTIMETERS_PER_INCH     1 / INCHES_PER_CENTIMETER

#define  QUARTS_PER_LITER         1.057
#define  LITERS_PER_QUART         1 / QUARTS_PER_LITER

#define  OUNCES_PER_GRAM          0.035
#define  GRAMS_PER_OUNCE          1 / OUNCES_PER_GRAM
   ...
```

Suppose you entered the previous definitions into a separate file on the system called metric.h. Any program that subsequently needed to use any of the definitions contained in the metric.h file could then do so by simply issuing the preprocessor directive

```
#include "metric.h"
```

This statement must appear before any of the defines contained in metric.h are referenced and is typically placed at the beginning of the source file. The preprocessor looks for the specified file on the system and effectively copies the contents of the file into the program at the precise point that the #include statement appears. So, any statements inside the file are treated just as if they had been directly typed into the program at that point.

The double quotation marks around the include filename instruct the preprocessor to look for the specified file in one or more file directories (typically first in the same directory that contains the source file, but the actual places the preprocessor searches are system dependent). If the file isn't located, the preprocessor automatically searches other *system* directories as described next.

Enclosing the filename within the characters < and > instead, as in

```
#include <stdio.h>
```

causes the preprocessor to look for the include file in the special system include file directory or directories. Once again, these directories are system dependent. On Unix systems (including Mac OS X systems), the system include file directory is /usr/include, so the standard header file stdio.h can be found in /usr/include/stdio.h.

To see how include files are used in an actual program example, type the six defines given previously into a file called metric.h. Then type in and run Program 12.3.

Program 12.3   **Using the** #include **Statement**

```
/* Program to illustrate the use of the #include statement
   Note: This program assumes that definitions are
   set up in a file called metric.h              */

#include <stdio.h>
#include "metric.h"
```

```
int main (void)
{
    float  liters, gallons;

    printf ("*** Liters to Gallons ***\n\n");
    printf ("Enter the number of liters: ");
    scanf ("%f", &liters);

    gallons = liters * QUARTS_PER_LITER / 4.0;
    printf ("%g liters = %g gallons\n", liters, gallons);

    return 0;
}
```

Program 12.3 **Output**

```
*** Liters to Gallons ***

Enter the number of liters: 55.75
55.75 liters = 14.73 gallons.
```

The preceding example is a rather simple one because it only shows a single defined value (QUARTS_PER_LITER) being referenced from the included file metric.h. Nevertheless, the point is well made: After the definitions have been entered into metric.h, they can be used in any program that uses an appropriate #include statement.

One of the nicest things about the include file capability is that it enables you to centralize your definitions, thus ensuring that all programs reference the same value. Furthermore, errors discovered in one of the values contained in the include file need only be corrected in that one spot, thus eliminating the need to correct each and every program that uses the value. Any program that references the incorrect value simply needs to be recompiled and does not have to be edited.

You can actually put anything you want in an include file—not just #define statements, as might have been implied. Using include files to centralize commonly used preprocessor definitions, structure definitions, prototype declarations, and global variable declarations is good programming technique.

One last point to be made about include files in this chapter: Include files can be nested. That is, an include file can itself include another file, and so on.

System Include Files

It was noted that the include file <stddef.h> contains a define for NULL and is often used for testing to see whether a pointer has a null value. Earlier in this chapter, it was also noted that the header file <math.h> contains the definition M_PI, which is set to an approximation for the value of π.

The <stdio.h> header file contains information about the I/O routines contained in the standard I/O library. This header file is described in more detail in Chapter 15, "Input and Output Operations in C." You should include this file whenever you use any I/O library routine in your program.

Two other useful system include files are <limits.h> and <float.h>. The first file, <limits.h>, contains system-dependent values that specify the sizes of various character and integer data types. For instance, the maximum size of an int is defined by the name INT_MAX inside this file. The maximum size of an unsigned long int is defined by ULONG_MAX, and so on.

The <float.h> header file gives information about floating-point data types. For example, FLT_MAX specifies the maximum floating-point number, and FLT_DIG specifies the number of decimal digits of precision for a float type.

Other system include files contain prototype declarations for various functions stored inside the system library. For example, the include file <string.h> contains prototype declarations for the library routines that perform character string operations, such as copying, comparing, and concatenating.

For more details on these header files, consult Appendix B.

Conditional Compilation

The C preprocessor offers a feature known as *conditional compilation*. Conditional compilation is often used to create one program that can be compiled to run on different computer systems. It is also often used to switch on or off various statements in the program, such as debugging statements that print out the values of various variables or trace the flow of program execution.

The #ifdef, #endif, #else, and #ifndef Statements

You were shown earlier in this chapter how you could make the rotate() function from Chapter 11 more portable. You saw there how the use of a #define would help in this regard. The definition

```
#define  kIntSize  32
```

was used to isolate the dependency on the specific number of bits contained in an unsigned int. It was noted in several places that this dependency does not have to be made at all because the program can itself determine the number of bits stored inside an unsigned int.

Unfortunately, a program sometimes must rely on system-dependent parameters—on a filename, for example—that might be specified differently on different systems or on a particular feature of the operating system.

If you had a large program that had many such dependencies on the particular hardware and/or software of the computer system (and this should be minimized as much as possible), you might end up with many defines whose values would have to be changed when the program was moved to another computer system.

You can help reduce the problem of having to change these defines when the program is moved and can incorporate the values of these defines for each different machine into the program by using the conditional compilation capabilities of the preprocessor. As a simple example, the statements

```
#ifdef  UNIX
#    define  DATADIR      "/uxn1/data"
#else
#    define  DATADIR      "\usr\data"
#endif
```

have the effect of defining DATADIR to "/uxn1/data" if the symbol UNIX has been previously defined and to "\usr\data" otherwise. As you can see here, you are allowed to put one or more spaces after the # that begins a preprocessor statement.

The #ifdef, #else, and #endif statements behave as you would expect. If the symbol specified on the #ifdef line has been already defined—through a #define statement or through the command line when the program is compiled—then lines that follow up to a #else, #elif, or #endif are processed by the compiler; otherwise, they are ignored.

To define the symbol UNIX to the preprocessor, the statement

```
#define  UNIX    1
```

or even just

```
#define  UNIX
```

suffices. Most compilers also permit you to define a name to the preprocessor when the program is compiled by using a special option to the compiler command. The gcc command line

```
gcc -D UNIX program.c
```

defines the name UNIX to the preprocessor, causing all #ifdef UNIX statements inside program.c to evaluate as TRUE (note that the -D UNIX must be typed *before* the program name on the command line). This technique enables names to be defined *without* having to edit the source program.

A value can also be assigned to the defined name on the command line. For example,

```
gcc -D GNUDIR=/c/gnustep program.c
```

invokes the gcc compiler, defining the name GNUDIR to be the text /c/gnustep.

Avoiding Multiple Inclusion of Header Files

The #ifndef statement follows along the same lines as the #ifdef. This statement is used the same way the #ifdef statement is used, except that it causes the subsequent lines to be processed if the indicated symbol is *not* defined. This statement is often used to avoid multiple inclusion of a file in a program. For example, inside a header file, if you want to make certain it is included only once in a program, you can define a unique identifier that can be tested later. Consider the sequence of statements:

```
#ifndef _MYSTDIO_H
#define _MYSTDIO_H
  ...
#endif /* _MYSTDIO_H */
```

Suppose you typed this into a file called `mystdio.h`. If you included this file in your program with a statement like this:

```
#include "mystdio.h"
```

the `#ifndef` inside the file would test whether `_MYSTDIO_H` were defined. Because it wouldn't be, the lines between the `#ifndef` and the matching `#endif` would be included in the program. Presumably, this would contain all of the statements that you want included in your program from this header file. Notice that the very next line in the header file defines `_MYSTDIO_H`. If an attempt were made to again include the file in the program, `_MYSTDIO_H` would be defined, so the statements that followed (up to the `#endif`, which presumably is placed at the very end of your header file) would not be included in the program, thus avoiding multiple inclusion of the file in the program.

This method as shown is used in the system header files to avoid their multiple inclusion in your programs. Take a look at some and see!

The `#if` and `#elif` Preprocessor Statements

The `#if` preprocessor statement offers a more general way of controlling conditional compilation. The `#if` statement can be used to test whether a constant expression evaluates to nonzero. If the result of the expression is nonzero, subsequent lines up to a `#else`, `#elif`, or `#endif` are processed; otherwise, they are skipped. As an example of how this might be used, assume you define the name OS, which is set to 1 if the operating system is Macintosh OS, to 2 if the operating system is Windows, to 3 if the operating system is Linux, and so on. You could write a sequence of statements to conditionally compile statements based upon the value of OS as follows:

```
#if    OS == 1  /* Mac OS */
  ...
#elif  OS == 2  /* Windows */
   ...
#elif  OS == 3  /* Linux  */
   ...
#else
   ...
#endif
```

With most compilers, you can assign a value to the name OS on the command line using the `-D` option discussed earlier. The command line

```
gcc -D OS=2 program.c
```

compiles `program.c` with the name `OS` defined as `2`. This causes the program to be compiled to run under Windows.

The special operator

```
defined (name)
```

can also be used in `#if` statements. The set of preprocessor statements

```
#if  defined (DEBUG)
    ...
#endif
```

and

```
#ifdef DEBUG
    ...
#endif
```

does the same thing. The statements

```
#if defined (WINDOWS) || defined (WINDOWSNT)
#  define BOOT_DRIVE "C:/"
#else
#  define BOOT_DRIVE "D:/"
#endif
```

define `BOOT_DRIVE` as `"C:/"` if either `WINDOWS` or `WINDOWSNT` is defined and as `"D:/"` otherwise.

The **#undef** Statement

On some occasions, you might need to cause a defined name to become undefined. This is done with the #undef statement. To remove the definition of a particular `name`, you write

```
#undef  name
```

So the statement

```
#undef  LINUX
```

removes the definition of `LINUX`. Subsequent `#ifdef LINUX` or `#if defined (LINUX)` statements will evaluate as FALSE.

This concludes the discussion of the preprocessor. You have seen how the preprocessor can be used to make programs easier to read, write, and modify. You've also seen how you can use include files to group common definitions and declarations together into a file that can be shared among different files. Some other preprocessor statements that weren't described here are described in Appendix A, "C Language Summary."

In the next chapter, you'll learn more about data types and type conversions. Before proceeding, try the following exercises.

Exercises

1. Type in and run the three programs presented in this chapter, remembering to type in the `.h` include file associated with Program 12.3. Compare the output produced by each program with the output presented in the text.

2. Locate the system header files `<stdio.h>`, `<limits.h>`, and `<float.h>` on your system (on Unix systems, look inside the `/usr/include` directory). Examine the files to see what's in them.

3. Define a macro `MIN` that gives the minimum of two values. Then write a program to test the macro definition.

4. Define a macro `MAX3` that gives the maximum of three values. Write a program to test the definition.

5. Write a macro `SHIFT` to perform the identical purpose as the `shift` function of Program 11.3.

6. Write a macro `IS_UPPER_CASE` that gives a nonzero value if a character is an uppercase letter.

7. Write a macro `IS_ALPHABETIC` that gives a nonzero value if a character is an alphabetic character. Have the macro use the `IS_LOWER_CASE` macro defined in the chapter text and the `IS_UPPER_CASE` macro defined in exercise 6.

8. Write a macro `IS_DIGIT` that gives a nonzero value if a character is a digit `'0'` through `'9'`. Use this macro in the definition of another macro `IS_SPECIAL`, which gives a nonzero result if a character is a special character; that is, not alphabetic and not a digit. Be certain to use the `IS_ALPHABETIC` macro developed in exercise 7.

9. Write a macro `ABSOLUTE_VALUE` that computes the absolute value of its argument. Make certain that an expression such as

   ```
   ABSOLUTE_VALUE (x + delta)
   ```

   is properly evaluated by the macro.

10. Consider the definition of the `printint` macro from this chapter:

    ```
    #define printint(n)   printf ("%i\n", x ## n)
    ```

    Could the following be used to display the values of the 100 variables `x1`–`x100`? Why or why not?

    ```
    for (i = 1; i < 100; ++i)
        printx (i);
    ```

11. Test the system library functions that are equivalent to the macros you developed in the preceding three exercises. The library functions are called `isupper`, `isalpha`, and `isdigit`. You need to include the *system* header file `<ctype.h>` in your program in order to use them.

## 13

Extending Data Types with the Enumerated Data Type, Type Definitions, and Data Type Conversions

This chapter introduces you to a data type that has not yet been described: the enumerated data type. You also learn about the `typedef` statement, which enables you to assign your own names to basic data types or to derived data types. Finally, in this chapter you see the precise rules that are used by the compiler in the conversion of data types in an expression. Although the three topics covered in this chapter are diverse, understanding them is an important step in maximizing the power of data use in your programs. The topics covered include

- Using enumerated data types
- Creating your own labels of C's existing data types with the `typedef` statement
- Converting existing data types to others

Enumerated Data Types

Wouldn't it be nice if you could define a variable and specify the valid values that could be stored into that variable? For example, suppose you had a variable called `myColor` and you wanted to use it to store only one of the primary colors, `red`, `yellow`, or `blue`, and no other values. This type of capability is provided by the enumerated data type.

An enumerated data type definition is initiated by the keyword `enum`. Immediately following this keyword is the name of the enumerated data type, followed by a list of identifiers (enclosed in a set of curly braces) that define the permissible values that can be assigned to the type. For example, the statement

```
enum primaryColor { red, yellow, blue };
```

defines a data type `primaryColor`. Variables declared to be of this data type can be assigned the values `red`, `yellow`, and `blue` inside the program, *and no other values*. That's the theory anyway! An attempt to assign another value to such a variable causes some compilers to issue an error message. Other compilers simply don't check.

To declare a variable to be of type `enum primaryColor`, you again use the keyword `enum`, followed by the enumerated type name, followed by the variable list. So the statement

```
enum primaryColor  myColor, gregsColor;
```

defines the two variables `myColor` and `gregsColor` to be of type `primaryColor`. The only permissible values that can be assigned to these variables are the names `red`, `yellow`, and `blue`. So statements such as

```
myColor = red;
```

and

```
if ( gregsColor == yellow )
   . . .
```

are valid. As another example of an enumerated data type definition, the following defines the type `enum month`, with permissible values that can be assigned to a variable of this type being the months of the year:

```
enum  month  { January, February, March, April, May, June,
               July, August, September, October, November, December };
```

The C compiler actually treats enumeration identifiers as integer constants. Beginning with the first name in the list, the compiler assigns sequential integer values to these names, starting with 0. If your program contains these two lines:

```
enum month  thisMonth;
   . . .
thisMonth = February;
```

the value 1 is assigned to `thisMonth` (and not the name `February`) because it is the second identifier listed inside the enumeration list.

If you want to have a specific integer value associated with an enumeration identifier, the integer can be assigned to the identifier when the data type is defined. Enumeration identifiers that subsequently appear in the list are assigned sequential integer values beginning with the specified integer value plus 1. For example, in the definition

```
enum  direction  { up, down, left = 10, right };
```

an enumerated data type `direction` is defined with the values `up`, `down`, `left`, and `right`. The compiler assigns the value 0 to `up` because it appears first in the list; 1 to `down` because it appears next; 10 to `left` because it is explicitly assigned this value; and 11 to `right` because it appears immediately after `left` in the list.

Program 13.1 shows a simple program using enumerated data types. The enumerated data type month sets January to 1 so that the month numbers 1 through 12 correspond to the enumeration values January, February, and so on. The program reads a month number and then enters a switch statement to see which month was entered. Recall that enumeration values are treated as integer constants by the compiler, so they're valid case values. The variable days is assigned the number of days in the specified month, and its value is displayed after the switch is exited. A special test is included to see if the month is February.

Program 13.1   **Using Enumerated Data Types**

```
//  Program to print the number of days in a month

#include <stdio.h>

int main (void)
{
    enum  month  { January = 1, February, March, April, May, June,
                   July, August, September, October, November, December };
    enum  month  aMonth;
    int          days;

    printf ("Enter month number: ");
    scanf ("%i", &aMonth);

    switch (aMonth ) {
       case January:
       case March:
       case May:
       case July:
       case August:
       case October:
       case December:
               days = 31;
               break;
       case April:
       case June:
       case September:
       case November:
               days = 30;
               break;
       case February:
               days = 28;
               break;
       default:
               printf ("bad month number\n");
               days = 0;
```

```
            break;
    }

    if ( days != 0 )
        printf ("Number of days is %i\n", days);

    if ( aMonth  == february )
        printf ("...or 29 if it's a leap year\n");

    return 0;
}
```

Program 13.1 **Output**

```
Enter month number: 5
Number of days is 31
```

Program 13.1 **Output (Rerun)**

```
Enter month number: 2
Number of days is 28
...or 29 if it's a leap year
```

Enumeration identifiers can share the same value. For example, in

```
enum  switch  { no=0, off=0, yes=1, on=1 };
```

assigning either the value no or off to an enum switch variable assigns it the value 0; assigning either yes or on assigns it the value 1.

Explicitly assigning an integer value to an enumerated data type variable can be done with the type cast operator. So if monthValue is an integer variable that has the value 6, for example, the expression

```
thisMonth = (enum month) (monthValue - 1);
```

is permissible and assigns the value 5 to thisMonth.

When writing programs with enumerated data types, try not to rely on the fact that the enumerated values are treated as integers. Instead, try to treat them as distinct data types. The enumerated data type gives you a way to associate a symbolic name with an integer number. If you subsequently need to change the value of that number, you must change it only in the place where the enumeration is defined. If you make assumptions based on the actual value of the enumerated data type, you defeat this benefit of using an enumeration.

The variations permitted when defining an enumerated data type are similar to those permitted with structure definitions: The name of the data type can be omitted, and variables can be declared to be of the particular enumerated data type when the type is defined. As an example showing both of these options, the statement

```
enum { east, west, south, north }  direction;
```

defines an (unnamed) enumerated data type with values east, west, south, or north, and declares a variable direction to be of that type.

Enumerated type definitions behave like structure and variable definitions as far as their scope is concerned: Defining an enumerated data type within a block limits the scope of that definition to the block. On the other hand, defining an enumerated data type at the beginning of the program, outside of any function, makes the definition global to the file.

When defining an enumerated data type, you must make certain that the enumeration identifiers are unique with respect to other variable names and enumeration identifiers defined within the same scope.

The typedef Statement

C provides a capability that enables you to assign an alternate name to a data type. This is done with a statement known as typedef. The statement

```
typedef  int   Counter;
```

defines the name Counter to be equivalent to the C data type int. Variables can subsequently be declared to be of type Counter, as in the following statement:

```
Counter  j, n;
```

The C compiler actually treats the declaration of the variables j and n, shown in the preceding code, as normal integer variables. The main advantage of the use of the typedef in this case is in the added readability that it lends to the definition of the variables. It is clear from the definition of j and n what the intended purpose of these variables is in the program. Declaring them to be of type int in the traditional fashion would not have made the intended use of these variables at all clear. Of course, choosing more meaningful variable names would have helped as well!

In many instances, a typedef statement can be equivalently substituted by the appropriate #define statement. For example, you could have instead used the statement

```
#define  Counter  int
```

to achieve the same results as the preceding statement. However, because the typedef is handled by the C compiler proper, and not by the preprocessor, the typedef statement provides more flexibility than does the #define when it comes to assigning names to derived data types. For example, the following typedef statement:

```
typedef  char  Linebuf [81];
```

defines a type called Linebuf, which is an array of 81 characters. Subsequently declaring variables to be of type Linebuf, as in

```
Linebuf  text, inputLine;
```

has the effect of defining the variables `text` and `inputLine` to be arrays containing 81 characters. This is equivalent to the following declaration:

```
char   text[81], inputLine[81];
```

Note that, in this case, `Linebuf` could *not* have been equivalently defined with a `#define` preprocessor statement.

The following `typedef` defines a type name `StringPtr` to be a `char` pointer:

```
typedef   char *StringPtr;
```

Variables subsequently declared to be of type `StringPtr`, as in

```
StringPtr   buffer;
```

are treated as character pointers by the C compiler.

To define a new type name with `typedef`, follow these steps:

1. Write the statement as if a variable of the desired type were being declared.

2. Where the name of the declared variable would normally appear, substitute the new type name.

3. In front of everything, place the keyword `typedef`.

As an example of this procedure, to define a type called `Date` to be a structure containing three integer members called `month`, `day`, and `year`, you write out the structure definition, substituting the name `Date` where the variable name would normally appear (before the last semicolon). Before everything, you place the keyword `typedef`:

```
typedef   struct
          {
              int    month;
              int    day;
              int    year;
          } Date;
```

With this `typedef` in place, you can subsequently declare variables to be of type `Date`, as in

```
Date   birthdays[100];
```

This defines `birthdays` to be an array containing 100 `Date` structures.

When working on programs in which the source code is contained in more than one file (as described in Chapter 14, "Working with Larger Programs"), it's a good idea to place the common `typedef` statements into a separate file that can be included into each source file with an `#include` statement.

As another example, suppose you're working on a graphics package that needs to deal with drawing lines, circles, and so on. You probably will be working very heavily with the coordinate system. Here's a `typedef` statement that defines a type named `Point`, where a `Point` is a structure containing two `float` members `x` and `y`:

```
typedef  struct
{
    float  x;
    float  y;
} Point;
```

You can now proceed to develop your graphics library, taking advantage of this `Point` type. For example, the declaration

```
Point  origin = { 0.0, 0.0 }, currentPoint;
```

defines `origin` and `currentPoint` to be of type `Point` and sets the `x` and `y` members of `origin` to 0.0.

Here's a function called `distance` that calculates the distance between two points.

```
#include <math.h>

double  distance (Point p1, Point p2)
{
    double  diffx, diffy;

    diffx = p1.x - p2.x;
    diffy = p1.y - p2.y;

    return sqrt (diffx * diffx + diffy * diffy);
}
```

As previously noted, `sqrt` is the square root function from the standard library. It is declared in the system header file `math.h`, thus the reason for the `#include`.

Remember, the `typedef` statement does not actually define a new type—only a new type name. So the `Counter` variables `j` and `n`, as defined in the beginning of this section, would in all respects be treated as normal `int` variables by the C compiler.

Data Type Conversions

Chapter 3, "Variables, Data Types, and Arithmetic Expressions," briefly addressed the fact that sometimes conversions are implicitly made by the system when expressions are evaluated. The case you examined was with the data types `float` and `int`. You saw how an operation that involved a `float` and an `int` was carried out as a floating-point operation, the integer data item being automatically converted to floating point.

You have also seen how the type cast operator can be used to explicitly dictate a conversion. So in the statement

```
average = (float) total / n;
```

the value of the variable `total` is converted to type `float` before the operation is performed, thereby guaranteeing that the division will be carried out as a floating-point operation.

The C compiler adheres to strict rules when it comes to evaluating expressions that consist of different data types.

The following summarizes the order in which conversions take place in the evaluation of two operands in an expression:

1. If either operand is of type `long double`, the other is converted to `long double`, and that is the type of the result.

2. If either operand is of type `double`, the other is converted to `double`, and that is the type of the result.

3. If either operand is of type `float`, the other is converted to `float`, and that is the type of the result.

4. If either operand is of type `_Bool`, `char`, `short int`, `bit field`, or of an enumerated data type, it is converted to `int`.

5. If either operand is of type `long long int`, the other is converted to `long long int`, and that is the type of the result.

6. If either operand is of type `long int`, the other is converted to `long int`, and that is the type of the result.

7. If this step is reached, both operands are of type `int`, and that is the type of the result.

This is actually a simplified version of the steps that are involved in converting operands in an expression. The rules get more complicated when unsigned operands are involved. For the complete set of rules, refer to Appendix A, "C Language Summary."

Realize from this series of steps that whenever you reach a step that says "that is the type of the result," you're done with the conversion process.

As an example of how to follow these steps, see how the following expression would be evaluated, where f is defined to be a `float`, i an `int`, l a `long int`, and s a `short int` variable:

```
f * i + l / s
```

Consider first the multiplication of f by i, which is the multiplication of a `float` by an `int`. From step 3, you find that, because f is of type `float`, the other operand, i, is also converted to type `float`, and that is the type of the result of the multiplication.

Next, the division of l by s occurs, which is the division of a `long int` by a `short int`. Step 4 tells you that the `short int` is promoted to an `int`. Continuing, you find from step 6 that because one of the operands (l) is a `long int`, the other operand is converted to a `long int`, which is also the type of the result. This division, therefore, produces a value of type `long int`, with any fractional part resulting from the division truncated.

Finally, step 3 indicates that if one of the operands in an expression is of type float (as is the result of multiplying f * i), the other operand is converted to type float, which is the type of the result. Therefore, after the division of 1 by s has been performed, the result of the operation is converted to type float and then added into the product of f and i. The final result of the preceding expression is, therefore, a value of type float.

Remember, the type cast operator can always be used to explicitly force conversions and thereby control the way that a particular expression is evaluated.

So, if you didn't want the result of dividing 1 by s to be truncated in the preceding expression evaluation, you could have type cast one of the operands to type float, thereby forcing the evaluation to be performed as a floating-point division:

```
f * i + (float) 1 / s
```

In this expression, 1 would be converted to float before the division operation was performed, because the type cast operator has higher precedence than the division operator. Because one of the operands of the division would then be of type float, the other (s) would be automatically converted to type float, and that would be the type of the result.

Sign Extension

Whenever a signed int or signed short int is converted into an integer of a larger size, the sign is extended to the left when the conversion is performed. This ensures that a short int having a value of –5, for example, will also have the value –5 when converted to a long int. Whenever an unsigned integer is converted to an integer of a larger size, as you would expect, no sign extension occurs.

On some systems, characters are treated as signed quantities. This means that when a character is converted to an integer, sign extension occurs. As long as characters are used from the standard ASCII character set, this fact will never pose a problem. However, if a character value is used that is not part of the standard character set, its sign might be extended when converted to an integer. For example on a Mac, the character constant '\377' is converted to the value –1 because its value is negative when treated as a signed, eight-bit quantity.

Recall that the C language permits character variables to be declared unsigned, thus avoiding this potential problem. That is, an unsigned char variable will never have its sign extended when converted to an integer; its value will always be greater than or equal to 0. For the typical eight-bit character, a signed character variable, therefore, has the range of values from –128 to +127, inclusive. An unsigned character variable can range in value from 0 to 255, inclusive.

If you want to force sign extension on your character variables, you can declare such variables to be of type signed char. This ensures that sign extension will occur when the character value is converted to an integer, even on machines that don't do so by default.

Argument Conversion

You have used prototype declarations for all the functions that you have written in this book. In Chapter 7, "Working with Functions," you learned this was prudent because you can physically locate the function either before or after its call, or even in another source file, with a prototype declaration. It was also noted that the compiler automatically converts your arguments to the appropriate types as long as it knows the types of arguments the function expects. The only way it can know this is by having previously encountered the actual function definition or a prototype declaration.

Recall that, if the compiler sees neither the function definition nor a prototype declaration before it encounters a call to a function, it assumes the function returns an int. The compiler also makes assumptions about its argument types. In the absence of information about the argument types to a function, the compiler automatically converts _Bool, char, or short arguments to ints and converts float arguments to double.

For example, assume that the compiler encounters in your program

```
float  x;
   ...
y = absoluteValue (x);
```

Having not previously seen the definition of the absoluteValue function, and with no prototype declaration for it either, the compiler generates code to convert the value stored inside the float variable x to double and passes the result to the function. The compiler also assumes the function returns an int.

If the absoluteValue function is defined inside another source file like this:

```
float  absoluteValue (float  x)
{
    if ( x < 0.0 )
       x = -x;

    return x;
}
```

you're in trouble. First, the function returns a float, yet the compiler thinks it returns an int. Second, the function expects to see a float argument, but you know the compiler will pass a double.

Remember, the bottom line here is that you should always include prototype declarations for the functions you use. This prevents the compiler from making mistaken assumptions about return types and argument types.

Now that you have learned more about data types, it's time to learn about how to work with programs that can be split into multiple source files. Chapter 14 covers this topic in detail. Before you start that chapter, try the following exercises to make certain you understand the concepts you just learned.

Exercises

1. Define a type FunctionPtr() (using typedef) that represents a pointer to a function that returns an int and that takes no arguments. Refer to Chapter 10, "Pointers," for the details on how to declare a variable of this type.

2. Write a function called monthName() that takes as its argument a value of type enum month (as defined in this chapter) and returns a pointer to a character string containing the name of the month. In this way, you can display the value of an enum month variable with a statement such as:

   ```
   printf ("%s\n", monthName (aMonth));
   ```

3. Given the following variable declarations:

   ```
   float     f = 1.00;
   short int i = 100;
   long int  l = 500L;
   double    d = 15.00;
   ```

   and the seven steps outlined in this chapter for conversion of operands in expressions, determine the type and value of the following expressions:

   ```
   f + i
   l / d
   i / l + f
   l * i
   f / 2
   i / (d + f)
   l / (i * 2.0)
   l + i / (double) l
   ```

## 14

Working with Larger Programs

The programs that have been illustrated throughout this book have all been very small and relatively simple. Unfortunately, the programs that you will have to develop to solve your particular problems will probably be neither as small nor as simple. Learning the proper techniques for dealing with such programs is the topic of this chapter. As you will see, C provides all the features necessary for the efficient development of large programs. In addition, developing with an Integrated Development Environment (IDE) or using one of several utility programs—which are briefly mentioned in this chapter—can make working with large projects easier.

This chapter covers a number of topics that are specific to whichever operating system and development environment you use, but the concepts are good to learn in case you find yourself using different development environments. Some of the topics covered include:

- Breaking larger programs into multiple files
- Compiling several files into one executable
- Working with external variables
- Extending the use of header files
- Improving your programs with utilities

Dividing Your Program into Multiple Files

In every program that you've seen so far, it was assumed that the entire program was entered into a single file—presumably via some text editor that came with your C compiler, or a stand-alone product such as emacs, vim, or some Windows-based editor—and then compiled and executed. In this single file, all the functions that the program used were included—except, of course, for the system functions, such as printf() and scanf(). Standard header files such as <stdio.h> and <stdbool.h> were also included for definitions and function declarations. This approach works fine when dealing with small programs—that is, programs that contain up to 100 statements or so. However, when you start dealing with larger programs, this approach no longer suffices. As the number of statements in the program increases, so does the time it takes to edit the program and to subsequently recompile it. Not only that, large programming applications frequently require the efforts of more than one programmer. Having everyone work on the same source file, or even on their own copy of the same source file, is unmanageable.

C supports the notion of modular programming in that it does not require that all the statements for a particular program be contained in a single file. This means that you can enter your code for a particular module into one file, for another module into a different file, and so on. Here, the term *module* refers either to a single function or to a number of related functions that you choose to group logically.

If you're working with a windows-based project management tool, such as Metrowerks' CodeWarrior, Code::Blocks, Microsoft Visual Studio, Apple's Xcode, or other IDEs, working with multiple source files is easy. You simply have to identify the particular files that belong to the project on which you are working, and the software handles the rest for you. The next section describes how to work with multiple files if you're not using such a tool. That is, the next section assumes you are compiling programs from the command line by directly issuing gcc or cc commands, for example.

Compiling Multiple Source Files from the Command Line

Suppose you have conceptually divided your program into three modules and have entered the statements for the first module into a file called mod1.c, the statements for the second module into a file called mod2.c, and the statements for your main() routine into the file main.c. To tell the system that these three modules actually belong to the same program, you simply include the names of all three files when you enter the command to compile the program. For example, using gcc, the command

```
$ gcc mod1.c mod2.c main.c -o dbtest
```

has the effect of separately compiling the code contained in mod1.c, mod2.c, and main.c. Errors discovered in mod1.c, mod2.c, and main.c are separately identified by the compiler. For example, if the gcc compiler gives output that looks like this:

```
mod2.c:10: mod2.c: In function 'foo':
mod2.c:10: error: 'i' undeclared (first use in this function)
mod2.c:10: error: (Each undeclared identifier is reported only once
mod2.c:10: error: for each function it appears in.)
```

then the compiler indicates that mod2.c has an error at line 10, which is in the function foo. Because no messages are displayed for mod1.c and main.c, no errors are found compiling those modules.

Typically, if there are errors discovered in a module, you have to edit the module to correct the mistakes.[1] In this case, because an error was discovered only inside mod2.c, you have to edit

---

1. *The error might be due to a problem with a header file included by that module, for example, which means the header file and not the module would have to be edited.*

only this file to fix the mistake. You can then tell the C compiler to recompile your modules after the correction has been made:

```
$ gcc mod1.c mod2.c main.c -o dbtest
$
```

Because no error message was reported, the executable was placed in the file dbtest.

Normally, the compiler generates intermediate object files for each source file that it compiles. The compiler places the resulting object code from compiling mod.c into the file mod.o by default. (Most Windows compilers work similarly, only they might place the resulting object code into .obj files instead of .o files.) Typically, these intermediate object files are automatically deleted after the compilation process ends. Some C compilers (and, historically, the standard Unix C compiler) keep these object files around and do not delete them when you compile more than one file at a time. This fact can be used to your advantage for recompiling a program after making a change to only one or several of your modules. So in the previous example, because mod1.c and main.c had no compiler errors, the corresponding .o files— mod1.o and main.o—would still be around after the gcc command completed. Replacing the c from the filename mod.c with an o tells the C compiler to use the object file that was produced the last time mod.c was compiled. So, the following command line could be used with a compiler (in this case, cc) that does not delete the object code files:

```
$ cc mod1.o mod2.c main.o -o dbtest
```

So, not only do you not have to reedit mod1.c and main.c if no errors are discovered by the compiler, but you also don't have to recompile them.

If your compiler automatically deletes the intermediate .o files, you can still take advantage of performing incremental compilations by compiling each module separately and using the -c command-line option. This option tells the compiler not to link your file (that is, not to try to produce an executable) and to retain the intermediate object file that it creates. So, typing

```
$ gcc -c mod2.c
```

compiles the file mod2.c, placing the resulting executable in the file mod2.o.

So, in general, you can use the following sequence to compile your three-module program dbtest using the incremental compilation technique:

```
$ gcc -c mod1.c                        Compile mod1.c => mod1.o
$ gcc -c mod2.c                        Compile mod2.c => mod2.o
$ gcc -c main.c                        Compile main.c => main.o
$ gcc mod1.o mod2.o mod3.o -o dbtest   Create executable
```

The three modules are compiled separately. The previous output shows no errors were detected by the compiler. If any were, the file could be edited and incrementally recompiled. The last line that reads

```
$ gcc mod1.o mod2.o mod3.o
```

lists only object files and no source files. In this case, the object files are just linked together to produce the executable output file dbtest.

If you extend the preceding examples to programs that consist of many modules, you can see how this mechanism of separate compilations can enable you to develop large programs more efficiently. For example, the commands

```
$ gcc -c legal.c                        Compile legal.c, placing output in legal.o
$ gcc legal.o makemove.o exec.o enumerator.o evaluator.o display.o -o superchess
```

could be used to compile a program consisting of six modules, in which only the module legal.c needs to be recompiled.

As you'll see in the last section of this chapter, the process of incremental compilation can be automated by using a tool called make. The IDE tools that were mentioned at the beginning of this chapter invariably have this knowledge of what needs recompilation, and they only recompile files as necessary.

Communication Between Modules

Several methods can be used so that the modules contained in separate files can effectively communicate. If a function from one file needs to call a function contained inside another file, the function call can be made in the normal fashion, and arguments can be passed and returned in the usual way. Of course, in the file that calls the function, you should *always make certain to include a prototype declaration so the compiler knows the function's argument types and the type of the return value*. As noted in Chapter 13, "Extending Data Types with the Enumerated Data Type, Type Definitions, and Data Type Conversions," in the absence of any information about a function, the compiler assumes it returns an int and converts short or char arguments to ints and float arguments to doubles when the function is called.

It's important to remember that even though more than one module might be specified to the compiler at the same time on the command line, *the compiler compiles each module independently*. That means that no knowledge about structure definitions, function return types, or function argument types is shared across module compilations by the compiler. It's totally up to you to ensure that the compiler has sufficient information about such things to correctly compile each module.

External Variables

Functions contained in separate files can communicate through *external variables*, which are effectively an extension to the concept of the global variable discussed in Chapter 7, "Working with Functions."

An external variable is one whose value can be accessed and changed by another module. Inside the module that wants to access the external variable, the variable is declared in the normal fashion and the keyword extern is placed before the declaration. This signals to the system that a globally defined variable from another file is to be accessed.

Suppose you want to define an `int` variable called moveNumber, whose value you want to access and possibly modify from within a function contained in another file. In Chapter 7, you learned that if you wrote the statement

```
int   moveNumber = 0;
```

at the beginning of your program, *outside* of any function, then its value could be referenced by any function within that program. In such a case, moveNumber was defined as a global variable.

Actually, this same definition of the variable moveNumber also makes its value accessible by functions contained in other files. Specifically, the preceding statement defines the variable moveNumber not just as a global variable, but also as an *external* global variable. To reference the value of an external global variable from another module, you must declare the variable to be accessed, preceding the declaration with the keyword `extern`, as follows:

```
extern int   moveNumber;
```

The value of moveNumber can now be accessed and modified by the module in which the preceding declaration appears. Other modules can also access the value of moveNumber by incorporating a similar `extern` declaration in the file.

You must obey an important rule when working with external variables. The variable has to be *defined* in some place among your source files. This is done in one of two ways. The first way is to declare the variable outside of any function, *not* preceded by the keyword `extern`, as follows:

```
int   moveNumber;
```

Here, an initial value can be optionally assigned to the variable, as was shown previously.

The second way to define an external variable is to declare the variable outside of any function, placing the keyword `extern` in front of the declaration, and *explicitly assigning an initial value to it*, as follows:

```
extern int moveNumber = 0;
```

Note that these two ways are mutually exclusive.

When dealing with external variables, the keyword `extern` can only be omitted in one spot throughout your source files. If you don't omit the keyword in any one spot, in exactly one place, you must assign the variable an initial value.

Take a look at a small program example to illustrate the use of external variables. Suppose you type the following code into a file called `main.c`:

```
#include <stdio.h>

int  i = 5;

int main (void)
{
    printf ("%i  ", i);
```

```
    foo ();

    printf ("%i\n", i);

    return 0;
}
```

The definition of the global variable i in the preceding program makes its value accessible by any module that uses an appropriate extern declaration. Suppose you now type the following statements into a file called foo.c:

```
extern int i;

void foo (void)
{
    i = 100;
}
```

Compiling the two modules main.c and foo.c together with a command like

```
$ gcc main.c foo.c
```

and subsequently executing the program produces the following output at the terminal:

```
5  100
```

This output verifies that the function foo is able to access and change the value of the external variable i.

Because the value of the external variable i is referenced *inside* the function foo, you could have placed the extern declaration of i inside the function itself, as follows:

```
void foo (void)
{
    extern int  i;

    i = 100;
}
```

If many functions in the file foo.c need to access the value of i, it is easier to make the extern declaration just once at the front of the file. However, if only one function or a small number of functions need to access this variable, there is something to be said for making separate extern declarations in each such function: It makes the program more organized and isolates the use of the particular variable to those functions that actually use it.

When declaring an external array, it is not necessary to give its size. Thus, the declaration

```
extern char  text[];
```

enables you to reference a character array `text` that is defined elsewhere. As with formal parameter arrays, if the external array is multidimensional, all but the first dimension must be specified. Thus, the declaration

```
extern int  matrix[] [50];
```

suffices to declare a two-dimensional external array `matrix` that contains 50 columns.

Static Versus **Extern** Variables and Functions

You now know that any variable defined outside of a function is not only a global variable, but is also an external variable. Many situations arise in which you want to define a variable to be global but *not* external. In other words, you want to define a global variable to be local to a particular module (file). It makes sense to want to define a variable this way if no functions other than those contained inside a particular file need access to the particular variable. This can be accomplished in C by defining the variable to be `static`.

The statement

```
static int  moveNumber = 0;
```

if made outside of any function, makes the value of `moveNumber` accessible from any subsequent point in the file in which the definition appears, *but not from functions contained in other files*.

If you need to define a global variable whose value does not have to be accessed from another file, declare the variable to be `static`. This is a cleaner approach to programming: The `static` declaration more accurately reflects the variable's usage and no conflicts can be created by two modules that unknowingly both use different external global variables of the same name.

As mentioned earlier in this chapter, you can directly call a function defined in another file. Unlike variables, no special mechanisms are required; that is, to call a function contained in another file, you don't need an `extern` declaration for that function.

When a function is *defined*, it can be declared to be `extern` or `static`, the former case being the default. A static function can be called only from within the same file as the function appears. So, if you have a function called `squareRoot`, placing the keyword `static` before the function header declaration for this function makes it callable only from within the file in which it is defined:

```
static double  squareRoot (double x)
{
   . . .
}
```

The definition of the `squareRoot` function effectively becomes local to the file in which it is defined. It cannot be called from outside the file.

The same motivations previously cited for using static variables also apply to the case of static functions.

Figure 14.1 summarizes communication between different modules. Here two modules are depicted, mod1.c and mod2.c.

```
double x;
static double result;

static void doSquare (void)
{
    double square (void);

    x = 2.0;
    result = square ();
}

int main (void)
{
    doSquare ();
    printf ("%g\n", result);

    return 0;
}
```

```
extern double x;


double square(void)
{

    return x * x;
}
```

                    mod1.c   mod2.c

Figure 14.1   Communication between modules.

mod1.c defines two functions: doSquare() and main(). The way things are set up here, main() calls doSquare(), which in turn calls square(). This last function is defined in the module mod2.c.

Because doSquare() is declared static, it can only be called from within mod1.c, and by no other module.

mod1.c defines two global variables: x and result, both of type double. x can be accessed by any module that is linked together with mod1.c. On the other hand, the keyword static in front of the definition of result means that it can only be accessed by functions defined inside mod1.c (namely main() and doSquare()).

When execution begins, the main() routine calls doSquare(). This function assigns the value 2.0 to the global variable x and then calls the function square(). Because square() is defined in another source file (inside mod2.c), and because it doesn't return an int, doSquare() properly includes an appropriate declaration at the beginning of the function.

The square() function returns as its value the square of the value of the global variable x. Because square wants to access the value of this variable, which is defined in another source file (in mod1.c), an appropriate extern declaration appears in mod2.c (and, in this case, it makes no difference whether the declaration occurs inside or outside the square() function).

The value that is returned by `square()` is assigned to the global variable `result` inside `doSquare()`, which then returns back to `main()`. Inside `main()`, the value of the global variable `result` is displayed. This example, when run, produces a result of 4.0 at the terminal (because that's obviously the square of 2.0).

Study the example until you feel comfortable with it. This small—albeit impractical—example illustrates very important concepts about communicating between modules, and it's necessary that you understand these concepts to work effectively with larger programs.

Using Header Files Effectively

In Chapter 12, "The Preprocessor," you were introduced to the concept of the include file. As stated there, you can group all your commonly used definitions inside such a file and then simply include the file in any program that needs to use those definitions. Nowhere is the usefulness of the `#include` facility greater than in developing programs that have been divided into separate program modules.

If more than one programmer is working on developing a particular program, include files provide a means of standardization: Each programmer is using the same definitions, which have the same values. Furthermore, each programmer is thus spared the time-consuming and error-prone task of typing these definitions into each file that must use them. These last two points are made even stronger when you start placing common structure definitions, external variable declarations, `typedef` definitions, and function prototype declarations into include files. Various modules of a large programming system invariably deal with common data structures. By centralizing the definition of these data structures into one or more include files, you eliminate the error that is caused by two modules that use different definitions for the same data structure. Furthermore, if a change has to be made to the definition of a particular data structure, it can be done in one place only—inside the include file.

Recall your `date` structure from Chapter 8, "Working with Structures;" following is an include file that might be similar to one you would set up if you have to work with a lot of dates within different modules: It is also a good example of how to tie together many of the concepts you've learned up to this point.

```
// Header file for working with dates


#include <stdbool.h>


// Enumerated types

enum kMonth { January=1, February, March, April, May, June,
        July, August, September, October, November, December };

enum kDay { Sunday, Monday, Tuesday, Wednesday, Thursday, Friday };
```

```
struct  date
{
    enum  kMonth month;
    enum  kDay   day;
    int          year;
};

// Date type
typedef struct date Date;

// Functions that work with dates
Date  dateUpdate (Date today);
int   numberOfDays (Date d);
bool  isLeapYear (Date d);

// Macro to set a date in a structure
#define setDate(s,mm,dd,yy)   s = (Date) {mm, dd, yy}

// External variable reference
extern Date todaysDate;
```

The header file defines two enumerated data types, kMonth and kDay, and the date structure (and note the use of the enumerated data types); uses typedef to create a type called Date; and declares functions that use this type, a macro to set a date to specific values (using compound literals), and an external variable called todaysDate, that will presumably be set to today's date (and is defined in one of the source files).

As an example using this header file, the following is a rewritten version of the dateUpdate function from Chapter 8.

```
#include "date.h"

// Function to calculate tomorrow's date

Date dateUpdate (Date today)
{
    Date  tomorrow;

    if ( today.day != numberOfDays (today) )
        setDate (tomorrow, today.month, today.day + 1, today.year);
    else if ( today.month == December )      // end of year
        setDate (tomorrow, January, 1, today.year + 1);
    else                              // end of month
        setDate (tomorrow, today.month + 1, 1, today.year);

    return tomorrow;
}.
```

Other Utilities for Working with Larger Programs

As briefly mentioned previously, the IDE can be a powerful tool for working with larger programs. If you still want to work from the command line, there are tools you might want to learn how to use. These tools are not part of the C language. However, they can help speed your development time, which is what it's all about.

Following is a list of tools you might want to consider when working with larger programs. If you are running Unix, you will find a plethora of commands at your disposal that can also help you in your development efforts. This is just the tip of the iceberg here. Learning how to write programs in a scripting language, such as the Unix shell, can also prove useful when dealing with large numbers of files.

The make Utility

This powerful utility (or its GNU version gnumake) allows you to specify a list of files and their dependencies in a special file known as a Makefile. The make program automatically recompiles files only when necessary. This is based on the modification times of a file. So, if make finds that your source (.c) file is newer than your corresponding object (.o) file, it automatically issues the commands to recompile the source file to create a new object file. You can even specify source files that depend on header files. For example, you can specify that a module called datefuncs.o is dependent on its source file datefunc.c as well as the header file date.h. Then, if you change anything inside the date.h header file, the make utility automatically recompiles the datefuncs.c file. This is based on the simple fact that the header file is newer than the source file.

Following is a simple Makefile that you could use for the three-module example from this chapter. It is assumed here that you've placed this file in the same directory as your source files.

```
$ cat Makefile
SRC = mod1.c mod2.c main.c
OBJ = mod1.o mod2.o main.o
PROG = dbtest

$(PROG): $(OBJ)
        gcc $(OBJ) -o $(PROG)


$(OBJ): $(SRC)
```

A detailed explanation of how this Makefile works is not provided here. In a nutshell, it defines the set of source files (SRC), the corresponding set of object files (OBJ), the name of the executable (PROG), and some dependencies. The first dependency,

```
$(PROG): $(OBJ)
```

says that the executable is dependent on the object files. So, if one or more object files change, the executable needs to be rebuilt. The way to do that is specified on the following gcc command line, which must be typed with a leading tab, as follows:

```
gcc $(OBJ) -o $(PROG)
```

The last line of the Makefile,

```
$(OBJ): $(SRC)
```

says that each object file depends on its corresponding source file. So, if a source file changes, its corresponding object file must be rebuilt. The make utility has built-in rules that tell it how to do that.

Here's what happens the first time you run make:

```
$ make
gcc    -c -o mod1.o mod1.c
gcc    -c -o mod2.o mod2.c
gcc    -c -o main.o main.c
gcc mod1.o mod2.o main.o -o dbtest
$
```

That's kind of nice! make compiled each individual source file and then linked the resulting object files to create the executable.

If you instead had an error in mod2.c, here's what the output from make would have looked like:

```
$ make
gcc    -c -o mod1.o mod1.c
gcc    -c -o mod2.o mod2.c
mod2.c: In function 'foo2':
mod2.c:3: error: 'i' undeclared (first use in this function)
mod2.c:3: error: (Each undeclared identifier is reported only once
mod2.c:3: error: for each function it appears in.)
make: *** [mod2.o] Error 1
$
```

Here, make found there was an error in compiling mod2.c and stopped the make process, which is its default action.

If you correct mod2.c and run make again, here's what happens:

```
$ make
gcc    -c -o mod2.o mod2.c
gcc    -c -o main.o main.c
gcc mod1.o mod2.o main.o -o dbtest
$
```

Notice that make didn't recompile mod1.c. That's because it knew it didn't have to. Therein lies the real power and elegance of the make utility.

Even with this simple example, you can use the sample Makefile to start using make for your own programs. Appendix E, "Resources," tells you where you can turn for more information on this powerful utility.

The `cvs` Utility

This is one of several utilities for managing source code. It provides for automatic version-tracking of source code, and keeps track of changes that are made to a module. This allows you to re-create a particular version of a program if needed (either to roll back code or to re-create an older version for customer support, for example). With `cvs` (which stands for Concurrent Versions System), you "check out" a program (using the `cvs` command with the checkout option), make your changes to it, and then "check it back in" (using the `cvs` command with the `commit` option). This mechanism avoids the potential conflict that can arise if more than one programmer wants to edit the same source file. With `cvs`, programmers can be at multiple locations and can all work on the same source code over a network.

Unix Utilities: `ar`, `grep`, `sed`, and so on

A wide assortment of commands available under Unix makes large program development easier and more productive. For example, you can use `ar` to create your own library. This is useful, for example, if you create a bunch of utility functions that you frequently use or want to share. Just as you linked your program with the `-lm` option whenever you used a routine from the standard math library, so too can you specify your own library at link time, using the option `-llib`. During the link edit phase, the library is automatically searched to locate functions that you reference from the library. Any such functions are pulled from the library and linked together with your program.

Other commands such as `grep` and `sed` are useful for searching for strings in a file or making global changes to a set of files. For example, combined with a little shell programming skills, you can easily use `sed` to change all occurrences of one particular variable name to another across a set of source files. The `grep` command simply searches a file or files for a specified string. This is useful for locating a variable or function in a set of source files, or a macro in a set of header files, for example. So the command

```
$ grep todaysDate main.c
```

can be used to search the file `main.c` for all lines containing the string `todaysDate`. The command

```
$ grep -n todaysDate *.c *.h
```

searches all source and header files in the current directory and displays each match preceded by its relative line number within the file (the use of the -n option). You have seen how the C language supports division of your program into smaller modules and incremental and independent compilation of those modules. Header files provide the "glue" between your modules when you use them to specify shared prototype declarations, macros, structure definitions, enumerations, and so on.

If you are using an IDE, managing multiple modules in a program is straightforward. The IDE application keeps track of the files that need to be recompiled when you make changes. If you're instead using a command-line compiler, like `gcc`, you either have to keep track of the files that need to be recompiled yourself, or you should resort to a tool such as make to automatically keep track for you. If you are compiling from the command line, you'll want to look into other tools that can help you search your source files, make global changes to them, and create and maintain program libraries.

15

Input and Output Operations in C

All reading and writing of data up to this point has been done through your output window, otherwise known as the console or terminal. When you wanted to input some information, you either used the `scanf()` or `getchar()` functions. All program results were displayed in your window with a call to the `printf()` function.

The C language itself does not have any special statements for performing input/output (I/O) operations; all I/O operations in C must be carried out through function calls. These functions are contained in the standard C library. This chapter covers some additional input and output functions as well as how to work with files. Topics covered include

- Covering basic I/O with `putchar()` and `getchar()`
- Maximizing `printf()` and `scanf()` with flags and modifiers
- Redirecting input and output from files
- Using file functions and pointers. Recall the use of the following `include` statement from previous programs that used the `printf()` or `scanf()` function:

```
#include <stdio.h>
```

This include file contains function declarations and macro definitions associated with the I/O routines from the standard library. Therefore, whenever using a function from this library, you should include this file in your program.

In this chapter, you learn about many of the I/O functions that are provided in the standard library. Unfortunately, space does not permit lengthy details about these functions or discussions of each function that is offered. Refer to Appendix B, "The Standard C Library," for a list of most of the functions in the library.

Character I/O: `getchar()` and `putchar()`

The `getchar()` function proved convenient when you wanted to read data a single character at a time. You saw how you could develop a function called `readLine()` to read an entire line of text that the user inputted. This function repeatedly called `getchar()` until a newline character was read.

There is an analogous function for writing data a single character at a time. The name of this function is `putchar()`.

A call to the `putchar()` function is quite simple: The only argument it takes is the character to be displayed. So, the call

```
putchar (c);
```

in which c is defined as type `char`, has the effect of displaying the character contained in c.

The call

```
putchar ('\n');
```

has the effect of displaying the newline character, which, as you know, causes the cursor to move to the beginning of the next line.

Formatted I/O: `printf()` and `scanf()`

You have been using the `printf()` and `scanf()` functions throughout this book. In this section, you learn about all of the options that are available for formatting data with these functions.

The first argument to both `printf()` and `scanf()` is a character pointer. This points to the format string. The format string specifies how the remaining arguments to the function are to be displayed in the case of `printf()`, and how the data that is read is to be interpreted in the case of `scanf()`.

The `printf()` Function

You have seen in various program examples how you could place certain characters between the % character and the specific so-called conversion character to more precisely control the formatting of the output. For example, you saw in Program 4.3A how an integer value before the conversion character could be used to specify a *field width*. The format characters `%2i` specified the display of an integer value right-justified in a field width of two columns. You also saw in exercise 6 in Chapter 4, "Program Looping," how a minus sign could be used to left-justify a value in a field.

The general format of a `printf()` conversion specification is as follows:

```
%[flags] [width] [.prec] [hlL] type
```

Optional fields are enclosed in brackets and must appear in the order shown.

Tables 15.1, 15.2, and 15.3 summarize all possible characters and values that can be placed directly after the % sign and before the `type` specification inside a format string.

Table 15.1   `printf()` **Flags**

Flag	Meaning
-	Left-justify value
+	Precede value with + or -
(*space*)	Precede positive value with space character
0	Zero fill numbers
#	Precede octal value with 0, hexadecimal value with 0x (or 0X); display decimal point for floats; leave trailing zeroes for g or G format

Table 15.2   `printf()` **Width and Precision Modifiers**

Specifier	Meaning
number	Minimum size of field
*	Take next argument to `printf()` as size of field
.*number*	Minimum number of digits to display for integers; number of decimal places for e or f formats; maximum number of significant digits to display for g; maximum number of characters for s format
.*	Take next argument to `printf` as precision (and interpret as indicated in preceding row)

Table 15.3   `printf()` **Type Modifiers**

Type	Meaning
hh	Display integer argument as a character
h*	Display short integer
l*	Display long integer
ll*	Display long long integer
L	Display long double
j*	Display intmax_t or uintmax_t value

Type	Meaning
t*	Display `ptrdiff_t` value
z*	Display `size_t` value

Note: These modifiers can also be placed in front of the n conversion character to indicate the corresponding pointer argument is of the specified type.

Table 15.4 lists the conversion characters that can be specified in the format string.

Table 15.4 `printf()` Conversion Characters

Char	Use to Display
i or d	Integer
u	Unsigned integer
o	Octal integer
x	Hexadecimal integer, using a–f
X	Hexadecimal integer, using A–F
f or F	Floating-point number, to six decimal places by default
e or E	Floating-point number in exponential format (e places lowercase e before the exponent, E places uppercase E before exponent)
g	Floating-point number in f or e format
G	Floating-point number in f or E format
a or A	Floating-point number in the hexadecimal format 0x*d.ddddp±d*
c	Single character
s	Null-terminated character string
p	Pointer
n	Doesn't print anything; stores the number of characters written so far by this call inside the `int` pointed to by the corresponding argument (see note from Table 15.3)
%	Percent sign

Tables 15.1 to 15.4 might appear a bit overwhelming. As you can see, many different combinations can be used to precisely control the format of your output. The best way to become familiar with the various possibilities is through experimentation. Just make certain that the number

of arguments you give to the `printf()` function matches the number of % signs in the format string (with %% as the exception, of course). And, in the case of using an * in place of an integer for the field width or precision modifiers, remember that `printf()` is expecting an argument for each asterisk as well.

Program 15.1 shows some of the formatting possibilities using `printf()`.

Program 15.1   Illustrating the `printf()` Formats

```c
// Program to illustate various printf() formats
#include <stdio.h>

int main (void)
{
    char           c = 'X';
    char           s[] = "abcdefghijklmnopqrstuvwxyz";
    int            i = 425;
    short int      j = 17;
    unsigned int   u = 0xf179U;
    long int       l = 75000L;
    long long int  L = 0x1234567812345678LL;
    float          f = 12.978F;
    double         d = -97.4583;
    char           *cp = &c;
    int            *ip = &i;
    int            c1, c2;

    printf ("Integers:\n");
    printf ("%i  %o  %x  %u\n", i, i, i, i);
    printf ("%x  %X  %#x %#X\n", i, i, i, i);
    printf ("%+i % i %07i %.7i\n", i, i, i, i);
    printf ("%i  %o  %x  %u\n", j, j, j, j);
    printf ("%i  %o  %x  %u\n", u, u, u, u);
    printf ("%ld %lo %lx %lu\n", l, l, l, l);
    printf ("%lli %llo %llx %llu\n", L, L, L, L);

    printf ("\nFloats and Doubles:\n");
    printf ("%f  %e  %g\n", f, f, f);
    printf ("%.2f  %.2e\n", f, f);
    printf ("%.0f  %.0e\n", f, f);
    printf ("%7.2f  %7.2e\n", f, f);
    printf ("%f  %e  %g\n", d, d, d);
    printf ("%.*f\n", 3, d);
    printf ("%*.*f\n", 8, 2, d);

    printf ("\nCharacters:\n");
    printf ("%c\n", c);
```

```
        printf ("%3c%3c\n", c, c);
        printf ("%x\n", c);

        printf ("\nStrings:\n");
        printf ("%s\n", s);
        printf ("%.5s\n", s);
        printf ("%30s\n", s);
        printf ("%20.5s\n", s);
        printf ("%-20.5s\n", s);

        printf ("\nPointers:\n");
        printf ("%p  %p\n\n", ip, cp);

        printf ("This%n is fun.%n\n\n", &c1, &c2);
        printf ("c1 = %i, c2 = %i\n", c1, c2);

        return 0;
}
```

Program 15.1   **Output**

```
Integers:
425   651   1a9   425
1a9   1A9   0x1a9 0X1A9
+425   425 0000425 0000425
17   21   11   17
61817   170571   f179   61817
75000   222370   124f8   75000
1311768465173141112 1106425474022150531701 234567812345678 1311768465173141112

Floats and Doubles:
12.978000  1.297800e+01   12.978
12.98  1.30e+01
13   1e+01
  12.98  1.30e+01
-97.458300  -9.745830e+01  -97.4583
-97.458
  -97.46

Characters:
X
  X  X
58
```

```
Strings:
abcdefghijklmnopqrstuvwxyz
abcde
    abcdefghijklmnopqrstuvwxyz
                abcde
abcde

Pointers:
0xbffffc20  0xbffffbf0

This is fun.
c1 = 4, c2 = 12
```

It's worthwhile to take some time to explain the output in detail. The first set of output deals with the display of integers: short, long, unsigned, and "normal" ints. The first line displays i in decimal (%i), octal (%o), hexadecimal (%x), and unsigned (%u) formats. Notice that octal numbers are not preceded by a leading 0 when they are displayed.

The next line of output displays the value of i again. First, i is displayed in hexadecimal notation using %x. The use of a capital X (%#X) causes printf() to use uppercase letters A–F instead of lowercase letters when displaying numbers in hexadecimal. The # modifier (%#x) causes a leading 0x to appear before the number and causes a leading 0X to appear when the capital X is used as the conversion character (%#X).

The fourth printf() call first uses the + flag to force a sign to appear, even if the value is positive (normally, no sign is displayed). Then, the space modifier is used to force a leading space in front of a positive value. (Sometimes this is useful for aligning data that might be positive or negative; the positive values have a leading space; the negative ones have a minus sign.) Next, %07 is used to display the value of i right-justified within a field width of seven characters. The 0 flag specifies zero fill. Therefore, four leading zeroes are placed in front of the value of i, which is 425. The final conversion in this call, %.7i is used to display the value of i using a minimum of seven digits. The net effect is the same as specifying %07i: Four leading zeroes are displayed, followed by the three-digit number 425.

The fifth printf() call displays the value of the short int variable j in various formats. Any integer format can be specified to display the value of a short int.

The next printf() call shows what happens when %i is used to display the value of an unsigned int. Because the value assigned to u is larger than the maximum positive value that can be stored in a signed int on the machine on which this program was run, it is displayed as a negative number when the %i format characters are used.

The next-to-last printf() call in this set shows how the l modifier is used to display long integers, and the final printf() call in the set shows how long long integers can be displayed.

The second set of output illustrates various formatting possibilities for displaying floats and doubles. The first output line of this set shows the result of displaying a float value using %f, %e, and %g formats. As mentioned, unless specified otherwise, the %f and %e formats default to six decimal places. With the %g format, printf() decides whether to display the value in either %e or %f format, depending upon the magnitude of the value and on the specified precision. If the exponent is less than −4 or greater than the optionally specified precision (remember, the default is 6), %e is used; otherwise, %f is used. In either case, trailing zeroes are automatically removed, and a decimal point is displayed only if nonzero digits follow it. In general, %g is the best format to use for displaying floating-point numbers in the most aesthetically pleasing format.

In the next line of output, the precision modifier .2 is specified to limit the display of f to two decimal places. As you can see, printf() is nice enough to automatically round the value of f for you. The line that immediately follows shows the use of the .0 precision modifier to suppress the display of any decimal places, including the decimal point, in the %f format. Once again, the value of f is automatically rounded.

The modifiers 7.2, as used for generating the next line of output, specify that the value is to be displayed in a minimum of seven columns, to two decimal places of accuracy. Because both values need fewer than seven columns to be displayed, printf() right-justifies the value (adding spaces on the left) within the specified field width.

In the next three lines of output, the value of the double variable d is displayed with various formats. The same format characters are used for the display of floats and double values, because, as you'll once again recall, floats are automatically converted to doubles when passed as arguments to functions. The printf() call

```
printf ("%.*f\n", 3, d);
```

specifies that the value of d is to be displayed to three decimal places. The asterisk after the period in the format specification instructs printf() to take the next argument to the function as the value of the precision. In this case, the next argument is 3. This value could also have been specified by a variable, as in

```
printf ("%.*f\n", accuracy, d);
```

which makes this feature useful for dynamically changing the format of a display.

The final line of the floats and doubles set shows the result of using the format characters %*.*f for displaying the value of d. In this case, both the field width and the precision are given as arguments to the function, as indicated by the two asterisks in the format string. Because the first argument after the format string is 8, this is taken as the field width. The next argument, 2, is taken as the precision. The value of d is, therefore, displayed to two decimal places in a field size of eight characters. Notice that the minus sign as well as the decimal point are included in the field-width count. This is true for any field specifier.

In the next set of program output, the character c, which was initially set to the character X, is displayed in various formats. The first time it is displayed using the familiar %c format characters. On the next line, it is displayed twice with a field-width specification of 3. This results in the display of the character with two leading spaces.

A character can be displayed using any integer format specification. In the next line of output, the value of c is displayed in hexadecimal. The output indicates that on this machine the character X is internally represented by the number hexadecimal 58.

In the final set of program output, the character string s is displayed. The first time it is displayed with the normal %s format characters. Then, a precision specification of 5 is used to display just the first five characters from the string. This results in the display of the first five letters of the alphabet.

In the third output line from this set, the entire character string is once again displayed, this time using a field-width specification of 30. As you can see, the string is displayed right-justified in the field.

The final two lines from this set show five characters from the string s being displayed in a field-width size of 20. The first time, these five characters are displayed right-justified in the field. The second time, the minus sign results in the display of the first five letters left-justified in the field. The vertical bar character was printed to verify that the format characters %-20.5s actually result in the display of 20 characters at the terminal (five letters followed by 15 spaces).

The %p characters are used to display the value of a pointer. Here, you are displaying the integer pointer ip and the character pointer cp. You should note that you will probably get different values displayed on your system because your pointers will most likely contain different addresses.

The format of the output when using %p is implementation-defined, but in this example, the pointers are displayed in hexadecimal format. According to the output, the pointer variable ip contained the address bffffc20 hexadecimal, and the pointer cp contained the address bffffbf0.

The final set of output shows the use of the %n format characters. In this case, the corresponding argument to printf() must be of type pointer to int, unless a type modifier of h, hh, h, l, ll, j, z, or t is specified. printf() actually stores the number of characters it has written so far into the integer pointed to by this argument. So, the first occurrence of %n causes printf to store the value 4 inside the integer variable c1 because that's how many characters have been written so far by this call. The second occurrence of %n causes the value 12 to be stored inside c2. This is because 12 characters had been displayed at that point by printf(). Notice that inclusion of the %n inside the format string has no effect on the actual output produced by printf().

The scanf() Function

Like the printf() function, many more formatting options can be specified inside the format string of a scanf() call than have been illustrated up to this point. As with printf(), scanf() takes optional modifiers between the % and the conversion character. These optional modifiers are summarized in Table 15.5. The possible conversion characters that can be specified are summarized in Table 15.6.

When the scanf() function searches the input stream for a value to be read, it always bypasses any leading so-called *whitespace* characters, where *whitespace* refers to either a blank space, horizontal tab ('\t'), vertical tab ('\v'), carriage return ('\r'), newline ('\n'), or form-feed character ('\f'). The exceptions are in the case of the %c format characters—in which case the next character from the input, no matter what it is, is read—and in the case of the bracketed character string read—in which case, the characters contained in the brackets (or *not* contained in the brackets) specify the permissible characters of the string.

Table 15.5   `scanf()` **Conversion Modifiers**

Modifier	Meaning
*	Field is to be skipped and not assigned
size	Maximum size of the input field
hh	Value is to be stored in a `signed` or `unsigned char`
h	Value is to be stored in a `short int`
l	Value is to be stored in a `long int`, double, or wchar_t
j, z, or t	Value is to be stored in a `size_t` (%j), `ptrdiff_t` (%z), `intmax_t`, or `uintmax_t` (%t)
ll	Value is to be stored in a `long long int`
L	Value is to be stored in a `long double`
type	Conversion character

Table 15.6   `scanf()` **Conversion Characters**

Character	Action
d	The value to be read is expressed in decimal notation; the corresponding argument is a pointer to an `int` unless the h, l, or ll modifier is used, in which case the argument is a pointer to a `short`, `long`, or `long long int`, respectively.
i	Like `%d`, except numbers expressed in octal (leading 0) or hexadecimal (leading 0x or 0X) also can be read.
u	The value to be read is an integer, and the corresponding argument is a pointer to an `unsigned int`.
o	The value to be read is expressed in octal notation and can be optionally preceded by a 0. The corresponding argument is a pointer to an `int`, unless h, l, or ll precedes the letter o, in which case the argument is a pointer to a `short`, `long`, or `long long`, respectively.
x	The value to be read is expressed in hexadecimal notation and can be optionally preceded by a leading 0x or 0X; the corresponding argument is a pointer to an `unsigned int`, unless h, l, or ll modifies the x.

Character	Action
a, e, f, or g	The value to be read is expressed in floating-point notation; the value can be optionally preceded by a sign and can optionally be expressed in exponential notation (as in 3.45 e-3); the corresponding argument is a pointer to float, unless an l or L modifier is used, in which case it is a pointer to a double or to a long double, respectively.
c	The value to be read is a single character; the next character that appears on the input is read, even if it is a space, tab, newline, or form-feed character. The corresponding argument is a pointer to char; an optional count before the c specifies the number of characters to be read.
s	The value to be read is a sequence of characters; the sequence begins with the first nonwhitespace character and is terminated by the first whitespace character. The corresponding argument is a pointer to a character array, which must contain enough characters to contain the characters that are read plus the null character that is automatically added to the end. If a number precedes the s, the specified number of characters is read, unless a whitespace character is encountered first.
[...]	Characters enclosed within brackets indicate that a character string is to be read, as in %s; the characters within the brackets indicate the permissible characters in the string. If any character other than that specified in the brackets is encountered, the string is terminated; the sense of how these characters are treated can be "inverted" by placing a ^ as the first character inside the brackets. In such a case, the subsequent characters are taken to be the ones that will terminate the string; that is, if any of the subsequent characters are found on the input, the string is terminated.
n	Nothing gets read. The number of characters read so far by this call is written into the int pointed to by the corresponding argument.
p	The value to be read is a pointer expressed in the same format as is displayed by printf() with the %p conversion characters. The corresponding argument is a pointer to a pointer to void.
%	The next nonwhitespace character on input must be a %.

When scanf() reads in a particular value, reading of the value terminates as soon as the number of characters specified by the field width is reached (if supplied) or until a character that is not valid for the value being read is encountered. In the case of integers, valid characters are an optionally signed sequence of digits that are valid for the base of the integer that is being read (decimal: 0–9, octal: 0–7, hexadecimal: 0–9, a–f, or A–F). For floats, permissible characters are an optionally signed sequence of decimal digits, followed by an optional decimal point and another sequence of decimal digits, all of which can be followed by the letter e (or E) and an optionally signed exponent. In the case of %a, a hexadecimal floating value can be supplied in the format of a leading 0x, followed by a sequence of hexadecimal digits with an optional decimal point, followed by an optional exponent preceded by the letter p (or P).

For character strings read with the %s format, any nonwhitespace character is valid. In the case of %c format, all characters are valid. Finally, in the case of the bracketed string read, valid characters are only those enclosed within the brackets (or not enclosed within the brackets if the ^ character is used after the open bracket).

Recall from Chapter 8, "Working with Structures," when you wrote the programs that prompted the user to enter the time from the terminal, any nonformat characters that were specified in the format string of the scanf() call were expected on the input. So, for example, the scanf() call

```
scanf ("%i:%i:%i", &hour, &minutes, &seconds);
```

means that three integer values are to be read in and stored in the variables hour, minutes, and seconds, respectively. Inside the format string, the : character specifies that colons are expected as separators between the three integer values.

To specify that a percent sign is expected as input, double percent signs are included in the format string, as follows:

```
scanf ("%i%%", &percentage);
```

Whitespace characters inside a format string match an arbitrary number of whitespace characters on the input. So, the call

```
scanf ("%i%c", &i, &c);
```

with the line of text

```
29    w
```

assigns the value 29 to i and a space character to c because this is the character that appears immediately after the characters 29 on the input. If the following scanf() call is made instead:

```
scanf ("%i %c", &i, &c);
```

and the same line of text is entered, the value 29 is assigned to i and the character 'w' to c because the blank space in the format string causes the scanf() function to ignore any leading whitespace characters after the characters 29 have been read.

Table 15.5 indicates that an asterisk can be used to skip fields. If the scanf() call

```
scanf ("%i %5c %*f %s", &i1, text, string);
```

is executed and the following line of text is typed in:

```
144abcde    736.55      (wine and cheese)
```

the value 144 is stored in i1; the five characters abcde are stored in the character array text; the floating value 736.55 is matched but not assigned; and the character string "(wine" is stored in string, terminated by a null. The next call to scanf() *picks up where the last one left off*. So, a subsequent call such as

```
scanf ("%s %s %i", string2, string3, &i2);
```

has the effect of storing the character string "and" in string2 and the string "cheese)" in string3, and causes the function to wait for an integer value to be typed.

Remember that scanf expects pointers to the variables where the values that are read in are to be stored. You know from Chapter 10, "Pointers," why this is necessary—so that scanf() can make changes to the variables; that is, store the values that it reads into them. Remember also that to specify a pointer to an array, only the name of the array needs be specified. So, if text is defined as an appropriately sized array of characters, the scanf() call

```
scanf ("%80c", text);
```

reads the next 80 characters from the input and stores them in text.

The scanf() call

```
scanf ("%[^/]", text);
```

indicates that the string to be read can consist of any character except for a slash. Using the preceding call on the following line of text

```
(wine and cheese)/
```

has the effect of storing the string "(wine and cheese)" in text because the string is not terminated until the / is matched (which is also the character read by scanf on the next call).

To read an entire line from the terminal into the character array buf, you can specify that the newline character at the end of the line is your string terminator:

```
scanf ("%[^\n]\n", buf);
```

The newline character is repeated outside the brackets so that scanf() matches it and does not read it the next time it's called. (Remember, scanf() always continues reading from the character that terminated its last call.)

When a value is read that does not match a value expected by scanf() (for example, typing in the character x when an integer is expected), scanf() does not read any further items from the input and immediately returns. Because the function returns the number of items that were successfully read and assigned to variables in your program, this value can be tested to determine if any errors occurred on the input. For example, the call

```
if ( scanf ("%i %f %i", &i, &f, &l) != 3 )
    printf ("Error on input\n");
```

tests to make certain that scanf() successfully read and assigned three values. If not, an appropriate message is displayed.

Remember, the return value from scanf() indicates the number of values read *and assigned*, so the call

```
scanf ("%i %*d %i", &i1, &i3)
```

returns 2 when successful and not 3 because you are reading and assigning *two* integers (skipping one in between). Note also that the use of %n (to obtain the number of characters read so far) does not get included in the value returned by scanf().

Experiment with the various formatting options provided by the scanf() function. As with the printf() function, a good understanding of these various formats can be obtained only by trying them in actual program examples.

Input and Output Operations with Files

So far, when a call was made to the scanf() function by one of the programs in this book, the data that was requested by the call was always read in from keyboard input by your program's user. Similarly, all calls to the printf() function resulted in the display of the desired information to your active window. To improve the utility of your programs, you need to be able to read data from, and write data to, files, which are covered in this section.

Redirecting I/O to a File

Both read and write file operations can be easily performed under many operating systems, including Windows, Linux, and Unix, without anything special being done at all to the program. Type Program 15.2, a very simple example that takes a number, then performs some very simple calculations on it.

Program 15.2   **A Simple Example**

```
//Taking a single number and outputting several calculations
#include <stdio.h>

main()
{

    float d = 6.5;
    float half, square, cube;

    half = d/2;
    square = d*d;
    cube = d*d*d;

    printf("\nYour number is %.2f\n", d);
    printf("Half of it is %.2f\n", half);
    printf("Square it to get %.2f\n", square);
    printf("Cube it to get %.2f\n", cube);

    return 0;
}
```

Simple enough, but suppose you want to keep the results in a file. If you want to write the results from this program into a file called `results.txt`, for example, all that you need to do under Unix or Windows if running from a command prompt is to redirect the output from the program into the file `results.txt` by executing the program with the following command:

```
program1502 > results.txt
```

This command instructs the system to execute the program `program1502` but to redirect the output normally written to the command prompt into a file called results.txt instead. So, any values displayed by `printf()` do not appear in your window but are instead written into the file called `results.txt`.

While program 15.2 is interesting, it would be even more valuable to prompt the user to enter a number and then perform the calculations on the number and display the results. Program 15.3 shows that slightly tweaked program.

Program 15.3   A Simple, yet More Interactive, Example

```c
//Inputting a single number and outputting several calculations
#include <stdio.h>

main()
{

    float d ;
    float half, square, cube;

    printf("Enter a number between 1 and 100: \n");
    scanf("%f", &d);
    half = d/2;
    square = d*d;
    cube = d*d*d;

    printf("\nYour number is %.2f\n", d);
    printf("Half of it is %.2f\n", half);
    printf("Square it to get %.2f\n", square);
    printf("Cube it to get %.2f\n", cube);

    return 0;
}
```

Now suppose you want to save the data from this program to a file, called `results2.txt`. You would type the following line at your command prompt:

```
program1503 > results.txt
```

This time, it may look as though the program is hung up and not responding. This is partially true. The program is not advancing because it is waiting for input from the user—looking for the user to enter a number to perform the calculations on. This is the downside to directing output to a file in this manner. All output goes into the file, even the `printf()` statement used to prompt the user for data entry. If you examine the contents of `results2.txt`, you would get the following, assuming you entered 6.5 as your number.

```
Enter a number between 1 and 100:
```

```
Your number is 6.50
Half of it is 3.25
Square it to get 42.25
Cube it to get 274.63
```

This verifies that the output from the program went into the file `results2.txt` as described previously. You might want to try running the program with different filenames and different numbers to see that it works repeatedly.

You can do a similar type of redirection for the input to your programs. Any call to a function that normally reads data from your window, such as `scanf()` and `getchar()`, can be easily made to read its information from a file. Create a file with just a single number in it (for this example, the filename is `simp4.txt`, and contains simply the number 4), and then run program1503 again, but use the following command line:

```
program1503 < simp4.txtn
```

The following output appears at the terminal after this command is entered:

```
Enter a number between 1 and 100:
```

```
Your number is 4.00
Half of it is 2.00
Square it to get 16.00
Cube it to get 64.00
```

Notice that the program requested that a number be entered but did not wait for you to type in a number. This is because the input to program1503—but not its output—was redirected from the file called `simp4.txt`. Therefore, the `scanf()` call from the program had the effect of reading the value from the file `simp4.txt` and not from your command prompt. The information must be entered in the file the same way that it would be typed in. The `scanf()` function itself does not actually know (or care) whether its input is coming from your window or from a file; all it cares about is that it is properly formatted.

Naturally, you can redirect the input and the output to a program at the same time. The command

```
program1503 < simp4.txt > results3.txt
```

causes execution of the program contained in program1503 to read all program input from the file `simp4.txt` and to write all program results into the file `results3.txt`.

The method of redirecting the program's input and/or its output is often practical. For example, suppose you are writing an article for a magazine and have typed the text into a file called article. Program 9.8 counted the number of words that appeared in lines of text entered at the terminal. You could use this very same program to count the number of words in your article simply by typing in the following command[1]:

```
wordcount < article
```

Of course, you have to remember to include an extra carriage return at the end of the article file because your program was designed to recognize an end-of-data condition by the presence of a single newline character on a line.

Note that I/O redirection, as described here, is not actually part of the ANSI definition of C. This means that you might find operating systems that don't support it. Luckily, most do.

End of File

The preceding point about end of data is worthy of more discussion. When dealing with files, this condition is called *end of file*. An end-of-file condition exists when the final piece of data has been read from a file. Attempting to read past the end of the file might cause the program to terminate with an error, or it might cause the program to go into an infinite loop if this condition is not checked by the program. Luckily, most of the functions from the standard I/O library return a special flag to indicate when a program has reached the end of a file. The value of this flag is equal to a special name called EOF, which is defined in the standard I/O include file <stdio.h>.

As an example of the use of the EOF test in combination with the getchar() function, Program 15.4 reads in characters and echoes them back in the terminal window until an end of file is reached. Notice the expression contained inside the while loop. As you can see, an assignment does not have to be made in a separate statement.

Program 15.4   **Copying Characters from Standard Input to Standard Output**

```
// Program to echo characters until an end of file

#include <stdio.h>

int main (void)
{
    int  c;

    while ( (c = getchar ()) != EOF )
        putchar (c);

    return 0;
}
```

---

1. *Unix systems provide a* wc *command, which can also count words. Also, recall that this program was designed to work on text files, not word processing files, such as MS Word .doc files.*

If you compile and execute Program 15.4, redirecting the input to a file with a command such as

```
program1504 < infile
```

the program displays the contents of the file `infile` at the terminal. Try it and see! Actually, the program serves the same basic function as the `cat` command under Unix, and you can use it to display the contents of any text file you choose.

In the `while` loop of Program 15.4, the character that is returned by the `getchar()` function is assigned to the variable `c` and is then compared against the defined value `EOF`. If the values are equal, this means that you have read the final character from the file. One important point must be mentioned with respect to the `EOF` value that is returned by the `getchar()` function: The function actually returns an `int` and not a `char`. This is because the `EOF` value must be unique; that is, it cannot be equal to the value of any character that would normally be returned by `getchar()`. Therefore, the value returned by `getchar()` is assigned to an `int` and not a `char` variable in the preceding program. This works out okay because C allows you to store characters inside `int`s, even though, in general, it might not be the best of programming practices.

If you store the result of the `getchar()` function inside a `char` variable, the results are unpredictable. On systems that do sign extension of characters, the code might still work okay. On systems that don't do sign extension, you might end up in an infinite loop.

The bottom line is to always remember to store the result of `getchar()` inside an `int` so that you can properly detect an end-of-file condition.

The fact that you can make an assignment inside the conditional expression of the `while` loop illustrates the flexibility that C provides in the formation of expressions. The parentheses are required around the assignment because the assignment operator has lower precedence than the not equals operator.

Special Functions for Working with Files

It is very likely that many of the programs you will develop will be able to perform all their I/O operations using just the `getchar()`, `putchar()`, `scanf()`, and `printf()` functions and the notion of I/O redirection. However, situations do arise when you need more flexibility to work with files. For example, you might need to read data from two or more different files or to write output results into several different files. To handle these situations, special functions have been designed expressly for working with files. Several of these functions are described in the following sections.

The **fopen** Function

Before you can begin to do any I/O operations on a file, the file must first be *opened*. To open a file, you must specify the name of the file. The system then checks to make certain that this file actually exists and, in certain instances, creates the file for you if it does not. When a file is opened, you must also specify to the system the type of I/O operations that you intend to perform with the file. If the file is to be used to read in data, you normally open the file in *read mode*. If you want to write data into the file, you open the file in *write mode*. Finally, if you want to append information to the end of a file that already contains some data, you open the file in *append mode*. In the latter two cases, write and append mode, if the specified file does not exist on the system, the system creates the file for you. In the case of read mode, if the file does not exist, an error occurs.

Because a program can have many different files open at the same time, you need a way to identify a particular file in your program when you want to perform some I/O operation on the file. This is done by means of a *file pointer*.

The function called fopen() in the standard library serves the function of opening a file on the system and of returning a unique file pointer with which to subsequently identify the file. The function takes two arguments: The first is a character string specifying the name of the file to be opened; the second is also a character string that indicates the mode in which the file is to be opened. The function returns a file pointer that is used by other library functions to identify the particular file.

If the file cannot be opened for some reason, the function returns the value NULL, which is defined inside the header file <stdio.h>.[2] Also defined in this file is the definition of a type called FILE. To store the result returned by the fopen() function in your program, you must define a variable of type "pointer to FILE."

If you take the preceding comments into account, the statements

```
#include <stdio.h>

FILE  *inputFile;

inputFile = fopen ("data", "r");
```

have the effect of opening a file called data in read mode. (Write mode is specified by the string "w", and append mode is specified by the string "a".) The fopen() call returns an identifier for the opened file that is assigned to the FILE pointer variable inputFile. Subsequent testing of this variable against the defined value NULL, as in the following:

```
if ( inputFile == NULL )
    printf ("*** data could not be opened.\n");
else
    // read the data from the file
```

tells you whether the open was successful.

You should always check the result of an fopen() call to make certain it succeeds. Using a NULL pointer can produce unpredictable results.

---

2. *NULL is "officially" defined in the header file* <stddef.h>; *however, it is most likely also defined in* <stdio.h>.

Frequently, in the fopen() call, the assignment of the returned FILE pointer variable and the test against the NULL pointer are combined into a single statement, as follows:

```
if ( (inputFile = fopen ("data", "r")) == NULL )
    printf ("*** data could not be opened.\n");
```

The fopen() function also supports three other types of modes, called *update* modes ("r+", "w+", and "a+"). All three update modes permit both reading and writing operations to be performed on a file. Read update ("r+") opens an existing file for both reading and writing. Write update ("w+") is like write mode (if the file already exists, the contents are destroyed; if one doesn't exist, it's created), but once again both reading and writing are permitted. Append update ("a+") opens an existing file or creates a new one if one doesn't exist. Read operations can occur anywhere in the file, but write operations can only add data to the end.

Under operating systems such as Windows, which distinguish text files from binary files, a b must be added to the end of the mode string to read or write a binary file. If you forget to do this, you will get strange results, even though your program will still run. This is because on these systems, carriage return/line feed character pairs are converted to return characters when they are read from or written to text files. Furthermore, on input, a file that contains a Ctrl+Z character causes an end-of-file condition if the file was not opened as a binary file. So,

```
inputFile = fopen ("data", "rb");
```

opens the binary file data for reading.

The getc() and putc() Functions

The function getc() enables you to read in a single character from a file. This function behaves identically to the getchar() function described previously. The only difference is that getc() takes an argument: a FILE pointer that identifies the file from which the character is to be read. So, if fopen() is called as shown previously, then subsequent execution of the statement

```
c = getc (inputFile);
```

has the effect of reading a single character from the file data. Subsequent characters can be read from the file simply by making additional calls to the getc() function.

The getc() function returns the value EOF when the end of file is reached, and as with the getchar() function, the value returned by getc() should be stored in a variable of type int.

As you might have guessed, the putc() function is equivalent to the putchar() function, only it takes two arguments instead of one. The first argument to putc() is the character that is to be written into the file. The second argument is the FILE pointer. So the call

```
putc ('\n', outputFile);
```

writes a newline character into the file identified by the FILE pointer outputFile. Of course, the identified file must have been previously opened in either write or append mode (or in any of the update modes) for this call to succeed.

The `fclose()` Function

One operation that you can perform on a file, which must be mentioned, is that of closing the file. The `fclose()` function, in a sense, does the opposite of what the `fopen()` does: It tells the system that you no longer need to access the file. When a file is closed, the system performs some necessary housekeeping chores (such as writing all the data that it might be keeping in a buffer in memory to the file) and then dissociates the particular file identifier from the file. After a file has been closed, it can no longer be read from or written to unless it is reopened.

When you have completed your operations on a file, it is a good habit to close the file. When a program terminates normally, the system automatically closes any open files for you. It is generally better programming practice to close a file as soon as you are done with it. This can be beneficial if your program has to deal with a large number of files, as there are practical limits on the number of files that can be kept simultaneously open by a program. Your system might have various limits on the number of files that you can have open simultaneously. This might only be an issue if you are working with multiple files in your program.

By the way, the argument to the `fclose()` function is the FILE pointer of the file to be closed. So, the call

```
fclose (inputFile);
```

closes the file associated with the FILE pointer `inputFile`.

With the functions `fopen()`, `putc()`, `getc()`, and `fclose()`, you can now proceed to write a program that will copy one file to another. Program 15.5 prompts the user for the name of the file to be copied and the name of the resultant copied file. This program is based upon Program 15.4. You might want to refer to that program for comparison purposes.

Assume that the following three lines of text have been previously typed into the file `copyme`:

```
This is a test of the file copy program
that we have just developed using the
fopen, fclose, getc, and putc functions.
```

Program 15.5 Copying Files

```c
// Program to copy one file to another

#include <stdio.h>

int main (void)
{
    char   inName[64], outName[64];
    FILE   *in, *out;
    int    c;

    // get file names from user
```

```
    printf ("Enter name of file to be copied: ");
    scanf ("%63s", inName);
    printf ("Enter name of output file: ");
    scanf ("%63s", outName);

    // open input and output files

    if ( (in = fopen (inName, "r"))  ==  NULL ) {
        printf ("Can't open %s for reading.\n", inName);
        return 1;
    }

    if  ( (out = fopen (outName, "w"))  ==  NULL ) {
        printf ("Can't open %s for writing.\n", outName);
        return 2;
    }

    // copy in to out

    while ( (c = getc (in)) != EOF )
        putc (c, out);

    // Close open files

    fclose (in);
    fclose (out);

    printf ("File has been copied.\n");


    return 0;
}
```

Program 15.5 **Output**

```
Enter name of file to be copied: copyme
Enter name of output file: here
File has been copied.
```

Now examine the contents of the file here. The file should contain the same three lines of text as contained in the copyme file.

The scanf() function call in the beginning of the program is given a field-width count of 63 just to ensure that you don't overflow your inName or outName character arrays. The program then opens the specified input file for reading and the specified output file for writing. If the output file already exists and is opened in write mode, its previous contents are overwritten on most systems.

If either of the two fopen() calls is unsuccessful, the program displays an appropriate message at the terminal and proceeds no further, returning a nonzero exit status to indicate the failure. Otherwise, if both opens succeed, the file is copied one character at a time by means of successive getc() and putc() calls until the end of the file is encountered. The program then closes the two files and returns a zero exit status to indicate success.

The **feof** Function

To test for an end-of-file condition on a file, the function feof() is provided. The single argument to the function is a FILE pointer. The function returns an integer value that is nonzero if an attempt has been made to read past the end of a file, and is zero otherwise. So, the statements

```
if ( feof (inFile) ) {
    printf ("Ran out of data.\n");
    return 1;
}
```

have the effect of displaying the message "Ran out of data" at the terminal if an end-of-file condition exists on the file identified by inFile.

Remember, feof() tells you that an attempt has been made to read past the end of the file, which is not the same as telling you that you just read the last data item from a file. You have to read one past the last data item for feof() to return nonzero.

The **fprintf()** and **fscanf()** Functions

The functions fprintf() and fscanf() are provided to perform the analogous operations of the printf() and scanf() functions on a file. These functions take an additional argument, which is the FILE pointer that identifies the file to which the data is to be written or from which the data is to be read. So, to write the character string "Programming in C is fun.\n" into the file identified by outFile, you can write the following statement:

```
fprintf (outFile, "Programming in C is fun.\n");
```

Similarly, to read in the next floating-point value from the file identified by inFile into the variable fv, the statement

```
fscanf (inFile, "%f", &fv);
```

can be used. As with scanf(), fscanf() returns the number of arguments that are successfully read and assigned or the value EOF, if the end of the file is reached before any of the conversion specifications have been processed.

The **fgets()** and **fputs()** Functions

For reading and writing entire lines of data from and to a file, the fputs() and fgets() functions can be used. The fgets() function is called as follows:

```
fgets (buffer, n, filePtr);
```

buffer is a pointer to a character array where the line that is read in will be stored; *n* is an integer value that represents the maximum number of characters to be stored into *buffer*; and *filePtr* identifies the file from which the line is to be read.

The `fgets()` function reads characters from the specified file until a newline character has been read (which *will* get stored in the buffer) or until *n-1* characters have been read, whichever occurs first. The function automatically places a null character after the last character in *buffer*. It returns the value of *buffer* (the first argument) if the read is successful, and the value NULL if an error occurs on the read or if an attempt is made to read past the end of the file.

The `fgets()` function can be combined with `sscanf()` (see Appendix B, "The Standard C Library") to perform line-oriented reading in a more orderly and controlled fashion than by using `scanf()` alone.

The `fputs()` function writes a line of characters to a specified file. The function is called as follows:

```
fputs (buffer, filePtr);
```

Characters stored in the array pointed to by *buffer* are written to the file identified by *filePtr* until the null character is reached. The terminating null character is *not* written to the file.

There are also analogous functions called `gets()` and `puts()` that can be used to read a line from the terminal and write a line to the terminal, respectively. These functions are described in Appendix B.

stdin, stdout, and stderr

When a C program is executed, three files are automatically opened by the system for use by the program. These files are identified by the *constant* FILE pointers stdin, stdout, and stderr, which are defined in <stdio.h>. The FILE pointer stdin identifies the standard input of the program and is normally associated with your terminal window. All standard I/O functions that perform input and do not take a FILE pointer as an argument get their input from stdin. For example, the scanf() function reads its input from stdin, and a call to this function is equivalent to a call to the fscanf() function with stdin as the first argument. So, the call

```
fscanf (stdin, "%i", &i);
```

reads in the next integer value from the standard input, which is normally your terminal window. If the input to your program has been redirected to a file, this call reads the next integer value from the file to which the standard input has been redirected.

As you might have guessed, stdout refers to the standard output, which is normally also associated with your terminal window. So, a call such as

```
printf ("hello there.\n");
```

can be replaced by an equivalent call to the `fprintf()` function with `stdout` as the first argument:

```
fprintf (stdout, "hello there.\n");
```

The `FILE` pointer `stderr` identifies the standard error file. This is where most of the error messages produced by the system are written and is also normally associated with your terminal window. The reason `stderr` exists is so that error messages can be logged to a device or file other than where the normal output is written. This is particularly desirable when the program's output is redirected to a file. In such a case, the normal output is written into the file, but any system error messages still appear in your window. You might want to write your own error messages to `stderr` for this same reason. As an example, the `fprintf()` call in the following statement:

```
if ( (inFile = fopen ("data", "r")) == NULL )
{
    fprintf (stderr, "Can't open data for reading.\n");
    ...
}
```

writes the indicated error message to `stderr` if the file `data` cannot be opened for reading. In addition, if the standard output has been redirected to a file, this message still appears in your window.

The `exit()` Function

At times, you might want to force the termination of a program, such as when an error condition is detected by a program. You know that program execution is automatically terminated whenever the last statement in `main()` is executed or when executing a `return` from `main()`. To explicitly terminate a program, no matter from what point you are executing, the `exit()` function can be called. The function call

```
exit (n);
```

has the effect of terminating (exiting from) the current program. Any open files are automatically closed by the system. The integer value n is called the *exit status*, and has the same meaning as the value returned from `main()`.

The standard header file `<stdlib.h>` defines `EXIT_FAILURE` as an integer value that you can use to indicate the program has failed and `EXIT_SUCCESS` to be one that you can use to indicate it has succeeded.

When a program terminates simply by executing the last statement in `main`, its exit status is undefined. If another program needs to use this exit status, you mustn't let this happen. In such a case, make certain that you exit or return from `main()` with a defined exit status.

As an example of the use of the `exit()` function, the following function causes the program to terminate with an exit status of `EXIT_FAILURE` if the file specified as its argument cannot be opened for reading. Naturally, you might want to return the fact that the open failed instead of taking such a drastic action by terminating the program.

```c
#include <stdlib.h>
#include <stdio.h>

FILE *openFile (const char *file)
{
    FILE  *inFile;

    if ( (inFile = fopen (file, "r")) == NULL ) {
        fprintf (stderr, "Can't open %s for reading.\n", file);
        exit (EXIT_FAILURE);
    }

    return inFile;
}
```

Remember that there's no real difference between exiting or returning from `main()`. They both terminate the program, sending back an exit status. The main difference between `exit()` and `return()` is when they're executed from inside a function other than `main()`. The `exit()` call terminates the program *immediately* whereas `return()` simply transfers control back to the calling routine.

Renaming and Removing Files

The `rename()` function from the library can be used to change the name of a file. It takes two arguments: the old filename and the new filename. If for some reason the renaming operation fails (for example, if the first file doesn't exist, or the system doesn't allow you to rename the particular file), `rename()` returns a nonzero value. The code

```c
if ( rename ("tempfile", "database") ) {
    fprintf (stderr, "Can't rename tempfile\n");
    exit (EXIT_FAILURE);
}
```

renames the file called `tempfile` to `database` and checks the result of the operation to ensure it succeeded.

The `remove()` function deletes the file specified by its argument. It returns a nonzero value if the file removal fails. The code

```c
if ( remove ("tempfile") )
{
    fprintf (stderr, "Can't remove tempfile\n");
    exit (EXIT_FAILURE);
}
```

attempts to remove the file `tempfile` and writes an error message to standard error and exit if the removal fails.

Incidentally, you might be interested in using the `perror()` function to report errors from standard library routines. For more details, consult Appendix B.

This concludes our discussion of I/O operations under C. As mentioned, not all of the library functions are covered here due to lack of space. The standard C library contains a wide selection of functions for performing operations with character strings, for *random* I/O, mathematical calculations, and dynamic memory management. Appendix B lists many of the functions inside this library.

Exercises

1. Type in and run the three programs presented in this chapter. Compare the output produced by each program with the output presented in the text.

2. Go back to programs developed earlier in this book and experiment with redirecting their input and output to files.

3. Write a program to copy one file to another, replacing all lowercase characters with their uppercase equivalents.

4. Write a program that merges lines alternately from two files and writes the results to `stdout`. If one file has fewer lines than the other, the remaining lines from the larger file should simply be copied to `stdout`.

5. Write a program that writes columns m through n of each line of a file to `stdout`. Have the program accept the values of m and n from the terminal window.

6. Write a program that displays the contents of a file at the terminal 20 lines at a time. At the end of each 20 lines, have the program wait for a character to be entered from the terminal. If the character is the letter `q`, the program should stop the display of the file; any other character should cause the next 20 lines from the file to be displayed.

## 16

Miscellaneous and Advanced Features

This chapter discusses some miscellaneous features of the C language that have not yet been covered and provides a discussion of some more advanced topics, such as command-line arguments and dynamic memory allocation. The topics presented in this chapter are varied, but they are important to know as you will see many of these concepts in C programs you encounter. Topics covered include

- Understanding the goto statement, and why you should avoid it
- Maximizing space by using unions
- Adding the null statement to your programs
- Implementing statements that include the comma operator
- Using command-line arguments with your programs
- Dynamically allocating memory with `malloc()` and `calloc()`, and cleaning it up with `free()`

Miscellaneous Language Statements

This section discusses two statements you haven't encountered to this point: the goto and the *null* statements.

The `goto` Statement

Anyone who has learned about structured programming knows of the bad reputation afforded to the goto statement. Virtually every computer language has such a statement.

Execution of a goto statement causes a direct branch to be made to a specified point in the program. This branch is made immediately and unconditionally upon execution of the goto. To identify where in the program the branch is to be made, a *label* is needed. A label is a name that is formed with the same rules as variable names and must be immediately followed by a colon. The label is placed directly before the statement to which the branch is to be made and must appear in the same function as the `goto`.

So, for example, the statement

```
goto out_of_data;
```

causes the program to branch immediately to the statement that is preceded by the label `out_of_data:`. This label can be located anywhere in the function, before or after the `goto`, and might be used as shown:

```
out_of_data:  printf ("Unexpected end of data.\n");
   ...
```

Programmers who are lazy frequently abuse the `goto` statement to branch to other portions of their code. The `goto` statement interrupts the normal sequential flow of a program. As a result, programs are harder to follow. Using many `goto`s in a program can make it impossible to decipher. This style of programming is often derisively referred to as "spaghetti code." For this reason, `goto` statements are not considered part of good programming style.

The null Statement

C permits a solitary semicolon to be placed wherever a normal program statement can appear. The effect of such a statement, known as the *null* statement, is that nothing is done. Although this might seem useless, it is often used by C programmers in `while`, `for`, and `do` loops. For example, the purpose of the following statement is to store all the characters read in from the standard input into the character array pointed to by `text` until a newline character is encountered.

```
while ( (*text++ = getchar ()) != '\n' )
   ;
```

All of the operations are performed inside the looping-conditions part of the `while` statement. The null statement is needed because the compiler takes the statement that follows the looping expression as the body of the loop. Without the null statement, whatever statement that follows in the program is treated as the body of the program loop by the compiler.

The following `for` statement copies characters from the standard input to the standard output until the end of file is encountered:

```
for (  ; (c = getchar ()) != EOF;  putchar (c) )
   ;
```

The next `for` statement counts the number of characters that appear in the standard input:

```
for ( count = 0;  getchar () != EOF;  ++count )
   ;
```

As a final example illustrating the null statement, the following loop copies the character string pointed to by `from` to the one pointed to by `to`.

```
while ( (*to++ = *from++) != '\0' )
    ;
```

The reader is advised that there is a tendency among certain programmers to try to squeeze as much as possible into the condition part of the `while` or into the condition or looping part of the `for`. Try not to become one of those programmers. In general, only those expressions involved with testing the condition of a loop should be included inside the condition part. Everything else should form the body of the loop. The only case to be made for forming such complex expressions might be one of execution efficiency. Unless execution speed is that critical, you should avoid using these types of expressions.

The preceding `while` statement is easier to read when written like this:

```
while ( *from != '\0' )
    *to++ = *from++;


*to = '\0';
```

Working with Unions

One of the more unusual constructs in the C programming language is the *union*. This construct is used mainly in more advanced programming applications in which it is necessary to store different types of data in the same storage area. For example, if you want to define a single variable called x, which could be used to store a single character, a floating-point number, or an integer, you could first define a union called, perhaps, `mixed`:

```
union  mixed
{
    char   c;
    float  f;
    int    i;
};
```

The declaration for a union is identical to that of a structure, except the keyword `union` is used where the keyword `struct` is otherwise specified. The real difference between structures and unions has to do with the way memory is allocated. Declaring a variable to be of type `union mixed`, as in

```
union mixed  x;
```

does *not* define x to contain three distinct members called c, f, and i; rather, it defines x to contain a *single* member that is called *either* c, f, or i. In this way, the variable x can be used to store either a `char` or a `float` or an `int`, but not all three (or not even two of the three). You can store a character in the variable x with the following statement:

```
x.c = 'K';
```

The character stored in x can subsequently be retrieved in the same manner. So, to display its value at the terminal, for example, the following could be used:

```
printf ("Character = %c\n", x.c);
```

To store a floating-point value in x, the notation x.f is used:

```
x.f = 786.3869;
```

Finally, to store the result of dividing an integer count by 2 in x, the following statement can be used:

```
x.i = count / 2;
```

Because the float, char, and int members of x all exist in the same place in memory, only one value can be stored in x at a time. Furthermore, it is your responsibility to ensure that the value retrieved from a union is consistent with the way it was last stored in the union.

A union member follows the same rules of arithmetic as the type of the member that is used in the expression. So in

```
x.i / 2
```

the expression is evaluated according to the rules of integer arithmetic because x.i and 2 are both integers.

A union can be defined to contain as many members as desired. The C compiler ensures that enough storage is allocated to accommodate the largest member of the union. Structures can be defined that contain unions, as can arrays. When defining a union, the name of the union is not required, and variables can be declared at the same time that the union is defined. Pointers to unions can also be declared, and their syntax and rules for performing operations are the same as for structures.

One of the members of a union variable can be initialized. If no member name is specified, the *first* member of the union is set to the specified value, as in:

```
union mixed  x = { '#' };
```

This sets the first member of x, which is c, to the character #.

By specifying the member name, any member of the union can be initialized like so:

```
union mixed x = { .f = 123.456; };
```

This sets the floating member f of the union mixed variable x to the value 123.456.

An automatic union variable can also be initialized to another union variable of the same type:

```
void foo (union mixed x)
{
    union mixed  y = x;

    ...
}
```

Here, the function `foo` assigns to the automatic union variable `y` the value of the argument `x`.

The use of a union enables you to define arrays that can be used to store elements of different data types. For example, the statement

```
struct
{
    char            *name;
    enum symbolType  type;
    union
    {
        int    i;
        float  f;
        char   c;
    }              data;
} table [kTableEntries];
```

sets up an array called `table`, consisting of `kTableEntries` elements. Each element of the array contains a structure consisting of a character pointer called `name`, an enumeration member called `type`, and a union member called `data`. Each `data` member of the array can contain either an `int`, a `float`, or a `char`. The member `type` might be used to keep track of the type of value stored in the member `data`. For example, you could assign it the value `INTEGER` if it contained an `int`, `FLOATING` if it contained a `float`, and `CHARACTER` if it contained a `char`. This information would enable you to know how to reference the particular `data` member of a particular array element.

To store the character `'#'` in `table[5]`, and subsequently set the `type` field to indicate that a character is stored in that location, the following two statements could be used:

```
table[5].data.c = '#';
table[5].type = CHARACTER;
```

When sequencing through the elements of `table`, you could determine the type of data value stored in each element by setting up an appropriate series of test statements. For example, the following loop would display each name and its associated value from `table` at the terminal:

```
enum symbolType { INTEGER, FLOATING, CHARACTER };

    ...

for ( j = 0;  j < kTableEntries;  ++j ) {
    printf ("%s  ", table[j].name);

    switch ( table[j].type ) {
        case INTEGER:
            printf ("%i\n", table[j].data.i);
            break;
        case FLOATING:
            printf ("%f\n", table[j].data.f);
            break;
```

```
         case CHARACTER:
               printf ("%c\n", table[j].data.c);
               break;
         default:
               printf ("Unknown type (%i), element %i\n", table[j].type, j );
               break;
      }
}
```

The type of application illustrated might be practical for storage of a symbol table, for example, which might contain the name of each symbol, its type, and its value (and perhaps other information about the symbol as well).

The Comma Operator

At first glance, you might not realize that a comma can be used in expressions as an operator. The comma operator is at the bottom of the precedence totem pole, so to speak. In Chapter 4, "Program Looping," you learned that inside a for statement you could include more than one expression in any of the fields by separating each expression with a comma. For example, the for statement that begins

```
for ( i = 0, j = 100;  i != 10;  ++i, j -= 10 )
    ...
```

initializes the value of i to 0 *and* j to 100 before the loop begins, and increments the value of i *and* subtracts 10 from the value of j each time after the body of the loop is executed.

The comma operator can be used to separate multiple expressions anywhere that a valid C expression can be used. The expressions are evaluated from left to right. So, in the statement

```
while ( i < 100 )
    sum += data[i], ++i;
```

the value of data[i] is added into sum and then i is incremented. Note that you don't need braces here because just one statement follows the while statement. (It consists of two expressions separated by the comma operator.)

Because all operators in C produce a value, the value of the comma operator is that of the rightmost expression.

Note that a comma, used to separate arguments in a function call, or variable names in a list of declarations, for example, is a separate syntactic entity and is *not* an example of the use of the comma operator.

Type Qualifiers

The following qualifiers can be used in front of variables to give the compiler more information about the intended use of the variable and, in some cases, to help it generate better code.

The `register` Qualifier

If a function uses a particular variable heavily, you can request that access to the variable be made as fast as possible by the compiler. Typically, this means requesting that it be stored in one of the machine's registers when the function is executed. This is done by prefixing the declaration of the variable by the keyword `register`, as follows:

```
register int    index;
register char   *textPtr;
```

Both local variables and formal parameters can be declared as `register` variables. The types of variables that can be assigned to registers vary among machines. The basic data types can usually be assigned to registers, as well as pointers to any data type.

Even if your compiler enables you to declare a variable as a `register` variable, it is still not guaranteed that it will do anything with that declaration. It is up to the compiler.

You might want to also note that you cannot apply the address operator to a `register` variable. Other than that, `register` variables behave just as ordinary automatic variables.

The `volatile` Qualifier

The `volatile` qualifier is sort of the inverse to `const`. It tells the compiler explicitly that the specified variable *will* change its value. It's included in the language to prevent the compiler from optimizing away seemingly redundant assignments to a variable, or repeated examination of a variable without its value seemingly changing. A good example is to consider an I/O port. Suppose you have an output port that's pointed to by a variable in your program called `outPort`. If you want to write two characters to the port, for example an O followed by an N, you might have the following code:

```
*outPort = 'O';
*outPort = 'N';
```

A smart compiler might notice two successive assignments to the same location and, because `outPort` isn't being modified in between, simply remove the first assignment from the program. To prevent this from happening, you declare `outPort` to be a `volatile` pointer, as follows:

```
volatile char   *outPort;
```

The `restrict` Qualifier

Like the `register` qualifier, `restrict` is an optimization hint for the compiler. As such, the compiler can choose to ignore it. It is used to tell the compiler that a particular pointer is the only reference (either indirect or direct) to the value it points to throughout its scope. That is, the same value is not referenced by any other pointer or variable within that scope.

The lines

```
int * restrict intPtrA;
int * restrict intPtrB;
```

tell the compiler that, for the duration of the scope in which intPtrA and intPtrB are defined, they will never access the same value. Their use for pointing to integers inside an array, for example, is mutually exclusive.

Command-line Arguments

Many times, a program is developed that requires the user to enter a small amount of information at the terminal. This information might consist of a number indicating the triangular number that you want to have calculated or a word that you want to have looked up in a dictionary.

Rather than having the program request this type of information from the user, you can supply the information to the program at the time the program is executed. This capability is provided by what is known as *command-line arguments*.

As pointed out previously, the only distinguishing quality of the function main() is that its name is special; it specifies where program execution is to begin. In fact, the function main() is actually *called* upon at the start of program execution by the C system (known more formally as the *runtime* system), just as you call a function from within your own C program. When main() completes execution, control is returned to the runtime system, which then knows that your program has completed execution.

When main() is called by the runtime system, two arguments are actually passed to the function. The first argument, which is called argc by convention (for *arg*ument *c*ount), is an integer value that specifies the number of arguments typed on the command line. The second argument to main() is an array of character pointers, which is called argv by convention (for *argu*ment *v*ector). There are argc + 1 character pointers contained in this array, where argc always has a minimum value of 0. The first entry in this array is a pointer to the name of the program that is executing or is a pointer to a null string if the program name is not available on your system. Subsequent entries in the array point to the values that were specified in the same line as the command that initiated execution of the program. The last pointer in the argv array, argv[argc], is defined to be null.

To access the command-line arguments, the main() function must be appropriately declared as taking two arguments. The conventional declaration that is used appears as follows:

```
int  main (int  argc, char  *argv[])
{
    ...
}
```

Remember, the declaration of `argv` defines an array that contains elements of type "pointer to char." As a practical use of command-line arguments, recall Program 9.10, which looked up a word inside a dictionary and printed its meaning. You can make use of command-line arguments so that the word whose meaning you want to find can be specified at the same time that the program is executed, as in the following command:

```
lookup aerie
```

This eliminates the need for the program to prompt the user to enter a word because it is entered on the command line.

If the previous command is executed, the system automatically passes to `main()` a pointer to the character string `"aerie"` in `argv[1]`. Recall that `argv[0]` contains a pointer to the name of the program, which in this case is `"lookup"`.

The `main()` routine might appear as follows:

```
#include <stdlib.h>
#include <stdio.h>

int main (int argc, char *argv[])
{
    const struct entry dictionary[100] =
        { { "aardvark", "a burrowing African mammal"      },
          { "abyss",    "a bottomless pit"                },
          { "acumen",   "mentally sharp; keen"            },
          { "addle",    "to become confused"              },
          { "aerie",    "a high nest"                     },
          { "affix",    "to append; attach"               },
          { "agar",     "a jelly made from seaweed"       },
          { "ahoy",     "a nautical call of greeting"     },
          { "aigrette", "an ornamental cluster of feathers" },
          { "ajar",     "partially opened"                } };

    int     entries = 10;
    int     entryNumber;
    int     lookup (const struct entry dictionary [], const char search[],
                    const int entries);

    if ( argc != 2 )
    {
        fprintf (stderr, "No word typed on the command line.\n");
        return EXIT_FAILURE;
    }

    entryNumber = lookup (dictionary, argv[1], entries);

    if ( entryNumber != -1 )
        printf ("%s\n", dictionary[entryNumber].definition);
```

```
    else
        printf ("Sorry, %s is not in my dictionary.\n", argv[1]);

    return EXIT_SUCCESS;
}
```

The main() routine tests to make certain that a word was typed after the program name when the program was executed. If it wasn't, or if more than one word was typed, the value of argc is not equal to 2. In this case, the program writes an error message to standard error and terminates, returning an exit status of EXIT_FAILURE.

If argc is equal to 2, the lookup function is called to find the word pointed to by argv[1] in the dictionary. If the word is found, its definition is displayed.

As another example of command-line arguments, Program 15.3 was a file-copy program. Program 16.1, which follows, takes the two filenames from the command line rather than prompting the user to type them in.

Program 16.1 File Copy Program Using Command-line Arguments

```
// Program to copy one file to another — version 2


#include <stdio.h>

int main (int  argc, char  *argv[])
{
    FILE   *in, *out;
    int    c;

    if ( argc != 3 ) {
        fprintf (stderr, "Need two files names\n");
        return 1;
    }

    if ( (in = fopen (argv[1], "r"))  ==  NULL ) {
        fprintf (stderr, "Can't read %s.\n", argv[1]);
        return 2;
    }

    if ( (out = fopen (argv[2], "w")) == NULL ) {
        fprintf (stderr, "Can't write %s.\n", argv[2]);
        return 3;
    }

    while ( (c = getc (in)) != EOF )
        putc (c, out);
```

```
    printf ("File has been copied.\n");

    fclose (in);
    fclose (out);

    return 0;
}
```

The program first checks to make certain that two arguments were typed after the program name. If so, the name of the input file is pointed to by argv[1], and the name of the output file by argv[2]. After opening the first file for reading and the second file for writing, and after checking both opens to make certain they succeeded, the program copies the file character by character as before.

Note that there are four different ways for the program to terminate: incorrect number of command-line arguments, can't open the file to be copied for reading, can't open the output file for writing, and successful termination. Remember, if you're going to use the exit status, you should *always* terminate the program with one. If your program terminates by falling through the bottom of main(), it returns an *undefined* exit status.

If Program 16.1 were called copyf and the program was executed with the following command line:

```
copyf foo foo1
```

then the argv array would look like Figure 16.1 when main is entered.

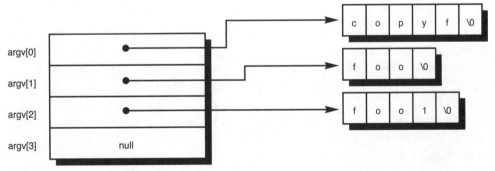

Figure 16.1   argv array on startup of copyf.

Remember that command-line arguments are *always* stored as character strings. Execution of the program power with the command-line arguments 2 and 16, as in

```
power 2 16
```

stores a pointer to the character string "2" inside argv[1], and a pointer to the string "16" inside argv[2]. If the arguments are to be interpreted as numbers by the program (as you might suspect is the case in the power program), they must be converted by the program itself. Several routines are available in the program library for doing such conversions, such as `sscanf()`, `atof()`, `atoi()`, `strtod()`, and `strtol()`. These are described in Appendix B, "The Standard C Library."

Dynamic Memory Allocation

Whenever you define a variable in C—whether it is a simple data type, an array, or a structure—you are effectively reserving one or more locations in the computer's memory to contain the values that will be stored in that variable. The C compiler automatically allocates the correct amount of storage for you.

It is frequently desirable, if not necessary, to be able to *dynamically* allocate storage while a program is running. Suppose you have a program that is designed to read in a set of data from a file into an array in memory. Suppose, however, that you don't know how much data is in the file until the program starts execution. You have three choices:

- Define the array to contain the maximum number of possible elements at compile time.
- Use a variable-length array to dimension the size of the array at runtime.
- Allocate the array dynamically using one of C's memory allocation routines.

Using the first approach, you have to define your array to contain the maximum number of elements that would be read into the array, as in the following:

```
#define  kMaxElements    1000

struct dataEntry  dataArray [kMaxElements];
```

Now, as long as the data file contains 1,000 elements or less, you're in business. But if the number of elements exceeds this amount, you must go back to the program, change the value of `kMaxElements`, and recompile it. Of course, no matter what value you select, you always have the chance of running into the same problem again in the future.

With the second approach, if you can determine the number of elements you need before you start reading in the data (perhaps from the size of the file, for example), you can then define a variable-length array as follows:

```
struct dateEntry dataArray [dataItems];
```

Here, it is assumed that the variable `dataItems` contains the aforementioned number of data items to read in.

Using the dynamic memory allocation functions, you can get storage as you need it. That is, this approach enables you to allocate memory as the program is executing. To use dynamic memory allocation, you must first learn about three functions and one new operator.

The `calloc()` and `malloc()` Functions

In the standard C library, two functions, called `calloc()` and `malloc()`, can be used to allocate memory at runtime. The `calloc()` function takes two arguments that specify the number of elements to be reserved and the size of each element in *bytes*. The function returns a pointer to the beginning of the allocated storage area in memory. The storage area is also automatically set to 0.

The `calloc()` function returns a pointer to `void`, which is C's generic pointer type. Before storing this returned pointer inside a pointer variable in your program, it can be converted into a pointer of the appropriate type using the type cast operator.

The `malloc()` function works similarly, except that it only takes a single argument—the total number of bytes of storage to allocate—and also doesn't automatically set the storage area to 0.

The dynamic memory allocation functions are declared in the standard header file `<stdlib.h>`, which should be included in your program whenever you want to use these routines.

The `sizeof` Operator

To determine the size of data elements to be reserved by `calloc()` or `malloc()` in a machine-independent way, the C `sizeof` operator should be used. The `sizeof` operator returns the size of the specified item in bytes. The argument to the `sizeof` operator can be a variable, an array name, the name of a basic data type, the name of a derived data type, or an expression. For example, writing

```
sizeof (int)
```

gives the number of bytes needed to store an integer. On a Pentium 4 machine, this has the value 4 because an integer occupies 32 bits on that machine. If x is defined to be an array of 100 integers, the expression

```
sizeof (x)
```

gives the amount of storage required for the 100 integers of x (or the value 400 on a Pentium 4). The expression

```
sizeof (struct dataEntry)
```

has as its value the amount of storage required to store one `dataEntry` structure. Finally, if data is defined as an array of `struct dataEntry` elements, the expression

```
sizeof (data) / sizeof (struct dataEntry)
```

gives the number of elements contained in data (data must be a previously defined array, and not a formal parameter or externally referenced array). The expression

```
sizeof (data) / sizeof (data[0])
```

also produces the same result. The macro

```
#define  ELEMENTS(x)    (sizeof(x) / sizeof(x[0]))
```

simply generalizes this technique. It enables you to write code like

```
if ( i >= ELEMENTS (data) )
    ...
```

and

```
for ( i = 0; i < ELEMENTS (data); ++i )
    ...
```

You should remember that `sizeof` is actually an operator, and not a function, even though it looks like a function. This operator is evaluated at compile time and not at runtime, unless a variable-length array is used in its argument. If such an array is not used, the compiler evaluates the value of the `sizeof` expression and replaces it with the result of the calculation, which is treated as a constant.

Use the `sizeof` operator wherever possible to avoid having to calculate and hard-code sizes into your program.

Getting back to dynamic memory allocation, if you want to allocate enough storage in your program to store 1,000 integers, you can call `calloc()` as follows:

```
#include <stdlib.h>
    ...
int  *intPtr;
    ...
intPtr = (int *) calloc (sizeof (int), 1000);
```

Using `malloc()`, the function call looks like this:

```
intPtr = (int *) malloc (1000 * sizeof (int));
```

Remember that both `malloc()` and `calloc()` are defined to return a pointer to `void` and, as noted, this pointer should be type cast to the appropriate pointer type. In the preceding example, the pointer is type cast to an integer pointer and then assigned to `intPtr`.

If you ask for more memory than the system has available, `calloc()` (or `malloc()`) returns a null pointer. Whether you use `calloc()` or `malloc()`, be certain to test the pointer that is returned to ensure that the allocation succeeded.

The following code segment allocates space for 1,000 integer pointers and tests the pointer that is returned. If the allocation fails, the program writes an error message to standard error and then exits.

```
#include <stdlib.h>
#include <stdio.h>
    ...
int  *intPtr;
    ...
intptr = (int *) calloc (sizeof (int), 1000);

if ( intPtr == NULL )
```

```
{
    fprintf (stderr, "calloc failed\n");
    exit (EXIT_FAILURE);
}
```

If the allocation succeeds, the integer pointer variable intptr can be used as if it were pointing to an array of 1,000 integers. So, to set all 1,000 elements to –1, you could write

```
for ( p = intPtr; p < intPtr + 1000; ++p )
    *p = -1;
```

assuming p is declared to be an integer pointer.

To reserve storage for n elements of type struct dataEntry, you first need to define a pointer of the appropriate type

```
struct dataEntry  *dataPtr;
```

and could then proceed to call the calloc() function to reserve the appropriate number of elements

```
dataPtr = (struct dataEntry *) calloc (n, sizeof (struct dataEntry));
```

Execution of the preceding statement proceeds as follows:

1. The calloc() function is called with two arguments, the first specifying that storage for n elements is to be dynamically allocated and the second specifying the size of each element.

2. The calloc() function returns a pointer in memory to the allocated storage area. If the storage cannot be allocated, the null pointer is returned.

3. The pointer is type cast into a pointer of type "pointer to struct dataEntry" and is then assigned to the pointer variable dataPtr.

Once again, the value of dataPtr should be subsequently tested to ensure that the allocation succeeded. If it did, its value is nonnull. This pointer can then be used in the normal fashion, as if it were pointing to an array of n dataEntry elements. For example, if dataEntry contains an integer member called index, you can assign 100 to this member as pointed to by dataPtr with the following statement:

```
dataPtr->index = 100;
```

The **free** Function

When you have finished working with the memory that has been dynamically allocated by calloc() or malloc(), you should give it back to the system by calling the free() function. The single argument to the function is a pointer to the beginning of the allocated memory, as returned by a calloc() or malloc() call. So, the call

```
free (dataPtr);
```

returns the memory allocated by the `calloc()` call shown previously, provided that the value of `dataPtr` still points to the *beginning* of the allocated memory.

The `free()` function does not return a value.

The memory that is released by `free()` can be reused by a later call to `calloc()` or `malloc()`. For programs that need to allocate more storage space than would otherwise be available if it were all allocated at once, this is worth remembering. Make certain you give the `free()` function a valid pointer to the beginning of some previously allocated space.

Dynamic memory allocation is invaluable when dealing with linked structures, such as linked lists. When you need to add a new entry to the list, you can dynamically allocate storage for one entry in the list and link it into the list with the pointer returned by `calloc()` or `malloc()`. For example, assume that `listEnd` points to the end of a singly linked list of type `struct entry`, defined as follows:

```
struct entry
{
    int         value;
    struct entry   *next;
};
```

Here is a function called `addEntry()` that takes as its argument a pointer to the start of the linked list and that adds a new entry to the end of the list.

```
#include <stdlib.h>
#include <stddef.h>

// add new entry to end of linked list

struct entry *addEntry (struct entry *listPtr)
{
    // find the end of the list

    while ( listPtr->next != NULL )
        listPtr = listPtr->next;

    // get storage for new entry

    listPtr->next = (struct entry *) malloc (sizeof (struct entry));

    // add null to the new end of the list

    if ( listPtr->next != NULL )
        (listPtr->next)->next = (struct entry *) NULL;

    return listPtr->next;
}
```

If the allocation succeeds, a null pointer is placed in the `next` member of the newly allocated linked-list entry (pointed to by `listPtr->next`).

The function returns a pointer to the new list entry, or the null pointer if the allocation fails (verify that this is, in fact, what happens). If you draw a picture of a linked list and trace through the execution of `addEntry()`, it will help you to understand how the function works.

Another function, called `realloc()`, is associated with dynamic memory allocation. It can be used to shrink or expand the size of some previously allocated storage. For more details, consult Appendix B.

This chapter concludes coverage of the features of the C language. In Chapter 17, "Debugging Programs," you learn some techniques that will help you to debug your C programs. One involves using the preprocessor. The other involves the use of a special tool, called an interactive debugger.

Exercises

1. Type in and run the program presented in this chapter. Check the program's results by comparing the original file you chose to copy with the filename you entered to copy and ensure the two are the same.

2. Finish the program that takes a word as a command-line argument and looks up the word to see whether it is in the array of terms and definitions, providing the definition if it is found, or informs the user that the term is not in the program's glossary if it isn't found.

Debugging Programs

This chapter teaches you two techniques you can use to debug your programs. One involves using the preprocessor to allow for the conditional inclusion of debugging statements in your program. The other technique involves the use of an interactive debugger. In this chapter, you are introduced to a popular debugger called gdb. Even if you use a different debugger (such as dbx, or one built in to an IDE tool), it is likely that your debugger will have similarities to gdb.

Again, as discussed in the opening of Chapter 14, "Working with Larger Programs," some of the topics covered in this chapter may not seem applicable to you depending on the operating system and development environment you use, but the concepts are important and universal.

Debugging with the Preprocessor

As noted in Chapter 12, "The Preprocessor," conditional compilation is useful when debugging programs. The C preprocessor can be used to insert debugging code into your program. By appropriate use of #ifdef statements, the debugging code can be enabled or disabled at your discretion. Program 17.1 is a program (admittedly contrived) that reads in three integers and prints out their sum. Note that when the preprocessor identifier DEBUG is defined, the debugging code (which prints to stderr) is compiled with the rest of the program, and when DEBUG isn't defined, the debugging code is left out.

Program 17.1 **Adding Debug Statements with the Preprocessor**

```
#include <stdio.h>
#define DEBUG

int process (int i, int j, int k)
{
    return i + j + k;
}

int main (void)
```

```
{
    int  i, j, k, nread;

    nread = scanf ("%d %d %d", &i, &j, &k);

#ifdef DEBUG
    fprintf (stderr, "Number of integers read = %i\n", nread);
    fprintf (stderr, "i = %i, j = %i, k = %i\n", i, j, k);
#endif

    printf ("%i\n", process (i, j, k));
    return 0;
}
```

Program 17.1 **Output**

```
1 2 3
Number of integers read = 3
i = 1, j = 2, k = 3
6
```

Program 17.1 **Output (Rerun)**

```
1 2 e
Number of integers read = 2
i = 1, j = 2, k = 0
3
```

Note that the value displayed for k can be anything because its value was not set by the scanf() call and it was not initialized by the program.

The statements

```
#ifdef DEBUG
    fprintf (stderr, "Number of integers read = %i\n", nread);
    fprintf (stderr, "i = %d, j = %d, k = %d\n", i, j, k);
#endif
```

are analyzed by the preprocessor. If the identifier DEBUG has been previously defined (#ifdef DEBUG), the preprocessor sends the statements that follow up to the #endif (the two fprintf() calls) to the compiler to be compiled. If DEBUG hasn't been defined, the two fprintf() calls never make it to the compiler (they're removed from the program by the preprocessor). As you can see, the program prints out messages after it reads in the integers. The second time the program is run, an invalid character is entered (e). The debugging output informs you of the error. Note that to turn off the debugging code, all you have to do is remove (or comment out) the line

```
#define DEBUG
```

and the `fprintf()` statements are not compiled with the rest of the program. Although this program is so short you might not feel it's worth the bother, consider how easy it is to turn debugging code on and off in a program several hundreds of lines long by simply changing one line.

You can even control the debugging from the command line when the program is compiled. If you're using `gcc`, the command

```
gcc -D DEBUG debug.c
```

compiles the file `debug.c`, defining the preprocessor variable `DEBUG` for you. This is equivalent to putting the following line in your program:

```
#define DEBUG
```

Take a look at a slightly longer program. Program 17.2 takes up to two command-line arguments. Each of these is converted into an integer value and is assigned to the corresponding variables `arg1` and `arg2`. To convert the command-line arguments into integers, the standard library function `atoi()` is used. This function takes a character string as its argument and returns its corresponding representation as an integer. The `atoi()` function is declared in the header file `<stdlib.h>`, which is included at the beginning of Program 17.2.

After processing the arguments, the program calls the `process()` function, passing the two command-line values as arguments. This function simply returns the product of these two arguments. As you can see, when the `DEBUG` identifier is defined, various debugging messages are printed, and when it isn't defined, only the result is printed.

Program 17.2 **Compiling in Debug Code**

```
#include <stdio.h>
#include <stdlib.h>

int process (int i1, int i2)
{
    int  val;

#ifdef DEBUG
    fprintf (stderr, "process (%i, %i)\n", i1, i2);
#endif
    val = i1 * i2;
#ifdef DEBUG
    fprintf (stderr, "return %i\n", val);
#endif
    return val;
}

int main (int argc, char *argv[])
{
```

```
    int arg1 = 0, arg2 = 0;

    if (argc > 1)
    arg1 = atoi (argv[1]);
    if (argc == 3)
        arg2 = atoi (argv[2]);
#ifdef DEBUG
    fprintf (stderr, "processed %i arguments\n", argc - 1);
    fprintf (stderr, "arg1 = %i, arg2 = %i\n", arg1, arg2);
#endif
    printf ("%i\n", process (arg1, arg2));

    return 0;
}
```

Program 17.2   **Output**

```
$ gcc -D DEBUG p18-2.c     Compile with DEBUG defined
$ a.out 5 10
processed 2 arguments
arg1 = 5, arg2 = 10
process (5, 10)
return 50
50
```

Program 17.2   **Output (Rerun)**

```
$ gcc p18-2.c              Compile without DEBUG defined
$ a.out 2 5
10
```

When the program is ready for distribution, the debugging statements can be left in the source file without affecting the executable code, as long as DEBUG isn't defined. If a bug is found at some later time, the debugging code can be compiled in and the output examined to see what's happening.

The previous method is still rather clumsy because the programs themselves tend to be difficult to read. One thing you can do is change the way the preprocessor is used. You can define a macro that can take a variable number of arguments to produce your debugging output:

```
#define DEBUG(fmt, ...) fprintf (stderr, fmt, __VA_ARGS__)
```

and use it instead of fprintf as follows:

```
DEBUG ("process (%i, %i)\n", i1, i2);
```

This gets evaluated as follows:

```
fprintf (stderr, "process (%i, %i)\n", i1, i2);
```

The DEBUG macro can be used throughout a program, and the intent is quite clear, as shown in Program 17.3.

Program 17.3   **Defining a** DEBUG **Macro**

```
#include <stdio.h>
#include <stdlib.h>

#define DEBUG(fmt, ...) fprintf (stderr, fmt, __VA_ARGS__)

int process (int i1, int i2)
{
    int  val;

    DEBUG ("process (%i, %i)\n", i1, i2);
    val = i1 * i2;
    DEBUG ("return %i\n", val);

    return val;
}

int main (int argc, char *argv[])
{
    int arg1 = 0, arg2 = 0;

    if (argc > 1)
    arg1 = atoi (argv[1]);
    if (argc == 3)
       arg2 = atoi (argv[2]);

    DEBUG ("processed %i arguments\n", argc - 1);
    DEBUG ("arg1 = %i, arg2 = %i\n", arg1, arg2);
    printf ("%d\n", process (arg1, arg2));

    return 0;
}
```

Program 17.3   **Output**

```
$ gcc pre3.c
$ a.out 8 12
processed 2 arguments
arg1 = 8, arg2 = 12
process (8, 12)
return 96
96
```

As you can see, the program is much more readable in this form. When you no longer need debugging output, simply define the macro to be nothing:

```
#define DEBUG(fmt, ...)
```

This tells the preprocessor to replace calls to the DEBUG macro with nothing, so all uses of DEBUG simply turn into null statements.

You can expand on the notion of the DEBUG macro a little further to allow for both compile-time and execution-time debugging control: Declare a global variable Debug that defines a debugging level. All DEBUG statements less than or equal to this level produce output. DEBUG now takes at least two arguments; the first is the level:

```
DEBUG (1, "processed data\n");
DEBUG (3, "number of elements = %i\n", nelems)
```

If the debugging level is set to 1 or 2, only the first DEBUG statement produces output; if the debugging level is set to 3 or more, both DEBUG statements produce output. The debugging level can be set via a command-line option at execution time as follows:

a.out –d1   *Set debugging level to 1*
a.out –d3   *Set debugging level to 3*

The definition for DEBUG is straightforward:

```
#define DEBUG(level, fmt, ...) \
  if (Debug >= level) \
   fprintf (stderr, fmt, __VA_ARGS__)
```

So

```
DEBUG (3, "number of elements = %i\n", nelems);
```

becomes

```
if (Debug >= 3)
 fprintf (stderr, "number of elements = %i\n", nelems);
```

Again, if DEBUG is defined to be nothing, the DEBUG calls become null statements.

The following definition provides all the mentioned features, as well as the ability to control the definition of DEBUG at compile time.

```
#ifdef DEBON
#  define DEBUG(level, fmt, ...) \
     if (Debug >= level) \
          fprintf (stderr, fmt, __VA_ARGS__)
#else
#  define DEBUG(level, fmt, ...)
#endif
```

When compiling a program containing the previous definition (which you can conveniently place inside a header file and include in your program), you either define DEBON or not. If you compile prog.c as follows:

```
$ gcc prog.c
```

it compiles in the null definition for DEBUG based on the #else clause shown in the previous preprocessor statements. On the other hand, if you compile your program like this:

```
$ gcc -D DEBON prog.c
```

the DEBUG macro that calls fprintf based on the debug level is compiled in with the rest of your code.

At runtime, if you have compiled in the debugging code, you can select the debug level. As noted, this can be done with a command-line option as follows:

```
$ a.out -d3
```

Here, the debug level is set to 3. Presumably, you would process this command-line argument in your program and store the debug level in a variable (probably global) called Debug. And in this case, only DEBUG macros that specify a level of 3 or greater cause the fprintf calls to be made.

Note that a.out -d0 sets the debugging level to zero and no debugging output is generated even though the debugging code is still in there.

To summarize, you have seen here a two-tiered debugging scheme: Debugging code can be compiled in or out of the code, and when compiled in, different debugging levels can be set to produce varying amounts of debugging output.

Debugging Programs with gdb

gdb is a powerful interactive debugger that is frequently used to debug programs compiled with GNU's gcc compiler. It allows you to run your program, stop at a predetermined location, display and/or set variables, and continue execution. It allows you to trace your program's execution and even execute it one line at a time. gdb also has a facility for determining where *core dumps* occur. A core dump occurs due to some abnormal event, possibly division by zero or attempts to access past the end of an array. This results in the creation of a file named core that contains a snapshot of the contents of the process's memory at the time it terminated.[1]

Your C program must be compiled with the gcc compiler using the -g option to make full use of gdb's features. The -g option causes the C compiler to add extra information to the output file, including variable and structure types, source filenames, and C statement to machine code mappings.

Program 17.4 shows a program that attempts to access elements past the end of an array.

---

1. *Your system might be configured to disable the automatic creation of this* core *file, often due to the large size of these files. Sometimes, this has to do with the maximum file creation size, which can be changed with the* ulimit *command.*

Program 17.4   **A Simple Program for Use with** gdb

```
#include <stdio.h>

int main (void)
{
    const int  data[5] = {1, 2, 3, 4, 5};
    int  i, sum;

    for (i = 0; i >= 0; ++i)
        sum += data[i];

    printf ("sum = %i\n", sum);

    return 0;
}
```

Here's what happens when the program is run on a Mac OS X system from a terminal window (on other systems you might get a different message displayed when you run the program):

```
$ a.out
Segmentation fault
```

Use gdb to try to track down the error. This is certainly a contrived example; nevertheless, it is illustrative.

First, make sure you compile the program with the –g option. Then, you can start up gdb on the executable file, which is a.out by default. This might result in lines of introductory messages being displayed on your system:

```
$ gcc -g p18.4.c        Recompile with debugging information for gdb
$ gdb a.out             Start up gdb on the executable file
GNU gdb 5.3-20030128 (Apple version gdb-309) (Thu Dec  4 15:41:30 GMT 2003)
Copyright 2003 Free Software Foundation, Inc.
GDB is free software, covered by the GNU General Public License, and you are
welcome to change it and/or distribute copies of it under certain conditions.
Type "show copying" to see the conditions.
There is absolutely no warranty for GDB. Type "show warranty" for details.
This GDB was configured as "powerpc-apple-darwin".
Reading symbols for shared libraries .. done
```

When gdb is ready to accept commands, it displays a (gdb) prompt. In our simple example, you're simply telling it to run your program by entering the run command. This causes gdb to start execution of your program until it finishes or an abnormal event occurs:

```
(gdb) run
Starting program: /Users/stevekochan/MySrc/c/a.out
Reading symbols for shared libraries . done

Program received signal EXC_BAD_ACCESS, Could not access memory.
```

```
0x00001d7c in main () at p18-4.c:9
9                   sum += data[i];
(gdb)
```

So your program receives an error (as it did before), but it still remains under the control of gdb. That's the nice part because now you can see what it was doing when the error occurred as well as look at the values of variables at the time of the error.

As you can see from the previous display, the program tried to perform an invalid memory access at line 9 in your program. The actual line in question is automatically displayed from your source file. To gain a little context around that line, you can use the list command, which displays a window of 10 lines around the specified line (5 lines before and 4 lines after):

```
(gdb) list 9
4       {
5               const int  data[5] = {1, 2, 3, 4, 5};
6               int  i, sum;
7
8               for (i = 0; i >= 0; ++i)
9                   sum += data[i];
10
11              printf ("sum = %i\n", sum);
12
13              return 0;
(gdb)
```

You can look at variables by using the print command. Take a look at what the value of sum was at the time the program stopped with an error:

```
(gdb) print sum
$1 = -1089203864
```

This value for sum is obviously out of whack (and on your system might differ from what's shown here). The $n notation is used by gdb to keep track of the values you've previously displayed, so you can easily reference them again later.

Take a look at what the index variable i is set to:

```
(gdb) print i
$2 = 232
```

Oops! That's not good. You have only five elements in the array and you tried to access the 233rd element when the error occurred. On your system, the error might occur earlier or later. But eventually, you should get an error.

Before you exit from gdb, look at another variable. See how nicely gdb deals with variables like arrays and structures:

```
(gdb) print data            Show the contents of the data array
$3 = {1, 2, 3, 4, 5}
(gdb) print data[0]         Show the value of the first element
$4 = 1
```

You'll see an example of a structure a little later. To complete this first example with gdb, you need to learn how to get out. You can do that with the quit command:

```
(gdb) quit
The program is running. Exit anyway? (y or n) y
$
```

Even though the program had an error, technically speaking, it was still active inside gdb; the error merely caused your program's execution to be suspended, but not terminated. That's the reason gdb asked for confirmation about quitting.

Working with Variables

gdb has two basic commands that allow you to work with variables in your program. One you've seen already is print. The other allows you to set the value of a variable. This is done with the set var command. The set command actually takes a number of different options, but var is the one you want to use to assign a value to a variable:

```
(gdb) set var i=5
(gdb) print i
$1 = 5
(gdb) set var i=i*2        You can write any valid expression
(gdb) print i
$2 = 10
(gdb) set var i=$1+20      You can use so-called "convenience variables"
(gdb) print i
$3 = 25
```

A variable must be accessible by the current function, and the process must be *active*, that is, running. gdb maintains an idea of a current line (like an editor), a current file (the source file of the program), and a current function. When gdb starts up without a core file, the current function is main(), the current file is the one that contains main(), and the current line is the first executable line in main(); otherwise, the current line, file, and procedure are set to the location where the program aborted.

If a local variable with the specified name doesn't exist, gdb looks for an external variable of the same name. In the previous example, the function executing at the time the invalid access occurred was main(), and i was a variable local to main.

A function can be specified as part of the variable name in the form *function::variable* to reference a variable local to a specific routine, for example,

```
(gdb) print main::i        Display contents of i in main
$4 = 25
(gdb) set var main::i=0    Set value of i in main
```

Note that attempting to set a variable in an inactive function (that is, a function that is not either currently executing or waiting for another function to return to continue its own execution) is an error and results in the following message:

```
No symbol "var" in current context.
```

Global variables can be directly referenced as `'file'::var`. This forces gdb to access an external variable as defined in the file *file* and ignore any local variable of the same name in the current function.

Structure and union members can be accessed using standard C syntax. If `datePtr` is a pointer to a `date structure`, `print datePtr->year` prints the year member of the structure pointed to by `datePtr`.

Referencing a structure or union without a member causes the contents of the entire structure or union to be displayed.

You can force gdb to display a variable in a different format, for example hexadecimal, by following the `print` command with a `/` and a letter that specifies the format to use. Many gdb commands can be abbreviated with a single letter. In the following example, the abbreviation for the `print` command, which is p, is used:

```
(gdb) set var i=35      Set i to 3
(gdb) p /x i            Display i in hexadecimal
$1 = 0x23
```

Source File Display

gdb provides several commands that give you access to the source files. This enables you to debug the program without having to reference a source listing or open your source files in other windows.

As mentioned earlier, gdb maintains an idea of what the current line and file are. You've seen how you can display the area around the current line with the `list` command, which can be abbreviated as `l`. Each time you subsequently type the `list` command (or more simply, just press the *Enter* or *Return* key), the next 10 lines from the file are displayed. This value of `10` is the default and can be set to any value by using the `listsize` command.

If you want to display a range of lines, you can specify the starting and ending line numbers, separated by a comma, as follows:

```
(gdb) list 10,15        List lines 10 through 15
```

Lines from a function can be listed by specifying the function's name to the `list` command:

```
(gdb) list foo          Display lines for function foo
```

If the function is in another source file, gdb automatically switches to that file. You can find the name of the current source file being displayed with gdb by typing in the command `info source`.

Typing a + after the `list` command causes the next 10 lines from the current file to be displayed, which is the same action that occurs if just `list` is typed. Typing a – causes the previous 10 lines to be displayed. Both the + and – options can also be followed by a number to specify a relative offset to be added or subtracted from the current line.

Controlling Program Execution

Displaying lines from a file doesn't modify the way a program is executed. You must use other commands for that. You've seen two commands that control the execution of a program in gdb: run, which runs the program from the beginning, and quit, which terminates execution of the current program.

The run command can be followed by command-line arguments and/or redirection (< or >), and gdb handles them properly. Subsequent use of the r command without any arguments reuses the previous arguments and redirection. You can display the current arguments with the command show args.

Inserting Breakpoints

The break command can be used to set *breakpoints* in your program. A breakpoint is just as its name implies—a point in your program that, when reached during execution, causes the program to "break" or pause. The program's execution is suspended, which allows you to do things such as look at variables and determine precisely what's going on at the point.

A breakpoint can be set at any line in your program by simply specifying the line number to the command. If you specify a line number but no function or filename, the breakpoint is set on that line in the current file; if you specify a function, the breakpoint is set on the first executable line in that function.

```
(gdb) break 12                    Set breakpoint on line 12
Breakpoint 1 at 0x1da4: file mod1.c, line 12.
(gdb) break main                  Set breakpoint at start of main
Breakpoint 2 at 0x1d6c: file mod1.c, line 3.
(gdb) break mod2.c:foo            Breakpoint in function foo in file mod2.c
Breakpoint 3 at 0x1dd8: file mod2.c, line 4.
```

When a breakpoint is reached during program execution, gdb suspends execution of your program, returns control to you, and identifies the breakpoint and the line of your program at which it stopped. You can do anything you want at that point: You can display or set variables, set or unset breakpoints, and so on. To resume execution of the program, you can simply use the continue command, which can be abbreviated as simply c.

Single Stepping

Another useful command for controlling program execution is the step command, which can be abbreviated as s. This command single steps your program, meaning that one line of C code in your program is executed for each step command you enter. If you follow the step command with a number, then that many lines are executed. Note that a line might contain several C statements; however, gdb is line oriented, and executes all statements on a line as a single step. If a statement spans several lines, single stepping the first line of the statement causes all the lines of the statement to be executed. You can single step your program at any time that a continue is appropriate (after a signal or breakpoint).

If the statement contains a function call and you step, gdb takes you into the function (provided it's not a system library function; these are typically not entered). If you use the next command instead of step, gdb makes the function call and does not step you into it.

Try some of gdb's features on Program 17.5, which otherwise serves no useful purpose.

Program 17.5 **Working with gdb**

```c
#include <stdio.h>
#include <stdlib.h>

struct date {
    int month;
    int day;
    int year;
};


struct date foo (struct date x)
{
    ++x.day;

    return x;
}

int main (void)
{
    struct date today = {10, 11, 2014};
    int         array[5] = {1, 2, 3, 4, 5};
    struct date *newdate, foo ();
    char        *string = "test string";
    int         i = 3;

    newdate = (struct date *) malloc (sizeof (struct date));
    newdate->month = 11;
    newdate->day = 15;
    newdate->year = 2014;

    today = foo (today);

    free (newdate);

    return 0;
}
```

In the sample session for Program 17.5, your output might be slightly different, depending on which version and on what system you are running gdb.

Program 17.5   **gdb Session**

```
$ gcc -g p18-5.c
$ gdb a.out
GNU gdb 5.3-20030128 (Apple version gdb-309) (Thu Dec  4 15:41:30 GMT 2003)
Copyright 2003 Free Software Foundation, Inc.
GDB is free software, covered by the GNU General Public License, and you are
welcome to change it and/or distribute copies of it under certain conditions.
Type "show copying" to see the conditions.
There is absolutely no warranty for GDB. Type "show warranty" for details.
This GDB was configured as "powerpc-apple-darwin".
Reading symbols for shared libraries .. done
(gdb) list main
14
15          return x;
16      }
17
18      int main (void)
19      {
20          struct date today = {10, 11, 2014};
21          int        array[5] = {1, 2, 3, 4, 5};
22          struct date *newdate, foo ();
23          char       *string = "test string";
(gdb) break main             Set breakpoint in main
Breakpoint 1 at 0x1ce8: file p18-5.c, line 20.
(gdb) run                    Start program execution
Starting program: /Users/stevekochan/MySrc/c/a.out
Reading symbols for shared libraries . done

Breakpoint 1, main () at p18-5.c:20
20          struct date today = {10, 11, 2014};
(gdb) step                   Execute line 20
21          int        array[5] = {1, 2, 3, 4, 5};
(gdb) print today
$1 = {
  month = 10,
  day = 11,
  year = 2014
}
(gdb) print array            This array hasn't been initialized yet
$2 = {-1881069176, -1880816132, -1880815740, -1880816132, -1880846287}
(gdb) step                   Run another line
23          char       *string = "test string";
(gdb) print array            Now try it
$3 = {1, 2, 3, 4, 5}         That's better
(gdb) list 23,28
23          char       *string = "test string";
```

```
24          int        i = 3;
25
26          newdate = (struct date *) malloc (sizeof (struct date));
27          newdate->month = 11;
28          newdate->day = 15;
(gdb) step 5                 Execute 5 lines
29          newdate->year = 2014;
(gdb) print string
$4 = 0x1fd4 "test string"
(gdb) print string[1]
$5 = 101 'e'
(gdb) print array[i]            The program set i to 3
$6 = 4
(gdb) print newdate            This is a pointer variable
$7 = (struct date *) 0x100140
(gdb) print newdate->month
$8 = 11
(gdb) print newdate->day + i  Arbitrary C expression
$9 = 18
(gdb) print $7                 Access previous value
$10 = (struct date *) 0x100140
(gdb) info locals            Show the value of all local variables
today = {
  month = 10,
  day = 11,
  year = 2014
}
array = {1, 2, 3, 4, 5}
newdate = (struct date *) 0x100140
string = 0x1fd4 "test string"
i = 3
(gdb) break foo            Put a breakpoint at the start of foo
Breakpoint 2 at 0x1c98: file p18-5.c, line 13.
(gdb) continue            Continue execution
Continuing.

Breakpoint 2, foo (x={month = 10, day = 11, year = 2014}) at p18-5.c:13
13          ++x.day; 0x8e in foo:25: {
 (gdb) print today            Display value of today
 No symbol "today" in current context
(gdb) print main::today      Display value of today from main
$11 = {
  month = 10,
  day = 11,
  year = 2014
}
 (gdb) step
```

```
15              return x;
(gdb) print x.day
$12 = 12
(gdb) continue
Continuing.
Program exited normally.
(gdb)
```

Note one feature of gdb: After a breakpoint is reached or after single stepping, it lists the line that will be executed next when you resume execution of your program, and not the last executed line. That's why array was still not initialized the first time it was displayed. Single stepping one line caused it to be initialized. Also note that declarations that initialize automatic variables are considered executable lines (they actually do cause the compiler to produce executable code).

Listing and Deleting Breakpoints

Once set, breakpoints remain in a program until gdb exits or until you delete them. You can see all the breakpoints that you have set by using the info break command, as follows:

```
(gdb) info break
Num Type           Disp Enb Address    What
1   breakpoint     keep y   0x00001c9c in main at p18-5.c:20
2   breakpoint     keep y   0x00001c4c in foo at p18-5.c:13
```

You can delete a breakpoint at a particular line with the clear command followed by the line number. You can delete a breakpoint at the start of a function by specifying the function's name to the clear command instead:

```
(gdb) clear 20      Remove breakpoint from line 20
Deleted breakpoint 1
(gdb) info break
Num Type           Disp Enb Address    What
2   breakpoint     keep y   0x00001c4c in foo at p18-5.c:13
(gdb) clear foo     Remove breakpoint on entry into foo
Deleted breakpoint 2
(gdb) info break
No breakpoints or watchpoints.
(gdb)
```

Getting a Stack Trace

Sometimes, you'll want to know exactly where you are in terms of the hierarchy of function calls when a program gets interrupted. This is useful information when examining a core file. You can take a look at the *call stack* by using the backtrace command, which can be abbreviated as bt. The following is an example use of Program 17.5.

```
(gdb) break foo
Breakpoint 1 at 0x1c4c: file p18-5.c, line 13.
(gdb) run
Starting program: /Users/stevekochan/MySrc/c/a.out
Reading symbols for shared libraries . done

Breakpoint 1, foo (x={month = 10, day = 11, year = 2014}) at p18-5.c:13
13          ++x.day;
(gdb) bt              Print stack trace
#0  foo (x={month = 10, day = 11, year = 2014}) at p18-5.c:13
#1  0x00001d48 in main () at p18-5.c:31
(gdb)
```

When the break is taken on entry to foo(), the backtrace command is entered. The output shows two functions on the call stack: foo() and main(). As you can see, the arguments to the functions are also listed. Various commands (such as up, down, frame, and info args) that are not covered here allow you to work your way around in the stack so that you can more easily examine arguments passed to a particular function or work with its local variables.

Calling Functions and Setting Arrays and Structures

You can use function calls in gdb expressions as follows:

```
(gdb) print foo(*newdate)    Call foo with date structure pointed to by newdate
$13 = {
  month = 11,
  day = 16,
  year = 2014
}
(gdb)
```

Here, the function foo() is as defined in Program 17.5.

You can assign values to an array or structure by listing them inside a set of curly braces, as follows:

```
(gdb) print array
$14 = {1, 2, 3, 4, 5}
(gdb) set var array = {100, 200}
(gdb) print array
$15 = {100, 200, 0, 0}          Unspecified values set to zero
(gdb) print today
$16 = {
  month = 10,
  day = 11,
  year = 2014
}
(gdb) set var today={8, 8, 2014}
```

```
(gdb) print today
$17 = {
  month = 8,
  day = 8,
  year = 2014
}
(gdb)
```

Getting Help with gdb Commands

You can use the built-in help command to get information about various commands or types of commands (called *classes* by gdb).

The command help, without any arguments, lists all the available classes:

```
(gdb) help
List of classes of commands:

aliases -- Aliases of other commands
breakpoints -- Making program stop at certain points
data -- Examining data
files -- Specifying and examining files
internals -- Maintenance commands
obscure -- Obscure features
running -- Running the program
stack -- Examining the stack
status -- Status inquiries
support -- Support facilities
tracepoints -- Tracing of program execution without stopping the program
user-defined -- User-defined commands

Type "help" followed by a class name for a list of commands in that class.
Type "help" followed by command name for full documentation.
Command name abbreviations are allowed if unambiguous.
```

Now, you can give the help command one of those listed classes, as follows:

```
(gdb) help breakpoints
Making program stop at certain points.

List of commands:

awatch -- Set a watchpoint for an expression
break -- Set breakpoint at specified line or function
catch -- Set catchpoints to catch events
clear -- Clear breakpoint at specified line or function
commands -- Set commands to be executed when a breakpoint is hit
condition -- Specify breakpoint number N to break only if COND is true
```

```
delete -- Delete some breakpoints or auto-display expressions
disable -- Disable some breakpoints
enable -- Enable some breakpoints
future-break -- Set breakpoint at expression
hbreak -- Set a hardware assisted breakpoint
ignore -- Set ignore-count of breakpoint number N to COUNT
rbreak -- Set a breakpoint for all functions matching REGEXP
rwatch -- Set a read watchpoint for an expression
save-breakpoints -- Save current breakpoint definitions as a script
set exception-catch-type-regexp -
        Set a regexp to match against the exception type of a caughtobject
set exception-throw-type-regexp -
        Set a regexp to match against the exception type of a thrownobject
show exception-catch-type-regexp -
        Show a regexp to match against the exception type of a caughtobject
show exception-throw-type-regexp -
        Show a regexp to match against the exception type of a thrownobject
tbreak -- Set a temporary breakpoint
tcatch -- Set temporary catchpoints to catch events
thbreak -- Set a temporary hardware assisted breakpoint
watch -- Set a watchpoint for an expression

Type "help" followed by command name for full documentation.
Command name abbreviations are allowed if unambiguous.
(gdb)
```

Alternatively, you can specify a command, such as one from the previous list:

```
(gdb_ help break
Set breakpoint at specified line or function.
Argument may be line number, function name, or "*" and an address.
If line number is specified, break at start of code for that line.
If function is specified, break at start of code for that function.
If an address is specified, break at that exact address.
With no arg, uses current execution address of selected stack frame.
This is useful for breaking on return to a stack frame.

Multiple breakpoints at one place are permitted, and useful if conditional.

break ... if <cond> sets condition <cond> on the breakpoint as it is created.

Do "help breakpoints" for info on other commands dealing with breakpoints.
(gdb)
```

So, you can see that you have a lot of help information built right in to the gdb debugger. Be sure to take advantage of it!

Odds and Ends

Many other features are available with gdb that can't be covered here for space reasons. These
include the ability to

- Set temporary breakpoints that are automatically removed when they are reached.

- Enable and disable breakpoints without having to clear them.

- Dump memory locations in a specified format.

- Set a watchpoint that allows for your program's execution to be stopped whenever the
  value of a specified expression changes (for example, when a variable changes its value).

- Specify a list of values to be displayed whenever the program stops.

- Set your own "convenience variables" by name.

In addition, if you are using an integrated development environment (IDE), most have their
own debugging tools, many of which are similar to the gdb commands described in this
chapter. It's impossible to cover each individual IDE in this chapter, so the best way to explore
the options available to you is run the debugging tools on your programs—even introduce
some errors that you have to hunt down with your debugger.

Table 17.1 lists the gdb commands covered in this chapter. A leading bold character for a
command name shows how the command can be abbreviated.

Table 17.1   **Common gdb Commands**

Command	Meaning
Source File	
List [n]²	Displays lines around line n or next 10 lines if n is not specified
list m,n	Displays lines m through n
list +[n]	Displays lines around line n lines forward in file or 10 lines forward if n is not specified
list -[n]	Displays lines around line n lines back in file or 10 lines back if n is not specified
list func	Displays lines from function func
listsize n	Specifies number of lines to display with list command
info source	Shows current source filename
Variables and Expressions	
print /fmt expr	Prints expr according to format fmt, which can be d (decimal), u (unsigned), o (octal), x (hexadecimal), c (character), f (floating point), t (binary), or a (address)

Command	Meaning
`info locals`	Shows value of local variables in current function
`set var var=expr`	Sets variable *var* to value of *expr*
Breakpoints	
`break n`	Sets breakpoint at line *n*
`break func`	Sets breakpoint at start of function *func*
`info break`	Shows all breakpoints
`clear [n]`	Removes breakpoint at line *n* or at next line if not specified
`clear func`	Removes breakpoint at start of function *func*
Program Execution	
`run [args] [<file] [>file]`	Starts program execution from the beginning
`continue`	Continues program execution
`step [n]`	Executes next program line or next *n* program lines
`next [n]`	Executes next program line or next *n* program lines without stepping into functions
`quit`	Quits `gdb` execution
Help	
`help [cmd]`	Displays classes of commands or help about specific
`help [class]`	command *cmd* or *class*

2. Note that each command that takes a line number or function name can be preceded by an optional filename followed by a colon (for example, `list main.c:1,10` or `break main.c:12`)

## 18

Object-Oriented Programming

Because object-oriented programming (or OOP) is so popular, and because many of the widely used OOP languages—such as C++, C#, Java, and Objective-C—are based on the C language, a brief introduction to this topic is presented here. The chapter starts with an overview about the concepts of OOP, and then shows you a simple program in three of the four aforementioned OOP languages (I picked the three that contain the word "C"!). The idea here is not to teach you how to program in these languages or even to describe their main features so much as it is to give you a quick taste. This chapter includes

- Understanding the basic concepts of OOP, including objects, classes, and methods.

- Explaining the basic differences between how a structured programming language approaches a problem versus how an object-oriented language does it.

- Comparing how three different object-oriented languages, specifically Objective-C, C++, and C#, approach a simple programming task.

What Is an Object Anyway?

An object is a *thing*. Think about object-oriented programming as a thing and something you want to do to that thing. This is in contrast to a programming language such as C, more formally known as a procedural programming language. In C, you typically think about what you want to do first (and maybe write some functions to accomplish those tasks), and then you worry about the objects—almost the opposite from object orientation.

As an example from everyday life, assume you own a car. That car is obviously an object—one that you own. You don't have just any car; you have a particular car that was manufactured from the factory, perhaps in Detroit, perhaps in Japan, or perhaps someplace else. Your car has a vehicle identification number (VIN) that uniquely identifies your car.

In object-oriented parlance, *your* car is an *instance* of a car. And continuing with the terminology, *car* is the name of the *class* from which this instance was created. So, each time a new car gets manufactured, a new instance from the class of cars gets created. Each instance of the car is also referred to as an *object*.

Now, your car might be silver, it might have a black interior, it might be a convertible or hardtop, and so on. In addition, there are certain things, or actions, you do with your car. For example, you drive your car, you fill it up with gas, you (hopefully) wash your car, you take it in for service, and so on. This is depicted in Table 18.1.

Table 18.1   **Actions on Objects**

Object	What You Do with It
Your car	Drive it
	Fill it with gas
	Wash it
	Service it

The actions listed in Table 18.1 can be done with your car, and they can also be done with other cars. For example, your sister can drive her car, wash it, fill it up with gas, and so on.

Instances and Methods

A unique occurrence of a class is an instance. The actions that you perform are called *methods*. In some cases, a method can be applied to an instance of the class or to the class itself. For example, washing your car applies to an instance (in fact, all of the methods listed in Table 18.1 are considered instance methods). Finding out how many different types of cars a manufacturer makes applies to the class, so it is a class method.

In C++, you invoke a method on an instance using the following notation:

```
Instance.method ();
```

A C# method is invoked with the same notation as follows:

```
Instance.method ();
```

An Objective-C message call follows this format:

```
[Instance  method]
```

Go back to the previous list and write a message expression in this new syntax. Assume that yourCar is an object from the Car class. Table 18.2 shows what message expressions might look like in the three OOP languages.

Table 18.2   **Message Expressions in OOP Languages**

C++	C#	Objective-C	Action
yourCar.drive()	yourCar.drive()	[yourCar drive]	Drive your car
yourCar.getGas()	yourCar.getGas()	[yourCar getGas]	Put gas in your car
yourCar.wash()	yourCar.wash()	[yourCar wash]	Wash your car
yourCar.service()	yourCar.service()	[yourCar service]	Service your car

And if your sister has a car, called suesCar, for example, then she can invoke the same methods on her car, as follows:

```
suesCar.drive()     suesCar.drive()     [suesCar drive]
```

This is one of the key concepts behind object-oriented programming (that is, applying the same methods to different objects).

Another key concept, known as polymorphism, allows you to send the same message to instances from different classes. For example, if you have a Boat class, and an instance from that class called myBoat, then polymorphism allows you to write the following message expressions in C++:

```
myBoat.service()
myBoat.wash()
```

The key here is that you can write a method for the Boat class that knows about servicing a boat, that can be (and probably is) completely different from the method in the Car class that knows how to service a car. This is the key to polymorphism.

The important distinction for you to understand about OOP languages versus C, is that in the former case you are working with objects, such as cars and boats. In the latter, you are typically working with functions (or procedures). In a so-called procedural language like C, you might write a function called service and then inside that function write separate code to handle servicing different vehicles, such as cars, boats, or bicycles. If you ever want to add a new type of vehicle, you have to modify all functions that deal with different vehicle types. In the case of an OOP language, you just define a new class for that vehicle and add new methods to that class. You don't have to worry about the other vehicle classes; they are independent of your class, so you don't have to modify their code (to which you might not even have access).

The classes you work with in your OOP programs will probably not be cars or boats. More likely, they'll be objects such as windows, rectangles, clipboards, and so on. The messages you'll send (in a language like C#) will look like this:

```
myWindow.erase()                        Erase the window
myRect.getArea()                        Calculate the area of the rectangle
userText.spellCheck()                   Spell check some text
deskCalculator.setAccumulator(0.0)      Clear the accumulator
favoritePlaylist.showSongs()            Show songs in favorite playlist
```

Writing a C Program to Work with Fractions

Suppose you need to write a program to work with fractions. Perhaps you need to deal with adding, subtracting, multiplying them, and so on. You could define a structure to hold a fraction, and then develop a set of functions to manipulate them.

The basic setup for a fraction using C might look like Program 18.1. Program 18.1 sets the numerator and denominator and then displays the value of the fraction.

Program 18.1   **Working with Fractions in C**

```c
// Simple program to work with fractions
#include <stdio.h>

typedef struct {
    int numerator;
    int denominator;
} Fraction;

int main (void)
{
    Fraction myFract;

    myFract.numerator = 1;
    myFract.denominator = 3;

    printf ("The fraction is %i/%i\n", myFract.numerator, myFract.denominator);

    return 0;
}
```

Program 18.1   **Output**

```
The fraction is 1/3
```

The next three sections illustrate how you might work with fractions in Objective-C, C++, and C#, respectively. The discussion about OOP that follows the presentation of Program 18.2 applies to OOP in general, so you should read these sections in order.

Defining an Objective-C Class to Work with Fractions

The Objective-C language was invented by Brad Cox in the early 1980s. The language was based on a language called SmallTalk-80 and was licensed by NeXT Software in 1988. When Apple acquired NeXT in 1988, it used NEXTSTEP as the basis for its Mac OS X operating system. Most of the applications found today on Mac OS X, as well as a number of iPad and iPhone apps, are written in Objective-C.

Program 18.2 shows how you can define and use a `Fraction` class in Objective-C.

Program 18.2   **Working with Fractions in Objective-C**

```
// Program to work with fractions - Objective-C version

#import <stdio.h>
#import <objc/Object.h>

//------- @interface section -------

@interface Fraction: Object
{
    int      numerator;
    int      denominator;
}
-(void) setNumerator: (int) n;
-(void) setDenominator: (int) d;
-(void) print;

@end

//------- @implementation section -------


@implementation Fraction;

// getters

-(int) numerator
{
    return numerator;
}

-(int) denominator
{
    return denominator;
}
// setters
```

```
-(void) setNumerator: (int) num
{
    numerator = num;
}

-(void) setDenominator: (int) denom
{
    denominator = denom;
}

// other

-(void) print
{
    printf ("The value of the fraction is %i/%i\n", numerator, denominator);
}

@end


//------- program section -------


int main (void)
{
    Fraction    *myFract;


    myFract = [Fraction new];

    [myFract setNumerator: 1];
    [myFract setDenominator: 3];

    printf ("The numerator is %i, and the denominator is %i\n",
        [myFract numerator], [myFract denominator]);
    [myFract print];    // use the method to display the fraction


    [myFract free];

    return 0;
}
```

Program 18.2 **Output**

```
The numerator is 1, and the denominator is 3
The value of the fraction is 1/3
```

As you can see from the comments in Program 18.2, the program is logically divided into three sections: the @interface section, the @implementation section, and the program section. These sections are typically placed in separate files. The @interface section is usually put into a header file that gets included in any program that wants to work with that particular class. It tells the compiler what variables and methods are contained in the class.

The @implementation section contains the actual code that implements these methods. Finally, the program section contains the program code to carry out the intended purpose of the program.

The name of the new class is Fraction, and its parent class is Object. Classes inherit methods and variables from their parents.

As you can see in the @interface section, the declarations

```
int   numerator;
int   denominator;
```

say that a Fraction object has two integer members called numerator and denominator.

The members declared in this section are known as the instance variables. Each time you create a new object, a new and unique set of instance variables is created. Therefore, if you have two fractions, one called fracA and another called fracB, each has its own set of instance variables. That is, fracA and fracB each has its own separate numerator and denominator.

You have to define methods to work with your fractions. You need to be able to set the value of a fraction to a particular value. Because you don't have direct access to the internal representation of a fraction (in other words, direct access to its instance variables), you must write methods to set the numerator and denominator (these are known as *setters*). You also need methods to retrieve the values of your instance variables (such methods are known as *getters*).[1]

The fact that the instance variables for an object are kept hidden from the user of the object is another key concept of OOP known as *data encapsulation*. This assures someone extending or modifying a class that all the code that accesses the data (that is, the instance variables) for that class is contained in the methods. Data encapsulation provides a nice layer of insulation between the programmer and the class developer.

Here's what one such setter method declaration looks like:

```
-(int) numerator;
```

The leading minus sign (-) says that the method is an instance method. The only other option is a plus sign (+), which indicates a class method. A class method is one that performs some operation on the class itself, such as creating a new instance of the class. This is similar to manufacturing a new car, in that the car is the class and you want to create a new one—which would be a class method.

---

1. *You can get direct access to the instance variables, but it's generally considered poor programming practice.*

An instance method performs some operation on a particular instance of a class, such as setting its value, retrieving its value, displaying its value, and so on. Referring to the car example, after you have manufactured the car, you might need to fill it with gas. The operation of filling it with gas is performed on a particular car, so it is analogous to an instance method.

When you declare a new method (and similar to declaring a function), you tell the Objective-C compiler whether the method returns a value, and if it does, what type of value it returns. This is done by enclosing the return type in parentheses after the leading minus or plus sign. So, the declaration

```
-(int) numerator;
```

specifies that the instance method called `numerator` returns an integer value. Similarly, the line

```
-(void) setNumerator: (int) num;
```

defines a method that doesn't return a value that can be used to set the numerator of your fraction.

When a method takes an argument, you append a colon to the method name when referring to the method. Therefore, the correct way to identify these two methods is `setNumerator:` and `setDenominator:`—each of which takes a single argument. Also, the identification of the numerator and denominator methods without a trailing colon indicates that these methods do not take any arguments.

The `setNumerator:` method takes the integer argument you called `num` and simply stores it in the instance variable `numerator`. Similarly, `setDenominator:` stores the value of its argument `denom` in the instance variable `denominator`. Note that methods have direct access to their instance variables.

The last method defined in your Objective-C program is called `print`. Its use is to display the value of a fraction. As you see, it takes no arguments and returns no results. It simply uses `printf()` to display the numerator and denominator of the fraction, separated by a slash.

Inside `main()`, you define a variable called `myFract` with the following line:

```
Fraction *myFract;
```

This line says that `myFract` is an object of type `Fraction`; that is, `myFract` is used to store values from your new `Fraction` class. The asterisk (*) in front of `myFraction` says that `myFract` is actually a pointer to a `Fraction`. In fact, it points to the structure that contains the data for a particular instance from the `Fraction` class.

Now that you have an object to store a `Fraction`, you need to create one, just like you ask the factory to build you a new car. This is done with the following line:

```
myFract = [Fraction new];
```

You want to allocate memory storage space for a new fraction. The expression

```
[Fraction new]
```

sends a message to your newly created `Fraction` class. You are asking the `Fraction` class to apply the new method, but you never defined a new method, so where did it come from? The method was inherited from a parent class.

You are now ready to set the value of your `Fraction`. The program lines

```
[myFract setNumerator: 1];
[myFract setDenominator: 3];
```

do just that. The first message statement sends the `setNumerator:` message to `myFract`. The argument that is supplied is the value `1`. Control is then sent to the `setNumerator:` method you defined for your `Fraction` class. The Objective-C runtime system knows that it is the method from this class to use because it knows that `myFract` is an object from the `Fraction` class.

Inside the `setNumerator:` method, the single program line in that method takes the value passed in as the argument and stores it in the instance variable `numerator`. So, you have effectively set the numerator of `myFract` to `1`.

The message that invokes the `setDenominator:` method on `myFract` follows next, and works in a similar way.

With the fraction being set, Program 18.2 then calls the two getter methods `numerator` and `denominator` to retrieve the values of the corresponding instance variables from `myFract`. The results are then passed to `printf()` to be displayed.

The program next invokes the `print` method. This method displays the value of the fraction that is the receiver of the message. Even though you saw in the program how the numerator and denominator could be retrieved using the getter methods, a separate `print` method was also added to the definition of the `Fraction` class for illustrative purposes.

The last message in the program

```
[myFract free];
```

frees the memory that was used by your `Fraction` object.

Defining a C++ Class to Work with Fractions

Program 18.3 shows how a program to implement a `Fraction` class might be written using the C++ language. C++ was invented by Bjarne Stroustroup at Bell Laboratories, and was the first object-oriented programming language based on C—at least to my knowledge! Note when compiling this program—if you are using an integrated development environment (IDE) that can compile C and C++ programs, and you have been writing C programs to this point, your IDE might try to save the program as a .c file. That would then generate a series of error messages that can be avoided by saving the file with a .cpp extension, ensuring that your IDE compiles the program as a C++ program.

Program 18.3 **Working with Fractions in C++**

```cpp
#include <iostream>

class Fraction
{
 private:
    int numerator;
    int denominator;

 public:
    void setNumerator (int num);
    void setDenominator (int denom);
    int  Numerator (void);
    int  Denominator (void);
    void print (Fraction f);
};

void Fraction::setNumerator (int num)
{
    numerator = num;
}

void Fraction::setDenominator (int denom)
{
    denominator = denom;
}

int Fraction::Numerator (void)
{
    return numerator;
}

int Fraction::Denominator (void)
{
    return denominator;
}

void Fraction::print (Fraction f)
{
    std::cout << "The value of the fraction is " << numerator << '/'
            << denominator << '\n';
}

int main (void)
{
    Fraction  myFract;
```

```
    myFract.setNumerator (1);
    myFract.setDenominator (3);

    myFract.print (myFract);

    return 0;
}
```

Program 18.3   **Output**

```
The value of the fraction is 1/3
```

The C++ members (instance variables) `numerator` and `denominator` are labeled `private` to enforce data encapsulation; that is, to prevent them from being directly accessed from outside the class.

The `setNumerator` method is declared as follows:

```
void Fraction::setNumerator (int num)
```

The method is preceded by the notation `Fraction::` to identify that it belongs to the `Fraction` class.

A new instance of a `Fraction` is created like a normal variable in C, as in the following declaration in `main()`:

```
Fraction  myFract;
```

The numerator and denominator of the fraction are then set to 1 and 3, respectively, with the following method calls:

```
myFract.setNumerator (1);
myFract.setDenominator (3);
```

The value of the fraction is then displayed using the fraction's `print` method.

Probably the oddest-appearing statement from Program 18.3 occurs inside the `print` method as follows:

```
std::cout << "The value of the fraction is " << numerator << '/'
          << denominator << '\n';
```

`cout` is the name of the standard output stream, analogous to `stdout` in C. The `<<` is known as the *stream insertion operator*, and it provides an easy way to get output. You might recall that `<<` is also C's left shift operator. This is one significant aspect of C++: a feature known as *operator overloading* that allows you to define operators that are associated with a class. Here, the left shift operator is overloaded so that when it is used in this context (that is, with a stream as its left operand), it invokes a method to write a formatted value to an output stream, instead of trying to actually perform a left shift operation.

As another example of overloading, you might want to override the addition operator + so that if you try to add two fractions together, as in

```
myFract + myFract2
```

an appropriate method from your Fraction class is invoked to handle the addition.

Each expression that follows the << is evaluated and written to the standard output stream. In this case, first the string "The value of the fraction is " gets written, followed by the fraction's numerator, followed by a /, the fraction's denominator, and then a newline character.

The C++ language is rich with features. Consult Appendix E, "Resources," for recommendations on a good tutorial.

Note that in the previous C++ example, the getter methods Numerator () and Denominator () were defined in the Fraction class but were not used.

Defining a C# Class to Work with Fractions

As the final example in this chapter, Program 18.4 shows the fraction example written in C#, a programming language developed by Microsoft, Inc. C# is part of Microsoft's Visual Studio suite and is a key development tool in the .NET Framework. If you want to try C#, visit www.visualstudio.com/en-US/products/visual-studio-express-vs to download a free express version of the full product.

Program 18.4   **Working with Fractions in C#**

```csharp
using System;

class Fraction
{
    private int numerator;
    private int denominator;

    public int Numerator
    {
        get
        {
            return numerator;
        }

        set
        {
            numerator = value;
        }
    }

    public int Denominator
```

```
    {
        get
        {
            return denominator;
        }

        set
        {
            denominator = value;
        }
    }

    public void print ()
    {
        Console.WriteLine("The value of the fraction is {0}/{1}",
            numerator, denominator);
    }
}

class example
{
    public static void Main()
    {
        Fraction myFract = new Fraction();

        myFract.Numerator = 1;
        myFract.Denominator = 3;

        myFract.print ();

    }
}
```

Program 18.4 **Output**

```
The value of the fraction is 1/3
```

You can see the C# program looks a little different from the other two OOP programs, but you can probably still determine what's happening. The Fraction class definition begins by declaring the two instance variables numerator and denominator as private. The Numerator and Denominator methods each have their getter and setter method defined as *properties*. Take a closer look at Numerator:

```
public int Numerator
{
    get
    {
        return numerator;
```

```
        }

        set
        {
            numerator = value;
        }
    }
}
```

The "get" code is executed when the value of the numerator is needed in an expression, such as in

```
num = myFract.Numerator;
```

The "set" code is executed when a value is assigned to the method, as in

```
myFract.Numerator = 1;
```

The actual value that is assigned gets stored in the variable value when the method gets called. Note that parentheses do not follow the setter and getter methods here.

Naturally, you can define methods that optionally take arguments, or setter methods that take multiple arguments. For example, this C# method invocation might be used to set the value of a fraction to 2/5 with a single call:

```
myFract.setNumAndDen (2, 5)
```

Returning to Program 18.4, the statement

```
Fraction myFract = new Fraction();
```

is used to create a new instance from the Fraction class and assign the result to the Fraction variable myFract. The Fraction is then set to 1/3 using the Fraction's setters.

The print method is invoked next on myFract to display the value of the fraction. Inside the print method, the WriteLine method from the Console class is used to display output. Similar to printf's % notation, {0} specifies in the string where the first value is to be substituted, {1} where the second value is to be displayed, and so on. Unlike the printf routine, you don't need to worry here about the types being displayed.

As with the C++ example, the getter methods for the C# Fraction class were not exercised here. They were included for illustrative purposes.

This concludes this brief introduction to object-oriented programming. Hopefully, this chapter has given you a better idea about what object-oriented programming is all about and how programming in an OOP language differs from a language such as C. You have seen how you can write a simple program in one of three OOP languages to work with objects that represent fractions. If you were serious about working with fractions in your programs, you would probably extend your class definition to support operations such as addition, subtraction, multiplication, division, inversion, and reduction of fractions, for example. This would be a relatively straightforward task for you to do.

To continue your studies further, get a good tutorial on a particular OOP language, such as one listed in Appendix E.

A

C Language Summary

This section summarizes the C language in a format suitable for quick reference. It is not intended that this section be a complete definition of the language, but rather a more informal description of its features. You should thoroughly read the material in this section after you have completed the text. Doing so not only reinforces the material you have learned, but also provides you with a better global understanding of C.

This summary is based on the ANSI C11 (ISO/IEC 9899:2011) standard.

1.0 Digraphs and Identifiers

1.1 Digraph Characters

Table A.1 lists special two-character sequences (digraphs) that are equivalent to the listed single-character punctuators.

Table A.1 **Digraph Characters**

Digraph	Meaning
<:	[
:>	]
<%	{
%>	}
%:	#
%:%:	##

1.2   Identifiers

An *identifier* in C consists of a sequence of letters (upper- or lowercase), *universal character names* (Section 1.2.1), digits, or underscore characters. The first character of an identifier must be a letter, underscore, or a universal character name. The first 31 characters of an identifier are guaranteed to be significant in an external name, and the first 63 characters are guaranteed to be significant for an internal identifier or macro name.

1.2.1   Universal Character Names

A universal character name is formed by the characters \u followed by four hexadecimal numbers or the characters \U followed by eight hexadecimal numbers. If the first character of an identifier is specified by a universal character, its value cannot be that of a digit character. Universal characters, when used in identifier names, can also not specify a character whose value is less than $A0_{16}$ (other than 24_{16}, 40_{16}, or 60_{16}) or a character in the range $D800_{16}$ through $DFFF_{16}$, inclusive.

Universal character names can be used in identifier names, character constants, and character strings.

1.2.2   Keywords

The identifiers listed in Table A.2 are keywords that have a special meaning to the C compiler.

Table A.2   **Keywords**

_Bool	default	inline	struct
_Complex	do	int	switch
_Generic	double	long	typedef
_Imaginary	else	register	union
auto	enum	restrict	unsigned
break	extern	return	void
case	float	short	volatile
char	for	signed	while
const	goto	sizeof	
continue	if	static	

2.0   Comments

You can insert comments into a program in two ways. A comment can begin with the two characters //. Any characters that follow on the line are ignored by the compiler.

A comment can also begin with the two characters /* and end when the characters */ are encountered. Any characters can be included inside the comment, which can extend over multiple lines of the program. A comment can be used anywhere in the program where a blank space is allowed. Comments, however, cannot be nested, which means that the first */ characters encountered end the comment, no matter how many /* characters you use.

3.0   Constants

3.1   Integer Constants

An integer constant is a sequence of digits, optionally preceded by a plus or minus sign. If the first digit is 0, the integer is taken as an octal constant, in which case all digits that follow must be from 0 to 7. If the first digit is 0 and is immediately followed by the letter x (or X), the integer is taken as a hexadecimal constant, and the digits that follow can be in the range from 0 to 9 or from a to f (or from A to F).

The suffix letter 1 or L can be added to the end of a decimal integer constant to make it a `long int` constant. If the value can't fit into a `long int`, it's treated as a `long long int`. If the suffix letter 1 or L is added to the end of an octal or a hexadecimal constant, it is taken as a `long int` if it can fit; if it cannot fit, it is taken as a `long long int`. Finally, if it cannot fit in a `long long int`, it is taken as an `unsigned long long int` constant.

The suffix letters 11 or LL can be added to the end of a decimal integer constant to make it a `long long int`. When added to the end of an octal or a hexadecimal constant, it is taken as a `long long int` first, and if it cannot fit there, it is taken as an `unsigned long long int` constant.

The suffix u or U can be added to the end of an integer constant to make it `unsigned`. If the constant is too large to fit inside an `unsigned int`, it's taken as an `unsigned long int`. If it's too large for an `unsigned long int`, it's taken as an `unsigned long long int`.

Both an `unsigned` and a `long` suffix can be added to an integer constant to make it an `unsigned long int`. If the constant is too large to fit in an `unsigned long int`, it's taken as an `unsigned long long int`.

Both an `unsigned` and a `long long` suffix can be added to an integer constant to make it an `unsigned long long int`.

If an unsuffixed decimal integer constant is too large to fit into a `signed int`, it is treated as a `long int`. If it's too large to fit into a `long int`, it's treated as a `long long int`.

If an unsuffixed octal or hexadecimal integer constant is too large to fit into a `signed int`, it is treated as an `unsigned int`. If it's too large to fit into an `unsigned int`, it's treated as a `long int`, and if it's too large to fit into a `long int`, it's treated as an `unsigned long int`. If it's too large for an `unsigned long int`, it's taken as a `long long int`. Finally, if it's too large to fit into a `long long int`, the constant is treated as an `unsigned long long int`.

3.2   Floating-Point Constants

A floating-point constant consists of a sequence of decimal digits, a decimal point, and another sequence of decimal digits. A minus sign can precede the value to denote a negative value. Either the sequence of digits before the decimal point or after the decimal point can be omitted, but not both.

If the floating-point constant is immediately followed by the letter e (or E) and an optionally signed integer, the constant is expressed in scientific notation. This integer (the *exponent*) represents the power of 10 by which the value preceding the letter e (the *mantissa*) is multiplied (for example, `1.5e-2` represents 1.5×10^{-2} or .015).

A *hexadecimal* floating constant consists of a leading `0x` or `0X`, followed by one or more decimal or hexadecimal digits, followed by a p or P, followed by an optionally signed binary exponent. For example, `0x3p10` represents the value 3×2^{10}.

Floating-point constants are treated as `double` precision values by the compiler. The suffix letter f or F can be added to specify a `float` constant instead of a `double` constant. The suffix letter l or L can be added to specify a `long double` constant.

3.3   Character Constants

A character enclosed within single quotation marks is a character constant. How the inclusion of more than one character inside the single quotation marks is handled is implementation-defined. A universal character (Section 1.2.1) can be used in a character constant to specify a character not included in the standard character set.

3.3.1   Escape Sequences

Special escape sequences are recognized and are introduced by the backslash character. These escape sequences are listed in Table A.3.

Table A.3 **Special Escape Sequences**

Character	Meaning
\a	Audible alert
\b	Backspace
\f	Form feed

Character	Meaning
\n	Newline
\r	Carriage return
\t	Horizontal tab
\v	Vertical tab
\\	Backslash
\"	Double quote
\'	Single quote
\?	Question mark
\nnn	Octal character value
\unnnn	Universal character name
\Unnnnnnnn	Universal character name
\xnn	Hexadecimal character value

In the octal character case, from one to three octal digits can be specified. In the last three cases, hexadecimal digits are used.

3.3.2 Wide Character Constants

A *wide character constant* is written as `L'x'`. The type of such a constant is `wchar_t`, as defined in the standard header file `<stddef.h>`. Wide character constants provide a way to express a character from a character set that cannot be fully represented with the normal `char` type.

3.4 Character String Constants

A sequence of zero or more characters enclosed within double quotation marks represents a character string constant. Any valid character can be included in the string, including any of the escape characters listed previously. The compiler automatically inserts a null character (`'\0'`) at the end of the string.

Normally, the compiler produces a pointer to the first character in the string and the type is "pointer to `char`." However, when the string constant is used with the `sizeof` operator to initialize a character array, or with the `&` operator, the type of the string constant is "array of `char`."

Character string constants cannot be modified by the program.

3.4.1 Character String Concatenation

The preprocessor automatically concatenates adjacent character string constants together. The strings can be separated by zero or more whitespace characters. So, the following three strings

```
"a" " character "
   "string"
```

are equivalent to the single string

```
"a character string"
```

after concatenation.

3.4.2   Multibyte Characters

Implementation-defined sequences of characters can be used to *shift* back and forth between different states in a character string so that multibyte characters can be included.

3.4.3   Wide Character String Constants

Character string constants from an extended character set are expressed using the format `L"..."`. The type of such a constant is "pointer to `wchar_t`," where `wchar_t` is defined in `<stddef.h>`.

3.5   Enumeration Constants

An identifier that has been declared as a value for an enumerated type is taken as a constant of that particular type and is otherwise treated as type `int` by the compiler.

4.0   Data Types and Declarations

This section summarizes the basic data types, derived data types, enumerated data types, and `typedef`. Also summarized in this section is the format for declaring variables.

4.1   Declarations

When defining a particular structure, union, enumerated data type, or `typedef`, the compiler does not automatically reserve any storage. The definition merely tells the compiler about the particular data type and (optionally) associates a name with it. Such a definition can be made either inside or outside a function. In the former case, only the function knows of its existence; in the latter case, it is known throughout the remainder of the file.

After the definition has been made, variables can be declared to be of that particular data type. A variable that is declared to be of *any* data type *does* have storage reserved for it, unless it is an `extern` declaration, in which case it might or might not have storage allocated (see Section 6.0).

The language also enables storage to be allocated at the same time that a particular structure, union, or enumerated data type is defined. This is done by simply listing the variables before the terminating semicolon of the definition.

4.2 Basic Data Types

The basic C data types are summarized in Table A.4. A variable can be declared to be of a particular basic data type using the following format:

```
type  name = initial_value;
```

The assignment of an initial value to the variable is optional, and is subject to the rules summarized in Section 6.2. More than one variable can be declared at once using the following general format:

```
type  name = initial_value, name = initial_value, ... ;
```

Before the type declaration, an optional storage class might also be specified, as summarized in Section 6.2. If a storage class is specified, and the type of the variable is int, then int can be omitted. For example,

```
static  counter;
```

declares counter to be a static int variable.

Table A.4 **Summary of Basic Data Types**

Type	Meaning
int	Integer value; that is, a value that contains no decimal point; guaranteed to contain at least 16 bits of precision.
short int	Integer value of reduced precision; takes half as much memory as an int on some machines; guaranteed to contain at least 16 bits of precision.
long int	Integer value of extended precision; guaranteed to contain at least 32 bits of precision.
long long int	Integer value of extraextended precision; guaranteed to contain at least 64 bits of precision.
unsigned int	Positive integer value; can store positive values up to twice as large as an int; guaranteed to contain at least 16 bits of precision.
float	Floating-point value; that is, a value that can contain decimal places; guaranteed to contain at least six digits of precision.
double	Extended accuracy floating-point value; guaranteed to contain at least 10 digits of precision.
long double	Extraextended accuracy floating-point value; guaranteed to contain at least 10 digits of precision.

Type	Meaning
char	Single character value; on some systems, sign extension might occur when used in an expression.
unsigned char	Same as char, except ensures that sign extension does not occur as a result of integral promotion.
signed char	Same as char, except ensures that sign extension does occur as a result of integral promotion.
_Bool	Boolean type; large enough to store the values 0 or 1.
float _Complex	Complex number.
double _Complex	Extended accuracy complex number.
long double _Complex	Extraextended accuracy complex number.
void	No type; used to ensure that a function that does not return a value is not used as if it does return one, or to explicitly "discard" the results of an expression. Also used as a generic pointer type (void *).

Note that the signed modifier can also be placed in front of the short int, int, long int, and long long int types. Because these types are signed by default anyway, this has no effect.

_Complex and -_Imaginary data types enable complex and imaginary numbers to be declared and manipulated, with functions in the library for supporting arithmetic on these types. Normally, you should include the file <complex.h> in your program, which defines macros and declares functions for working with complex and imaginary numbers. For example, a double_Complex variable c1 can be declared and initialized to the value 5 + 10.5i with a statement such as:

```
double _Complex  c1 = 5 + 10.5 * I;
```

Library routines such as creal and cimag can then be used to extract the real and imaginary part of c1, respectively.

An implementation is not required to support types _Complex and _Imaginary, or it can optionally support one but not the other.

The header file <stdbool.h> can be included in a program to make working with Boolean variables easier. In that file, the macros bool, true, and false are defined, enabling you to write statements such as:

```
bool  endOfData = false;
```

4.3   Derived Data Types

A derived data type is one that is built up from one or more of the basic data types. Derived data types are arrays, structures, unions, and pointers. A function that returns a value of a specified type is also considered a derived data type. Each of these, with the exception of functions, is summarized in the following sections. Functions are separately covered in Section 7.0.

4.3.1   Arrays

Single-Dimensional Arrays

Arrays can be defined to contain any basic data type or any derived data type. Arrays of functions are not permitted (although arrays of function pointers are).

The declaration of an array has the following basic format:

```
type   name[n]    = { initExpression, initExpression, ... };
```

The expression *n* determines the number of elements in the array *name* and can be omitted provided a list of initial values is specified. In such a case, the size of the array is determined based on the number of initial values listed or on the largest index element referenced if *designated initializers* are used.

Each initial value must be a constant expression if a global array is defined. There can be fewer values in the initialization list than there are elements in the array, but there cannot be more. If fewer values are specified, only that many elements of the array are initialized. The remaining elements are set to 0.

A special case of array initialization occurs in the event of character arrays, which can be initialized by a constant character string. For example,

```
char today[] = "Monday";
```

declares `today` as an array of characters. This array is initialized to the characters `'M'`, `'o'`, `'n'`, `'d'`, `'a'`, `'y'`, and `'\0'`, respectively.

If you explicitly dimension the character array and don't leave room for the terminating null, the compiler does not place a null at the end of the array:

```
char today[6] = "Monday";
```

This declares `today` as an array of six characters and sets its elements to the characters `'M'`, `'o'`, `'n'`, `'d'`, `'a'`, and `'y'`, respectively.

By enclosing an element number in a pair of brackets, specific array elements can be initialized in any order. For example

```
int     x = 1233;
int     a[] = { [9] = x + 1, [3] = 3, [2] = 2, [1] = 1 };
```

defines a 10-element array called a (based on the highest index into the array), and initializes the last element to the value of `x + 1` (1234), and the first three elements to 1, 2, and 3, respectively.

4.3.1.1 Variable-Length Arrays

Inside a function or block, you can dimension an array using an expression containing variables. In that case, the size is calculated at runtime. For example, the function

```
int makeVals (int n)
{
    int valArray[n];
    ...
}
```

defines an automatic array called `valArray` with a size of n elements, where n is evaluated at runtime, and might vary between function calls. Variable-length arrays cannot be initialized at the time they are declared.

4.3.1.2 Multidimensional Arrays

The general format for declaring a multidimensional array is as follows:

```
type  name[d1][d2]...[dn] = initializationList;
```

The array *name* is defined to contain *d1* x *d2* x ... x *dn* elements of the specified type. For example,

```
int  three_d [5][2][20];
```

defines a three-dimensional array, `three_d`, containing 200 integers.

A particular element is referenced from a multidimensional array by enclosing the desired subscript for each dimension in its own set of brackets. For example, the statement

```
three_d [4][0][15] = 100;
```

stores 100 in the indicated element of the array `three_d`.

Multidimensional arrays can be initialized in the same manner as one-dimensional arrays. Nested pairs of braces can be used to control the assignment of values to the elements in the array.

The following declares `matrix` to be a two-dimensional array containing four rows and three columns:

```
int matrix[4][3] =
            {  { 1, 2, 3 },
               { 4, 5, 6 },
               { 7, 8, 9 } };
```

Elements in the first row of `matrix` are set to the values 1, 2, and 3, respectively; elements in the second row are set to the values 4, 5, and 6, respectively; and in the third row, elements are set to the values 7, 8, and 9, respectively. The elements in the fourth row are set to 0 because no values are specified for that row. The declaration

```
static int matrix[4][3] =
            { 1, 2, 3, 4, 5, 6, 7, 8, 9 };
```

initializes `matrix` to the same values because the elements of a multidimensional array are initialized in "dimension-order"; that is, from leftmost to rightmost dimension.

The declaration

```
int matrix[4][3] =
        {  { 1 },
           { 4 },
           { 7 } };
```

sets the first element of the first row of `matrix` to 1, the first element of the second row to 4, and the first element of the third row to 7. All remaining elements are set to 0 by default.

Finally, the declaration

```
int matrix[4][3] = {  [0][0] = 1,  [1][1] = 5,  [2][2] = 9 };
```

initializes the indicated elements of the matrix to the specified values.

4.3.2   Structures

The general format for declaring a structure is as follows:

```
struct name
{
    memberDeclaration
    memberDeclaration
        . . .
}  variableList;
```

The structure `name` is defined to contain the members as specified by each `memberDeclaration`. Each such declaration consists of a type specification followed by a list of one or more member names.

Variables can be declared at the time that the structure is defined simply by listing them before the terminating semicolon, or they can subsequently be declared using the format

```
struct name  variableList;
```

This format cannot be used if `name` is omitted when the structure is defined. In that case, all variables of that structure type must be declared with the definition.

The format for initializing a structure variable is similar to that for arrays. Its members can be initialized by enclosing the list of initial values in a pair of curly braces. Each value in the list must be a constant expression if a global structure is initialized.

The declaration

```
struct  point
{
    float x;
    float y;
}  start = {100.0, 200.0};
```

defines a structure called `point` and a `struct point` variable called `start` with initial values as specified. Specific members can be designated for initialization in any order with the notation

```
.member = value
```

in the initialization list, as in

```
struct point  end = { .y = 500, .x = 200 };
```

The declaration

```
struct  entry
{
   char  *word;
   char  *def;
} dictionary[1000] = {
    { "a",        "first letter of the alphabet" },
    { "aardvark", "a burrowing African mammal" },
    { "aback",    "to startle"                   }
};
```

declares `dictionary` to contain 1,000 `entry` structures, with the first three elements initialized to the specified character string pointers. Using designated initializers, you could have also written it like this:

```
struct  entry
{
   char  *word;
   char  *def;
} dictionary[1000] = {
    [0].word = "a",        [0].def = "first letter of the alphabet",
    [1].word = "aardvark", [1].def = "a burrowing African mammal",
    [2].word = "aback",    [2].def = "to startle"
};
```

or equivalently like this:

```
struct  entry
{
   char  *word;
   char  *def;
} dictionary[1000] = {
    { .word = "a",        .def = "first letter of the alphabet" },
      { .word = "aardvark", .def = "a burrowing African mammal"} ,
      { .word = "aback",    .def = "to startle"}
};
```

An automatic structure variable can be initialized to another structure of the same type like this:

```
struct date  tomorrow = today;
```

This declares the date structure variable `tomorrow` and assigns to it the contents of the (previously declared) date structure variable `today`.

A *memberDeclaration* that has the format

```
type  fieldName : n
```

defines a `field` that is *n* bits wide inside the structure, where *n* is an integer value. Fields can be packed from left to right on some machines and from right to left on others. If *fieldName* is omitted, the specified number of bits are reserved, but cannot be referenced. If *fieldName* is omitted and *n* is 0, the field that follows is aligned on the next storage *unit* boundary, where a *unit* is implementation-defined. The type of field can be `_Bool`, `int`, `signed int`, or `unsigned int`. It is implementation-defined whether an `int` field is treated as `signed` or `unsigned`. The address operator (`&`) cannot be applied to a field, and arrays of fields cannot be defined.

4.3.3   Unions

The general format for declaring a union is as follows:

```
union   name
{
      memberDeclaration
      memberDeclaration
            . . .
}   variableList;
```

This defines a union called *name* with members as specified by each *memberDeclaration*. Each member of the union shares overlapping storage space, and the compiler takes care of ensuring that enough space is reserved to contain the largest member of the union.

Variables can be declared at the time that the union is defined, or they can be subsequently declared using the notation

```
union   name   variableList;
```

provided the union was given a name when it was defined.

It is the programmer's responsibility to ensure that the value retrieved from a union is consistent with the last value that was stored inside the union. The *first* member of a union can be initialized by enclosing the initial value, which, in the case of a global union variable, must be a constant expression, inside a pair of curly braces:

```
union   shared
{
    long long  int  l;
    long int       w[2];
} swap = { 0xffffffff };
```

This declares the union variable `swap` and sets the `l` member to hexadecimal `ffffffff`. A different member can be initialized instead by specifying the member name, as in

```
union shared swap2 = {.w[0] = 0x0,  .w[1] = 0xffffffff;  }
```

An automatic union variable can also be initialized to a union of the same type, as in

```
union shared swap2 = swap;
```

4.3.4   Pointers

The basic format for declaring a pointer variable is as follows:

```
type  *name;
```

The identifier *name* is declared to be of type "pointer to *type*," which can be a basic data type, or a derived data type. For example,

```
int  *ip;
```

declares `ip` to be a pointer to an `int`, and the declaration

```
struct  entry  *ep;
```

declares `ep` to be a pointer to an `entry` structure.

Pointers that point to elements in an array are declared to point to the type of element contained in the array. For example, the previous declaration of `ip` can also be used to declare a pointer into an array of integers.

More advanced forms of pointer declarations are also permitted. For example, the declaration

```
char *tp[100];
```

declares `tp` to be an array of 100 character pointers, and the declaration

```
struct entry (*fnPtr) (int);
```

declares `fnPtr` to be a pointer to a function that returns an `entry` structure and that takes a single `int` argument.

A pointer can be tested to see if it's null by comparing it against a constant expression whose value is `0`. The implementation can choose to internally represent a null pointer with a value other than `0`. However, a comparison between such an internally represented null pointer and a constant value of `0` must prove equal.

The manner in which pointers are converted to integers, and integers are converted to pointers, is machine dependent, as is the size of the integer required to hold a pointer.

The type "pointer to `void`" is the generic pointer type. The language guarantees that a pointer of any type can be assigned to a `void` pointer and back again without changing its value.

Other than this special case, assignment of different pointer types is not permitted, and typically results in a warning message from the compiler if attempted.

4.4   Enumerated Data Types

The general format for declaring enumerated data types is as follows:

```
enum   name { enum_1, enum_2, ... } variableList;
```

The enumerated type *name* is defined with enumeration values *enum_1, enum_2, ...*, each of which is an identifier or an identifier followed by an equal sign and a constant expression. *variableList* is an optional list of variables (with optional initial values) declared to be of type enum *name*.

The compiler assigns sequential integers to the enumeration identifiers starting at zero. If an identifier is followed by = and a constant expression, the value of that expression is assigned to the identifier. Subsequent identifiers are assigned values beginning with that constant expression plus 1. Enumeration identifiers are treated as constant integer values by the compiler.

If it is desired to declare variables to be of a previously defined (and named) enumeration type, the construct

```
enum   name   variableList;
```

can be used.

A variable declared to be of a particular enumerated type can only be assigned a value of the same data type, although the compiler might not flag this as an error.

4.5   The `typedef` Statement

The `typedef` statement is used to assign a new name to a basic or derived data type. The `typedef` does not define a new type but simply a new name for an existing type. Therefore, variables declared to be of the newly named type are treated by the compiler exactly as if they were declared to be of the type associated with the new name.

In forming a `typedef` definition, proceed as though a normal variable declaration were being made. Then, place the new type name where the variable name would normally appear. Finally, in front of everything, place the keyword `typedef`.

As an example,

```
typedef struct
        {
              float  x;
              float  y;
        } Point;
```

associates the name `Point` with a structure containing two floating-point members called x and y. Variables can subsequently be declared to be of type `Point`, as in

```
Point  origin = { 0.0, 0.0 };
```

4.6   Type Modifiers `const`, `volatile`, and `restrict`

The keyword `const` can be placed before a type declaration to tell the compiler that the value cannot be modified. So the declaration

```
const int x5 = 100;
```

declares `x5` to be a constant integer (that is, it won't be set to anything else during the program's execution). The compiler is *not* required to flag attempts to change the value of a `const` variable.

The `volatile` modifier explicitly tells the compiler that the value changes (usually dynamically). When a `volatile` variable is used in an expression, its value is accessed each place it appears.

To declare `port17` to be of type "`volatile` pointer to `char`," write

```
volatile char *port17;
```

The `restrict` keyword can be used with pointers. It is a hint to the compiler for optimization (like the `register` keyword for variables). The `restrict` keyword specifies to the compiler that the pointer is the only reference to a particular object; that is, it is not referenced by any other pointer within the same scope. The lines

```
int  * restrict intPtrA;
int  * restrict intPtrB;
```

tell the compiler that for the duration of the scope in which `intPtrA` and `intPtrB` are defined, they will never access the same value. Their use for pointing to integers (in an array, for example) is mutually exclusive.

5.0   Expressions

Variable names, function names, array names, constants, function calls, array references, and structure and union references are all considered expressions. Applying a unary operator (where appropriate) to one of these expressions is also an expression, as is combining two or more of these expressions with a binary or ternary operator. Finally, an expression enclosed within parentheses is also an expression.

An expression of any type other than `void` that identifies a data object is called an `lvalue`. If it can be assigned a value, it is known as a *modifiable lvalue*.

Modifiable lvalue expressions are required in certain places. The expression on the left-hand side of an assignment operator must be a modifiable lvalue. Furthermore, the increment and decrement operators can only be applied to modifiable lvalues, as can the unary address operator `&` (unless it's a function).

5.1 Summary of C Operators

Table A.5 summarizes the various operators in the C language. These operators are listed in order of decreasing precedence. Operators grouped together have the same precedence.

Table A.5 **Summary of C Operators**

Operator	Description	Associativity
()	Function call	
[]	Array element reference	
->	Pointer to structure member reference	Left to right
.	Structure member reference	
-	Unary minus	
+	Unary plus	
++	Increment	
--	Decrement	
!	Logical negation	
~	Ones complement	Right to left
*	Pointer reference (indirection)	
&	Address	
sizeof	Size of an object	
(type)	Type cast (conversion)	
*	Multiplication	
/	Division	Left to right
%	Modulus	
+	Addition	Left to right
-	Subtraction	
<<	Left shift	Left to right
>>	Right shift	
<	Less than	
<=	Less than or equal to	Left to right
>	Greater than	
=>	Greater than or equal to	
==	Equality	Left to right
!=	Inequality	

Operator	Description	Associativity
&	Bitwise AND	Left to right
^	Bitwise XOR	Left to right
|	Bitwise OR	Left to right
&&	Logical AND	Left to right
||	Logical OR	Left to right
? :	Conditional	Right to left
= *= /= %= += -= &= ^= |= <<= >>=	Assignment operators	Right to left
,	Comma operator	Right to left

As an example of how to use Table A.5, consider the following expression:

```
b | c & d * e
```

The multiplication operator has higher precedence than both the bitwise OR and bitwise AND operators because it appears above both of these in Table A.5. Similarly, the bitwise AND operator has higher precedence than the bitwise OR operator because the former appears above the latter in the table. Therefore, this expression is evaluated as

```
b | ( c & ( d * e ) )
```

Now consider the following expression:

```
b % c * d
```

Because the modulus and multiplication operator appear in the same grouping in Table A.5, they have the same precedence. The associativity listed for these operators is left to right, indicating that the expression is evaluated as

```
( b % c ) * d
```

As another example, the expression

```
++a->b
```

is evaluated as

```
++(a->b)
```

because the -> operator has higher precedence than the ++ operator.

Finally, because the assignment operators group from right to left, the statement

```
a = b = 0;
```

is evaluated as

```
a = (b = 0);
```

which has the net result of setting the values of a and b to 0. In the case of the expression

```
x[i] + ++i
```

it is not defined whether the compiler evaluates the left side of the plus operator or the right side first. Here, the way that it's done affects the result because the value of i might be incremented before x[i] is evaluated.

Another case in which the order of evaluation is not defined is in the following expression:

```
x[i] = ++i
```

In this situation, it is not defined whether the value of i is incremented before or after its value is used to index into x.

The order of evaluation of function arguments is also undefined. Therefore, in the function call

```
f (i, ++i);
```

i might be incremented first, thereby causing the same value to be sent as the two arguments to the function.

The C language guarantees that the && and || operators are evaluated from left to right. Furthermore, in the case of &&, it is guaranteed that the second operand is not evaluated if the first is 0; and in the case of ||, it is guaranteed that the second operand is not evaluated if the first is nonzero. This fact is worth bearing in mind when forming expressions such as

```
if ( dataFlag || checkData (myData) )
   . . .
```

because, in this case, checkData is called only if the value of dataFlag is 0. To take another example, if the array a is defined to contain n elements, the statement that begins

```
if (index >= 0 && index < n && a[index] == 0))
   . . .
```

references the element contained in the array only if index is a valid subscript in the array.

5.2 Constant Expressions

A constant expression is an expression in which each of the terms is a constant value. Constant expressions are *required* in the following situations:

1. As the value after a case in a `switch` statement

2. For specifying the size of an array that is initialized or globally declared

3. For assigning a value to an enumeration identifier

4. For specifying the bit field size in a structure definition

5. For assigning initial values to static variables

6. For assigning initial values to global variables

7. As the expression following the `#if` in a `#if` preprocessor statement

In the first four cases, the constant expression must consist of integer constants, character constants, enumeration constants, and `sizeof` expressions. The only operators that can be used are the arithmetic operators, the bitwise operators, the relational operators, the conditional expression operator, and the type cast operator. The `sizeof` operator cannot be used on an expression with a variable-length array because the result is evaluated at runtime and is, therefore, not a constant expression.

In the fifth and sixth cases, in addition to the rules cited earlier, the address operator can be implicitly or explicitly used. However, it can only be applied to global or static variables or functions. So, for example, the expression

```
&x + 10
```

is a valid constant expression, provided that x is a global or static variable. Furthermore, the expression

```
&a[10] - 5
```

is a valid constant expression if a is a global or static array. Finally, because `&a[0]` is equivalent to the expression a,

```
a + sizeof (char) * 100
```

is also a valid constant expression.

For the last situation that requires a constant expression (after the `#if`), the rules are the same as for the first four cases, except the `sizeof` operator, enumeration constants, and the type cast operator cannot be used. However, the special `defined` operator is permitted (see Section 9.2.3).

5.3   Arithmetic Operators

Given that

a, b	are expressions of any basic data type except `void`;
i, j	are expressions of any integer data type;

then the expression

`-a`	negates the value of a
`+a`	gives the value of a
`a + b`	adds a with b
`a - b`	subtracts b from a
`a * b`	multiplies a by b
`a / b`	divides a by b
`i % j`	gives the remainder of i divided by j

In each expression, the usual arithmetic conversions are performed on the operands (see Section 5.17). If a is unsigned, $-a$ is calculated by first applying integral promotion to it, subtracting it from the largest value of the promoted type, and adding 1 to the result.

If two integral values are divided, the result is truncated. If either operand is negative, the direction of the truncation is not defined (that is, $-3 / 2$ might produce -1 on some machines and -2 on others); otherwise, truncation is always toward zero (3 / 2 always produces 1). See Section 5.15 for a summary of arithmetic operations with pointers.

5.4   Logical Operators

Given that

`a, b`	are expressions of any basic data type except `void`, or are both pointers

then the expression

`a && b`	has the value 1 if both a and b are nonzero, and 0 otherwise (and b is evaluated only if a is nonzero)
`a || b`	has the value 1 if either a or b is nonzero, and 0 otherwise (and b is evaluated only if a is zero)
`! a`	has the value 1 if a is zero, and 0 otherwise

The usual arithmetic conversions are applied to a and b (see Section 5.17). The type of the result in all cases is `int`.

5.5   Relational Operators

Given that

`a, b`	are expressions of any basic data type except `void`, or are both pointers

then the expression

a < b	has the value 1 if a is less than b, and 0 otherwise
a <= b	has the value 1 if a is less than or equal to b, and 0 otherwise
a > b	has the value 1 if a is greater than b, and 0 otherwise
a >= b	has the value 1 if a is greater than or equal to b, and 0 otherwise
a == b	has the value 1 if a is equal to b, and 0 otherwise
a != b	has the value 1 if a is not equal to b, and 0 otherwise

The usual arithmetic conversions are performed on a and b (see Section 5.17). The first four relational tests are only meaningful for pointers if they both point into the same array or to members of the same structure or union. The type of the result in each case is int.

5.6   Bitwise Operators

Given that

i, j, n	are expressions of any integer data type

then the expression

i & j	performs a bitwise AND of i and j
i | j	performs a bitwise OR of i and j
i ^ j	performs a bitwise XOR of i and j
~i	takes the ones complement of i
i << n	shifts i to the left n bits
i >> n	shifts i to the right n bits

The usual arithmetic conversions are performed on the operands, except with << and >>, in which case just integral promotion is performed on each operand (see Section 5.17). If the shift count is negative or is greater than or equal to the number of bits contained in the object being shifted, the result of the shift is undefined. On some machines, a right shift is arithmetic (sign fill) and on others logical (zero fill). The type of the result of a shift operation is that of the promoted left operand.

5.7   Increment and Decrement Operators

Given that

lv	is a modifiable lvalue expression, whose type is not qualified as const

then the expression

`++lv`	increments `lv` and then uses its value as the value of the expression
`lv++`	uses `lv` as the value of the expression and then increments `lv`
`--lv`	decrements `lv` and then uses its value as the value of the expression
`lv--`	uses `lv` as the value of the expression and then decrements `lv`

Section 5.15 describes these operations on pointers.

5.8 Assignment Operators

Given that

`lv`	is a modifiable `lvalue` expression, whose type is not qualified as `const`
`op`	is any operator that can be used as an assignment operator (see Table A.5)
`a`	is an expression

then the expression

`lv = a`	stores the value of `a` into `lv`
`lv op= a`	applies `op` to `lv` and `a`, storing the result in `lv`

In the first expression, if `a` is one of the basic data types (except `void`), it is converted to match the type of `lv`. If `lv` is a pointer, `a` must be a pointer to the same type as `lv`, a `void` pointer, or the *null* pointer.

If `lv` is a `void` pointer, `a` can be of any pointer type. The second expression is treated as if it were written `lv = lv op (a)`, except `lv` is only evaluated once (consider `x[i++] += 10`).

5.9 Conditional Operators

Given that

`a, b, c`	are expressions

then the expression

`a ? b : c`	has as its value `b` if `a` is nonzero, and `c` otherwise; only expression `b` or `c` is evaluated

Expressions b and c must be of the same data type. If they are not, but are both arithmetic data types, the usual arithmetic conversions are applied to make their types the same. If one is a pointer and the other is zero, the latter is taken as a null pointer of the same type as the former. If one is a pointer to void and the other is a pointer to another type, the latter is converted to a pointer to void, and that is the resulting type.

5.10   Type Cast Operator

Given that

type	is the name of a basic data type, an enumerated data type (preceded by the keyword enum), a typedef-defined type, or is a derived data type
a	is an expression

then the expression

(*type*)	converts a to the specified type

5.11   sizeof Operator

Given that

type	is as described previously
a	is an expression

then the expression

sizeof (*type*)	has as its value the number of bytes needed to contain a value of the specified type
sizeof a	has as its value the number of bytes required to hold the result of the evaluation of a

If *type* is char, the result is defined to be 1. If a is the name of an array that has been dimensioned (either explicitly or implicitly through initialization) and is not a formal parameter or undimensioned extern array, sizeof a gives the number of bytes required to store the elements in a.

If a is the name of a class, then sizeof (a) gives the size of the data structure needed to hold an instance of a.

The type of integer produced by the `sizeof` operator is `size_t`, which is defined in the standard header file `<stddef.h>`.

If `a` is a variable-length array, the `sizeof` operator is evaluated at runtime; otherwise `a` is evaluated at compile time and the result can be used in constant expressions (see Section 5.2).

5.12   Comma Operator

Given that

`a, b`	are expressions

then the expression

`a, b`	causes `a` to be evaluated and then `b` to be evaluated; the type and value of the expression is that of `b`

5.13   Basic Operations with Arrays

Given that

`a`	is declared as an array of `n` elements
`i`	is an expression of any integer data type
`v`	is an expression

then the expression

`a[0]`	references the first element of `a`
`a[n - 1]`	references the last element of `a`
`a[i]`	references element number `i` of `a`
`a[i] = v`	stores the value of `v` into `a[i]`

In each case, the type of the result is the type of the elements contained in `a`. See Section 5.15 for a summary of operations with pointers and arrays.

5.14   Basic Operations with Structures[1]

Given that

x	is a modifiable lvalue expression of type `struct s`
y	is an expression of type `struct s`
m	is the name of one of the members of the structure `s`
v	is an expression

then the expression

x	references the entire structure and is of type `struct s`
y.m	references the member m of the structure y and is of the type declared for the member m
x.m = v	assigns v to the member m of x and is of the type declared for the member m
x = y	assigns y to x and is of type `struct s`
f (y)	calls the function f, passing contents of the structure y as the argument; inside f, the formal parameter must be declared to be of type `struct s`
return y;	returns the structure y; the return type declared for the function must be `struct s`

5.15   Basic Operations with Pointers

Given that

x	is an `lvalue` expression of type t
pt	is a modifiable lvalue expression of type "pointer to t"
v	is an expression

then the expression

&x	produces a pointer to x and has type "pointer to t"
pt = &x	sets pt pointing to x and has type "pointer to t"
pt = 0	assigns the null pointer to pt
pt == 0	tests to see if pt is null
*pt	references the value pointed to by pt and has type t
*pt = v	stores the value of v into the location pointed to by pt and has type t

---

1. Also applies to unions.

Pointers to Arrays

Given that

a	is an array of elements of type t
pa1	is a modifiable lvalue expression of type "pointer to t" that points to an element in a
pa2	is an lvalue expression of type "pointer to t" that points to an element in a, or to one past the last element in a
v	is an expression
n	is an integral expression

then the expression

a, &a, &a[0]	produces a pointer to the first element
&a[n]	produces a pointer to element number n of a and has type "pointer to t"
*pa1	references the element of a that pa1 points to and has type t
*pa1 = v.	stores the value of v in the element pointed to by pa1, and has type t
++pa1	sets pa1 pointing to the next element of a, no matter what type of elements are contained in a and has type "pointer to t"
--pa1	sets pa1 pointing to the previous element of a, no matter what type of elements are contained in a, and has type "pointer to t"
*++pa1	increments pa1 and then references the value in a that pa1 points to, and has type t
*pa1++	references the value in a that pa1 points to before incrementing pa1 and has type t
pa1 + n	produces a pointer that points n elements further into a than pa1 and has type "pointer to t"
pa1 - n	produces a pointer to a that points n elements previous to that pointed to by pa1 and has type "pointer to t"
*(pa1 + n) = v	stores the value of v in the element pointed to by pa1 + n and has type t
pa1 < pa2	tests if pa1 is pointing to an earlier element in a than is pa2 and has type int (any relational operators can be used to compare two pointers)
pa2 - pa1	produces the number of elements in a contained between the pointers pa2 and pa1 (assuming that pa2 points to an element further in a than pa1) and has integer type
a + n	produces a pointer to element number n of a, has type "pointer to t," and is in all ways equivalent to the expression &a[n]
*(a + n)	references element number n of a, has type t, and is in all ways equivalent to the expression a[n]

The actual type of the integer produced by subtracting two pointers is specified by `ptrdiff_t`, which is defined in the standard header file `<stddef.h>`.

Pointers to Structures[2]

Given that

x	is an `lvalue` expression of type `struct s`
ps	is a modifiable lvalue expression of type "pointer to `struct s`"
m	is the name of a member of the structure `s` and is of type `t`
v	is an expression

then the expression

`&x`	produces a pointer to x and is of type "pointer to `struct s`"
`ps = &x`	sets `ps` pointing to x and is of type "pointer to `struct s`"
`ps->m`	references member `m` of the structure pointed to by `ps` and is of type `t`
`(*ps).m`	also references this member and is in all ways equivalent to the expression `ps->m`
`ps->m = v`	stores the value of `v` into the member `m` of the structure pointed to by `ps` and is of type `t`

5.16   Compound Literals

A compound literal is a type name enclosed in parentheses followed by an initialization list. It creates an unnamed value of the specified type, which has scope limited to the block in which it is created, or global scope if defined outside of any block. In the latter case, the initializers must all be constant expressions.

As an example,

```
(struct point) {.x = 0, .y = 0}
```

is an expression that produces a structure of type `struct point` with the specified initial values. This can be assigned to another `struct point` structure, as in

```
origin = (struct point) {.x = 0, .y = 0};
```

or passed to a function expecting an argument of `struct point`, as in

```
moveToPoint ((struct point) {.x = 0, .y = 0});
```

---

2. Also applies to unions.

Types other than structures can be defined as well, for example, if `intPtr` is of type `int *`, the statement

```
intPtr = (int [100]) {[0] = 1, [50] = 50, [99] = 99 };
```

(which can appear anywhere in the program) sets `intptr` pointing to an array of 100 integers, whose three elements are initialized as specified.

If the size of the array is not specified, it is determined by the initializer list.

5.17   Conversion of Basic Data Types

The C language converts operands in arithmetic expressions in a predefined order, known as the *usual arithmetic conversions*.

Step 1. If either operand is of type `long double`, the other is converted to `long double`, and that is the type of the result.

Step 2. If either operand is of type `double`, the other is converted to `double`, and that is the type of the result.

Step 3. If either operand is of type `float`, the other is converted to `float`, and that is the type of the result.

Step 4. If either operand is of type `_Bool`, `char`, `short int`, `int` bit field, or of an enumerated data type, it is converted to `int`, if an `int` can fully represent its range of values; otherwise, it is converted to `unsigned int`. If both operands are of the same type, that is the type of the result.

Step 5. If both operands are signed or both are unsigned, the smaller integer type is converted to the larger integer type, and that is the type of the result.

Step 6. If the unsigned operand is equal in size or larger than the signed operand, then the signed operand is converted to the type of the unsigned operand, and that is the type of the result.

Step 7. If the signed operand can represent all of the values in the unsigned operand, the latter is converted to the type of the former if it can fully represent its range of values, and that is the type of the result.

Step 8. If this step is reached, both operands are converted to the unsigned type corresponding to the type of the signed type.

Step 4 is known more formally as *integral promotion*.

Conversion of operands is well behaved in most situations, although the following points should be noted:

1. Conversion of a `char` to an `int` might involve sign extension on some machines, unless the `char` is declared as `unsigned`.

2. Conversion of a signed integer to a longer integer results in extension of the sign to the left; conversion of an unsigned integer to a longer integer results in zero fill to the left.

3. Conversion of any value to a _Bool results in 0 if the value is zero and 1 otherwise.

4. Conversion of a longer integer to a shorter one results in truncation of the integer on the left.

5. Conversion of a floating-point value to an integer results in truncation of the decimal portion of the value. If the integer is not large enough to contain the converted floating-point value, the result is not defined, as is the result of converting a negative floating-point value to an unsigned integer.

6. Conversion of a longer floating-point value to a shorter one might or might not result in rounding before the truncation occurs.

6.0   Storage Classes and Scope

The term *storage class* refers to the manner in which memory is allocated by the compiler in the case of variables and to the scope of a particular function definition. Storage classes are auto, static, extern, and register. A storage class can be omitted in a declaration and a default storage class is assigned, as discussed later in this chapter.

The term *scope* refers to the extent of the meaning of a particular identifier within a program. An identifier defined outside any function or statement block (herein referred to as a *BLOCK*) can be referenced anywhere subsequent in the file. Identifiers defined within a BLOCK are local to that BLOCK and can locally redefine an identifier defined outside it. Label names are known throughout the BLOCK, as are formal parameter names. Labels, instance variables, structure and structure member names, union and union member names, and enumerated type names do not have to be distinct from each other or from variable or function names. However, enumeration identifiers *do* have to be distinct from variable names and from other enumeration identifiers defined within the same scope.

6.1   Functions

If a storage class is specified when a function is defined, it must be either static or extern. Functions that are declared as static can only be referenced from within the same file that contains the function. Functions that are specified as extern (or that have no class specified) can be called by functions from other files.

6.2   Variables

Table A.6 summarizes the various storage classes that can be used in declaring variables as well as their scope and methods of initialization.

Table A.6   **Variables: Summary of Storage Classes, Scope, and Initialization**

If Storage Class is	And Variable is declared	Then it can be referenced	And can be initialized with	Comments
static	Outside any BLOCK	Anywhere within the file	Constant expression only	Variables are initialized only once at the start of program execution; values are retained through BLOCKs; default value is 0.
	Inside a BLOCK	Within the BLOCK		
extern	Outside any BLOCK	Anywhere within the file	Constant expression only	Variable must be declared in at least one place without the extern keyword, or in one place using the keyword extern and assigned an initial value.
	Inside a BLOCK	Within the BLOCK		
auto	Inside a BLOCK	Within the BLOCK	Any valid expression	Variable is initialized each time the BLOCK is entered; no default value.
register	Inside a BLOCK	Within the BLOCK	Any valid expression	Assignment to register not guaranteed; varying restrictions on types of variables that can be declared; cannot take the address of a register variable; initialized each time BLOCK is entered; no default value.
omitted	Outside any BLOCK	Anywhere within the file or by other files that contain appropriate declarations	Constant expressions only	This declaration can appear in only one place; variable is initialized at the start of program execution; default value is 0; defaults to auto.
	Inside a BLOCK	(See auto)	(See auto)	

7.0   Functions

This section summarizes the syntax and operation of functions.

7.1   Function Definition

The general format for declaring a function definition is as follows:

```
returnType   name ( type1 param1, type2 param2, ... )
{
    variableDeclarations

    programStatement
    programStatement
    ...
    return expression;
}
```

The function called *name* is defined, which returns a value of type *returnType* and has formal parameters *param1*, *param2*, ... *param1* is declared to be of type *type1*, *param2* is declared to be of type *type2*, and so on.

Local variables are typically declared at the beginning of the function, but that's not required. They can be declared anywhere, in which case their access is limited to statements appearing after their declaration in the function.

If the function does not return a value, *returnType* is specified as void.

If just void is specified inside the parentheses, the function takes no arguments. If . . . is used as the last (or only) parameter in the list, the function takes a variable number of arguments, as in

```
int  printf (char *format, ...)
{
   ...
}
```

Declarations for single-dimensional array arguments do not have to specify the number of elements in the array. For multidimensional arrays, the size of each dimension except the first must be specified.

See Section 8.9 for a discussion of the return statement.

The keyword inline can be placed in front of a function definition as a hint to the compiler. Some compilers replace the function call with the actual code for the function itself, thus providing for faster execution. An example is

```
inline int min (int a, int b)
{
    return ( a < b ? a : b);
}
```

7.2   Function Call

The general format for declaring a function call is as follows:

```
name ( arg1, arg2, ... )
```

The function called `name` is called and the values `arg1`, `arg2`, ... are passed as arguments to the function. If the function takes no arguments, just the open and closed parentheses are specified (as in `initialize ()`).

If you are calling a function that is defined after the call, or in another file, you should include a *prototype declaration* for the function, which has the following general format:

```
returnType  name  (type1  param1, type2  param2, ... );
```

This tells the compiler the function's return type, the number of arguments it takes, and the type of each argument. As an example, the line

```
long double  power (double x, int n);
```

declares `power` to be a function that returns a `long double` and that takes two arguments, the first a `double` and the second an `int`. The argument names inside the parentheses are actually dummy names and can be omitted if desired, so

```
long double  power (double, int);
```

works just as well.

If the compiler has previously encountered the function definition or a prototype declaration for the function, the type of each argument is automatically converted (where possible) to match the type expected by the function when the function is called.

If neither the function's definition nor a prototype declaration has been encountered, the compiler assumes the function returns a value of type `int`, automatically converts all `float` arguments to type `double`, and performs integral promotion on any integer arguments as outlined in Section 5.17. Other function arguments are passed without conversion.

Functions that take a variable number of arguments must be declared as such. Otherwise, the compiler is at liberty to assume the function takes a fixed number of arguments based upon the number actually used in the call.

A function whose return type is declared as `void` causes the compiler to flag any calls to that function that try to make use of a returned value.

All arguments to a function are passed by value; therefore, their values cannot be changed by the function. If a pointer is passed to a function, the function *can* change values referenced by the pointer, but it still cannot change the value of the pointer variable itself.

7.3   Function Pointers

A function name, without a following set of parentheses, produces a pointer to that function. The address operator can also be applied to a function name to produce a pointer to it.

If `fp` is a pointer to a function, the corresponding function can be called either by writing

```
fp ()
```

or

```
(*fp) ()
```

If the function takes arguments, they can be listed inside the parentheses.

8.0   Statements

A program statement is any valid expression (usually an assignment or function call) that is immediately followed by a semicolon, or it is one of the special statements described in the following sections. A *label* can optionally precede any statement, and consists of an identifier followed immediately by a colon (see Section 8.6).

8.1   Compound Statements

Program statements that are contained within a pair of braces are known collectively as a *compound* statement or *block* and can appear anywhere in the program that a single statement is permitted. A block can have its own set of variable declarations, which override any similarly named variables defined outside the block. The scope of such local variables is the block in which they are defined.

8.2   The **break** Statement

The general format for declaring a `break` statement is as follows:

```
break;
```

Execution of a `break` statement from within a `for`, `while`, `do`, or `switch` statement causes execution of that statement to be immediately terminated. Execution continues with the statement that immediately follows the loop or switch.

8.3   The **continue** Statement

The general format for declaring the `continue` statement is as follows:

```
continue;
```

Execution of the `continue` statement from within a loop causes any statements that follow the `continue` in the loop to be skipped. Execution of the loop otherwise continues as normal.

8.4   The **do** Statement

The general format for declaring the do statement is as follows:

```
do
      programStatement
while ( expression );
```

programStatement is executed as long as *expression* evaluates as nonzero. Note that, because *expression* is evaluated each time *after* the execution of *programStatement*, it is guaranteed that *programStatement* will be executed at least once.

8.5   The **for** Statement

The general format for declaring the for statement is as follows:

```
for ( expression_1;   expression_2;  expression_3 )
     programStatement
```

expression_1 is evaluated once when execution of the loop begins. Next, *expression_2* is evaluated. If its value is nonzero, *programStatement* is executed and then *expression_3* is evaluated. Execution of *programStatement* and the subsequent evaluation of *expression_3* continues as long as the value of *expression_2* is nonzero. Note that, because *expression_2* is evaluated each time before *programStatement* is executed, *programStatement* might never be executed if the value of *expression_2* is 0 when the loop is first entered.

Variables local to the for loop can be declared in *expression 1*. The scope of such variables is the scope of the for loop. For example,

```
for ( int i = 0; i < 100; ++i)
    . . .
```

declares the integer variable i and sets its initial value to 0 when the loop begins. The variable can be accessed by any statements inside the loop, but is not accessible after the loop is terminated.

8.6   The **goto** Statement

The general format for declaring the goto statement is as follows:

```
goto identifier;
```

Execution of the goto causes control to be sent directly to the statement labeled *identifier*. The labeled statement must be located in the same function as the goto.

8.7   The **if** Statement

One general format for declaring an if statement is as follows:

```
if ( expression )
    programStatement
```

If the result of evaluating *expression* is nonzero, *programStatement* is executed; otherwise, it is skipped.

Another general format for declaring an if statement is as follows:

```
if ( expression )
    programStatement_1
else
    programStatement_2
```

If the value of *expression* is nonzero, the *programStatement_1* is executed; otherwise, *programStatement_2* is executed. If *programStatement_2* is another if statement, an if-else if chain is effected:

```
if ( expression_1 )
    programStatement_1
else if ( expression_2 )
    programStatement_2
    ...
else
    programStatement_n
```

An else clause is always associated with the last if statement that does not contain an else. Braces can be used to change this association if necessary.

8.8   The null Statement

The general format for declaring the null statement is as follows:

```
;
```

Execution of a null statement has no effect and is used primarily to satisfy the requirement of a program statement in a for, do, or while loop. For example, in the following statement, which copies a character string pointed to by from to one pointed to by to:

```
while ( *to++ = *from++ )
    ;
```

the null statement is used to satisfy the requirement that a program statement appear after the looping expression of the while.

8.9   The return Statement

One general format for declaring the return statement is as follows:

```
return;
```

Execution of the return statement causes program execution to be immediately returned to the calling function. This format can only be used to return from a function that does not return a value.

If execution proceeds to the end of a function and a `return` statement is not encountered, it returns as if a `return` statement of this form had been executed. Therefore, in such a case, no value is returned.

A second general format for declaring the `return` statement is as follows:

```
return  expression;
```

The value of *expression* is returned to the calling function. If the type of *expression* does not agree with the return type declared in the function declaration, its value is automatically converted to the declared type before it is returned.

8.10   The `switch` Statement

The general format for declaring a `switch` statement is as follows:

```
switch ( expression )
{
    case constant_1:
        programStatement
        programStatement
          . . .
        break;
    case constant_2:
        programStatement
        programStatement
          . . .
        break;
    . . .
    case constant_n:
        programStatement
        programStatement
          . . .
        break;
    default:
        programStatement
        programStatement
          . . .
        break;
}
```

expression is evaluated and compared against the constant expression values *constant_1*, *constant_2*, ..., *constant_n*. If the value of *expression* matches one of these case values, the program statements that immediately follow are executed. If no case value matches the value of *expression*, the default case, if included, is executed. If the default case is not included, no statements contained in the switch are executed.

The result of the evaluation of *expression* must be of integral type and no two cases can have the same value. Omitting the break statement from a particular case causes execution to continue into the next case.

8.11   The while Statement

The general format for declaring the while statement is as follows:

```
while ( expression )
    programStatement
```

programStatement is executed as long as the value of *expression* is nonzero. Note that, because *expression* is evaluated each time *before* the execution of *programStatement*, *programStatement* might never be executed.

9.0   The Preprocessor

The preprocessor analyzes the source file before the compiler properly sees the code. The preprocessor does the following:

1. Replaces trigraph sequences (see Section 9.1) by their equivalents

2. Joins any lines that end with a backslash character (\) into a single line

3. Divides the program into a stream of tokens

4. Removes comments, replacing them with a single space

5. Processes preprocessor directives (see Section 9.2) and expands macros

9.1   Trigraph Sequences

To handle non-ASCII character sets, the three-character sequences (called *trigraphs*) listed in Table A.7 are recognized and treated specially wherever they occur inside a program (as well as inside character strings):

Table A.7   **Trigraph Sequences**

Trigraph	Meaning
??=	#
??(	[
??)	]
??<	{
??>	}

Trigraph	Meaning
??/	\
??'	^
??!	|
??-	~

9.2   Preprocessor Directives

All preprocessor directives begin with the character #, which must be the first nonwhitespace character on the line. The # can be optionally followed by one or more space or tab characters.

9.2.1   The #define Directive

The general format for declaring the #define directive is as follows:

```
#define name   text
```

This defines the identifier *name* to the preprocessor and associates with it whatever *text* appears after the first blank space after *name* to the end of the line. Subsequent use of *name* in the program causes *text* to be substituted directly into the program at that point.

Another general format for declaring the #define directive is as follows:

```
#define name(param_1, param_2, ..., param_n)   text
```

The macro *name* is defined to take arguments as specified by *param_1*, *param_2*, ..., *param_n*, each of which is an identifier. Subsequent use of *name* in the program with an argument list causes *text* to be substituted directly into the program at that point, with the arguments of the macro call replacing all occurrences of the corresponding parameters inside *text*.

If the macro takes a variable number of arguments, three dots are used at the end of the argument list. The remaining arguments in the list are collectively referenced in the macro definition by the special identifier __VA_ARGS__. As an example, the following defines a macro called myPrintf to take a leading format string followed by a variable number of arguments:

```
#define myPrintf(...)   printf ("DEBUG: " __VA_ARGS__);
```

Legitimate macro uses include

```
myPrintf ("Hello world!\n");
```

as well as

```
myPrintf ("i = %i, j = %i\n", i, j);
```

If a definition requires more than one line, each line to be continued must be ended with a backslash character. After a name has been defined, it can be used subsequently anywhere in the file.

The # operator is permitted in `#define` directives that take arguments. It is followed by the name of an argument to the macro. The preprocessor puts double quotation marks around the actual value passed to the macro when it's invoked. That is, it turns it into a character string. For example, the definition

```
#define  printint(x)   printf (# x " = %d\n", x)
```

with the call

```
printint (count);
```

is expanded by the preprocessor into

```
printf ("count" " = %i\n", count);
```

or, equivalently,

```
printf ("count = %i\n", count);
```

The preprocessor puts a \ character in front of any " or \ characters when performing this *stringizing* operation. So, with the definition

```
#define  str(x)   # x
```

the call

```
str (The string "\t" contains a tab)
```

expands to

```
"The string \"\\t\" contains a tab"
```

The ## operator is also allowed in `#define` directives that take arguments. It is preceded (or followed) by the name of an argument to the macro. The preprocessor takes the value that is passed when the macro is invoked and creates a single token from the argument to the macro and the token that follows (or precedes) it. For example, the macro definition

```
#define printx(n)  printf ("%i\n", x ## n );
```

with the call

```
printx (5)
```

produces

```
printf ("%i\n", x5);
```

The definition

```
#define printx(n) printf ("x" # n " = %i\n", x ## n );
```

with the call

```
printx(10)
```

produces

```
printf ("x10 = %i\n", x10);
```

after substitution and concatenation of the character strings.

Spaces are not required around the # and ## operators.

9.2.2   The #error Directive

The general format for declaring the #error directive is as follows:

```
#error text
    ...
```

The specified *text* is written as an error message by the preprocessor.

9.2.3   The #if Directive

One general format for declaring the #if directive is as follows:

```
#if constant_expression
    ...
    #endif
```

The value of *constant_expression* is evaluated. If the result is nonzero, all program lines up until the #endif directive are processed; otherwise, they are automatically skipped and are not processed by the preprocessor or by the compiler.

Another general format for declaring the #if directive is as follows:

```
#if constant_expression_1
    ...
#elif constant_expression_2
    ...
#elif constant_expression_n
    ...
#else
    ...
#endif
```

If *constant_expression_1* is nonzero, all program lines up until the #elif are processed, and the remaining lines up to the #endif are skipped. Otherwise, if *constant_expression_2* is nonzero, all program lines up until the next #elif are processed, and the remaining lines up to the #endif are skipped. If none of the constant expressions evaluates to nonzero, the lines after the #else (if included) are processed.

The special operator `defined` can be used as part of the constant expression, so

```
#if defined (DEBUG)
   ...
#endif
```

causes the code between the `#if` and `#endif` to be processed if the identifier `DEBUG` has been previously defined (see Section 9.2.4). The parentheses are not necessary around the identifier, so

```
#if defined DEBUG
```

works just as well.

9.2.4   The `#ifdef` Directive

The general format for declaring the `#ifdef` directive is as follows:

```
#ifdef identifier
   ...
#endif
```

If the value of *identifier* has been previously defined (either through a `#define` or with the -D command-line option when the program was compiled), all program lines up until the `#endif` are processed; otherwise, they are skipped. As with the `#if` directive, `#elif` and `#else` directives can be used with a `#ifdef` directive.

9.2.5   The `#ifndef` Directive

The general format for declaring the `#ifndef` directive is as follows:

```
#ifndef identifier
   ...
#endif
```

If the value of *identifier* has not been previously defined, all program lines up until the `#endif` are processed; otherwise, they are skipped. As with the `#if` directive, `#elif` and `#else` directives can be used with a `#ifndef` directive.

9.2.6   The `#include` Directive

One general format for declaring the `#include` directive is as follows:

```
#include "fileName"
```

The preprocessor searches an implementation-defined directory or directories first for the file *fileName*. Typically, the same directory that contains the source file is searched first. If the file is not found there, a sequence of implementation-defined standard places is searched. After it is found, the contents of the file is included in the program at the precise point that the `#include` directive appears. Preprocessor directives contained within the included file are analyzed, and, therefore, an included file can itself contain other `#include` directives.

Another general format for declaring the `#include` directive is as follows:

```
#include <fileName>
```

The preprocessor searches for the specified file only in the standard places. The action taken after the file is found is otherwise identical to that described previously.

In either format, a previously defined name can be supplied and expansion occurs. So the following sequence works:

```
#define DATABASE_DEFS    </usr/data/database.h>
    . . .
#include DATABASE_DEFS
```

9.2.7 The `#line` Directive

The general format for declaring the `#line` directive is as follows:

```
#line   constant  "fileName"
```

This directive causes the compiler to treat subsequent lines in the program as if the name of the source file were *fileName*, and as if the line number of all subsequent lines began at *constant*. If *fileName* is not specified, the filename specified by the last `#line` directive or the name of the source file (if no filename was previously specified) is used.

The `#line` directive is primarily used to control the filename and line number that are displayed whenever an error message is issued by the compiler.

9.2.8 The `#pragma` Directive

The general format for declaring the `#pragma` directive is as follows:

```
#pragma text
```

This causes the preprocessor to perform some implementation-defined action. For example,

```
#pragma loop_opt(on)
```

might cause special loop optimization to be performed on a particular compiler. If this pragma is encountered by a compiler that doesn't recognize the `loop_opt` pragma, it is ignored.

The special keyword `STDC` is used after the `#pragma` for special meaning. Current supported "switches" that can follow a `#pragma STDC` are `FP_CONTRACT`, `FENV_ACCESS`, and `CX_LIMITED_RANGE`.

9.2.9 The `#undef` Directive

The general format for declaring the `#undef` directive is as follows:

```
#undef  identifier
```

The specified *identifier* becomes undefined to the preprocessor. Subsequent #ifdef or #ifndef directives behave as if the identifier were never defined.

9.2.10   The # Directive

This is a null directive and is ignored by the preprocessor.

9.3   Predefined Identifiers

The identifiers listed in Table A.8 are defined by the preprocessor.

Table A.8   **Predefined Preprocessor Identifiers**

Identifier	Meaning
__LINE__	Current line number being compiled
__FILE__	Name of the current source file being compiled
__DATE__	Date the file is being compiled, in the format "*mm dd yyyy*"
__TIME__	Time the file is being compiled, in the format "*hh:mm:ss*"
__STDC__	Defined as 1 if the compiler conforms to the ANSI standard, 0 if not
__STDC_HOSTED__	Defined as 1 if the implementation is hosted, 0 if not
__STDC_VERSION__	Defined as 199901L

The Standard C Library

The standard C library contains a large selection of functions that might be called from a C program. This section does not list all of these functions, but rather most of the more commonly used ones. For a complete listing of all the functions that are available, consult the documentation that was included with your compiler, or check one of the resources listed in Appendix E, "Resources."

Among the routines not described in this appendix are ones for manipulating the date and time (such as time, ctime, and localtime), performing nonlocal jumps (setjmp and longjmp), generating diagnostics (assert), handling a variable number of arguments (va_list, va_start, va_arg, and va_end), handling signals (signal and raise), dealing with localization (as defined in <locale.h>), and dealing with wide character strings.

Standard Header Files

This section describes the contents of some standard header files: <stddef.h>, <stdbool.h>, <limits.h>, <float.h>, and <stdinit.h>.

<stddef.h>

This header file contains some standard definitions, such as the following:

Define	Meaning
NULL	A null pointer constant
offsetof (*structure*, *member*)	The offset in bytes of the member *member* from the start of the structure *structure*; the type of the result is size_t
ptrdiff_t	The type of integer produced by subtracting two pointers
size_t	The type of integer produced by the sizeof operator
wchar_t	The type of the integer required to hold a wide character (see Appendix A, "C Language Summary")

`<limits.h>`

This header file contains various implementation-defined limits for character and integer data types. Certain minimum values are guaranteed by the ANSI standard. These are noted at the end of each description inside parentheses.

Define	Meaning
CHAR_BIT	Number of bits in a `char` (8)
CHAR_MAX	Maximum value for object of type `char` (127 if sign extension is done on `char`s, 255 otherwise)
CHAR_MIN	Minimum value for object of type `char` (−127 if sign extension is done on `char`s, 0 otherwise)
SCHAR_MAX	Maximum value for object of type `signed char` (127)
SCHAR_MIN	Minimum value for object of type `signed char` (−127)
UCHAR_MAX	Maximum value for object of type `unsigned char` (255)
SHRT_MAX	Maximum value for object of type `short int` (32767)
SHRT_MIN	Minimum value for object of type `short int` (−32767)
USHRT_MAX	Maximum value for object of type `unsigned short int` (65535)
INT_MAX	Maximum value for object of type `int` (32767)
INT_MIN	Minimum value for object of type `int` (−32767)
UINT_MAX	Maximum value for object of type `unsigned int` (65535)
LONG_MAX	Maximum value for object of type `long int` (2147483647)
LONG_MIN	Minimum value for object of type `long int` (−2147483647)
ULONG_MAX	Maximum value for object of type `unsigned long int` (4294967295)
LLONG_MAX	Maximum value for object of type `long long int` (9223372036854775807)
LLONG_MIN	Minimum value for object of type `long long int` (−9223372036854775807)
ULLONG_MAX	Maximum value for object of type `unsigned long long int` (18446744073709551615)

`<stdbool.h>`

This header file contains definitions for working with Boolean variables (type `_Bool`).

Define	Meaning
bool	Substitute name for the basic `_Bool data type`
true	Defined as 1
false	Defined as 0

`<float.h>`

This header file defines various limits associated with floating-point arithmetic. Minimum magnitudes are noted at the end of each description inside parentheses. Note that all of the definitions are not listed here.

Define	Meaning
FLT_DIG	Number of digits of precision for a `float` (6)
FLT_EPSILON	Smallest value that, when added to 1.0, does not compare equal to 1.0 (1e−5)
FLT_MAX	Maximum size of a `float` (1e+37)
FLT_MAX_EXP	Maximum size of a `float` (1e+37)
FLT_MIN	Minimum size of a normalized `float` (1e−37)

Similar definitions exist for `double` and `long double` types. Just replace the leading `FLT` with `DBL` for `doubles`, and with `LDBL` for `long doubles`. For example, `DBL_DIG` gives the number of digits of precision for a `double`, and `LDBL_DIG` gives it for a `long double`.

You should also note that the header file `<fenv.h>` is used to get information and have more control over the floating-point environment. For example, there's a function called `fesetround` that allows you to specify the direction of rounding to a value as defined in `<fenv.h>`: `FE_TONEAREST`, `FE_UPWARD`, `FE_DOWNWARD`, or `FE_TOWARDZERO`. You also have the ability to clear, raise, or test floating-point exceptions, using the `feclearexcept`, `feraiseexcept`, and `fetextexcept` functions, respectively.

`<stdint.h>`

This header file defines various type definitions and constants that you can use to work with integers in a more machine-independent fashion. For example, the `typedef int32_t` can be used to declare a signed integer variable of exactly 32 bits, without having to know the exact 32-bit integer data type on the system on which the program is being compiled. Similarly, `int_least32_t` can be used to declare an integer with a width of at least 32 bits. Other types of `typedefs` allow you to select the fastest integer representations, for example. For more information, you can take a look at the file on your system or consult your documentation.

A few other useful definitions from this header file are as follows:

Define	Meaning
intptr_t	Integer guaranteed to hold any pointer value
uintptr_t	Unsigned integer guaranteed to hold any pointer value
intmax_t	Largest signed integer type
uintmax_t	Largest unsigned integer type

String Functions

The following functions perform operations on character arrays. In the description of these routines, *s*, *s1*, and *s2* represent pointers to null-terminated character arrays, *c* is an int, and *n* represents an integer of type size_t (defined in stddef.h). For the strnxxx routines, *s1* and *s2* can point to character arrays that aren't null-terminated.

To use any of these functions, you should include the header file <string.h> in your program:

#include <string.h>

```
char *strcat (s1, s2)
```

Concatenates the character string *s2* to the end of *s1*, placing a null character at the end of the final string. The function returns *s1*.

```
char *strchr (s, c)
```

Searches the string *s* for the first occurrence of the character *c*. If it is found, a pointer to the character is returned; otherwise, a null pointer is returned.

```
int strcmp (s1, s2)
```

Compares strings *s1* and *s2* and returns a value less than zero if *s1* is less than *s2*, equal to zero if *s1* is equal to *s2*, and greater than zero if *s1* is greater than *s2*.

```
char *strcoll (s1, s2)
```

Is like strcmp, except *s1* and *s2* are pointers to strings represented in the current locale.

```
char *strcpy (s1, s2)
```

Copies the string *s2* to *s1*, returning *s1*.

```
char *strerror (n)
```

Returns the error message associated with error number *n*.

```
size_t strcspn (s1, s2)
```

Counts the maximum number of initial characters in *s1* that consist of any characters but those in *s2*, returning the result.

```
size_t strlen (s)
```

Returns the number of characters in *s*, excluding the null character.

```
char *strncat (s1, s2, n)
```

Copies *s2* to the *end* of *s1* until either the null character is reached or *n* characters have been copied, whichever occurs first. Returns *s1*.

```
int strncmp (s1, s2, n)
```

Performs the same function as `strcmp`, except that at most n characters from the strings are compared.

```
char *strncpy (s1, s2, n)
```

Copies $s2$ to $s1$ until either the null character is reached or n characters have been copied, whichever occurs first. Returns $s1$.

```
char *strrchr (s, c)
```

Searches the string s for the last occurrence of the character c. If found, a pointer to the character in s is returned; otherwise, the null pointer is returned.

```
char *strpbrk (s1, s2)
```

Locates the first occurrence of any character from $s2$ inside $s1$, returning a pointer to it or the null pointer if not found.

```
size_t strspn (s1, s2)
```

Counts the maximum number of initial characters in $s1$ that consist only of characters from $s2$, returning the result.

```
char *strstr (s1, s2)
```

Searches the string $s1$ for the first occurrence of the string $s2$. If found, a pointer to the start of where $s2$ is located inside $s1$ is returned; otherwise, if $s2$ is not located inside $s1$, the null pointer is returned.

```
char *strtok (s1, s2)
```

Breaks the string $s1$ into tokens based on delimiter characters in $s2$. For the first call, $s1$ is the string being parsed and $s2$ contains a list of characters that delimit the tokens. The function places a null character in $s1$ to mark the end of each token as it is found and returns a pointer to the start of the token. On subsequent calls, $s1$ should be a null pointer. When no more tokens remain, a null pointer is returned.

```
size_t strxfrm (s1, s2, n)
```

Transforms up to n characters from the string $s2$, placing the result in $s1$. Two such transformed strings from the current locale can then be compared with `strcmp`.

Memory Functions

The following routines deal with arrays of characters. They are designed for efficient searching of memory and for copying data from one area of memory to another. They require the header file `<string.h>`:

```
#include <string.h>
```

In the description of these routines, *m1* and *m2* are of type void *, *c* is an int that gets converted by the routine to an unsigned char, and *n* is an integer of type size_t.

```
void  *memchr (m1, c, n)
```

Searches *m1* for the first occurrence of *c*, returning a pointer to it if found, or the null pointer, if not found after examining *n* characters.

```
void  *memcmp (m1, m2, n)
```

Compares the corresponding first *n* characters from *m1* and *m2*. Zero is returned if both arrays are identical in their first *n* characters. If they're not, the difference between the corresponding characters from *m1* and *m2* that caused the first mismatch is returned. So, if the disagreeing character from *m1* was less than the corresponding character from *m2*, a value less than zero is returned; otherwise, a value greater than zero is returned.

```
void  *memcpy (m1, m2, n)
```

Copies *n* characters from *m2* to *m1*, returning *m1*.

```
void  *memmove (m1, m2, n)
```

Is like memcpy, but is guaranteed to work even if *m1* and *m2* overlap in memory.

```
void  *memset (m1, c, n)
```

Sets the first *n* characters of *m1* to the value *c*. memset returns *m1*.

Note that these routines attach no special significance to null characters inside the arrays. They can be used with arrays other than character arrays provided you cast the pointers accordingly to void *. So, if data1 and data2 are each an array of 100 ints, the call

```
memcpy ((void *) data2, (void *) data1, sizeof (data1));
```

copies all 100 integers from data1 to data2.

Character Functions

The following functions deal with single characters. To use them, you must include the file <ctype.h> in your program:

```
#include <ctype.h>
```

Each of the functions that follow takes an int (*c*) as an argument and returns a TRUE value (nonzero), if the test is satisfied, and a FALSE (zero) value otherwise.

Name	Test
isalnum	Is *c* an alphanumeric character?
isalpha	Is *c* an alphabetic character?
isblank	Is *c* a blank character (space or horizontal tab)?

Name	Test
iscntrl	Is c a control character?
isdigit	Is c a digit character?
isgraph	Is c a graphics character (any printable character except a space)?
islower	Is c a lowercase letter?
isprint	Is c a printable character (including a space)?
ispunct	Is c a punctuation character (any character except a space or alphanumeric)?
isspace	Is c a whitespace character (space, newline, carriage return, horizontal or vertical tab, or formfeed)?
isupper	Is c an uppercase letter?
isxdigit	Is c a hexadecimal digit character?

The following two functions are provided for performing character translation:

    int tolower(c)

Returns the lowercase equivalent of c. If c is not an uppercase letter, c itself is returned.

    int toupper(c)

Returns the uppercase equivalent of c. If c is not a lowercase letter, c itself is returned.

I/O Functions

The following describes some of the more commonly used I/O functions from the C library. You should include the header file <stdio.h> at the front of any program that uses one of these functions, using the following statement:

#include <stdio.h>

Included in this file are declarations for the I/O functions and definitions for the names EOF, NULL, stdin, stdout, stderr (all constant values), and FILE.

In the descriptions that follow, *fileName*, *fileName1*, *fileName2*, *accessMode*, and *format* are pointers to null-terminated strings, *buffer* is a pointer to a character array, *filePtr* is of type "pointer to FILE," *n* and *size* are positive integer values of type size_t, and *i* and *c* are of type int.

    void clearerr (filePtr)

Clears the end of file and error indicators associated with the file identified by *filePtr*.

    int fclose (filePtr)

Closes the file identified by *filePtr* and returns zero if the close is successful, or returns EOF if an error occurs.

```
int feof (filePtr)
```

Returns nonzero if the identified file has reached the end of the file and returns zero otherwise.

```
int ferror (filePtr)
```

Checks for an error condition on the indicated file and returns zero if an error exists, and returns nonzero otherwise.

```
int fflush (filePtr)
```

Flushes (writes) any data from internal buffers to the indicated file, returning zero on success and the value EOF if an error occurs.

```
int fgetc (filePtr)
```

Returns the next character from the file identified by *filePtr*, or the value EOF if an end-of-file condition occurs. (Remember that this function returns an int.)

```
int fgetpos (filePtr, fpos)
```

Gets the current file position for the file associated with *filePtr*, storing it into the fpos_t (defined in <stdio.h>) variable pointed to by *fpos*. fgetpos returns zero on success, and returns nonzero on failure. See also the fsetpos function.

```
char *fgets (buffer, i, filePtr)
```

Reads characters from the indicated file, until either *i* − 1 characters are read or a newline character is read, whichever occurs first. Characters that are read are stored into the character array pointed to by *buffer*. If a newline character is read, it *will* be stored in the array. If an end of file is reached or an error occurs, the value NULL is returned; otherwise, *buffer* is returned.

```
FILE *fopen (fileName, accessMode)
```

Opens the specified file with the indicated access mode. Valid modes are "r" for reading, "w" for writing, "a" for appending to the end of an existing file, "r+" for read/write access starting at the beginning of an existing file, "w+" for read/write access (and the previous contents of the file, if it exists, are lost), and "a+" for read/write access with all writes going to the end of the file. If the file to be opened does not exist, it is created if the *accessMode* is write ("w", "w+") or append ("a", "a+"). If a file is opened in append mode ("a" or "a+"), it is not possible to overwrite existing data in the file.

On systems that distinguish binary from text files, the letter b must be appended to the access mode (as in "rb") to open a binary file.

If the fopen call is successful, a FILE pointer is returned to be used to identify the file in subsequent I/O operations; otherwise, a null pointer is returned.

```
int fprintf (filePtr, format, arg1, arg2, ..., argn)
```

Writes the specified arguments to the file identified by `filePtr`, according to the format specified by the character string `format`. Format characters are the same as for the `printf` function (see Chapter 15, "Input and Output Operations in C"). The number of characters written is returned. A negative return value indicates that an error occurred on output.

```
int fputc (c, filePtr)
```

Writes the value of `c` (converted to an `unsigned char`) to the file identified by `filePtr`, returning `c` if the write is successful, and the value `EOF` otherwise.

```
int fputs (buffer, filePtr)
```

Writes the characters in the array pointed to by `buffer` to the indicated file until the terminating null character in `buffer` is reached. A newline character is *not* automatically written to the file by this function. On failure, the value `EOF` is returned.

```
size_t fread (buffer, size, n, filePtr)
```

Reads `n` items of data from the identified file into `buffer`. Each item of data is `size` bytes in length. For example, the call

```
numread = fread (text, sizeof (char), 80, in_file);
```

reads 80 characters from the file identified by `in_file` and stores them into the array pointed to by `text`. The function returns the number of data items successfully read.

```
FILE *freopen (fileName, accessMode, filePtr)
```

Closes the file associated with `filePtr` and opens the file `fileName` with the specified `accessMode` (see the `fopen` function). The file that is opened is subsequently associated with `filePtr`. If the `freopen` call is successful, `filePtr` is returned; otherwise, a null pointer is returned. The `freopen` function is frequently used to reassign `stdin`, `stdout`, or `stderr` in the program. For example, the call

```
    if ( freopen ("inputData", "r", stdin) == NULL ) {
        ...
    }
```

has the effect of reassigning `stdin` to the file `inputData`, which is opened in read access mode. Subsequent I/O operations performed with `stdin` are performed with the file `inputData`, as if `stdin` had been redirected to this file when the program was executed.

```
int fscanf (filePtr, format, arg1, arg2, ..., argn)
```

Reads data items from the file identified by `filePtr`, according to the format specified by the character string `format`. The values that are read are stored in the arguments specified after `format`, each of which must be a pointer. The `format` characters that are allowed in `format` are the same as those for the `scanf` function (see Chapter 15). The `fscanf` function returns the number of items successfully read and assigned (excluding any %n assignments) or the value EOF if the end of file is reached before the first item is converted.

```
int fseek (filePtr, offset, mode)
```

Positions the indicated file to a point that is offset (a long int) bytes from the beginning of the file, from the current position in the file, or from the end of the file, depending upon the value of *mode* (an integer). If *mode* equals SEEK_SET, positioning is relative to the beginning of the file. If *mode* equals SEEK_CUR, positioning is relative to the current position in the file. If *mode* equals SEEK_END, positioning is relative to the end of the file. SEEK_SET, SEEK_CUR, and SEEK_END are defined in <stdio.h>.

On systems that distinguish between text and binary files, SEEK_END might not be supported for binary files. For text files, either *offset* must be zero or must be a value returned from a prior call to ftell. In the latter case, *mode* must be SEEK_SET.

If the fseek call is unsuccessful, a nonzero value is returned.

```
int fsetpos (filePtr, fpos)
```

Sets the current file position for the file associated with *filePtr* to the value pointed to by *fpos*, which is of type fpos_t (defined in <stdio.h>). Returns zero on success, and nonzero on failure. See also fgetpos.

```
long ftell (filePtr)
```

Returns the relative offset in bytes of the current position in the file identified by *filePtr*, or –1L on error.

```
size_t fwrite (buffer, size, n, filePtr)
```

Writes *n* items of data from *buffer* to the specified file. Each item of data is *size* bytes in length. Returns the number of items successfully written.

```
int getc (filePtr)
```

Reads and returns the next character from the indicated file. The value EOF is returned if an error occurs or if the end of the file is reached.

```
int getchar (void)
```

Reads and returns the next character from stdin. The value EOF is returned upon error or end of file.

```
char *gets (buffer)
```

Reads characters from stdin into *buffer* until a newline character is read. The newline character is *not* stored in *buffer*, and the character string is terminated with a null character. If an error occurs in performing the read, or if no characters are read, a null pointer is returned; otherwise, *buffer* is returned. This function has been removed from the ANSI C11 specification, but you may see this function in older code, so it is good to know what the function does.

```
void perror (message)
```

Writes an explanation of the last error to stderr, preceded by the string pointed to by *message*. For example, the code

```
#include <stdlib.h>
#include <stdio.h>

if ( (in = fopen ("data", "r")) == NULL ) {
    perror ("data file read");
    exit (EXIT_FAILURE);
}
```

produces an error message if the fopen call fails, possibly giving more details to the user about the reason for the failure.

```
int printf (format, arg1, arg2, ..., argn)
```

Writes the specified arguments to stdout, according to the format specified by the character string *format* (see Chapter 15). Returns the number of characters written.

```
int putc (c, filePtr)
```

Writes the value of *c* as an unsigned char to the indicated file. On success, *c* is returned; otherwise EOF is returned.

```
int putchar(c)
```

Writes the value of *c* as an unsigned char to stdout, returning *c* on success and EOF on failure.

```
int puts (buffer)
```

Writes the characters contained in buffer to stdout until a null character is encountered. A newline character is automatically written as the last character (unlike the fputs function). On error, EOF is returned.

```
int remove (fileName)
```

Removes the specified file. A nonzero value is returned on failure.

```
int rename (fileName1, fileName2)
```

Renames the file *fileName1* to *fileName2*, returning a nonzero result on failure.

```
void rewind (filePtr)
```

Resets the indicated file back to the beginning.

```
int scanf (format, arg1, arg2, ..., argn)
```

Reads items from stdin according to the format specified by the string *format* (see Chapter 15). The arguments that follow *format* must all be pointers. The number of items successfully read and assigned (excluding %n assignments) is returned by the function. The value EOF is returned if an end of file is encountered before any items have been converted.

```
FILE *tmpfile (void)
```

Creates and opens a temporary binary file in write update mode ("r+b"); it returns NULL if an error occurs. The temporary file is automatically removed when the program terminates. (A function called tmpnam is also available for creating unique, temporary file names.)

```
int ungetc (c, filePtr)
```

Effectively "puts back" a character to the indicated file. The character is not actually written to the file but is placed in a buffer associated with the file. The next call to getc returns this character. The ungetc function can only be called to "put back" one character to a file at a time; that is, a read operation must be performed on the file before another call to ungetc can be made. The function returns c if the character is successfully "put back"; otherwise, it returns the value EOF.

In-Memory Format Conversion Functions

The functions sprintf() and sscanf() are provided for performing data conversion in memory. These functions are analogous to the fprintf() and fscanf() functions, except a character string replaces the FILE pointer as the first argument. You should include the header file <stdio.h> in your program when using these routines.

```
int sprintf (buffer, format, arg1, arg2, ..., argn)
```

The specified arguments are converted according to the format specified by the character string *format* (see Chapter 15) and are placed into the character array pointed to by *buffer*. A null character is automatically placed at the end of the string inside *buffer*. The number of characters placed into *buffer* is returned, excluding the terminating null. As an example, the code

```
int  version = 2;
char fname[125];
  ...
sprintf (fname, "/usr/data%i/2015", version);
```

results in the character string "/usr/data2/2005" being stored in fname.

```
int sscanf (buffer, format, arg1, arg2, ..., argn)
```

The values as specified by the character string *format* are read from *buffer* and stored in the corresponding pointer arguments that follow *format* (see Chapter 15). The number of items successfully converted is returned by this function. As an example, the code

```
char  buffer[] = "July 16, 2014", month[10];
int   day, year;
  ...
sscanf (buffer, "%s %d, %d", month, &day, &year);
```

stores the string `"July"` inside `month`, the integer value `16` inside `day`, and the integer value `2014` inside `year`. The code

```
#include <stdio.h>
#include <stdlib.h>

if ( sscanf (argv[1], "%f", &fval) != 1 ) {
    fprintf (stderr, "Bad number: %s\n", argv[1]);
    exit (EXIT_FAILURE);
}
```

converts the first command-line argument (pointed to by `argv[1]`) to a floating-point number, and checks the value returned by `sscanf` to see if a number was successfully read from `argv[1]`. (See the routines described in the next section for other ways to convert strings to numbers.)

String-to-Number Conversion

The following routines convert character strings to numbers. To use any of the routines described here, include the header file `<stdlib.h>` in your program:

```
#include <stdlib.h>
```

In the descriptions that follow, *s* is a pointer to a null-terminated string, *end* is a pointer to a character pointer, and *base* is an `int`.

All routines skip leading whitespace characters in the string and stop their scan upon encountering a character that is invalid for the type of value being converted.

```
double atof (s)
```

Converts the string pointed to by *s* into a floating-point number, returning the result.

```
int atoi (s)
```

Converts the string pointed to by *s* into an `int`, returning the result.

```
int atol (s)
```

Converts the string pointed to by *s* into a `long int`, returning the result.

```
int atoll (s)
```

Converts the string pointed to by *s* into a `long long int`, returning the result.

```
double strtod (s, end)
```

Converts *s* to `double`, returning the result. A pointer to the character that terminated the scan is stored inside the character pointer pointed to by *end*, provided *end* is not a null pointer.

As an example, the code

```
#include <stdlib.h>
    ...
char    buffer[] = "  123.456xyz", *end;
```

```
double value;
  ...
value = strtod (buffer, &end);
```

has the effect of storing the value `123.456` inside `value`. The character pointer variable `end` is set by `strtod` to point to the character in `buffer` that terminated the scan. In this case, it is set pointing to the character `'x'`.

```
float strtof (s, end)
```

Is like `strtod`, except converts its argument to `float`.

```
long int strtol (s, end, base)
```

Converts `s` to `long int`, returning the result. `base` is an integer base number between 2 and 36, inclusive. The integer is interpreted according to the specified base. If `base` is 0, the integer can be expressed in either base 10, octal (leading `0`), or hexadecimal (leading `0x` or `0X`). If `base` is 16, the value can optionally be preceded by a leading `0x` or `0X`.

A pointer to the character that terminated the scan is stored inside the character pointer pointed to by `end`, provided `end` is not a null pointer.

```
long double strtold (s, end)
```

Is like `strtod`, except converts its argument to `long double`.

```
long long int strtoll (s, end, base)
```

Is like `strtol`, except a `long long int` is returned.

```
unsigned long int strtoul (s, end, base)
```

Converts `s` to `unsigned long int`, returning the result. The remaining arguments are interpreted as for `strtol`.

```
unsigned long long int strtoull (s, end, base)
```

Converts `s` to `unsigned long long int`, returning the result. The remaining arguments are interpreted as for `strtol`.

Dynamic Memory Allocation Functions

The following functions are available for allocating and freeing memory dynamically. For each of these functions, `n` and `size` represent integers of type `size_t`, and `pointer` represents a void pointer. To use these functions, include the following line in your program:

```
#include <stdlib.h>
```

```
void *calloc (n, size)
```

Allocates contiguous space for `n` items of data, where each item is `size` bytes in length. The allocated space is initially set to all zeroes. On success, a pointer to the allocated space is returned; on failure, the null pointer is returned.

```
void free (pointer)
```

Returns a block of memory pointed to by *pointer* that was previously allocated by a `calloc()`, `malloc()`, or `realloc()` call.

```
void *malloc (size)
```

Allocates contiguous space of *size* bytes, returning a pointer to the beginning of the allocated block if successful, and the null pointer otherwise.

```
void *realloc (pointer, size)
```

Changes the size of a previously allocated block to *size* bytes, returning a pointer to the new block (which might have moved), or a null pointer if an error occurs.

Math Functions

The following list identifies the math functions. To use these routines, include the following statement in your program:

```
#include <math.h>
```

The standard header file `<tgmath.h>` defines type-generic macros that can be used to call a function from the math or complex math libraries without worrying about the argument type. For example, you can use six different square root functions based upon the argument type and return type:

- `double sqrt (double x)`
- `float sqrtf (float x)`
- `long double sqrtl (long double x)`
- `double complex csqrt (double complex x)`
- `float complex csqrtf (float complex f)`
- `long double complex csqrtl (long double complex)`

Instead of having to worry about all six functions, you can include `<tgmath.h>` instead of `<math.h>` and `<complex.h>` and just use the "generic" version of the function under the name sqrt. The corresponding macro defined in `<tgmath.h>` ensures that the correct function gets called.

Returning to `<math.h>`, the following macros can be used to test specific properties of floating-point values given as argument(s):

```
int fpclassify (x)
```

Classifies *x* as NaN (`FP_NAN`), infinite (`FP_INFINITE`), normal (`FP_NORMAL`), subnormal (`FP_SUBNORMAL`), zero (`FP_ZERO`), or in some other implementation-defined category; each `FP_...` value is defined in `math.h`.

```
int isfin (x)
```

Does *x* represent a finite value?

```
int isinf (x)
```

Does *x* represent an infinite value?

```
int isgreater (x, y)
```

Is $x > y$?

```
int isgreaterequal (x, y)
```

Is $x \geq y$?

```
int islessequal (x, y)
```

Is $x \leq y$?

```
int islessgreater (x, y)
```

Is $x < y$ or is $x > y$?

```
int isnan (x)
```

Is *x* a NaN (that is, not a number)?

```
int isnormal (x)
```

Is *x* a normal value?

```
int isunordered (x, y)
```

Are *x* and *y* unordered (for example, one or both might be NaNs)?

```
int signbit (x)
```

Is the sign of *x* negative?

In the list of functions that follows, *x*, *y*, and *z* are of type `double`, *r* is an angle expressed in radians and is of type `double`, and *n* is an `int`.

For more information about how errors are reported by these functions, consult your documentation.

```
double acos (x)
```
[1]

Returns the arccosine of *x*, as an angle expressed in radians in the range [0, π]. *x* is in the range [−1, 1].

---

1. *The math library contains* `float`, `double`, *and* `long double` *versions of the math functions that take and return* `float`, `double`, *and* `long double` *values. The* `double` *versions are summarized here. The* `float` *versions have the same name with an* `f` *on the end (e.g.* `acosf`*). The* `long double` *versions have an* `l` *on the end instead (e.g.* `acosl`*).*

```
double acosh (x)
```

Returns the hyperbolic arccosine of x, $x \geq 1$.

```
double asin (x)
```

Returns the arcsine of x as an angle expressed in radians in the range $[-\pi/2, \pi/2]$. x is in the range $[-1, 1]$.

```
double asinh (x)
```

Returns the hyperbolic arcsine of x.

```
double atan (x)
```

Returns the arctangent of x as an angle expressed in radians in the range $[-\pi/2, \pi/2]$.

```
double atanh (x)
```

Returns the hyperbolic arctangent of x, $|x| \leq 1$.

```
double atan2 (y, x)
```

Returns the arctangent of y/x as an angle expressed in radians in the range $[-\pi, \pi]$.

```
double ceil (x)
```

Returns the smallest integer value greater than or equal to x. Note that the value is returned as a `double`.

```
double copysign (x, y)
```

Returns a value whose magnitude is that of x and whose sign is that of y.

```
double cos (r)
```

Returns the cosine of r.

```
double cosh (x)
```

Returns the hyperbolic cosine of x.

```
double erf (x)
```

Computes and returns the error function of x.

```
double erfc (x)
```

Computes and returns the complementary error function of x.

```
double exp (x)
```

Returns e^x.

```
double expm1 (x)
```

Returns $e^x - 1$.

```
double fabs (x)
```

Returns the absolute value of x.

```
double fdim (x, y)
```

Returns $x - y$ if $x > y$; otherwise, it returns 0.

```
double floor (x)
```

Returns the largest integer value less than or equal to x. Note that the value is returned as a `double`.

```
double fma (x, y, z)
```

Returns $(x \times y) + z$.

```
double fmax (x, y)
```

Returns the maximum of x and y.

```
double fmin (x, y)
```

Returns the minimum of x and y.

```
double fmod (x, y)
```

Returns the floating-point remainder of dividing x by y. The sign of the result is that of x.

```
double frexp (x, exp)
```

Divides x into a normalized fraction and a power of two. Returns the fraction in the range [1/2, 1] and stores the exponent in the integer pointed to by *exp*. If x is zero, both the value returned and the exponent stored are zero.

```
int hypot (x, y)
```

Returns the square root of the sum of $x^2 + y^2$.

```
int ilogb (x)
```

Extracts the exponent of x as a signed integer.

```
double ldexp (x, n)
```

Returns $x \times 2^n$.

```
double lgamma (x)
```

Returns the natural logarithm of the absolute value of the gamma of x.

```
double log (x)
```

Returns the natural logarithm of x, $x \geq 0$.

```
double logb (x)
```

Returns the signed exponent of *x*.

```
double log1p (x)
```

Returns the natural logarithm of $(x + 1)$, $x \geq -1$.

```
double log2 (x)
```

Returns $\log2 x$, $x \geq 0$.

```
double log10 (x)
```

Returns $\log10 x$, $x \geq 0$.

```
long int lrint (x)
```

Returns *x* rounded to the nearest `long` integer.

```
long long int llrint (x)
```

Returns *x* rounded to the nearest `long long` integer.

```
long long int llround (x)
```

Returns the value of *x* rounded to the nearest `long long int`. Halfway values are always rounded away from zero (so 0.5 always rounds to 1).

```
long int lround (x)
```

Returns the value of *x* rounded to the nearest `long int`. Halfway values are always rounded away from zero (so 0.5 always rounds to 1).

```
double modf (x, ipart)
```

Extracts the fractional and integral parts of *x*. The fractional part is returned and the integral part is stored in the `double` pointed to by *ipart*.

```
double nan (s)
```

Returns a NaN, if possible, according to the content specified by the string pointed to by *s*.

```
double nearbyint (x)
```

Returns the nearest integer to *x* in floating-point format.

```
double nextafter (x, y)
```

Returns the next representable value of *x* in the direction of *y*.

```
double nexttoward (x, ly)
```

Returns the next representable value of *x* in the direction of *y*. Similar to `nextafter`, except in this case the second argument is of type `long double`.

```
double pow (x, y)
```

Returns x^y. If x is less than zero, y must be an integer. If x is equal to zero, y must be greater than zero.

```
double remainder (x, y)
```

Returns the remainder of x divided by y.

```
double remquo (x, y, quo)
```

Returns the remainder of x divided by y, storing the quotient into the integer pointed to by *quo*.

```
double rint (x)
```

Returns the nearest integer to x in floating-point format. Might raise a floating-point exception if the value of the result is not equal to the argument x.

```
double round (x)
```

Returns the value of x rounded to the nearest integer in floating-point format. Halfway values are always rounded away from zero (so 0.5 always rounds to 1.0).

```
double scalbln (x, n)
```

Returns $x \times$ FLT_RADIX^n, where n is a `long int`.

```
double scalbn (x, n)
```

Returns $x \times$ FLT_RADIX^n.

```
double sin (r)
```

Returns the sine of r.

```
double sinh (x)
```

Returns the hyperbolic sine of x.

```
double sqrt (x)
```

Returns the square root of x, $x \geq 0$.

```
double tan (r)
```

Returns the tangent of r.

```
double tanh (x)
```

Returns the hyperbolic tangent of x.

```
double tgamma (x)
```

Returns the gamma of x.

```
double trunc (x)
```

Truncates the argument x to an integer value, returning the result as a `double`.

Complex Arithmetic

This header file `<complex.h>` defines various type definitions and functions for working with complex numbers. Listed next are several macros that are defined in this file, followed by functions for performing complex arithmetic.

Define	Meaning
complex	Substitute name for the type `_Complex`
_Complex_I	Macro used for specifying the imaginary part of a complex number (for example, `4 + 6.2 * _Complex_I` specifies 4 + 6.2i)
imaginary	Substitute name for the type `_Imaginary`; only defined if the implementation supports imaginary types
_Imaginary_I	Macro used to specify the imaginary part of an imaginary number

In the list of functions that follows, y and z are of type double complex, x is of type double, and n is an int.

```
double complex cabs (z)²
```

Returns the complex absolute value of z.

```
double complex cacos (z)
```

Returns the complex arc cosine of z.

```
double complex cacosh (z)
```

Returns the complex arc hyperbolic cosine of z.

```
double carg (z)
```

Returns the phase angle of z.

```
double complex casin (z)
```

Returns the complex arc sine of z.

```
double complex casinh (z)
```

Returns the complex arc hyperbolic sine of z.

```
double complex catan (z)
```

Returns the complex arc tangent of z.

---

2. The complex math library contains `float complex`, `double complex`, and `long double complex` versions of the functions that take and return `float complex`, `double complex`, and `long double complex` values. The `double complex` versions are summarized here. The `float complex` versions have the same name with an `f` on the end (e.g. `cacosf`). The `long double` versions have an `l` on the end instead (e.g. `cacosl`).

```
double complex catanh (z)
```

Returns the complex arc hyperbolic tangent of z.

```
double complex ccos (z)
```

Returns the complex cosine of z.

```
double complex ccosh (z)
```

Returns the complex hyperbolic cosine of z.

```
double complex cexp (z)
```

Returns the complex natural exponential of z.

```
double cimag (z)
```

Returns the imaginary part of z.

```
double complex clog (z)
```

Returns the complex natural logarithm of z.

```
double complex conj (z)
```

Returns the complex conjugate of z (inverts the sign of its imaginary part).

```
double complex cpow (y, z)
```

Returns the complex power function y^z.

```
double complex cproj (z)
```

Returns the projection of z onto the Riemann sphere.

```
double complex creal (z)
```

Returns the real part of z.

```
double complex csin (z)
```

Returns the complex sine of z.

```
double complex csinh (z)
```

Returns the complex hyperbolic sine of z.

```
double complex csqrt (z)
```

Returns the complex square root of z.

```
double complex ctan (z)
```

Returns the complex tangent of z.

```
double complex ctanh (z)
```

Returns the complex hyperbolic tangent of z.

General Utility Functions

Some routines from the library don't fit neatly into any of the previous categories. To use these routines, include the header file `<stdlib.h>`.

```
int abs (n)
```

Returns the absolute value of its `int` argument `n`.

```
void exit (n)
```

Terminates program execution, closing any open files and returning the exit status specified by its `int` argument `n`. `EXIT_SUCCESS` and `EXIT_FAILURE`, defined in `<stdlib.h>`, can be used to return a success or failure exit status, respectively.

Other related routines in the library that you might want to refer to are `abort` and `atexit`.

```
char *getenv (s)
```

Returns a pointer to the value of the environment variable pointed to by `s`, or a null pointer if the variable doesn't exist. This function operates in a system-dependent way.

As an example, under Unix, the code

```
char   *homedir;
       ...
homedir = getenv ("HOME");
```

could be used to get the value of the user's `HOME` variable, storing a pointer to it inside `homedir`.

```
long int labs (l)
```

Returns the absolute value of its `long int` argument `l`.

```
long long int llabs (ll)
```

Returns the absolute value of its `long long int` argument `ll`.

```
void qsort (arr, n, size, comp_fn)
```

Sorts the data array pointed to by the `void` pointer `arr`. There are `n` elements in the array, each `size` bytes in length. `n` and `size` are of type `size_t`. The fourth argument is of type "pointer to function that returns `int` and that takes two `void` pointers as arguments." `qsort` calls this function whenever it needs to compare two elements in the array, passing it pointers to the elements to compare. The function, which is user-supplied, is expected to compare the two elements and return a value less than zero, equal to zero, or greater than zero if the first element is less than, equal to, or greater than the second element, respectively.

Here is an example of how to use `qsort` to sort an array of 1,000 integers called `data`:

```
#include <stdlib.h>
   ...
int main (void)
{
    int data[1000], comp_ints (void *, void *);
       ...
    qsort (data, 1000, sizeof(int), comp_ints);
       ...
}

int comp_ints (void *p1, void *p2)
{
    int  i1 = * (int *) p1;
    int  i2 = * (int *) p2;
    return  i1 - i2;
}
```

Another routine called bsearch, which is not described here, takes similar arguments to qsort and performs a binary search of an ordered array of data.

```
int rand (void)
```

Returns a random number in the range [0, RAND_MAX], where RAND_MAX is defined in <stdlib.h> and has a minimum value of 32767. See also srand.

```
void srand (seed)
```

Seeds the random number generator to the unsigned int value seed.

```
int system (s)
```

Gives the command contained in the character array pointed to by s to the system for execution, returning a system-defined value. If s is the null pointer, system returns a nonzero value if a command processor is available to execute your commands.

As an example, under Unix, the call

```
system ("mkdir /usr/tmp/data");
```

causes the system to create a directory called /usr/tmp/data (assuming you have the proper permissions to do so).

C

Compiling Programs with gcc

This appendix summarizes some of the more commonly used gcc options. For information about all command-line options, under Unix, type the command man gcc. You can also visit the gcc website, http://gcc.gnu.org/onlinedocs, for complete online documentation.

This appendix summarizes the command-line options available in gcc, release 4.9, and does not cover extensions added by other vendors.

General Command Format

The general format of the gcc command is

```
gcc [options] file  [file ...]
```

Items enclosed in square brackets are optional.

Each file in the list is compiled by the gcc compiler. Normally, this involves preprocessing, compiling, assembling, and linking. Command-line options can be used to alter this sequence.

The suffix of each input file determines the way the file is interpreted. This can be overridden with the –x command-line option (consult the gcc documentation). Table C.1 contains a list of common suffixes.

Table C.1   **Common Source File Suffixes**

Suffix	Meaning
.c	C language source file
.cc, .cpp	C++ language source file
.h	Header file

Suffix	Meaning
.m	Objective-C source file
.pl	Perl source file
.o	Object (precompiled file)

Command-Line Options

Table C.2 contains a list of common options used for compiling C programs.

Table C.2   **Commonly Used** gcc **Options**

Option	Meaning	Example
--help	Displays summary of common command-line options.	gcc --help
-c	Does not link the files, saves the object files using .o for the suffix of each object file.	gcc -c enumerator.c
-dumpversion	Displays current version of gcc.	gcc -dumpversion
-g	Includes debugging information, typically for use with gdb (use -ggdb if multiple debuggers are supported).	gcc -g testprog.c -o testprog
-D id -D id=value	In the first case, defines the identifier id to the pre-processor with value 1. In the second case, defines the identifier id and sets its value to value.	gcc -D DEBUG=3 test.c
-E	Just preprocesses files and writes results to standard output; useful for examining the results of pre-processing.	gcc -E enumerator.c
-I dir	Adds directory dir to the list of directories to be searched for header files; this directory is searched before other standard directories.	gcc -I /users/ steve/include x.c
-llibrary	Resolves library references against the file specified by library. This option should be specified after the files that need functions from the library. The linker searches standard places (see the -L option) for a file named liblibrary.a.	gcc mathfuncs.c -lm
-L dir	Adds directory dir to the list of directories to be searched for library files. This directory is searched first before other standard directories.	gcc -L /users/ steve/lib x.c
-o execfile	Places the executable file in the file named execfile.	gcc dbtest.c -o dbtest

Option	Meaning	Example
`-Olevel`	Optimizes the code for execution speed according to the level specified by `level`, which can be 1, 2, or 3. If no level is specified, as in `-o`, then 1 is the default. Larger numbers indicate higher levels of optimization, and might result in longer compilation times and reduced debugging capability when using a debugger like `gdb`.	`gcc -O3 m1.c m2.c -o math-funcs`
`-std=standard`	Specifies the standard for C files.[1] Use `c11` for ANSI C11 without the GNU extensions.	`gcc -std=c99 mod1.c mod2.c`
`-warning`	Turns on warning messages specified by `warning`. Useful options are `all`, to get optional warnings that might be helpful for most programs, and `error`, which turns all warnings into errors, thereby forcing you to correct them.	`gcc -Werror mod1.c mod2.c`

1. The current default is gnu89 for ANSI C90 plus GNU extensions. Will be changed to gnu99 (for ANSI C99 plus GNU extensions) when all C99 features are implemented.

Common Programming Mistakes

The following list summarizes some of the more common programming mistakes made in C. They are not arranged in any particular order. Knowledge of these mistakes will hopefully help you avoid them in your own programs.

1. *Misplacing a semicolon.*

   Example

   ```
   if ( j == 100 );
       j = 0;
   ```

   In the previous statements, the value of j will always be set to 0 due to the misplaced semicolon after the closing parenthesis. Remember, this semicolon is syntactically valid (it represents the null statement), and, therefore, no error is produced by the compiler. This same type of mistake is frequently made in while and for loops.

2. *Confusing the operator = with the operator ==.*

   This mistake is usually made inside an if, while, or do statement.

   Example

   ```
   if ( a = 2 )
      printf ("Your turn.\n");
   ```

   The preceding statement is perfectly valid and has the effect of assigning 2 to a and then executing the printf() call. The printf() function will *always* be called because the value of the expression contained in the if statement will always be nonzero. (Its value will be 2.)

3. *Omitting prototype declarations.*

   Example

   ```
   result = squareRoot (2);
   ```

If squareRoot is defined later in the program, or in another file, and is not explicitly declared otherwise, the compiler assumes that the function returns an int. Furthermore, the compiler converts float arguments to double, and _Bool, char, and short arguments to int. No other conversion of arguments is done. Remember, it's always safest to include a prototype declaration for *all* functions that you call (either explicitly yourself or implicitly by including the correct header file in your program), even if they're defined earlier.

4. *Confusing the precedences of the various operators.*

   Examples

   ```
   while ( c = getchar ()   != EOF )
      . . .
   if ( x & 0xF  == y )
      . . .
   ```

   In the first example, the value returned by getchar is compared against the value EOF first. This is because the inequality test has higher precedence than the assignment operator. The value that is therefore assigned to c is the TRUE/FALSE result of the test: 1 if the value returned by getchar is not equal to EOF, and 0 otherwise. In the second example, the integer constant 0xF is compared against y first because the equality test has higher precedence than any of the bitwise operators. The result of this test (0 or 1) is then ANDed with the value of x.

5. *Confusing a character constant and a character string.*

   In the statement

   ```
   text = 'a';
   ```

   a single character is assigned to text. In the statement

   ```
   text = "a";
   ```

   a pointer to the character string "a" is assigned to text. Whereas, in the first case, text is normally declared to be a char variable, in the second case, it should be declared to be of type "pointer to char".

6. *Using the wrong bounds for an array.*

   Example

   ```
   int  a[100], i, sum = 0;
      . . .
   for ( i = 1;  i <= 100;  ++i )
      sum += a[i];
   ```

   Valid subscripts of an array range from 0 through the number of elements minus one. Therefore, the preceding loop is incorrect because the last valid subscript of a is 99 and not 100. The writer of this statement also probably intended to start with the first element of the array; therefore, i should have been initially set to 0.

7. *Forgetting to reserve an extra location in an array for the terminating null character of a string.*

   Remember to declare character arrays so that they are large enough to contain the terminating null character. For example, the character string `"hello"` would require six locations in a character array if you wanted to store a null at the end.

8. *Confusing the operator* `->` *with the operator* `.` *when referencing structure members.*

   Remember, the operator `.` is used for structure variables, whereas the operator `->` is used for structure *pointer* variables. So, if `x` is a structure variable, the notation `x.m` is used to reference the member `m` of `x`. On the other hand, if `x` is a pointer to a structure, the notation `x->m` is used to reference the member `m` of the structure pointed to by `x`.

9. *Omitting the ampersand before nonpointer variables in a* `scanf()` *call.*

   Example

   ```
   int   number;
      ...
   scanf ("%i", number);
   ```

   Remember that all arguments appearing after the format string in a `scanf()` call must be pointers.

10. *Using a pointer variable before it's initialized.*

    Example

    ```
    char  *char_pointer;
    *char_pointer = 'X';
    ```

    You can only apply the indirection operator to a pointer variable *after* you have set the variable pointing somewhere. In this example, `char_pointer` is never set pointing to anything, so the assignment is not meaningful.

11. *Omitting the* `break` *statement at the end of a case in a* `switch` *statement.*

    Remember that if a `break` is not included at the end of a case, then execution continues into the next case.

12. *Inserting a semicolon at the end of a preprocessor definition.*

    This usually happens because it becomes a matter of habit to end all statements with semicolons. Remember that everything appearing to the right of the defined name in the `#define` statement gets directly substituted into the program. So the definition

    ```
    #define    END_OF_DATA    999;
    ```

    leads to a syntax error if used in an expression such as

    ```
    if ( value == END_OF_DATA )
       ...
    ```

    because the compiler will see this statement after preprocessing:

    ```
    if ( value == 999; )
       ...
    ```

13. *Omitting parentheses around arguments in macro definitions.*

    Example

    ```
    #define    reciprocal(x)    1 / x
         ...
    w = reciprocal (a + b);
    ```

    The preceding assignment statement would be incorrectly evaluated as

    ```
    w = 1 / a + b;
    ```

14. *Omitting a closing parenthesis or closing quotation marks on any statement.*

    Example

    ```
    total_earning = (cash + (investments * inv_interest) + (savings * sav_interest);
    printf("Your total money to date is %.2f, total_earning);
    ```

    On the first line, the use of embedded parentheses to set apart each portion of the
    equation makes for a more readable line of code, but there is always the possibility of
    missing a closing parenthesis (or in some occasions, adding one too many). The second
    line also is missing a closing quotation mark for the string being sent to the `printf()`
    function. Both of these will generate a compiler error, but sometimes the error will be
    identified as coming on a different line, depending on whether the compiler uses a
    parenthesis or quotation mark on a subsequent line to complete the expression, and
    therefore move the missing character to a place later in the program.

15. *Failing to include the header file that includes the definition for a C-programming library
    function being used in the program.*

    Example

    ```
    double answer = sqrt(value1);
    ```

    If this program does not #include the <math.h> file, this will generate an error that
    sqrt() is undefined.

16. *Leaving a blank space between the name of a macro and its argument list in the* #define
    statement.

    Example

    ```
    #define MIN (a,b)  ( ( (a) < (b) ) ? (a) : (b) )
    ```

    This definition is incorrect, as the preprocessor considers the first blank space after the
    defined name as the start of the definition for that name. In this case, the statement

    ```
    minVal = MIN (val1, val2);
    ```

    gets expanded by the preprocessor into

    ```
    minVal = (a,b)  ( ( (a) < (b) ) ? (a) : (b) )(3,2);
    ```

    which is obviously not what is intended.

17. *Using an expression that has side effects in a macro call.*

Example

```
#define  SQUARE(x)   (x) * (x)
   ...
w = SQUARE (++v);
```

The invocation of the SQUARE macro causes v to be incremented *twice* because this statement is expanded by the preprocessor to

```
w = (++v) * (++v);
```

E

Resources

This appendix contains a selective list of resources you can turn to for more information. Some of the information might be online at a website or available from a book.

The C Programming Language

The C language has been around for more than 40 years now, so there's certainly no dearth of information on the subject. The following is just the tip of the iceberg.

Books

Kernighan, Brian W., and Dennis M. Ritchie. *The C Programming Language, 2nd Ed.* Englewood-Cliffs, NJ: Prentice Hall, Inc., 1988.

This has always been the bible as far as a reference for the language goes. It was the first book ever written about C, cowritten by Dennis Ritchie, who created the language. Despite being more than 25 years old, the second edition is the most recent edition, and it still is considered an indispensable reference.

Harbison, Samuel P. III, and Guy L. Steele Jr. *C: A Reference Manual, 5th Ed.* Englewood-Cliffs, NJ: Prentice Hall, Inc., 2002.

Another excellent reference book for C programmers.

Plauger, P. J. *The Standard C Library*. Englewood-Cliffs, NJ: Prentice Hall, Inc., 1992.

This book covers the standard C library, but as you can see from the publication date, does not cover any of the ANSI C99 additions (such as the complex math library).

Websites

www.ansi.org

This is the ANSI website. You can purchase the official ANSI C specification here. Type 9899:2011 into the search window to locate the ANSI C11 specifications.

www.opengroup.org/onlinepubs/007904975/idx/index.html

This is a great online reference source for library functions (there are also non-ANSI C functions here).

Newsgroup

comp.lang.c

This is a newsgroup devoted to the C programming language. You can ask questions here and help other people out as well—after you gain more experience. It's also useful just to observe the discussions. A good way to get access to this newsgroup is through http://groups.google.com.

C Compilers and Integrated Development Environments

Following is a list of websites where you can download and/or purchase C compilers and integrated development environments (IDEs), as well as obtain online documentation.

gcc

http://gcc.gnu.org/

The C compiler developed by the Free Software Foundation (FSF) is called gcc. You can download a C compiler for no charge from this website.

MinGW

www.mingw.org

If you want to get started writing C programs in a Windows environment, you can get a GNU gcc compiler from this website. Also consider downloading MSYS as an easy-to-use shell environment in which to work.

CygWin

www.cygwin.com

CygWin provides a Linux-like environment that runs under Windows. This development environment is available at no charge.

Visual Studio

http://msdn.microsoft.com/vstudio

Visual Studio is the Microsoft IDE that allows you to develop applications in a variety of different programming languages.

CodeWarrior

www.freescale.com/webapp/sps/site/homepage.jsp?code=CW_HOME

Originally offered by Metrowerks, but now from a company called Freescale, CodeWarrior offers professional IDE tools that run on a variety of operating systems, including Linux, Mac OS X, Solaris, and Windows.

Code::Blocks

www.codeblocks.org

Code::Blocks is a free IDE in which you can develop C, C++, and Fortran applications on a variety of platforms, including Windows, Linux, and Mac.

Miscellaneous

The following sections include resources for learning more about object-oriented programming and development tools.

Object-Oriented Programming

Budd, Timothy. *The Introduction to Object-Oriented Programming* (3rd Edition). Boston: Addison-Wesley Publishing Company, 2001.

This is considered a classic text that introduces object-oriented programming.

The C++ Language

Prata, Stephen. *C++ Primer Plus (6th Edition)*. Indianapolis: Addison-Wesley, 2011.

Stephen's tutorials have been well received. This one covers the C++ language.

Stroustrup, Bjarne. *The C++ Programming Language (4th Edition)*. Boston: Addison-Wesley Professional, 2013.

This is a recent update to the classic text on the language written by its inventor.

The C# Language

Petzold, Charles. *Programming in the Key of C#*. Redmond, WA: Microsoft Press, 2003.

This book has received recognition as a good book for beginners on C#.

Liberty, Jesse. *Programming C# 3.0,*. Cambridge, MA: O'Reilly & Associates, 2008.

A good introduction to C# for more experienced programmers.

Albahari, Joseph and Ben Albahari. *C# 5.0 in a Nutshell: The Definitive Reference.* Sebastopol, CA: 2012.

An excellent reference, particularly after you know the basics of the language.

The Objective-C Language

Kochan, Stephen. *Programming in Objective-C (Sixth Edition)*. Indianapolis: Sams Publishing, 2013.

Written by yours truly, it provides an introduction to the Objective-C language without assuming prior C or object-oriented programming experience. This edition covers OS X Mavericks and iOS 7. A new edition of the book, expected to be available in late 2014 or early 2015, will cover Apple's new Swift programming language.

https://developer.apple.com/library/mac/documentation/Cocoa/Conceptual/ProgrammingWithObjectiveC/Introduction/Introduction.html

While not a book per se, this online document is the official Apple introduction to how to program with the Objective-C language. It demonstrates many of the features of the language and provides examples of their use.

Development Tools

www.gnu.org/manual/manual.html

Here, you'll find a plethora of useful manuals, including ones on cvs, gdb, make, and other Unix command-line tools as well.

Index

E

F

G

Q-R

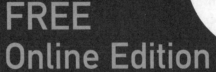

FREE
Online Edition

Your purchase of **Programming in C** includes access to a free online edition for 45 days through the Safari Books Online subscription service. Nearly every Addison-Wesley Professional book is available online through Safari Books Online, along with over thousands of books and videos from publishers such as Cisco Press, Exam Cram, IBM Press, O'Reilly Media, Prentice Hall, Que, Sams, and VMware Press.

Safari Books Online is a digital library providing searchable, on-demand access to thousands of technology, digital media, and professional development books and videos from leading publishers. With one monthly or yearly subscription price, you get unlimited access to learning tools and information on topics including mobile app and software development, tips and tricks on using your favorite gadgets, networking, project management, graphic design, and much more.

Activate your FREE Online Edition at
informit.com/safarifree

STEP 1:   Enter the coupon code: KRHSIWH.

STEP 2:   New Safari users, complete the brief registration form.
Safari subscribers, just log in.

If you have difficulty registering on Safari or accessing the online edition,
please e-mail customer-service@safaribooksonline.com